GRADUATE MANAGEMENT ADMISSION TEST

PREPARATION GUIDE

by

Jerry Bobrow, Ph.D.

Contributing Authors

William A. Covino, Ph.D.

Peter Z Orton, M.Ed.

Harold Nathan, Ph.D.

David A. Kay, M.S.

Dale Johnson, M.A.

INCORPORATED

LINCOLN, NEBRASKA   68501

ACKNOWLEDGMENTS

I would like to thank Michele Spence of Cliffs Notes for final editing and careful attention to the production process and Dr. Albert Upton for the use of excerpts from his outstanding book Design for Thinking. *I would also like to thank my wife, Susan, daughter, Jennifer, and sons Adam and Jonathan for their patience, moral support, and comic relief.*

CONTENTS

iii

PART III: PRACTICE-REVIEW-ANALYZE-PRACTICE
Three Full-Length Practice Tests

PREFACE

**Be prepared for the revised GMAT with the
Analytical Writing Assessment (AWA)**

YOUR GMAT SCORES MAKE THE DIFFERENCE! And better scores result from thorough preparation. With the addition of an Analytical Writing Assessment to the GMAT, your study time must be used more effectively than ever before. You need the most comprehensive test preparation guide that you can realistically complete in a reasonable time. It must be thorough, direct, precise, and easy to use, giving you all the information you need to do your best on the GMAT with the Analytical Writing Assessment.

In keeping with the fine tradition of Cliffs Notes, this guide was developed by leading experts in the field of test preparation as part of a series to specifically meet these standards. The testing strategies, techniques, and materials have been researched, tested, and evaluated, and are presently used at GMAT preparation programs at many leading colleges and universities. This guide features the PATTERNED PLAN OF ATTACK for each section and emphasizes the BOBROW TEST PREPARATION SERVICES approach which focuses on six major areas:

1. The Ability Tested
2. The Basic Skills Necessary
3. Understanding Directions
4. Analysis of Directions
5. Suggested Approaches with Samples
6. Practice-Review-Analyze-Practice

These major areas include important mathematical symbols, terminology, and formulas. THREE complete practice exams follow with answers and *in-depth* explanations.

This guide was written to give you the edge in doing your best by maximizing your effort in the minimum amount of time. If you take the time to follow the Study Guide Checklist in this book, you will get the best preparation possible.

STUDY GUIDE CHECKLIST

_____ 1. Read the GMAT Information Bulletin.

_____ 2. Become familiar with the Test Format, page 3.

_____ 3. Familiarize yourself with the answers to Questions Commonly Asked about the GMAT, page 5.

_____ 4. Learn the techniques of a Successful Overall Approach, page 7.

_____ 5. Carefully read Part II, Analysis of Exam Areas, beginning on page 13.

_____ 6. Review Math Symbols, Terminology, Formulas, and General Information, page 89.

_____ 7. Strictly observing time allotments, take Practice Test 1, section-by-section (review answers after each section), page 151.

_____ 8. Check your answers and analyze your results, page 206.

_____ 9. Fill out the Analysis Sheet for Problems Missed to pinpoint your mistakes, page 213.

_____ 10. While referring to each item of Practice Test 1, study ALL the Answers and Explanations that begin on page 217.

_____ 11. Review as necessary Basic Skills, Symbols, Terminology, Formulas, and General Information given in Part II of this book.

_____ 12. Strictly observing time allotments, take Practice Test 2, page 247.

_____ 13. Check your answers and analyze your results, page 303.

_____ 14. Fill out the Analysis Sheet for Problems Missed to pinpoint your mistakes, page 310.

_____ 15. While referring to each item of Practice Test 2, study ALL the Answers and Explanations that begin on page 313.

_____ 16. Again, selectively review materials as needed.

_____ 17. Strictly observing time allotments, selectively take sections of Practice Test 3 (those sections in which you want extra practice), page 339.

___ 18. Check your answers and analyze your results, page 395.

___ 19. Fill out the Analysis Sheet for Problems Missed to pinpoint your mistakes, page 402.

___ 20. While referring to each item of Practice Test 3, study ALL the Answers and Explanations that begin on page 405.

___ 21. Carefully reread Part II, Analysis of Exam Areas, beginning on page 13.

___ 22. Go over "FINAL PREPARATION" on page 431.

Part I: Introduction

COMMON FORMAT OF REVISED GMAT WITH NEW
ANALYTICAL WRITING ASSESSMENT

Section	Subject Area	Time (minutes)	Number of Questions
I	Analytical Writing Assessment		
	Essay 1	30	1
	Essay 2	30	1
II	Reading Comprehension	25	18–23
III	Problem Solving	25	16
IV	Data Sufficiency	25	20
V	Sentence Correction	25	22
VI	Problem Solving	25	16
VII	Critical Reasoning	25	16
VIII	Experimental (repeat of above)	25	varies

Total Time: 240 Minutes = 4 Hours   Approximately 133 Questions

NOTE: One of the sections on the exam will be experimental and will not count toward your score. However, you will not know which section is the experimental. The order of the *multiple-choice* sections will vary. The number of questions in each section may vary also.

GENERAL DESCRIPTION

The GMAT with the Analytical Writing Assessment (AWA) lasts approximately four hours and is composed of two 30-minute essays (Section I) and seven 25-minute multiple-choice sections. The essays are scored 0 to 6 while the multiple-choice questions are scored 200 to 800, with an average score of about 480. All multiple-choice questions have equal value. Two subscores are also generated: Verbal Ability, scored 0–60 (average score approximately 27), and Mathematical Ability, scored 0–60 (average score approximately 28).

The test is composed of the following sections:

ANALYTICAL WRITING ASSESSMENT—You will write two essays on topics provided. One essay will be an analysis of an issue, and the other will be an analysis of an argument.

READING COMPREHENSION—You will answer questions about reading passages from a variety of subjects.

DATA SUFFICIENCY—For each item you will decide how much of the mathematical data you are given is sufficient for answering a question.

SENTENCE CORRECTION—You will demonstrate your knowledge of correct and effective English expression.

PROBLEM SOLVING—You will solve general math and word-type problems.

CRITICAL REASONING—You will derive logical conclusions and relationships from a variety of situations and passages.

General college background is measured by these sections, not specific knowledge from any specialized course or courses. No formal background in business or management is required.

QUESTIONS COMMONLY ASKED
ABOUT THE GMAT

Q: WHO ADMINISTERS THE GMAT?

A: The GMAT is written and administered by Educational Testing Service (ETS). The Graduate Management Admissions Council, made up of representatives from 113 graduate schools of management, works with ETS in an advisory capacity.

Q: CAN I TAKE THE GMAT MORE THAN ONCE?

A: Yes. But be aware that if you take the test twice, *both* scores will appear on your score report. The score report will list the results from the immediate and the two most recent you have taken since August 1989.

Q: WHAT MATERIALS MAY I BRING TO THE GMAT?

A: Bring your registration form, positive identification, a watch, three or four sharpened Number 2 pencils, and a good eraser. You may *not* bring scratch paper, calculators, or books. You may do your figuring in the space provided in the test booklet.

Q: IF NECESSARY, MAY I CANCEL MY SCORE?

A: Yes. You may cancel your score on the day of the test by informing the test center supervisor, or you may contact ETS in writing *no later than seven days* after the test date. Your score report will record your cancellation as well as completed test scores.

Q: SHOULD I GUESS ON THE GMAT?

A: If you can eliminate one or more of the multiple-choice answers to a question, it is to your advantage to guess. Eliminating one or more answers increases your chance of choosing the right answer. To discourage wild guessing, a fraction of a point is subtracted for every wrong answer, but no points are subtracted if you leave the answer blank.

Q: HOW SHOULD I PREPARE FOR THE GMAT?

A: Understanding and practicing test-taking strategies will help a great deal, especially on the verbal sections. Subject-matter review is particularly useful for the math section. For the

Analytical Writing Assessment, practicing and reviewing analytical and argumentative essay writing would be valuable. Subject matter and strategies are fully covered in this book.

Q: WHEN IS THE GMAT ADMINISTERED?

A: The test is administered nationwide four times a year, in January, March, June, and October. These administrations are on Saturday mornings. Precise administration dates and test locations are published in the GMAT Bulletin, which is generally available at the Testing Office, Counseling Center, or Graduate Studies Office at your undergraduate institutions.

Q: HOW AND WHEN SHOULD I REGISTER?

A: Registration forms are included in the GMAT Bulletin. In order to avoid a late registration fee, you should register at least one month prior to the test date.

Q: IS WALK-IN REGISTRATION PROVIDED?

A: Yes, on a limited basis. If you are unable to meet regular registration deadlines, you may attempt to register on the day of the test (an additional fee is required). You will be seated only if space remains after preregistered students have been seated.

Q: HOW IS MY GMAT SCORE USED?

A: The GMAT is used as part of an assessment of your probable success in graduate business school. Other factors, such as undergraduate grades, interviews, and letters of recommendation, also figure into this assessment. The importance of GMAT scores varies from institution to institution, so you are wise to contact the graduate schools to which you are applying for further information.

Q: CAN I GET MORE INFORMATION?

A: Yes. If you require information which is not available in this book, write to: Graduate Management Admission Test, Educational Testing Service, P.O. Box 6103, Princeton, New Jersey 08541. Or telephone: (609) 771-7330.

TAKING THE GMAT:
A SUCCESSFUL OVERALL APPROACH

I. The "Plus-Minus" Strategy

Many who take the GMAT don't get the score that they are entitled to because they spend too much time dwelling on hard questions, leaving insufficient time to answer the easy questions they can get right. Don't let this happen to you. Use the following system to mark your answer sheet:

    1. Answer easy questions immediately.
    2. Place a "+" next to any problem that seems solvable but is too time-consuming.
    3. Place a "−" next to any problem that seems impossible. Act quickly. Don't waste time deciding whether a problem is a "+" or a "−."

After working all the problems you can do immediately, go back and work your "+" problems. If you finish them, try your "−" problems (sometimes when you come back to a problem that seemed impossible you will suddenly realize how to solve it).

Your answer sheet should look something like this after you finish working your easy questions:

    1. Ⓐ ● Ⓒ Ⓓ Ⓔ
+2. Ⓐ Ⓑ Ⓒ Ⓓ Ⓔ
    3. Ⓐ Ⓑ ● Ⓓ Ⓔ
−4. Ⓐ Ⓑ Ⓒ Ⓓ Ⓔ
+5. Ⓐ Ⓑ Ⓒ Ⓓ Ⓔ

Make sure to erase your "+" and "−" marks before your time is up. The scoring machine may count extraneous marks as wrong answers.

By using this overall approach, you are bound to achieve your best possible score.

II. The Elimination Strategy

Take advantage of being allowed to mark in your testing booklet. As you eliminate an answer choice from consideration, *make sure to mark it out in your question booklet* as follows:

~~(A)~~
?(B)
~~(C)~~
~~(D)~~
?(E)

Notice that some choices are marked with question marks, signifying that they may be possible answers. This technique will help you avoid reconsidering those choices you have already eliminated and will help you narrow down your possible answers.

These marks in your testing booklet do not need to be erased.

III. The Multiple Multiple-choice Strategy

You may encounter a few questions of the multiple multiple-choice type. This question type gives you answers marked with the roman numerals I, II, and III and then asks you if one, two, or possibly all three of the choices are correct answers. This question type can appear in the Reading Comprehension, Critical Reasoning, and Problem Solving sections. Here is an example:

Which of the following are equations with the only solution $x = 6$?

 I. $x^2 - 36 = 0$
 II. $x^2 - 7x + 6 = 0$
III. $x + 5 = 3x - 7$

(A) I only
(B) II only
(C) III only
(D) I and III only
(E) I, II, and III

A good strategy for this question type is to try to answer one of the roman numeral choices quickly. Then place a "T" or "F" by the numeral (for true or false) and go to the choices and eliminate possibilities. In the example, since I, $x^2 - 36 = 0$, gives you an answer of 6 and -6 ($x^2 = 36$ gives $x = 6$ or -6), it is false.

Immediately place an "F" by the roman numeral and eliminate the answer choices as shown here:

F I. $x^2 - 36 = 0$
  II. $x^2 - 7x + 6 = 0$
 III. $x + 5 = 3x - 7$

(A) I only
(B) II only
(C) III only
(D) I and III only
(E) I, II, and III

Now the answer must be (B) II or (C) III, since you've eliminated choices (A), (D), and (E) because they contain I. You can now work either answer II or answer III, since only one of them can be true. Working II gives

$$x^2 - 7x + 6 = 0$$
$$(x - 1)(x - 6) = 0$$
$$x - 1 = 0; x - 6 = 0$$
$$x = 1; x = 6$$

So II is not true. Therefore, the answer must be (C), III only. To finish the example, working III gives

$$x + 5 = 3x - 7$$

$$\begin{array}{rcr} x + 5 = & 3x - 7 \\ -5 & -5 \\ \hline x = & 3x - 12 \\ -3x & -3x \\ \hline -2x = & -12 \end{array}$$

$$\frac{-2x}{-2} = \frac{-12}{-2}$$

$$x = 6$$

So $x = 6$, and III and (C) are true.

Part II: Analysis of Exam Areas

This section is designed to introduce you to each GMAT area by carefully reviewing the

1. Ability Tested
2. Basic Skills Necessary
3. Directions
4. Analysis of Directions
5. Suggested Approach with Sample Questions

This section features the PATTERNED PLAN OF ATTACK for each subject area and emphasizes important test-taking techniques and strategies and how to apply them to a variety of problem types. It also includes some valuable math and verbal review.

INTRODUCTION TO
THE ANALYTICAL WRITING ASSESSMENT

The Analytical Writing Assessment section requires you to write two essays with a time limit of thirty minutes for each. You will be given two types of questions: (1) an *analysis of an issue,* which presents an issue to be discussed, and (2) an *analysis of an argument,* which presents an argument to be analyzed.

Ability Tested

This section tests your ability to think critically, to analyze issues and features of arguments, and to communicate complex ideas.

Basic Skills Necessary

You should possess good college-level writing, reading, and reasoning skills. You should be able to express your ideas in correct, clear, concise, and persuasive language. Your writing should be neat and legible.

Directions

Analysis of an issue: This section will require you to analyze and explain your views on the issue given. Consider many points of view as you develop your own position on the issue. There is no right or wrong answer to the question.

Read the statement and directions carefully. Make any notes in your test booklet. Then write your response on the separate answer document. Be sure to use the answer document that goes with this writing task.

Analysis of an argument: This section will require you to critique the argument given. Questioning underlying assumptions, finding alternative explanations or counterexamples, and delineating evidence to strengthen or weaken an argument are some possible approaches.

Read the argument and directions carefully. Make any notes in your test booklet. Then write your response on the separate answer document. Be sure to use the answer document that goes with this writing task.

Analysis

This section presents an analysis-of-an-issue topic and an analysis-of-an-argument topic, usually in about three or four sentences each. The topics are followed by several questions that set forth the tasks you must accomplish in your essays. Here is a typical set of such questions (notice the difference):

Analysis of an issue: Which point of view do you find more convincing? Explain your position with specific supporting details from your own experience, observations, or readings.

Analysis of an argument: Write an essay in which you evaluate the features of this argument. Is it convincing? Logical? Does it use evidence well? What would make it more persuasive?

Scoring the Analytical Writing Section

The two essays are scored holistically by university teachers skilled in the evaluation of writing. Their concern will be with the overall quality of the essays—the command of logic, clarity, and cogency—and not with minor errors of spelling or grammar.

The scoring guides for each type of essay (which follow) were developed by categorizing essay responses written during the devlopment of this section of the GMAT, rather than from a preconceived notion of what analytical essays should be like. Each of the two essays is given a score ranging from 0 (lowest) to 6 (highest) by two readers who are not aware of the other's score. If the two scores differ by more than two points, the paper is graded by a third reader. If the third reader's score is the same as that of one of the other readers, that score is assigned. If the score is between the two differing scores, the three grades are averaged. The scores of the issue analysis essay and the argument analysis essay are averaged, and the result is the final Analytical Writing Assessment score (a single grade ranging from 0 to 6).

Again, essay scores are determined by the quality of thought and the writing skill. A well-written, thoughtful essay will receive a high score regardless of what side of the issue or argument the writer chooses. Less-than-perfect handwriting, a minor spelling error, or a small error in grammar will not affect the final score. The readers are instructed to reward the essays for what they do well. Readers are chosen for their competence and experience (and to balance the group with regard to gender, ethnicity, and geography).

Analyzing the Scores

Grading the Analysis of an Issue Essay

Because the essays must be written in a limited period of time, minor errors of grammar or mechanics will not affect the scores. The essays scored at 6 will not be errorless, but they will be superior to the other essays.

Score of 6: Excellent

These papers are characterized by all of the following:

- coverage of all the tasks required by the exam question
- an understanding of the complexity of the issue
- cogent reasoning and logical development of a position
- relevant persuasive supporting details
- superior organization
- superior command of standard written English

Score of 5: Good

These papers are characterized by the following:

- coverage of all the tasks required by the exam question
- clear reasoning and development of a position
- use of well-chosen supporting evidence
- good organization
- good handling of standard written English

Score of 4: Competent

These papers are characterized by the following:

- coverage of all the tasks
- development of a position
- adequately reasoned and supported arguments
- competent organization
- adequate handling of standard written English

Score of 3: Limited

These papers are characterized by the following:

- failure to fully understand the issue and develop a position
- failure to respond to all the assigned tasks
- failure to use supporting details
- numerous minor errors in grammar or mechanics
- imperfect use of standard written English

Score of 2: Weak

These papers compound the deficiencies of papers in the 3 range. They are likely to fail in presenting a position on the issue or fail in employing supporting detail. The organization, grammar, diction, and mechanics are likely to be incompetent.

Score of 1: Poor

These papers compound the deficiencies in the 2 range. They display an inability to respond to the topic and write standard English prose. They are often unacceptably brief.

Score of 0

A score of zero is given to papers that are blank, unreadable, or wholly off-topic.

Grading the Analysis of an Argument Essay

Because the essays must be written in a limited period of time, minor errors of grammar or mechanics will not affect the scores. The essays scored at 6 will not be errorless, but will be superior to the other essays.

Score of 6: Excellent

These papers are characterized by all of the following:

- thorough coverage of all the tasks required by the exam question
- careful analysis of the important features of the argument
- cogent reasoning and logical development
- relevant supporting details of the critique
- superior organization
- superior command of standard written English

Score of 5: Good

These papers are characterized by the following:

- good coverage of all the tasks required by the exam question
- good analysis of the important features of the argument
- clear reasoning and development
- use of supporting evidence of the critique
- good organization
- good handling of standard written English

Score of 4: Competent

These papers are characterized by the following:

- some coverage of the tasks required by the exam question
- competent analysis of the important features of the argument
- adequately reasoned and supported points of the critique
- competent organization
- adequate handling of standard written English

Score of 3: Limited

These papers are characterized by one or more of the following weaknesses:

- failure to respond to all of the assigned tasks
- failure to understand or to analyze the important features of the argument
- failure to use supporting details of the critique
- numerous minor errors in grammar or mechanics
- imperfect use of standard written English

Score of 2: Weak

These papers compound the deficiencies of papers in the 3 range. They are likely to misunderstand the main features of the argument, fail in presenting an analysis, and fail in employing supporting detail. The organization, grammar, diction, and mechanics are likely to be incompetent.

Score of 1: Poor

These papers compound the deficiencies in the 2 range. They display an inability to respond to the topic and write standard English prose. They are often unacceptably brief.

Score of 0

A score of zero is given to papers that are blank, unreadable, or wholly off-topic.

Suggested Approach with Samples

Again, two distinct tasks are given in the Analytical Writing Assessment: (1) analyze an issue and (2) analyze an argument. To analyze an issue you are asked to take a position on the issue presented and support your position with relevant details or examples. To analyze an argument you are asked to analyze how logically convincing you find an argument that is presented. In explaining your point of view you must analyze the line of reasoning in the argument itself and its use of evidence or support.

For any timed writing task, you should envision three steps leading to the finished product:

      1. Preparing to write (prewriting)
      2. Writing
      3. Proofreading (editing)

Preparing to Write

- Note time and space constraints.

Before you begin analyzing the topic itself, you should be aware of the amount of time allotted for the assignment as well as the amount of paper available on which to write your essay. This will help you assess not only how much time you'll have to organize and write the essay, but also how long the essay should be and how much development it will require.

For the Analytical Writing Assessment, you have thirty minutes to write each essay. You will be given the equivalent of three sides of 8½-by-11-inch paper to complete your writing. Any organizing or scratch work is to be done on the essay topic sheet.

- Carefully read the topic.

Next, read and understand the topic. A major mistake is to give too little time and attention to this task. Remember that if you address the topic incorrectly, or even partially, your score is significantly lowered, no matter how well the essay is organized, supported, and written. Therefore, you must spend adequate time carefully reading and understanding the topic and its exact requirements.

Pay special attention to key words in the directions, like "describe," "compare," "explain," and "contrast." Be aware that "or" requires a choice, whereas "and" requires several elements. For example, "Present your opinions for or against . . ." means take one point of view, not both, whereas "for and against" means present both sides. "Analyze the line of reasoning . . ." means critique the features of the argument. Be careful to assess completely all the tasks required. You may find it helpful to read the topic several times, circling or marking the key words or tasks.

• Plan by brainstorming and organizing.

Remembering, inventing, and organizing information at short notice can be difficult unless you are prepared with an effective technique. Writing your essay immediately after reading the topic often results in a poorly organized, haphazard essay. Take time to organize your thoughts on paper before writing.

Brainstorming

The process of creating and accumulating ideas, examples, and illustrations is called "brainstorming." Brainstorming is simply jotting down on scratch paper as many thoughts, ideas, and possibilities as you can remember, invent, or otherwise bring to mind in order to address the topic. Neatness, order, and spelling are unimportant at this point.

Organizing

After generating as many illustrations as you can within the time allotted, assess these ideas. Remembering that development relies on specific examples, decide which examples best enable you to support your points. Eliminate (cross out) those you don't wish to use, and number those you'll want to address in your essay. Add any notes regarding more specific details or new thoughts that come to mind. However, don't worry about developing everything completely, since these planning notes are for your use. Your time will be better spent developing these points in your writing and not in your notes.

Writing

Opening Paragraph

A strong opening paragraph is essential. One type of introduction, easy to master and very effective, is a GENERALIZE-FOCUS-SURVEY structure. This is a three- to four-sentence paragraph in which the first sentence generalizes about the given topic, the second sentence focuses on what you have chosen to discuss, and the last one or two sentences survey the particulars you intend to present.

An effective first paragraph tells your reader what to expect in the body of the essay. The GENERALIZE-FOCUS-SURVEY paragraph points toward the specifics you will discuss and suggests the order in which you will discuss them.

Body

Writing the body of the essay involves presenting specific details and examples that are related to the aspects you have introduced. The body of the essay may consist of one longer paragraph or several shorter paragraphs. If you choose to break your discussion into several paragraphs, make sure that each paragraph consists of at least three sentences. Very short paragraphs may make your essay appear to be insubstantial and scattered.

Be realistic about *how much* you will be able to write. Your readers do not give more credit for longer essays. Although they want you to support your points adequately, they understand that you must write concisely in order to finish in time.

It will be important to provide at least one substantial example or "for instance" for each aspect you discuss in the body of your essay.

Conclusion

As you prepare to write the conclusion, you should be paying special attention to time. You must allow enough time both to write the conclusion and to proofread. The conclusion may function to (1) *complete* your response to the essay question, (2) *add* information that was not introduced earlier, or (3) *point toward the future.*

Proofreading

Always allow a few minutes to proofread your essay for errors in grammar, usage, and spelling. To make sure that you do not proofread hastily, try this: With a sheet of paper, cover all but the first line of your essay. Read that line carefully. Then reveal and read the second line, and so forth. Using this method, you are more assured of focused and careful proofreading.

If you detect an error, line it out carefully and insert the correction neatly. Keep in mind, both while you are writing and while you are correcting, that your handwriting must be *legible*.

One Approach: The "Why" Essay

One good way to approach a question which asks you to explain, analyze, or evaluate is to use a "why" essay format. A "why" essay is built around a thesis sentence. The thesis sentence begins with your opinion, followed by the word *because* and then a list of the most important reasons the opinion is valid, reasonable, or well-founded.

The "why" essay format could look like this in outline form:

Paragraph	"Why" Essay Format
1	Introduction—Thesis Sentence
2	Reason 1
3	Reason 2
4	Reason 3
5	Conclusion

Each paragraph should contain at least three to five sentences. The introduction invites the reader to read on. Your reasons (three are often sufficient) that follow should give examples or evidence to support each reason. Your concluding paragraph summarizes your reasons and restates the thesis statement.

Sample: Analysis of an Issue

More than half of the Americans recently surveyed expressed approval of the use of flogging to punish young offenders guilty of crimes such as vandalism. They believe the pain and mortification will be more effective deterrents to young offenders than fines paid by parents or community service hours. Opponents of flogging argue that the punishment is cruel and barbaric and that it leaves both physical and psychological scars.

Do you believe that flogging should be used in this country? Write an essay explaining your position with support from your observations, readings, and/or experience.

Sample Issue Essay

In light of the disturbing increase in crime in our cities and suburbs in recent years, many Americans have expressed an interest in the use of flogging to punish young offenders guilty of crimes such as vandalism. I am opposed to the use of flogging as punishment based on humanitarian, psychological, and moral grounds.

While I share the frustration of other law-abiding citizens who are trying to stem the tide of senseless destruction of personal property, I believe that flogging is a cruel and uncivilized form of punishment that has no place in our country. The public infliction of painful physical punishment was banished from civilized countries years ago with the disappearance of the stocks, pillories, and public whippings. As witnessed in the case of the American teenager who was sentenced to a caning for vandalism in Singapore, most civilized countries around the world objected vehemently to the severity and barbarism of this form of punishment for a nonviolent crime.

On psychological grounds, inflicting physical punishment to teach a lesson has been frowned upon for years by child psychologists and behavioral experts. Spankings, beltings, and beatings are all considered forms of abuse and have been proved to have only very negative affects on behavior. Studies have also supported the conclusion that violence begets violence, and it would seem very probable that the use of flogging to punish a young person who committed vandalism may well lead to a more violent expression of anger next time. The troubled individual whose antisocial behavior was directed toward property may well be incited to take his anger out in a physically violent way against people after being subjected to such treatment.

Finally, on moral grounds, we need to make the distinction between crimes against persons and crimes against property. In terms of the Biblical injunction of "an eye for an eye, a tooth for a tooth," inflicting physical injury on an offender who committed damage to property is hardly equitable. What is the lesson we are trying to teach? In the 1970s, the movie <u>A Clockwork Orange</u> dealt with the issue of violent crime in a futuristic setting and society's increasingly cruel methods of "rehabilitation." It left the viewer questioning which was more barbaric, the crime or the punishment?

In conclusion, we must continue to search for ways to reduce the incidence of crimes against property as well as persons, but we must above all keep sight of our humanity. Flogging is not the answer.

Evaluation of Issue Essay

This excellent analysis would probably be an example of a score of 6. The writer takes a stand and develops it with apt examples, referring to current events, a psychological film, and personal attitudes. Though it is *not* necessary to write a five-paragraph essay, this one shows well how easily and effectively such an essay can be organized. This first, introductory paragraph lists three grounds of opposition (humanitarian, psychological, and moral), and each of the next three paragraphs develops one of these. The final paragraph is a summing up. The essay is gracefully written and syntactically varied (the last paragraph, for example, plays a long sentence against a short one). Though the mechanics of the essay are not perfect (*affects* in the third paragraph should be *effects*), the writer's command of standard written English is first-rate.

Sample: Analysis of an Argument

Nothing overrides the public's right to know. When a person enters public life, whether it be in politics, sports, or entertainment, he or she must give up the rights to privacy that people who are less well-known enjoy. The Watergate scandal would never have been exposed without reporters who were willing to insist on the public's right to know.

Write an analysis of this argument, paying particular attention to its use of logic and its use of evidence. Are these convincing? What deficiencies, if any, do you find in this argument?

Sample Argument Essay

In the last twenty years, the role of the news media in public life has grown by leaps and bounds, encouraged by the battle cry of "the public's right to know." This fundamental right, as the news media sees it, comes straight from the First Amendment guaranteeing freedom of speech and freedom of the press. This "fundamental right" reasoning is the basis of this argument, but it ignores other conflicting rights. For example, what about the fundamental right to privacy that we protect by such means as the secret ballot or requirements for search warrants? This argument simply asserts there is a universal right to know, without ever explaining where this right comes from.

The second sentence of the argument is also flawed. Elected officials have a responsibility to the electorate who should be kept informed. But movie, football, television, or baseball stars have no such relation to public well-being. Does a public figure necessarily have to wave the rights to privacy which are accorded to the rest of us? And how do we define what constitutes a public figure? Obviously there are different issues involved in exposing private information about the president than there are regarding a sports star or entertainer.

This argument uses the specific example that the Watergate scandal would never have been exposed unless reporters were willing to insist on the public's right to know. Obviously, when national government is involved, and criminal acts are being committed that affect the welfare of our society, the media is doing us an invaluable and necessary service by uncovering the facts. On the other hand, the argument doesn't address the issue that prying into the personal habits, sex lives, and family relations of public figures serves no important purpose other than satisfying the prying, inquisitive wonderings of people who should be more concerned with their own lives. Just because "inquiring minds want to know" doesn't mean they have a right to.

The argument shows many deficiencies by not addressing the issues mentioned above. It also fails to consider that there is a fine line between responsible news coverage attempting to supply the public with needed information so that they can be informed citizens and the kind of tabloid journalism that panders to the prurient interests of the lowest common denominator.

Evaluation of Argument Essay

Though not without some flaws, this essay would probably exemplify the highest scoring response. It identifies clearly the weaknesses in this argument. By focusing one paragraph on each of the three sentences of the argument, its organization is logical. In each paragraph, the writer supports the critique with specific references. The writing is controlled and varied, and though there are a few minor slips (*media* is the plural of *medium,* so "as the news media sees" contains an agreement error, and *waive* is misspelled as *wave* in the next paragraph), this is a fine response to the question.

Extra Practice Topics

In addition to the topics and questions provided in each of the three practice tests, here are twelve sample topics for practicing analytical essay writing. Limit your time on each to thirty minutes to simulate the actual examination. Find someone skilled in writing to evaluate your essays using the checklist and grading scale following these extra practice topics.

Analysis of an Issue Questions

1. Some environmentalists believe that wood-burning stoves are among the best ways to conserve natural resources and protect the environment. But in many parts of the United States, wood is in short supply. Some wooded areas house animals. And wood smoke may be more harmful to air quality than emissions from fossil fuels like coal or oil.

    Which of these positions do you prefer? Explain your choice with support from your personal experience or knowledge of the issues.

2. Should students or the state be responsible for tuition costs at the state colleges and universities? In most of the country, tuition costs have risen steadily in the last ten years and no sign of their slowing down is in sight. Many students can no longer afford a higher education. But the result of tuition raises is a better education in the state colleges. Classes are no longer over-crowded. A far higher percentage of the entering first-year students complete their degrees in four years or fewer.

    Do you believe the benefits of higher tuition in state colleges outweigh the disadvantages? Make your opinion clear with specific support drawn from your observations or readings.

3. Since freedom of choice is a democratic ideal, there should be no doubt about the use of vouchers by which the government enables parents to pay tuition at *either* a public or private school. If fewer children attend public schools, the savings for the state should pay for the vouchers. The healthy competition for students will inevitably lead to an improvement of all schools.

Do you disagree with this statement? Write an essay supporting or opposing a voucher system to support education. Use your readings or personal experience to develop your argument.

4. By a 5-4 margin, the Supreme Court has ruled against statutes that prohibit the burning of an American flag on the grounds that flag burning is symbolic speech, and free speech must be protected. But protesters could easily use the desecration of other symbols to voice disapproval of such a national policy. Flag burning is like graffiti painting on the Liberty Bell.

Do you support or oppose the laws that forbid flag burning? Write an essay for or against the Supreme Court decision with support from your experience and/or reading.

5. Should people accused of stealing money be permitted to use that money to pay for their legal defense? Under the Constitution, they should be presumed to be innocent. But if they are found guilty, the money cannot be retrieved. The state-paid legal defense is not likely to be nearly as good as a well-paid private defense attorney's. But the Supreme Court has ruled that criminal defendants' assets can be frozen before their trials.

Write an essay defending or opposing the freezing of assets of accused thieves. Support your position by developing information in this paragraph and with additional ideas of your own.

6. "Experience should teach us to be most on our guard to protect liberty when the government's purposes are beneficent. Men born to freedom are naturally alert to repel invasion of their liberty by evil-minded rulers. The greatest dangers to liberty lurk in insidious encroachment by men of zeal, well-meaning but without understanding."

Would you assert that "men of zeal" are a greater threat to liberty than "evil-minded rulers?" Write an essay in which you explain your position for or against this position. Support your case with information from your reading or experience.

Analysis of an Argument Questions

1. More of this country's lawyers' time is spent in the services of the very rich than with anyone else. The people who really need legal representation cannot afford to hire lawyers. Publicly financed legal aid is virtually nonexistent. Since members of the bar have an uncontested monopoly on legal advising and representation, this unjust situation is unlikely to be changed.

   Write an essay in which you evaluate this argument. Is it convincing? Logical? Does it use evidence well? What would make it more persuasive?

2. War is the unavoidable consequence of our idea of manhood. The American notion of manhood is unchanging: aggressiveness, winning at all costs, physical supremacy, the primacy of work, the suppression of sensitivity. The results of these values in the twentieth century are two world wars and so many smaller conflicts that we lose count of them.

   How persuasive do you find this argument? Are its details convincing? Does it use evidence well? What would make its conclusion more convincing?

3. It is folly for the United States to put its soldiers at risk to keep the peace in countries of no strategic interest to us. There are always going to be areas in the world with civil unrest, poverty, or famine, and American soldiers will not prevent their recurrence. We should have learned the lesson of Vietnam: nonintervention is the best policy.

   Discuss the logic and the persuasiveness of the argument. Include commentary on its use of evidence and how you believe its case could be strengthened.

4. Self-censorship is a far better control of controversial expression than the law. Writers, filmmakers, and television producers who wish to reach an audience are likely to curb potentially offensive works more effectively than any state or city censorship panel. The attempt to throttle expression usually results in publicity that leads to the work's reaching a much larger audience.

Evaluate the logic and persuasiveness of this argument. Discuss what might be added to make this paragraph more convincing.

5. Some human laws prohibit cruelty to animals, but these laws do not give animals rights. Our laws allow us to kill animals for food or for sport, so animals do not have even a right to life. To set animal life above the human rights of progress and economic betterment is an inhumane denial of the value of human life.

Write an essay in which you evaluate the persuasiveness and logical development of this passage. Also discuss what argument might be used to undermine its conclusion.

6. Every ethnic community must be free to teach its heritage to its children, but this teaching should take place in the home, not in the public schools. Teaching multicultural values in schools will promote tension among different ethnic groups and undermine the bonds that hold this country together as one nation with liberty for all.

Evaluate this argument with special attention to its logic and use of evidence. Why do you suppose the author begins and ends the passage with references to "free" and "liberty"?

HOW TO SCORE YOUR ESSAYS

Have someone knowledgeable in the writing process evaluate your essays using the checklists and grading scales on the following page. Remember, because the essays must be written in a limited time period, minor errors of grammar or mechanics will not affect your scores.

Analysis of an Issue

	Yes, completely	Yes, partially	No
1. Does the essay focus on the assigned topic and cover all of the tasks?			
2. Does the essay show an understanding of the complexity of the issue?			
3. Does the essay show cogent reasoning and logical position development?			
4. Are there sufficient relevant persuasive supporting details?			
5. Is the essay well organized?			
6. Does the essay show a command of standard written English?			

Analysis of an Argument

	Yes, completely	Yes, partially	No
1. Does the essay focus on the assigned topic and cover all of the tasks?			
2. Does the essay carefully analyze the important features of the argument?			
3. Does the essay show cogent reasoning and logical development?			
4. Are there sufficient relevant supporting details of the critique?			
5. Is the essay well organized?			
6. Does the essay show a command of standard written English?			

A PATTERNED PLAN OF ATTACK

Analytical Writing Assessment

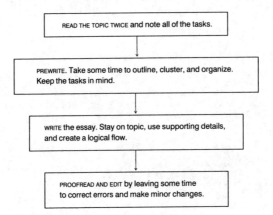

READ THE TOPIC TWICE and note all of the tasks.

PREWRITE. Take some time to outline, cluster, and organize. Keep the tasks in mind.

WRITE the essay. Stay on topic, use supporting details, and create a logical flow.

PROOFREAD AND EDIT by leaving some time to correct errors and make minor changes.

INTRODUCTION TO READING COMPREHENSION

Reading Comprehension is usually the first section of the GMAT and often appears again later in the test. It typically consists of three passages, each about 450 to 650 words in length, and contains a total of eighteen to twenty-three questions.

Ability Tested

This section tests your ability to understand, interpret, and analyze reading passages on a variety of topics. Passages are generally taken from the following categories:

- **Narrative**—passages from novels, short stories, essays, and biographies
- **Argumentative**—passages presenting different points of view
- **Biological science**—passages about botany, medicine, or zoology
- **Physical science**—passages about chemistry, physics, or astronomy
- **Humanities**—passages about art, literature, music, folklore, or philosophy
- **Social studies**—passages about history, government, economics, or sociology

The questions will frequently ask you

- about the **main idea, main point,** or **possible title** of the passage
- about **information** that is **directly stated** in the passage
- about **information** that is **implied, suggested,** or **can be inferred**
- to recognize **applications** of the author's **opinions** or **ideas**
- to evaluate how the author **develops** and **presents** the passage
- to recognize the **style** or **tone** of the passage

Basic Skills Necessary

Students who have read widely and know how to read and mark a passage actively and efficiently tend to do well on this section.

Directions

Each passage in this group is followed by questions based on its content. After reading a passage, choose the best answer to each question and blacken the corresponding space on the answer sheet. Answer all questions following a passage on the basis of what is *stated* or *implied* in that passage. You may refer back to the passage.

Analysis

Answer all the questions for one passage before moving to the next one. If you don't know the answer, take an educated guess or skip it.

Use only the information given or implied in a passage. Do not consider outside information, even if it seems more accurate than the given information.

Suggested Approach

• **Skim the *questions* first, marking words which give you a clue about what to look for when you read the passage.**

• **Skim the passage, reading only the first sentence of each paragraph. (optional)**

• **Read the passage, marking main points, important conclusions, names, definitions, places, and numbers. Make only a few marks per paragraph.**

WARM-UP PASSAGES

Following are two short and one full-length passage with questions for you to practice the techniques of skimming the questions, skimming the passage, and actively reading and marking the passage. (The first passage and questions have been marked.) The passages you will encounter in the Reading Comprehension section of the GMAT will be approximately the length of the full-length passage.

Short Passage 1

*By the time children start school, they have mastered the major part of the rules of their grammar. They have managed to accomplish this remarkable feat in such a short time by experimenting with and generalizing the rules all by themselves. Children, in effect, rediscover language in the first few years of their lives.

When it comes to vocabulary growth, it is a different story. Unlike grammar, the chief means through which vocabulary is learned is memorization. And some people have a hard time learning and remembering new words.

(The * indicates portions of the passage which refer directly to a question you've skimmed. Also marked are main points and key terms.)

Sample Questions with Explanations

1. Children have mastered many rules of grammar by about the age of
   (A) 3
   (B) 5
   (C) 8
   (D) 10
   (E) 18

The first sentence of the passage contains several words from this question, so it is likely to contain the correct answer. *By the time children start school* tells us that the answer is 5. Before choosing

(B), you should look at all the answers and cross out those which seem incorrect.

2. Although vocabulary growth involves memorization and grammar-learning doesn't, we may conclude that <u>both vocabulary and grammar make use of</u>
   - (A) memorization
   - (B) study skills
   - (C) words
   - (D) children
   - (E) teachers

The question asks you to simply use your common sense. Choice (A) is incorrect; it contradicts both the passage and the question itself. (D) and (E) make no sense. (B) is a possibility, but (C) is better because grammar-learning in young children does not necessarily involve study skills but does involve words.

3. The <u>last sentence</u> in the passage <u>implies</u> that
   - (A) some people have little difficulty learning and remembering new words
   - (B) some people have a hard time remembering new words
   - (C) grammar does not involve remembering words
   - (D) old words are not often remembered
   - (E) learning and remembering are kinds of growth

Implies tells us that the answer is something suggested but not explicitly stated in the passage. Choice (B) is explicitly stated in the passage, so it may be eliminated. But (B) implies the opposite: If *some* people have a hard time, then it must be true that *some* people don't. (A) is therefore the correct choice. Choices (C), (D), and (E) are altogether apart from the meaning of the last sentence.

Short Passage 2

St. Augustine was a contemporary of Jerome. After an early life of pleasure, he became interested in a philosophical religion called Manichaeism, a derivative of a Persian religion, in which the forces of good constantly struggle with those of evil. Augustine was eventually converted to Christianity by St. Ambrose of Milan. His *Confessions* was an autobiography that served as an inspiration to countless thousands who believed that virtue would ultimately win.

Sample Questions with Explanations

1. St. Augustine's conversion to Christianity was probably influenced by
   (A) his confessional leanings
   (B) his contemporaries
   (C) the inadequacy of a Persian religion to address Western moral problems
   (D) his earlier interest in the dilemma of retaining virtue
   (E) the ravages of a life of pleasure

Having skimmed this question, you should have marked the portion of the passage which mentions Augustine's conversion and paid attention to the events (influences) leading to it. (A) requires speculating beyond the facts in the paragraph; there is also no evidence in the passage to support (C) or (E). (B) is too vague and general to be the best answer. (D) points toward Augustine's earlier interest in Manichaeism, and the last sentence suggests that Augustine's interest in retaining virtue continued through his Christian doctrine. Well supported as it is, (D) is the best answer.

2. From the information in the passage, we must conclude that Augustine was a
   (A) fair-weather optimist
   (B) cockeyed optimist
   (C) hardworking optimist
   (D) failed optimist
   (E) glib optimist

Skimming *this* question is not very helpful; it does not point specifically to any information in the passage. Questions of this sort usually assess your overall understanding of the meaning, style, tone, or point of view of the passage. In this case, you should recognize that Augustine is a serious person; therefore, more lighthearted terms like "fair-weather" (A), "cockeyed" (B), and "glib" (E) are probably inappropriate. (D) contradicts Augustine's success as an *inspiration to countless thousands*. (C) corresponds with his ongoing, hopeful struggle to retain virtue in the world; it is the best answer.

3. Judging from the reaction of thousands to Augustine's *Confessions,* we may conclude that much of his world at that time was in a state of
   (A) opulence
   (B) misery
   (C) heresy
   (D) reformation
   (E) sanctification

Having skimmed this question, you should have marked the last sentence of the passage as the place to look for the answer. That Augustine's readers were inspired implies that they *required inspiration,* that they were in some sort of uninspiring, or *negative* situation. (A) and (E) must therefore be eliminated because they are positive terms. (D) is not necessarily a negative term, and so is probably not the best answer. (C), although a negative term, does not describe a state of being which thirsts for inspiration. (B) does, and (B) therefore is the best choice.

Full-length Passage

Woodrow Wilson is usually ranked among the country's great presidents in spite of his failures to win Senate approval of the League of Nations. Wilson had yearned for a political career all his life; he won his first office in 1910 when he was elected governor of New Jersey. Two years later he was elected president in one of the most rapid political rises in our history. For a while Wilson had practiced law but found it both boring and unprofitable; then he became a political scientist of great renown and finally president of Princeton University. He did an outstanding job at Princeton but lost out in a battle with Dean Andrew West for control of the graduate school. When he was asked by the Democratic boss of

New Jersey, Jim Smith, to run for governor, Wilson readily accepted because his position at Princeton was becoming untenable.

Until 1910, Wilson seemed to be a conservative Democrat in the Grover Cleveland tradition. He had denounced Bryan in 1896 and had voted for the National Democratic candidate who supported gold. In fact, when the Democratic machine first pushed Wilson's nomination in 1912, the young New Jersey progressives wanted no part of him. Wilson later assured them that he would champion the progressive cause, and so they decided to work for his election. It is easy to accuse Wilson of political expediency, but it is entirely possible that by 1912 he had changed his views as had countless other Americans. While governor of New Jersey, he carried out his election pledges by enacting an impressive list of reforms.

Wilson secured the Democratic nomination on the forty-sixth ballot after a fierce battle with Champ Clark of Missouri and Oscar W. Underwood of Alabama. Clark actually had a majority of votes but was unable to attract the necessary two-thirds. In the campaign, Wilson emerged as the middle-of-the-road candidate—between the conservative William H. Taft and the more radical Theodore Roosevelt. Wilson called his program the New Freedom, which he said was the restoration of free competition as it had existed before the growth of the trusts. In contrast, Theodore Roosevelt was advocating a New Nationalism, which seemed to call for massive federal intervention in the economic life of the nation. Wilson felt that the trusts should be destroyed, but he made a distinction between a trust and legitimately successful big business. Theodore Roosevelt, on the other hand, accepted the trusts as inevitable but said that the government should regulate them by establishing a new regulatory agency. The former president also felt that a distinction should be made between the "good" trusts and the "bad" trusts.

Sample Questions

1. The author's main purpose in writing this passage is to
   (A) argue that Wilson is one of the great U.S. presidents
   (B) survey the difference between Wilson, Taft, and Roosevelt
   (C) explain Wilson's concept of the New Freedom
   (D) discuss some major events of Wilson's career
   (E) suggest reasons that Wilson's presidency may have started World War I

2. The author implies which of the following about the New Jersey progressives?
   (A) They did not support Wilson after he was governor.
   (B) They were not conservative Democrats.
   (C) They were more interested in political expediency than in political causes or reforms.
   (D) Along with Wilson, they were supporters of Bryan in 1896.
   (E) They particularly admired Wilson's experience as president of Princeton University.

3. The passage supports which of the following conclusions about the progress of Wilson's political career?
   (A) Few politicians have progressed so rapidly toward the attainment of higher office.
   (B) Failures late in his career caused him to be regarded as a president who regressed instead of progressed.
   (C) Wilson encountered little opposition once he determined to seek the presidency.
   (D) The League of Nations marked the end of Wilson's reputation as a strong leader.
   (E) Wilson's political progress was aided by Champ Clark and Oscar Underwood.

4. In the statement "Wilson readily accepted because his position at Princeton was becoming untenable," the meaning of "untenable" is probably which of the following?
   (A) Unlikely to last for years
   (B) Filled with considerably less tension
   (C) Difficult to maintain or continue
   (D) Filled with achievements that would appeal to voters
   (E) Something he did not have a tenacious desire to continue

5. According to the passage, which of the following was probably true about the presidential campaign of 1912?
   (A) Woodrow Wilson won the election by an overwhelming majority.
   (B) The inexperience of Theodore Roosevelt accounted for his radical position.
   (C) Wilson was unable to attract two-thirds of the votes but won anyway.
   (D) There were three nominated candidates for the presidency.
   (E) Wilson's New Freedom did not represent Democratic interests.

Answers and Explanations

1. (D) Choices (A) and (E) are irrelevant to the information in the passage, and choices (B) and (C) mention *secondary* purposes rather than the primary one.

2. (B) In the second paragraph, Wilson's decision to *champion the progressive cause* after 1912 is contrasted with his earlier career, when *he seemed to be a conservative Democrat.* Thus, we may conclude that the progressives, whom Wilson finally joined, were not conservative Democrats, as was Wilson earlier in his career. Choices (A) and (D) contradict information in the paragraph, while choices (C) and (E) are not suggested by any information given in the passage.

3. (A) This choice is explicitly supported by the third sentence in paragraph one in which we are told that Wilson was *elected president in one of the most rapid political rises in our history.*

4. (C) On any reading comprehension test, it is best to be alert to the positive and negative connotations of words and phrases in each passage as well as in the questions themselves. In the case of *untenable,* the prefix *un-* suggests that the word has a negative connotation. The context in which the word occurs does so as well. Wilson *left* his position at Princeton; therefore, we may conclude that the position was somehow unappealing. Only two of the answer choices, (C) and (E), provide a negative definition. Although choice (E) may attract your attention because *tenacious* looks similar to *tenable,* the correct choice is (C), which is the conventional definition of *untenable*.

5. (D) Choices (A), (B), and (C) contain information that is not addressed in the passage. We may eliminate them as irrelevant. Choice (E) contradicts the fact that Wilson was a Democratic candidate. The discussion of Taft and Roosevelt as the candidates who finally ran against Wilson for the presidency supports choice (D).

A PATTERNED PLAN OF ATTACK

Reading Comprehension

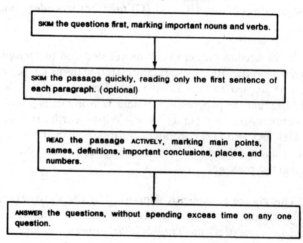

SKIM the questions first, marking important nouns and verbs.

SKIM the passage quickly, reading only the first sentence of each paragraph. (optional)

READ the passage ACTIVELY, marking main points, names, definitions, important conclusions, places, and numbers.

ANSWER the questions, without spending excess time on any one question.

INTRODUCTION TO PROBLEM SOLVING

The Problem Solving section contains sixteen questions, most of which are word problems. Occasionally, questions refer to a graph or chart.

Ability Tested

The Problem Solving section tests your ability to solve mathematical problems involving arithmetic, algebra, and geometry and word problems by using problem-solving insight, logic, and application of basic skills.

Basic Skills Necessary

The basic skills necessary to do well on this section include high school arithmetic, algebra, and intuitive geometry—no formal trigonometry or calculus is necessary. These skills, along with logical insight into problem-solving situations, are covered by the examination.

Directions

Solve each problem in this section by using the information given and your own mathematical calculations. Then select the *one* correct answer of the five choices given. Use the available space on the page for scratchwork.

Note: Some problems may be accompanied by figures or diagrams. These figures are drawn as accurately as possible *except* when it is stated in a specific problem that the figure is not drawn to scale. The figure is meant to provide information useful in solving the problem or problems.

Unless otherwise stated or indicated, all figures lie in a plane.

All numbers used are real numbers.

Analysis

All scratchwork is to be done in the test booklet; get used to doing this because no scratch paper is allowed into the testing area.

You are looking for the *one* correct answer; therefore, although other answers may be close, there is never more than one right answer.

Suggested Approach with Samples

• **Take advantage of being allowed to mark on the test booklet by always underlining or circling what you are looking for. This will ensure that you are answering the right question.**

If $x + 6 = 9$, then $3x + 1 =$
(A) 3
(B) 9
(C) 10
(D) 34
(E) 46

You should first circle or underline $3x + 1$, because this is what you are solving for. Solving for x leaves $x = 3$ and then substituting into $3x + 1$ gives $3(3) + 1$, or 10. The most common mistake is to solve for x, which is 3, and *mistakenly choose* (A) as your answer. But remember, you are solving for $3x + 1$, not just x. You should also notice that most of the other choices would all be possible answers if you made common or simple mistakes. The correct answer is (C). *Make sure that you are answering the right question.*

● **Substituting numbers for variables can often be an aid to understanding a problem. Remember to substitute simple numbers, since *you* have to do the work.**

If $x > 1$, which of the following decreases as x decreases?

  I. $x + x^2$

  II. $2x^2 - x$

III. $\dfrac{1}{x + 1}$

(A) I only
(B) II only
(C) III only
(D) I and II only
(E) II and III only

This problem is most easily solved by taking each situation and substituting simple numbers.

However, in the first situation, I, $x + x^2$, you should recognize that this expression will decrease as x decreases.

Trying $x = 2$ gives $2 + (2)^2$, which equals 6.

Now trying $x = 3$ gives $3 + (3)^2 = 12$.

Notice that choices (B), (C), and (E) are already eliminated because they do not contain I. You should also realize that now you only need to try the values in II; since III is not paired with I as a possible choice, III cannot be one of the answers.

Trying $x = 2$ in the expression $2x^2 - x$, gives $2(2)^2 - 2$, or $2(4) - 2$, which leaves 6.

Now trying $x = 3$ gives $2(3)^2 - 3$, or $2(9) - 3 = 18 - 3 = 15$. This expression also decreases as x decreases. Therefore the correct answer is choice (D). Once again notice that III was not even attempted, because it was not one of the possible choices.

• **Sometimes you will immediately recognize the proper formula or method to solve a problem. If this is not the situation, try a reasonable approach and then work from the answers.**

Barney can mow the lawn in 5 hours, and Fred can mow the lawn in 4 hours. How long will it take them to mow the lawn together?
(A) 5 hours
(B) 4½ hours
(C) 4 hours
(D) 2⅖ hours
(E) 1 hour

Suppose that you are unfamiliar with the type of equation for this problem. Try the "reasonable" method. Since Fred can mow the lawn in 4 hours by himself, he will take less than 4 hours if Barney helps him. Therefore, choices (A), (B), and (C) are ridiculous. Taking this method a little further, suppose that Barney could also mow the lawn in 4 hours. Then together it would take Barney and Fred 2 hours. But since Barney is a little slower than this, the total time should be more than 2 hours. The correct answer is (D), 2⅖ hours.

Using the equation for this problem would give the following calculations:

$$\frac{1}{5} + \frac{1}{4} = \frac{1}{x}$$

In 1 hour, Barney could do 1/5 of the job, and in 1 hour, Fred could do 1/4 of the job; unknown $1/x$ is the part of the job they could do together in one hour. Now, solving, you calculate as follows:

$$\frac{4}{20} + \frac{5}{20} = \frac{1}{x}$$

$$\frac{9}{20} = \frac{1}{x}$$

Cross multiplying gives $9x = 20$
Therefore, $x = $ ²⁰⁄₉, or 2⅖.

• **"Pulling" information out of the word problem structure can often give you a better look at what you are working with, and therefore, you gain additional insight into the problem.**

If a mixture is 3/7 alcohol by volume and 4/7 water by volume, what is the ratio of the volume of alcohol to the volume of water in this mixture?

(A) 3/7
(B) 4/7
(C) 3/4
(D) 4/3
(E) 7/4

The first bit of information that should be pulled out should be what you are looking for: "ratio of the volume of alcohol to the volume of water." Rewrite it as $A{:}W$ and then into its working form: A/W. Next, you should pull out the volumes of each; $A = 3/7$ and $W = 4/7$. Now the answer can be easily figured by inspection or substitution: using $(3/7)/(4/7)$, invert the bottom fraction and multiply to get $3/7 \times 7/4 = 3/4$. The ratio of the volume of alcohol to the volume of water is 3 to 4. The correct answer is (C). When pulling out information, actually write out the numbers and/or letters to the side of the problem, putting them into some helpful form and eliminating some of the wording.

• **Sketching diagrams or simple pictures can also be very helpful in problem solving, because the diagram may tip off either a simple solution or a method for solving the problem.**

What is the maximum number of pieces of birthday cake of size 4″ by 4″ that can be cut from a cake 20″ by 20″?

(A) 5
(B) 10
(C) 16
(D) 20
(E) 25

Sketching the cake and marking in as follows makes this a fairly simple problem.

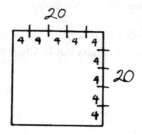

Notice that five pieces of cake will fit along each side, therefore 5 × 5 = 25. The correct answer is (E). Finding the total area of the cake and dividing it by the area of one of the 4 × 4 pieces would have also given you the correct answer, but beware of this method because it may not work if the pieces do not fit evenly into the original area.

• **Marking in diagrams as you read them can save you valuable time. Marking can also give you insight into how to solve a problem because you will have the complete picture clearly in front of you.**

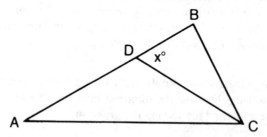

In the triangle, $\overline{CD}$ is an angle bisector, angle ACD is 30° and angle ABC is a right angle. Find the measurement of angle x in degrees.
(A) 80°
(B) 75°
(C) 60°
(D) 45°
(E) 30°

You should have read the problem and marked as follows:

In the triangle above, $\overline{CD}$ is an angle bisector (STOP AND MARK IN THE DRAWING), angle ACD is 30° (STOP AND MARK IN THE DRAWING), and angle ABC is a right angle (STOP AND MARK IN THE DRAWING). Find the measurement of angle x in degrees (STOP AND MARK IN OR CIRCLE WHAT YOU ARE LOOKING FOR IN THE DRAWING).

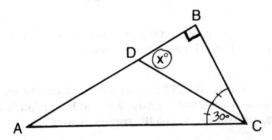

Now with the drawing marked in, it is evident that since angle ACD is 30°, angle BCD is also 30° because they are formed by an angle bisector (divides an angle into two equal parts). Since angle ABC is 90° (right angle) and BCD is 30°, then angle x is 60°, because there are 180° in a triangle; $180 - (90 + 30) = 60$. The correct answer is (C). ALWAYS MARK IN DIAGRAMS AS YOU READ THEIR DESCRIPTIONS AND INFORMATION ABOUT THEM. THIS INCLUDES WHAT YOU ARE LOOKING FOR.

• **If it appears that extensive calculations are going to be necessary to solve a problem, check to see how far apart the choices are, and then approximate. The reason for checking the answers first is to give you a guide for how freely you can approximate.**

The value for $(0.889 \times 55)/9.97$ to the nearest tenth is
(A) 0.5
(B) 4.63
(C) 4.9
(D) 7.7
(E) 49.1

Before starting any computations, take a glance at the answers to see how far apart they are. Notice that the only close answers are choices (B) and (C), except (B) is not possible, since it is to the nearest hundredth, not tenth. Now, making some quick approximations, $0.889 = 1$ and $9.97 = 10$, leaves the problem in this form

$$\frac{1 \times 55}{10} = \frac{55}{10} = 5.5$$

The closest answer is (C); therefore, it is the correct answer. Notice that choices (A) and (E) were not reasonable.

● **In some instances, it will be easier to work from the answers. Do not disregard this method, because it will at least eliminate some of the choices and could give you the correct answer.**

Find the counting number that is less than 15 and when divided by 3 has a remainder of 1 and divided by 4 has a remainder of 2.
(A) 13
(B) 12
(C) 10
(D) 8
(E) 5

By working from the answers, you eliminate wasting time on other numbers from 1 to 14. Choices (B) and (D) can be immediately eliminated because they are divisible by 4, leaving no remainder. Choices (A) and (E) can also be eliminated because they leave a remainder of 1 when divided by 4. Therefore the correct answer is (C); 10 leaves a remainder of 1 when divided by 3 and a remainder of 2 when divided by 4.

A PATTERNED PLAN OF ATTACK

Problem Solving

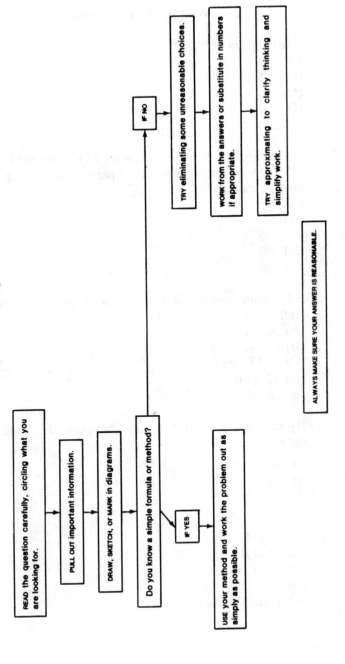

READ the question carefully, circling what you are looking for.

PULL OUT important information.

DRAW, SKETCH, OR MARK in diagrams.

Do you know a simple formula or method?

IF YES

USE your method and work the problem out as simply as possible.

IF NO

TRY eliminating some unreasonable choices.

WORK from the answers or substitute in numbers if appropriate.

TRY approximating to clarify thinking and simplify work.

ALWAYS MAKE SURE YOUR ANSWER IS REASONABLE.

WARM-UP PROBLEMS

1. What percent of 60 is 80?
   - (A) 133⅓
   - (B) 75
   - (C) 60
   - (D) 33⅓
   - (E) 25

2. On a map, 1 centimeter represents 35 kilometers. Two cities 245 kilometers apart would be separated on the map by how many centimeters?
   - (A)   5
   - (B)   7
   - (C)   9
   - (D) 210
   - (E) 280

3. If 5 machines can produce 20 units in 10 hours, how long would it take 20 machines to produce 100 units?
   - (A) 50 hours
   - (B) 40 hours
   - (C) 12.5 hours
   - (D) 12 hours
   - (E) 8 hours

4. If $g < 0$ and $f \neq 0$, which of these four expressions must have a positive sign?

   I. gf
   II. $g^2 f$
   III. gf^2
   IV. $(gf)^2$

   - (A) IV only
   - (B) I and III only
   - (C) I and IV only
   - (D) II and III only
   - (E) II and IV only

5. In ten years, David will be four times as old as Aaron. Twenty years ago, David was twice as old as Ellen. If David is seven years older than Ellen, how old is Aaron?
   (A) 1–5
   (B) 6–10
   (C) 11–15
   (D) 16–20
   (E) 21–25

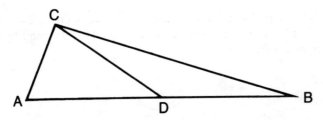

6. In the figure, $AB = BC$, $CD = BD$, and angle $CAD = 70°$. Therefore, what is the measure of angle ADC?
   (A) 50°
   (B) 60°
   (C) 70°
   (D) 80°
   (E) Cannot be determined

7. A girl runs k miles in n hours. How many miles will she run in x hours at the same rate?

   (A) knx

   (B) $\dfrac{k}{n}$

   (C) $\dfrac{kx}{n}$

   (D) kx

   (E) $\dfrac{kn}{x}$

8. If $ax + by = c$, then $b =$

   (A) $\dfrac{c}{y} - ax$

   (B) $c - ax - y$

   (C) $\dfrac{c}{ax} - y$

   (D) $\dfrac{c - ax}{y}$

   (E) $\dfrac{ax - c}{y}$

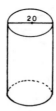

9. A right circular cylinder has a diameter of 20, as shown in the figure. If its height is 100, then its total surface area in square inches is approximately
   (A)   600
   (B)   3000
   (C)   6000
   (D)   6600
   (E) 30,000

10. Two airplanes take off from one airfield at noon. One flies due east at 200 miles per hour while the other flies directly northeast at 283 miles per hour. Approximately how many miles apart are the airplanes at 2 P.M.?
    (A) 166
    (B) 332
    (C) 400
    (D) 483
    (E) 566

11. At an elementary school, 70% of the faculty members are women and 60% of the faculty members are married. If ⅔ of the men are single, what fraction of the women are married?
    (A) 5/7
    (B) 7/10
    (C) ⅓
    (D) 7/30
    (E) Cannot be determined

12. At a party there were 5 times as many females as males. There were 3 times as many adults as children. Which of the following could not be the number of people at the party?
    (A) 384
    (B) 258
    (C) 216
    (D) 120
    (E) 72

13. Pete has some apples. He sold 40% more than he ate. If he sold 70 apples, how many did he eat?
    (A) 90
    (B) 50
    (C) 42
    (D) 28
    (E) 6

14. If $1/3 + 1/2 + 1/x = 4$, then $x =$
    (A) 18/5
    (B) 19/6
    (C) 24/11
    (D) 6/19
    (E) 5/18

15. While traveling from city A to city B, Sharon and Andy average 50 miles per hour. For the return trip, they average 40 miles per hour. What was their average speed for the round trip?
    (A) 45 mph
    (B) More than 45 mph
    (C) Less than 45 mph
    (D) More than 50 mph
    (E) Cannot be determined

16. If the @ of an integer is defined as the product of its cube root and its square root, then the @ of N equals 50% of N for which of the following?
    (A)   1
    (B)   64
    (C)   100
    (D)   144
    (E) 1,000,000

17. The Arnolds purchased 550 square feet of Kentucky Gem sod at $1.89 per square foot and 270 square feet of Zelzea Blue sod at $1.38 per square foot. What was the approximate average price per square foot paid for all the sod?
    (A) $1.63
    (B) $1.64
    (C) $1.68
    (D) $1.72
    (E) $1.76

18. How many combinations are possible if a person has 4 sport jackets, 5 shirts, and 3 pairs of slacks?
    (A)   4
    (B)   5
    (C)   12
    (D)   60
    (E) 120

19. John received a 10% raise each month for three consecutive months. What was his salary after the three raises if his starting salary was $1000 per month?
    (A) $1248
    (B) $1300
    (C) $1331
    (D) $1410
    (E) None of these

Question 20 refers to the graph.

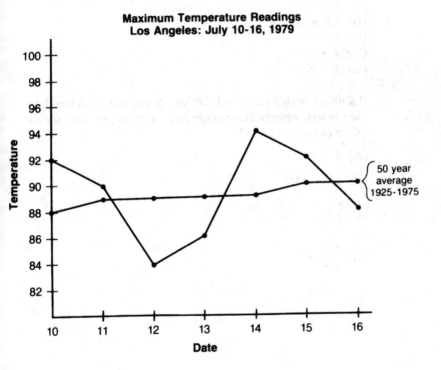

20. What was the percent increase in the maximum temperature from July 12 to July 14, 1979?
    (A) 10%
    (B) 10.6%
    (C) 10.9%
    (D) 11.9%
    (E) 13.6%

21. The greatest common factor of two positive integers is X. The least common multiple of these two integers is Y. If one of the integers is Z, what is the other?
    (A) XY/Z
    (B) $XZ + YZ$
    (C) $X/Z + Y$
    (D) $X + Y/Z$
    (E) $X + Z/Y$

22. If a man travels f miles an hour for t hours and r miles an hour for s hours, what is his average rate in miles per hour for the entire distance traveled?

    (A) $ft + rs$

    (B) $(ft + rs)/2$

    (C) $\dfrac{f}{t} + \dfrac{r}{s}$

    (D) $\dfrac{ft + rs}{t + s}$

    (E) $\dfrac{ft + rs}{t - s}$

23. If two numbers have only the number 1 as a common divisor, then they are called "relatively prime." Which of the following are NOT relatively prime?

    I.   3
    II. 4
    III. 7
    IV. 12

    (A) I and II, I and III
    (B) I and IV, II and IV
    (C) II and III, II and IV
    (D) II and IV, III and IV
    (E) I and II, I and IV

24. A square, with perimeter 16, is inscribed in a circle. What is the area of the circle?
    (A) 4π
    (B) 8π
    (C) 12π
    (D) 16π
    (E) 32π

25. Approximately how many revolutions will be made by a car tire with a 14-inch diameter if the car travels ½ mile?
    (A)   120
    (B)   180
    (C)   360
    (D)   720
    (E) 1440

Answers and Explanations

1. (A) One method is: $\dfrac{\text{is number}}{\text{of number}} = \dfrac{\text{percent}}{100}$

$$\frac{80}{60} = \frac{x}{100}$$

Cross-multiplying gives $60x = 8000$

Divide by 60 $x = \dfrac{8000}{60}$

Then $x = 133\frac{1}{3}\%$

Another method is making an equation by replacing "what percent" with $x/100$, "of" by times ($\cdot$) and "is" by equals ($=$) giving the equation

$$\frac{x}{100} \cdot 60 = 80$$

Simplifying gives $(3/5)x = 80$

Multiplying by $\dfrac{5}{3}$ $\left(\dfrac{5}{3}\right)(3/5)x = 80\left(\dfrac{5}{3}\right)$

$$x = \frac{400}{3}$$

Then $x = 133\frac{1}{3}$

2. (B) Solve by setting up a proportion.

If 1 cm = 35 km
then x cm = 245 km

and $\dfrac{1}{x} = \dfrac{35}{245}$

$$35x = 245$$

$$\frac{35x}{35} = \frac{245}{35}$$

$$x = 7$$

3. (C) If 5 machines can produce 20 units in 10 hours, then 20 machines can produce 80 units in 10 hours. Since 100 is 25% more than 80, the correct answer is 25% more than 10, or 12.5 hours.

4. (A) Since g is negative and f may be negative, it is necessary to square each of the two parameters to be assured of obtaining a positive expression. Note that $(gf)^2 = g^2f^2$.

5. (A) The solution to this problem can be seen through the following grid. The sequence of the solution is indicated by the arrows.

	20 years ago	now	in 10 years
David	4x − 30 ←	← 4x − 10 ←	← 4x
Ellen	2x − 15 ↕ ←	→ 2x + 5	
Aaron		x − 10 ←	← x

$$4x - 10 = (2x + 5) + 7$$
$$4x - 10 = 2x + 12$$
$$2x = 22$$
$$x = 11$$

Therefore Aaron is now $x - 10 = 1$

6. (D) Since $AB = BC$, angle CAD is equal to angle ACB (isoceles triangle ABC). Thus angle ACB is also 70°. This makes angle B equal to 40° (180° in a triangle). Also angle BCD equals 40° (same reason as above). Thus angle ADC equals 80° (external angle theorem: external angle of a triangle is equal to the sum of the opposite two angles).

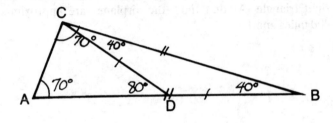

7. (C) Distance = rate × time

$d = rt$ Hence $d = rt$

$k = rn$

$r = \dfrac{k}{n}$ miles per hour

$$d = \dfrac{k}{n} \cdot (x) = \dfrac{kx}{n}$$

8. (D)

$$ax + by = c$$
$$\underline{-ax \qquad\qquad -ax}$$
$$by = c - ax$$
$$\dfrac{by}{y} = \dfrac{c - ax}{y}$$
$$b = \dfrac{c - ax}{y}$$

9. (D) To find the total surface area of a right circular cylinder, you must not only find the area of the "barrel" portion but also the area of the top and bottom circles. The area of the "barrel" portion equals the circumference of either the top or bottom circle times the height. $C = \pi d \cong 3 \times 20 = 60$. Thus the area of the "barrel" = $C \times h = 60 \times 100 = 6000$. Now to find the *total* surface area, add the areas of both top and bottom circles, or $2 \times \pi r^2 \cong 2 \times 3 \times 10^2 = 600$. Therefore the total surface area $\cong 6000 + 600 = 6600$.

10. (C) It is helpful to sketch a map of the positions, as shown on the following page. You should know that the northeast direction is 45° north of east, bisecting the north and east directions. After two hours the airplanes are at the arrowheads on the map. Since $566 \cong 400\sqrt{2}$, they are at two corners of a 45° right triangle. At that time, the airplanes are approximately 400 miles apart.

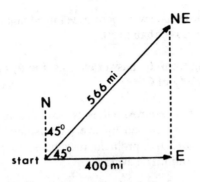

11. (A) Suppose there are 100 faculty members at the school. If 70% are women, then 30% are men. We then have 70 women and 30 men. If ⅔ of the men are single, then ⅓ of 30 = 10 men are married. 60% or 60 teachers are married. If 10 are men, then 50 are women. Therefore, the fraction of women who are married is ⁵⁰⁄₇₀ or ⁵⁄₇.

12. (B) From the first sentence, we see that the total number of persons at the party must be divisible by 6 (5:1). From the second sentence, the total must be divisible by 4 (3:1). Thus, the total must be a number divisible by both 6 and 4; such a number would be divisible by 12. The only number given that is not divisible by 12 is 258.

13. (B) Let x = number of apples Peter ate. Thus $x + 0.4x = 1.4x$ is the number of apples Peter sold. Thus $1.4x = 70; x = 70/1.4$, or 50. Notice answers (A), (D), and (E) are not reasonable.

14. (D) Multiplying the equation $1/3 + 1/2 + 1/x = 4$ by the common denominator $6x$, we get $6x/3 + 6x/2 + 6x/x = 4(6x)$. Reducing, we get

$$2x + 3x + 6 = 24x$$

$$5x + 6 = 24x$$

$$6 = 19x$$

$$6/19 = x$$

15. (C) Since more time was spent traveling at 40 mph, the average will be closer to 40 than to 50.

16. (B) Working from the answer choices, the @ of 64 = 4 × 8 = 32, which is 50% of 64.

17. (D) Notice that approximately two square feet of Kentucky Gem sod was purchased for every one square foot of Zelzea Blue. Therefore the problem may be simplified by using a simple 2 to 1 ratio. The average of

$$\begin{array}{ll} \text{2 square feet @ \$1.89} & = \$3.78 \\ \underline{\text{1 square foot @ \$1.38}} & = \underline{1.38} \\ \text{3 square feet} & \$5.16 \end{array}$$

Dividing $5.16 by 3 = $1.72 per square foot.

18. (D) Since each of the 4 sport jackets may be worn with 5 different shirts, we have 20 possible combinations. These may be worn with each of the 3 pairs of slacks for a total of 60 possible combinations. Stated simply, 5 × 4 × 3 = 60 possible combinations. Notice answers (A) and (B) are not reasonable.

19. (C) We have

10% of 1000 is 100. (1000 + 100) = 1100
10% of 1100 is 110. (1100 + 110) = 1210
10% of 1210 is 121. (1210 + 121) = 1331

20. (D) The increase was 94 − 84 = 10. The percent increase is found by dividing the increase by the *original* or *from* amount. Thus 10/84 = 11.9%.

21. (A) The product of the LCM and GCF of two numbers is the same as the product of the two original numbers. Thus, the answer is XY/Z.

22. (D) Average rate is total distance (found by multiplying rate times time and adding $ft + rs$) divided by total time $(t + s)$; therefore the average rate is $(ft + rs/t + s)$.

23. **(B)** Checking each possible pair of numbers for common divisions:

       I.   3 ⎤ Only common divisor 1
      II.   4 ⎦ These are relatively prime

      I.   3 ⎤ Only common divisor 1
     III. 7 ⎦ These are relatively prime

      I.   3 ⎤ Common divisors are 1 and 3
     IV. 12 ⎦ These are *not* relatively prime

Since I and IV are *not* relatively prime, check the choices to see which include I and IV. Notice that I and II are only in choices (B) and (E); therefore, those are the two possible choices. A closer look eliminates choice (E) because I and II have numbers that are relatively prime. For good measure, check II and IV:

      II.   4 ⎤ Common divisors are 1 and 4
     IV. 12 ⎦ These are *not* relatively prime

Therefore I and IV, and II and IV are *not* relatively prime giving the correct answer of (B).

24. **(B)** In square *ABCD*, each side is 4, since the perimeter is 16. Then by the Pythagorean theorem, $d = 4\sqrt{2}$.

$$4^2 + 4^2 = d^2$$
$$16 + 16 = d^2$$
$$32 = d^2$$
$$\sqrt{32} = d$$

Simplifying $d = \sqrt{32}$
$$= \sqrt{16 \times 2}$$
$$= \sqrt{16} \times \sqrt{2}$$
$$= 4\sqrt{2}$$

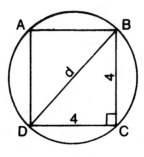

The radius is $r = \dfrac{d}{2}$

$$= \dfrac{4\sqrt{2}}{2}$$

$$= 2\sqrt{2}$$

The area of the circle $= \pi r^2$
$= \pi(2\sqrt{2})^2$
$= \pi \times 4 \times 2$
$= 8\pi$

Thus, (B) is correct. If you recognized DBC as a 45°-45°-90° triangle with side ratios $1{:}1{:}\sqrt{2}$, you could quickly find d by $4{:}4{:}4\sqrt{2}$.

25. (D) First calculate the circumference of the circle using the equation $C = \pi D$ (or $C = 2\pi r$). $C = (^{22}\!/_{7})14 = 44$. The circumference is 44 inches. Now change ½ mile to feet (2640) to inches, $2640 \times 12 = 31{,}680$. Dividing 31,680 by $44 = 720$ revolutions.

INTRODUCTION TO DATA SUFFICIENCY

The Data Sufficiency section contains twenty questions.

Ability Tested

Data Sufficiency tests your ability to analyze a problem, to recognize relevant or irrelevant information in determining the solution of that problem, and to determine when you have sufficient information to solve that problem.

Basic Skills Necessary

This section requires competence in high school arithmetic, algebra, and intuitive geometry. Mathematical insight and problem-solving skills are also necessary. No advanced mathematics is required.

Directions

Each of the problems below consists of a question and two statements, labeled (1) and (2), in which certain data are given. You must decide whether the data given in the statements are *sufficient* to answer the question. Using the data given in the statements *plus* your knowledge of mathematics and everyday facts (such as the number of days in July or the meaning of *counterclockwise*), you are to blacken space

- (A) if statement (1) ALONE is sufficient, but statement (2) alone is not sufficient to answer the question asked;
- (B) if statement (2) ALONE is sufficient, but statement (1) alone is not sufficient to answer the question asked;
- (C) if BOTH statements (1) and (2) TOGETHER are sufficient to answer the question asked, but NEITHER statement ALONE is sufficient;

67

(D) if EACH statement ALONE is sufficient to answer the question asked;

(E) if statements (1) and (2) TOGETHER are NOT sufficient to answer the question asked, and additional data specific to the problem are needed.

Analysis

The purpose here is to determine whether information given is *sufficient* to answer the question; therefore, *do not solve the problem* unless it is absolutely necessary.

The memory aid 12TEN will simplify the directions, making them easier to memorize and/or refer to. 12TEN stands for:

1 *First* statement ALONE is sufficient, not the second. CHOOSE (A).

2 *Second* statement ALONE is sufficient, not the first. CHOOSE (B).

T *Together* is the only way they are sufficient. CHOOSE (C).

E *Either* statement ALONE is sufficient. CHOOSE (D).

N *Neither* statement, TOGETHER or ALONE, is sufficient, CHOOSE (E).

REMEMBER: ONE, TWO, TOGETHER, EITHER, NEITHER, or 12TEN. (*Note: Either* means choose answer (D) *not* (E).)

Because of the structure of this type of question, you should always be able to eliminate some of the choices. If statement (1) ALONE is sufficient to answer the question, then the answer *must* be (A) or (D). If statement (1) ALONE is *not* sufficient to answer the question, then the answer *must* be (B), (C), or (E). If statements (1) and (2) ALONE are *not* sufficient, then the answer *must* be (C) or (E).

If statements (1) or (2) ALONE *are* sufficient, then you *never* try them TOGETHER.

Sometimes geometric figures are included; they should be used only for positional value, and are not to be measured as they are not necessarily drawn to scale.

Suggested Approach with Samples

● **Quickly decide what is the necessary basic information to answer the question. Then see if the data supplies that information.**

What is the area of circle O?
(1) The circumference is 12π.
(2) The diameter is 12.

To find the area of a circle, it is necessary to have the radius. (1) gives enough information to find the radius by substituting into the circumference formula, $C = 2\pi r$, and getting $12\pi = 2\pi r$. Then simply solve for r, which is 6. Thus this area is 36π. None of this solving was necessary, only knowing that you needed the radius and could find it from the information given. (2) also gives enough information to find the radius; therefore the answer is (D), either will be sufficient.

● **Don't solve unless it is absolutely necessary.**

What is the value of x?
(1) $3x + 12 = 36$
(2) $5x + 3y = 16$

This problem is most easily solved by inspecting the first bit of data and quickly noticing that (1) is enough to answer the question (one variable, one equation, solvable). (2) does not answer the question. This can also be determined by inspection (two variables, one equation, not solvable for a single value). The correct answer is (A), yet no actual solving had to be done.

● **Use a simple marking system to assist you in making your decision.**

What is the average height of Tom, Bob, and Luke?
(1) Bob is 4 inches shorter than Luke, and Tom is 4 inches taller than Luke.
(2) Luke is 5 feet 6 inches tall.

(1) is not sufficient, since no actual height is given; therefore mark a slash through (1). Note that the answer is immediately narrowed to (B), (C), or (E). (2) by itself is also not sufficient, as the other two, Tom and Bob, aren't mentioned; therefore, a slash should be made through (2). Notice that the answer is now narrowed to (C) or (E). Your markings should look as follows:

What is the average height of Tom, Bob, and Luke?
(1) Bob is 4 inches shorter than Luke, and Tom is 4 inches taller than Luke.
(2) Luke is 5 feet 6 inches tall.

Now trying them together, they are sufficient. The answer is (C). In marking the data, if you are in doubt whether it is sufficient or not, put a question mark by the data and try the next bit of data. Don't waste time trying one bit of data for over about 30 seconds.

● **Don't read in specialized knowledge; use only the information given and general or common knowledge.**

What is the runner's average speed in running around the track?
(1) One lap took 49 seconds.
(2) He ran 5 seconds faster than his previous best time.

Someone familiar with track and field would quickly assume that one lap is the standard 440 yards and would then *incorrectly answer* (A). This sort of assumption cannot be made as it is from specialized knowledge in the area and therefore is not general knowledge. The correct answer is (E) as the distance around the track is not given in either bit of data.

• **If a geometric figure is involved in the question, mark the figure with the information given and circle what you are looking for.**

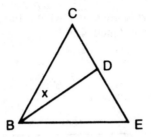

In the equilateral triangle above, what is the measure of angle *x*?
(1) $\overline{BD}$ is a median.
(2) Angle *BDE* is 90°.

Notice the markings from the information given:

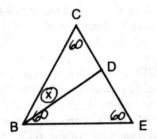

Mark in information given in data (1) as you read it, *but remember to erase that information before you try data* (2). (1) If $\overline{BD}$ is a median in an equilateral triangle, then it is also an angle bisector, making angle *x* equal to 30°. (Once again, the answer is not necessary, just the knowledge that it could be found.) (2) also gives enough information because if angle *BDE* is 90°, then angle *BDC* is 90°, and angle *x* is 30°, as there are 180° in a triangle. Marking the diagram makes the problem easier to solve.

• **If a geometric diagram is discussed, but no figure given, draw a simple diagram.**

If the legs of a trapezoid are equal, what is the area?
(1) The smaller base is 8 inches and the legs are 6 inches.
(2) The height is 5 inches.

Drawing the diagram helps give important insight into what is needed to answer the question.

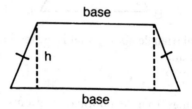

Now consider what is needed to find the area—height and length of each base since the area formula is $\frac{1}{2}h(b_1 + b_2)$ or $h(b_1 + b_2)/2$.

 (1) does not give sufficient information to find the larger base or the height. (2), by itself, does not give enough information to find the bases. (1) and (2) together give enough information to find the bases and the height. The answer is (C). The Pythagorean theorem would be necessary to find the length of the difference between the smaller and larger bases. Adding this difference to the length of the shorter base would give the longer base. You now have the necessary information. Notice the markings on the diagram below, to assist you in deciding what you have to work with.

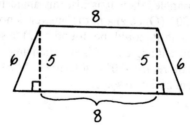

A PATTERNED PLAN OF ATTACK

Data Sufficiency

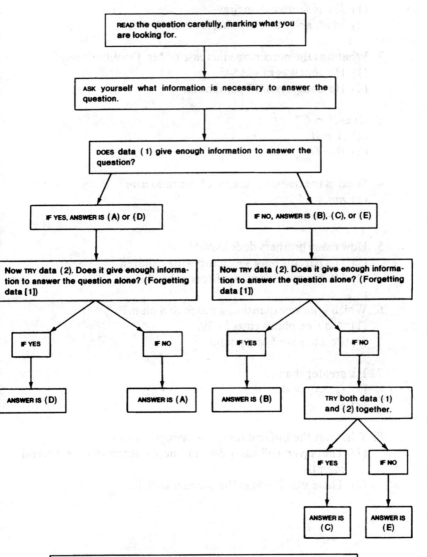

KEEP THE FOLLOWING TIPS IN MIND.
1. Don't solve unless it is absolutely necessary.
2. Use a simple marking system (slashes, question marks, etc.).
3. Don't read in specialized knowledge. Use only common information.
4. Mark in or draw geometric figures when appropriate.

WARM-UP PROBLEMS

1. Who is the tallest of four men?
   (1) Jim is shorter than Steve.
   (2) Mark and Steve are shorter than Walter.

2. What was the percentage increase of Mr. Doolittle's rent?
   (1) His rent was raised $45.
   (2) He now pays $315 per month.

3. Does $A = C$?
   (1) $A \neq B$
   (2) $B \neq C$

4. What is the numerical value of the ratio n/m?
   (1) $mn = 14$
   (2) $m = 6n$

5. How many brothers does David have?
   (1) His parents have seven surviving children.
   (2) He has twice as many sisters as brothers.

6. Which is more expensive, a peach or a plum?
   (1) A dozen plums costs $1.79.
   (2) Peaches are 69¢ a pound.

7. Is x greater than y?
   (1) $(x - y) > 0$
   (2) $x^2 < y^2$

8. What was the interest rate on a savings account?
   (1) The saver collected $42 in simple interest over several months.
   (2) There was $1680 in the account initially.

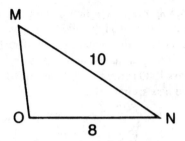

9. What is the perimeter of triangle *MNO*?
   (1) The area of triangle *MNO* is 24.
   (2) Angle *MON* equals 90°.

10. Which is the smallest of three numbers that average 7?
    (1) One of the numbers is 4.
    (2) One of the numbers is 6.

11. In the equation $3a - 7b + 14 = 0$, what is the value of b?
    (1) $a = b$
    (2) $a = 3$

12. What is the area of a circular garden?
    (1) The circumference is 314 feet.
    (2) The radius is 50 feet.

13. A hexagonal playing field is composed of six equilateral triangles, each the same size. If one player controls each triangle, how much area is controlled by all six players?
    (1) One edge of one triangular region equals 15 feet.
    (2) The perimeter of one triangular region equals 45 feet.

14. How many Mondays are in December of a particular year?
    (1) There are four Tuesdays that December.
    (2) There are four Saturdays that December.

15. How long is the diagonal through the center of a particular cube?
    (1) A diagonal across one face is 4.24 centimeters.
    (2) The surface area of the cube is 54 square centimeters.

16. Were more new sports cars or new sedans purchased in Wichita during the years 1980 through 1990?
    (1) In the years 1980 through 1990, one-fourth of the population of Wichita purchased new sedans.
    (2) In the years 1980 through 1990, one-third of the population purchased new sports cars.

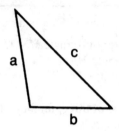

17. What is the length of side c?
    (1) $a = 6$
    (2) $b = 7$

18. Is x greater than y?
    (1) $x = \sqrt{3}$
    (2) y is a prime number.

19. What is the value of j if h is $k\%$ of j?
    (1) h is 25% of 40.
    (2) $k = 20$

20. Eloise's aquarium contains six tropical fish. If the largest fish is 4 ounces heavier than the smallest fish, how heavy is the smallest fish?
    (1) If the largest fish were 6 ounces heavier, it would weigh twice as much as the smallest fish.
    (2) The six fish average 14 ounces in weight.

Answers and Explanations

1. (C) From both statements, Jim must also be shorter than Walter, who is taller than any of the other men.

2. (C) His initial rent was $315 − $45 = $270, so the increase was 45 divided by 270 equals 16.7%.

3. (E) The relationship between two quantities is uncertain given merely that each is unequal to a third quantity.

4. (B) Statement (1) reveals a product, not a quotient. However, dividing both sides of equation (2) by $6/m$ demonstrates than $n/m = 1/6$.

5. (C) From the first statement, David has 6 sisters and brothers (he is the seventh child). Combining that piece of data with the second statement, he must have 4 sisters and 2 brothers.

6. (E) The first statement enables us to find the cost of one plum. But without the weight of one peach, we cannot use (2) to find the cost of a peach.

7. (A) Inequality (1) informs us that x exceeds y, whether positive, zero, or negative. Inequality (2) does not tell us so much, for the sign of the numbers is masked by the squaring.

8. (E) Simple interest equals principal times rate times time. We are not told the length of time the money was in the account.

9. (D) Since statement (1) tells us the area of triangle *MNO* is 24, its height must be 6. Note that side *MO* will be the height because 6-8-10 is a Pythagorean triple. Thus we can find the perimeter. Using statement (2) we know $\triangle MON$ is a right triangle and can use the Pythagorean theorem to find the third side.

10. (C) With both statements, we know that the third number must exceed 7, so the smallest number is 4. But with the first statement alone, all we know is $4 + x + y = 3.7$, and one of the unknown numbers could be less than 4.

11. (D) Either statement transforms the equation so there is only one unknown, which therefore could be found:

$$(1)\ 3b - 7b + 14 = 0$$
$$(2)\ 9 - 7b + 14 = 0$$

12. (D) The area can be calculated from $A = \pi r^2$ if we know the radius, which is given in the second statement. The first statement gives the circumference, from which the radius may be found by $r = C/2\pi$.

13. (D) Given the edge (N) of an equilateral triangle, one can determine its height ($N\sqrt{3}/2$) and therefore its area. So one can determine the area of all six equilateral triangular regions, each of the same size.

14. (C) You must know that December has 31 days. (For the GMAT, you should know the number of days in each month of the year.) Therefore, December has 4 weeks and 3 extra days. For the 7 days of the week, 4 occur 4 times and the other 3 occur 5 times. Since there are only 2 days between Saturday (statement 2) and Tuesday (statement 1), there must be 4 Sundays and Mondays that month.

15. (D) The diagonal through the center of a cube, from one corner to the opposite corner, may be found with the Pythagorean theorem providing that the length of the cube's edge is known. Statement (1) implies that the edge is $4.24/\sqrt{2}$ centimeters. Moreover, since the surface area (2) has 6 faces, each face has an area of $54/6 = 9$ cm^2, and so the edge is $\sqrt{9} = 3$ cm.

16. (E) Neither of the statements gives definitive information about the *number* of new sedans or the number of the new sports cars purchased. For example, although one-fourth of the population may have purchased new sedans, the members of that fraction of the population may have each purchased *several* new sedans, bringing the number of new sedans purchased above the number of new sports cars purchased.

17. (E) The Pythagorean theorem, $a^2 + b^2 = c^2$, can be employed only for a triangle known to have a right angle.

18. (C) The smallest prime is 2, which exceeds $\sqrt{3}$ (approximately 1.73). Consequently, x is less than y.

19. (C) From statement (1) we find $h = 10$. From (2), $k = 20$. Then the question translates to: The number 10 is 20% of what number j? Therefore, $10 = 0.2j$, and $j = 10/0.2 = 50$.

20. (A) From statement (1), the following equation may be derived:

$$L + 6 = 2S$$

From the information given in the question, the following equation may be derived:

$$L = S + 4$$

Using simultaneous equations, we may solve for both S and L. Notice that statement (2) tells nothing about the individual weight of any fish.

GRAPHS AND CHARTS

Graphs and charts used to appear in a separate section on the GMAT. Now there are occasional problems involving graphs, charts, and tables in the Problem Solving and Data Sufficiency sections of the exam.

Ability Tested

You will need to understand and to derive information from graphs, charts, and tables. Many of the problems require brief calculations based on the data, so your mathematical ability is also tested.

Basic Skills Necessary

The mathematics associated with diagrammatic interpretation does not go beyond high-school level. Your familiarity with a wide range of chart and graph types will help you feel comfortable with these problems and read the data accurately.

Directions

You are given data represented in chart or graph form. Following each set of data are questions based on that data. Select the *best* answer to each question by referring to the appropriate chart or graph and mark your choice on the answer sheet. Use only the given or implied information to determine your answer.

Analysis

Remember that you are looking for the *best* answer, not necessarily the perfect answer. Often, graph questions ask you for an *approximate* answer; if this happens, don't forget to round off numbers to make your work easier.

Use only the information given; never "read into" the information on a graph.

Suggested Approach with Samples

Here are some helpful strategies for extracting accurate information followed by some sample graph questions.

• **Skim the questions and quickly examine the whole graph before starting to work problems; this sort of prereading will tell you what to look for.**

• **Use your answer sheet as a straightedge in order to align points on the graph with their corresponding number values.**

• **Sometimes the answer to a question is available in supplementary information given with a graph (headings, scale factors, legends, etc.); be sure to read this information.**

• **Look for the obvious: dramatic trends, high points, low points, etc.—obvious information often leads directly to an answer.**

Graphs and Charts

Questions 1–3 refer to the graph.

**Gross Receipts of Several Fast-Food Restaurants
1970-1972**

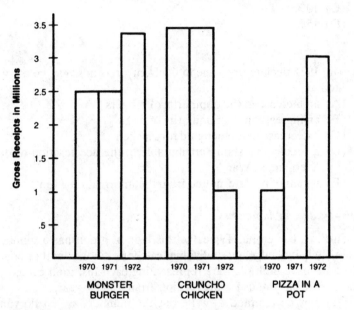

1. The 1970–72 gross receipts for Monster Burger exceeded those of Pizza In A Pot by approximately how much?
   - (A)   0.2 million
   - (B)   2 million
   - (C)   8.2 million
   - (D)   8.4 million
   - (E)   17 million

2. From 1971 to 1972, the percent increase in receipts for Pizza In A Pot exceeded the percent increase of Monster Burger by approximately how much?
   (A) 0%
   (B) 2%
   (C) 10%
   (D) 15%
   (E) 43%

3. The 1972 decline in Cruncho Chicken's receipts may be attributed to
   (A) an increase in the popularity of burgers
   (B) an increase in the popularity of pizza
   (C) a decrease in the demand for chicken
   (D) a predictable slump attributable to the deceleration of the Vietnamese War
   (E) it cannot be determined from the information given

Answers and Explanations

This is a bar graph. Typically, this type of graph has a number scale along one edge and individual categories along another edge. Here we have multiple bars representing each fast-food category; each single bar stands for the receipts from a single year.

You may be tempted to write out the numbers as you do your arithmetic (3.5 million = 3,500,000). This is unnecessary, as it often is on graphs which use large numbers. Since *all* measurements are in millions, adding zeros does not add precision to the numbers.

1. (B) Referring to the Monster Burger bars, we see that gross receipts are as follows: 1970 = 2.5, 1971 = 2.5, 1972 = 3.4 (use your answer sheet as a straightedge to determine this last number). Totalling the receipts for all three years, we get 8.4.

   Referring to the Pizza In A Pot bars, we see that gross receipts are as follows: 1970 = 1, 1971 = 2.1, 1972 = 3 (once again, use your straightedge, but do not designate numbers beyond the nearest tenth, since the graph numbers and the answer choices prescribe no greater accuracy than this). Totaling the receipts for all three years, we get 6.1.

So Monster Burger exceeds Pizza In A Pot by 2.3 million. The answer which best approximates this figure is (B).

2. (C) Several graph questions on the GMAT may ask you to calculate percent increase or percent decrease. The formula for figuring either of these is the same:

$$\frac{\text{amount of the change}}{\text{"starting" amount (follows the word } from)}$$

In this case, we may first calculate the percent increase for Monster Burger.

Gross receipts in 1971 = 2.5
Gross receipts in 1972 = 3.4
Amount of the change = 0.9

The 1971 amount is the "starting" or "from" amount.

$$\frac{\text{amount of the change}}{\text{"starting" amount}} = \frac{0.9}{2.5} = 0.36 = 36\%$$

Percent increase for Pizza In A Pot:

Gross receipts in 1971 = 2.1
Gross receipts in 1972 = 3
Amount of the change = 0.9

$$\frac{\text{amount of the change}}{\text{"starting" amount}} = \frac{0.9}{2.1} \cong 0.428 \cong 43\%$$

So, Pizza In A Pot exceeds Monster Burger by 7% (43% − 36%). The answer which best approximates this figure is (C).

3. (E) Never use information that you know is not given. In this case, the multiple factors which could cause a decline in receipts are not represented by the graph. All choices except (E) require you to speculate beyond the information given.

Questions 4–6 refer to the following pie charts.

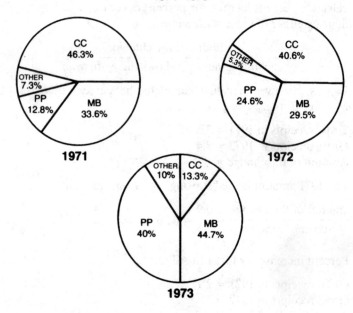

**Gross Receipts of All Major
Fast-Food Restaurants
1971–1973**

Gross Receipts for 1971: $7,500,000   MB—Monster Burger
Gross Receipts for 1972: $8,550,000   CC—Cruncho Chicken
Gross Receipts for 1973: $8,100,000   PP—Pizza In A Pot

4. The gross receipts for 1971 are approximately what percentage of the gross receipts for all three years?
   (A) 30%
   (B) 46.3%
   (C) 46.7%
   (D) 50%
   (E) It cannot be determined from the information given.

5. Over all three years, the average percentage of gross receipts for Cruncho Chicken exceeds the average percentage of gross receipts for Pizza In A Pot by approximately how much?
   (A) 53%
   (B) 30%
   (C) 23%
   (D) 8%
   (E) 4%

6. The gross receipts earned by other restaurants in 1973 amount to *precisely* how much?
   (A) $1,810,650
   (B) $810,000
   (C) $547,500
   (D) $453,150
   (E) A precise amount cannot be determined.

Answers and Explanations

   These are circle graphs, or pie charts. One hundred percent is represented by the whole circle, and the various "slices" represent portions of that 100 percent. The larger the slice, the higher the percentage.

4. (A) You can solve this problem without referring to the graphs; the necessary information is available in the list of gross receipts below the graphs. Don't write out all the zeros when calculating with these large figures; brief figures are easier to work with.

   Gross receipts for 1971 = 7.5 million.
   Gross receipts for all three years = 7.5 + 8.6 + 8.1 = 24.2 million.

$$\frac{7.5}{24.2} = 31\%$$

   The answer which best approximates 31% is 30%, (A). Notice that even without doing the calculations, you may approximate 30% by realizing that the gross receipts for any one year are about one-third of the total.

5. (D) To calculate the average percentage for Cruncho Chicken, add the percentages for each year and divide by 3.

$$46.3 + 40.6 + 13.3 = 100.2 \div 3 = 33.4\%$$

Do the same for Pizza In A Pot.

$$12.8 + 24.6 + 40 = 77.4 \div 3 = 25.8\%$$

Cruncho Chicken exceeds Pizza In A Pot by $33.4 - 25.8 = 7.6\%$. (D), 8%, best approximates this figure.

6. (B) In 1973, other restaurants earned precisely 10%. 10% of $8,100,000 = $810,000, (B).

A PATTERNED PLAN OF ATTACK

Graphs and Charts

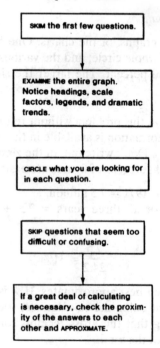

IMPORTANT SYMBOLS, TERMINOLOGY, FORMULAS, AND GENERAL MATHEMATICAL INFORMATION

COMMON MATH SYMBOLS AND TERMS

Symbol References:

= is equal to	≥ is greater than or equal to
≠ is not equal to	≤ is less than or equal to
> is greater than	‖ is parallel to
< is less than	⊥ is perpendicular to

Natural numbers—the counting numbers: 1, 2, 3, . . .

Whole numbers—the counting numbers beginning with zero: 0, 1, 2, 3, . . .

Integers—positive and negative whole numbers and zero: . . . -3, -2, -1, 0, 1, 2, . . .

Odd numbers—numbers not divisible by 2: 1, 3, 5, 7, . . .

Even numbers—numbers divisible by 2: 0, 2, 4, 6, . . .

Prime number—number divisible by only 1 and itself: 2, 3, 5, 7, 11, 13, . . .

Composite number—number divisible by more than just 1 and itself: 4, 6, 8, 9, 10, 12, 14, 15, . . .

Squares—the result when numbers are multiplied by themselves, $(2 \cdot 2 = 4)$ $(3 \cdot 3 = 9)$: 1, 4, 9, 16, 25, 36, . . .

Cubes—the result when numbers are multiplied by themselves twice, $(2 \cdot 2 \cdot 2 = 8)$, $(3 \cdot 3 \cdot 3 = 27)$: 1, 8, 27, . . .

MATH FORMULAS

Triangle	Perimeter $= s_1 + s_2 + s_3$
	Area $= \frac{1}{2}bh$
Square	Perimeter $= 4s$
	Area $= s \cdot s$, or s^2
Rectangle	Perimeter $= 2(b + h)$, or $2b + 2h$
	Area $= bh$, or lw

89

Parallelogram	Perimeter $= 2(l + w)$, or $2l + 2w$
	Area $= bh$
Trapezoid	Perimeter $= b_1 + b_2 + s_1 + s_2$
	Area $= \frac{1}{2}h(b_1 + b_2)$, or $h\left(\dfrac{b_1 + b_2}{2}\right)$
Circle	Circumference $= 2\pi r$, or πd
	Area $= \pi r^2$

Pythagorean theorem (for right triangles) $a^2 + b^2 = c^2$

The sum of the squares of the legs of a right triangle equals the square of the hypotenuse.

Cube	Volume $= s \cdot s \cdot s = s^3$
	Surface area $= s \cdot s \cdot 6$
Rectangular Prism	Volume $= l \cdot w \cdot h$
	Surface area $= 2(lw) + 2(lh) + 2(wh)$

IMPORTANT EQUIVALENTS

Memorizing the following can eliminate unnecessary computations:

$\frac{1}{100} = 0.01 = 1\%$

$\frac{1}{10} = 0.1 = 10\%$

$\frac{1}{5} = \frac{2}{10} = 0.2 = 0.20 = 20\%$

$\frac{3}{10} = 0.3 = 0.30 = 30\%$

$\frac{2}{5} = \frac{4}{10} = 0.4 = 0.40 = 40\%$

$\frac{1}{2} = \frac{5}{10} = 0.5 = 0.50 = 50\%$

$\frac{3}{5} = \frac{6}{10} = 0.6 = 0.60 = 60\%$

$\frac{7}{10} = 0.7 = 0.70 = 70\%$

$\frac{4}{5} = \frac{8}{10} = 0.8 = 0.80 = 80\%$

$\frac{9}{10} = 0.9 = 0.90 = 90\%$

$\frac{1}{4} = \frac{25}{100} = 0.25 = 25\%$

$\frac{3}{4} = \frac{75}{100} = 0.75 = 75\%$

$\frac{1}{3} = 0.33\frac{1}{3} = 33\frac{1}{3}\%$

$\frac{2}{3} = 0.66\frac{2}{3} = 66\frac{2}{3}\%$

$\frac{1}{8} = 0.125 = 0.12\frac{1}{2} = 12\frac{1}{2}\%$

$\frac{3}{8} = 0.375 = 0.37\frac{1}{2} = 37\frac{1}{2}\%$

$\frac{5}{8} = 0.625 = 0.62\frac{1}{2} = 62\frac{1}{2}\%$

$\frac{7}{8} = 0.875 = 0.87\frac{1}{2} = 87\frac{1}{2}\%$

$\frac{1}{6} = 0.16\frac{2}{3} = 16\frac{2}{3}\%$

$\frac{5}{6} = 0.83\frac{1}{3} = 83\frac{1}{3}\%$

$1 = 1.00 = 100\%$

$2 = 2.00 = 200\%$

$3\frac{1}{2} = 3.5 = 3.50 = 350\%$

MEASURES

Customary System, or English System

Length
12 inches (in) = 1 foot (ft)
3 feet = 1 yard (yd)
36 inches = 1 yard
1760 yards = 1 mile (mi)
5280 feet = 1 mile

Area
144 square inches (sq in) = 1 square foot (sq ft)
9 square feet = 1 square yard (sq yd)

Weight
16 ounces (oz) = 1 pound (lb)
2000 pounds = 1 ton (T)

Capacity
2 cups = 1 pint (pt)
2 pints = 1 quart (qt)
4 quarts = 1 gallon (gal)
4 pecks = 1 bushel

Time
365 days = 1 year
52 weeks = 1 year
10 years = 1 decade
100 years = 1 century

Metric System, or The International System of Units
(SI, *Le Système International d'Unités*)

Length—meter
Kilometer (km) = 1000 meters (m)
Hectometer (hm) = 100 meters
Dekameter (dam) = 10 meters

Meter
10 decimeters (dm) = 1 meter
100 centimeters (cm) = 1 meter
1000 millimeters (mm) = 1 meter

Volume—liter
    Common measures
        1000 milliliters (ml, or mL) = 1 liter (l, or L)
        1000 liters = 1 kiloliter (kl, or kL)

Mass—gram
    Common measures
        1000 milligrams (mg) = 1 gram (g)
        1000 grams = 1 kilogram (kg)
        1000 kilograms = 1 metric ton (t)

PROBLEM-SOLVING WORDS AND PHRASES

Words that signal an operation:

ADDITION
- Sum
- Total
- Plus
- Increase
- More than
- Greater than

SUBTRACTION
- Difference
- Less
- Decreased
- Reduced
- Fewer
- Have left

MULTIPLICATION
- Of
- Product
- Times
- At (sometimes)
- Total (sometimes)

DIVISION
- Quotient
- Divisor
- Dividend
- Ratio
- Parts

GEOMETRY TERMS AND BASIC INFORMATION

Angles

Vertical angles—Formed by two intersecting lines, across from each other, always equal

Adjacent angles—Next to each other, share a common side and vertex

Right angle—Measures 90°
Obtuse angle—Greater than 90°
Acute angle—Less than 90°
Straight angle, or line—Measures 180°
Angle bisector—Divides an angle into two equal angles
Supplementary angles—Two angles whose total is 180°
Complementary angles—Two angles whose total is 90°

Lines

Two points determine a line
Parallel lines—Never meet
Perpendicular lines—Meet at right angles

Polygons

Polygon—A many-sided (more than two sides) closed figure
Regular polygon—A polygon with all sides and all angles equal
Triangle—Three-sided polygon; the interior angles total 180°
    Equilateral triangle—All sides equal
    Isosceles triangle—Two sides equal
    Scalene triangle—All sides of different lengths
    Right triangle—A triangle containing a right angle
In a triangle—Angles opposite equal sides are equal
In a triangle—The longest side is across from the largest angle, and the shortest side is across from the smallest angle
In a triangle—The sum of any two sides of a triangle is larger than the third side.
In a triangle—An exterior angle is equal to the sum of the remote two angles
Median of a triangle—A line segment that connects the vertex and the midpoint of the opposite side.
Quadrilateral—Four-sided polygon; the interior angles total 360°
    Parallelogram—A quadrilateral with opposite sides parallel
      Rectangle—A parallelogram with all right angles
      Rhombus—A parallelogram with equal sides
      Square—A parallelogram with equal sides and all right angles
    Trapezoid—A quadrilateral with two parallel sides

Pentagon—A five-sided polygon
Hexagon—A six-sided polygon
Octagon—An eight-sided polygon

Circles

Radius of a circle—A line segment from the center of the circle to the circle itself
Diameter of a circle—A line segment than starts and ends on the circle and goes through the center
Chord—A line segment that starts and ends on the circle
Arc—A part of the circle
Circle—Composed of 360°

INTRODUCTION TO SENTENCE CORRECTION

The Sentence Correction section typically contains twenty-two questions.

Ability Tested

This section tests your knowledge of correct and effective English expression.

Basic Skills Necessary

Knowledge of basic rules of grammar and usage will help in this section.

Directions

Some part of each sentence below is underlined; sometimes the whole sentence is underlined. Five choices for rephrasing the underlined part follow each sentence; the first choice (A) repeats the original, and the other four are different. If choice (A) seems better than the alternatives, choose answer (A); if not, choose one of the others.

For each sentence, consider the requirements of standard written English. Your choice should be a correct and effective expression, not awkward or ambiguous. Focus on grammar, word choice, sentence construction, and punctuation. If a choice changes the meaning of the original sentence, do not select it.

Analysis

Several alternatives to an underlined portion may be correct; you are to pick the *best* (most clear and exact) one.

Any alternative which changes the meaning of the sentence should not be chosen, no matter how clear or correct it is.

Suggested Approach with Samples

• **Look for pronoun errors first. Focus upon words like** *he, him, she, her, we, us, they, them, who, whom, whoever, whomever, you, it, which,* **or** *that.*

The Rotary Club applauded Tom and I for our work helping the handicapped in town find secure jobs.
(A) The Rotary Club applauded Tom and I
(B) The Rotary club applauded Tom and I
(C) The Rotary Club applauded us both
(D) The Rotary Club applauded Tom and me
(E) The Rotary Club applauded both of us

Focus on *I*, because it's a pronoun. To test whether *I* is correct, remove "Tom and." The result is, "The Rotary Club applauded . . . I." *Me* would sound better, and in fact (D) is the correct choice. (C) and (E) change the meaning of the sentence.

• **If the sentence contains no pronouns or if the pronouns are correct, focus on the** *verb.*

The trunk containing costumes, makeup, and props were left at the stage entrance of the theater.
(A) costumes, makeup, and props were left
(B) costumes, makeup, and props were all left
(C) costumes, makeup, and props was left
(D) costumes, makeup, and props to be left
(E) costumes, makeup, and props left

The verb is *were left*. Since the subject is singular (*trunk*) the verb must be singular—*was* instead of *were*. Don't assume that the subject immediately precedes the verb; in this case, the subject and verb are some distance apart.

• **Another common error is faulty parallelism. Look for a series of items separated by commas and make sure each item has the same form.**

<u>To strive, to seek, to find, and not yielding</u> are the heroic goals of Ulysses in Tennyson's famous poem.
(A) To strive, to seek, to find, and not yielding
(B) To strive, to seek, to find, and to yield
(C) To strive, to seek, to find, and not to yield
(D) To strive, to seek, to find, and yet to yield
(E) Striving, seeking, finding and yielding

Not yielding is incorrect; it should have the "to _____" form of the other items. (C) is the best choice; (B), (D), and (E) are correct, but they change the meaning of the sentence.

• **Another verb error happens when the verb tense (past, present, future) is inconsistent. If there are two verbs in the sentence, make sure the verb tense of each is appropriate.**

<u>If he would have worked</u> harder, he could have gone to the movies.
(A) If he would have worked
(B) If he worked
(C) Working
(D) If he had worked
(E) After working

In general, if a sentence contains two "would haves," two "should haves," two "could haves," or any combination of these terms (in this case *would have* and *should have*), one of the verbs should be changed to *had*, to indicate that one of the actions (working) occurred earlier than the other (going to the movies). (D) is correct.

• **Sometimes a sentence contains an error in idiom; that is, it employs a word or phrase which is incorrect simply because it has not been established as standard usage. Such errors just don't "sound right."**

<u>After waiting on the arrival of a washer repairman for hours</u>, the customer resigned himself to using the laundromat.
(A) After waiting on the arrival of a washer repairman for hours
(B) With no arrival of a washer repairman for hours
(C) After hours of waiting for the arrival of a washer repairman
(D) Waiting after hours for the arrival of a washer repairman
(E) In the face of hours of waiting for a washer repairman

Waiting on is not idiomatic; the correct expression is *waiting for*. Choices (C), (D), and (E) employ this construction, but (D) and (E) significantly obscure and change the intended meaning of the original sentence.

• **Adjective or adverb misuse constitutes another type of error.**

<u>The tired mechanic, happily to be finished with a hard day's work</u>, closed the hood over the newly tuned engine.
(A) The tired mechanic, happily to be finished with a hard day's work
(B) Happily, the tired mechanic being finished with a hard day's work
(C) Tired but happy with a hard day's work being done, the mechanic
(D) The tired mechanic, happy to be finished with a hard day's work
(E) With the pleasant fatigue of a job well done, the mechanic

Happily is used here to describe a person, the mechanic. The correct part of speech for describing a person or thing is an adjective, *happy*. (D) is the correct choice—grammatically correct, logical, economical, and clear without unnecessarily changing the intended meaning of the original sentence.

• **A type of error that affects a whole phrase rather than just one word is a dangling element, or misplaced modifier, error.**

<u>Looking through the lens of a camera</u>, Mount Rushmore seemed much smaller and farther away than it had only seconds before.
(A) Looking through the lens of a camera
(B) With camera in hand
(C) Through the effects of the lens of a camera she looked through
(D) When she looked through the camera lens
(E) Against the camera

The sentence seems to say that Mount Rushmore is looking through the camera lens. Choice (D) makes it clear that a person is looking through the lens and does so without the excessive wordiness of choice (C).

• **A sentence may contain a comparison error.**

She wished that her career could be <u>as glamorous as the other women</u> but was not willing to work as hard as they had.
(A) as glamorous as the other women
(B) as glamorous as the other women's careers
(C) with the glamour of other women
(D) more glamorous than the careers of the other women
(E) glamorous

Here two very different *in*comparable things are being compared: her career is compared to the other women. Choice (B), the most clear, complete, and sensible construction, compares her career to the careers of other women.

Summary

Generally, watch out for pronouns, verbs, and awkward larger structures (illustrated by errors like faulty parallelism). Other possible errors which have not been explained above are fully explained in the answer sections following the practice tests.

A PATTERNED PLAN OF ATTACK

Sentence Correction

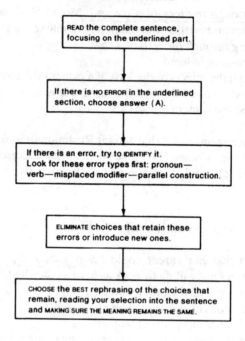

READ the complete sentence, focusing on the underlined part.

If there is NO ERROR in the underlined section, choose answer (A).

If there is an error, try to IDENTIFY it. Look for these error types first: pronoun— verb—misplaced modifier—parallel construction.

ELIMINATE choices that retain these errors or introduce new ones.

CHOOSE the BEST rephrasing of the choices that remain, reading your selection into the sentence and MAKING SURE THE MEANING REMAINS THE SAME.

WARM-UP PROBLEMS

1. Although the Contadora group of Central America has completed <u>their manifesto that address the political tensions in that area</u>, no easing of tensions has resulted.
   - (A) their manifesto that address the political tensions in that area
   - (B) their manifesto that addresses the political tensions in that area
   - (C) its manifesto that address the political tensions for that area
   - (D) its manifesto that addresses the political tensions with that area in mind
   - (E) its manifesto that addresses the political tensions in that area

2. <u>Secretly determined to break up the drug dealer's ring, the undercover agent with the local pushers joined forces,</u> without their realizing his identity.
   - (A) Secretly determined to break up the drug dealer's ring, the undercover agent with the local pushers joined forces,
   - (B) Secretly determined to break up the drug dealer's ring, the undercover agent joined forces with the local pushers,
   - (C) The undercover agent secretly joined forces with local pushers in order to destroy their ring,
   - (D) The undercover agent joined forces with the local pushers and secretly determined to destroy their ring,
   - (E) Secretly determined to destroy the rings, the local pushers and the undercover agent joined forces,

3. <u>In studying diabetes, many doctors have concluded</u> that early detection of the disease can permit control through diet.
   - (A) In studying diabetes, many doctors have concluded
   - (B) Many doctors, by studying diabetes, have concluded
   - (C) Many doctors studying diabetes have concluded
   - (D) Diabetes studies have led many doctors to conclude
   - (E) The conclusion of those doctors who have studied diabetes is

4. Although he is <u>liable to</u> make political enemies with the decision, the President will propose severe tax cuts that may both stimulate business and reduce the availability of home loans.
   (A) liable to
   (B) liable from
   (C) able to
   (D) of a mind to
   (E) acknowledging his liability to

5. <u>To bring to an end the 1984 Olympics, the festivities were highlighted</u> by the arrival of an "alien" spaceship that hovered mysteriously over the Coliseum, to the amazement and delight of thousands of spectators.
   (A) To bring to an end the 1984 Olympics, the festivities were highlighted
   (B) The festivities to bring to an end to the 1984 Olympics were highlighted
   (C) With the festivities that ended the 1984 Olympics highlighted
   (D) Festive highlights brought an end to the 1984 Olympics
   (E) The festive conclusion of the 1984 Olympics was highlighted

6. <u>To the behalf of many citizens who believe that some criminal statutes are unfair to the victims of crime</u>, legislators in California drafted a "Victim's Bill of Rights" law, which passed handily in the election.
   (A) To the behalf of many citizens who believe that some criminal statutes are unfair to the victims of crime
   (B) Listening for many citizens' belief that criminal statutes are unfair to the victims of crime
   (C) With the belief of their citizens that the victims of crime are unfairly served by some criminal statutes
   (D) On the behalf of many citizens who believe that some criminal statutes are unfair to the victims of crime
   (E) To believe on the behalf of many citizens about criminal statutes that are unfair to crime victims

7. The recent decrease in the prime interest rate has encouraged some economists and worried others, who recall all too vividly the skyrocketing rates and consequent economic stagnation of the late 1970s.
   - (A) The recent decrease in the prime interest rate
   - (B) Decreasing recently, the prime interest rate
   - (C) The recent rate of decrease in prime interest
   - (D) The prime interest rate, recently decreased,
   - (E) The recently decreasing prime interest rate

8. So many of us bemoan our lack of foresight by complaining that if we would have bought property twenty years ago, we could have taken advantage of the recent real estate boom.
   - (A) by complaining that if we would have bought property twenty years ago, we could have taken advantage of the recent real estate boom
   - (B) , looking backward to a potential property purchase twenty years ago and wishing we had done so for present purposes
   - (C) : with real estate available so cheaply twenty years ago, the advantages of the recent boom would be ours for the asking
   - (D) , complaining that if we had bought property twenty years ago, we could have taken advantage of the recent real estate boom
   - (E) , the complaint being our lack of purchasing property twenty years ago and the consequent absence of profit in the recent real estate boom

9. If the majority of your opponents have control, you may become defeated.
   - (A) If the majority of your opponents have control, you may become defeated.
   - (B) If the majority of your opponents take control, you may lose.
   - (C) If the majority of your opponents assumes control, you may see defeat.
   - (D) If the majority of your opponents has control, you may lose.
   - (E) Most of your opponents will have control, and you may lose.

10. Focusing across several generations, Alex Haley wrote *Roots,* a novel explaining both his family history and the history of American bigotry.
    (A) Focusing across several generations
    (B) Centering around several generations
    (C) Living through several generations
    (D) With an eye on several generations
    (E) Telling of several generations

11. Acting selfishly and impulsively, the chairperson adapted the committee's recommendations to meet his own needs, without considering the negative affects of his changes.
    (A) the chairperson adapted the committee's recommendations to meet his own needs, without considering the negative affects of his changes
    (B) without considering the negative affects of his changes, the chairperson adapted the committee's recommendations to meet his own needs
    (C) the chairperson adapted the committee's recommendations to meet his own needs, without considering the negative effects of his changes
    (D) necessarily, the chairperson adapted committee recommendations, despite negative effects
    (E) negative effects notwithstanding, the chairperson adapted the recommendations of the committee

12. Whatever he aspired to achieve, they were thwarted by his jealous older brothers, who controlled the stock in the family companies.
    (A) Whatever he aspired to achieve, they
    (B) Whatever he had any aspirations to, they
    (C) Whatever aspirations he had
    (D) Whatever be his aspirations, they
    (E) Many of his aspirations and goals

13. In the early fourteenth century, almost 200 years before Columbus reached the West Indies, and 250 years before the Reformation, Europe had been Catholic and the Church continued to influence virtually every phase of human life.
    - (A) Europe had been Catholic and the Church continued to influence virtually every phase of human life
    - (B) the Catholic Church continued to influence every phase of human life
    - (C) the Europe that had been Catholic was still influenced in virtually every phase of human life by the Church
    - (D) Europe was Catholic and the Church influenced virtually every phase of human life
    - (E) every phase of human life bore traces of the European influence of the Catholic Church

14. In the 1950s, toy stores sold thousands of play replicas of a gun popularized by the *Wyatt Earp* television series, the "Buntline Special," a long-barreled six-gun named after the legendary Ned Buntline.
    - (A) In the 1950s, toy stores sold thousands of play replicas of a gun popularized by the *Wyatt Earp* television series
    - (B) Popularized by the 1950s *Wyatt Earp* television series, toy stores sold thousands of play replicas of a gun
    - (C) In the 1950s, the *Wyatt Earp* television series popularized thousands of play replicas of a gun sold in toy stores
    - (D) A play replica of a gun popularized by the *Wyatt Earp* television series, which sold thousands in toy stores in the 1950s
    - (E) As toy stores sold thousands of the 1950s replicas of a gun popularized by the *Wyatt Earp* television series

15. The more the union stubbornly refused to budge from its original demand for a 20% across-the-board salary increase, <u>the more the district administration reiterated its original proposal of a mere 1% raise.</u>

   (A) the more the district administration reiterated its original proposal of a mere 1% raise

   (B) the district administration's original proposal for a mere 1% raise was reiterated all the more

   (C) proposing its original and mere 1% raise was the district administration's response, more and more

   (D) the district administration reiterated its proposal of a mere 1% raise

   (E) the more the district administration's original proposal of a mere 1% raise was reiterated

16. During the literary renaissance of the 1920s, a large number of new writers—William Faulkner, Ernest Hemingway, John Dos Passos, and F. Scott Fitzgerald—sought to record the inner life of Americans and to scrutinize the American dream, <u>the dream that anyone can earn his own fortune and live happily ever after through hard work, which had become tarnished.</u>

   (A) the dream that anyone can earn his own fortune and live happily ever after through hard work, which had become tarnished

   (B) the tarnished dream that anyone can make his own fortune and live happily ever after through hard work

   (C) the tarnished dream that anyone can, through hard work, make his own fortune and live happily ever after

   (D) the dream that anyone can earn his own fortune and live happily ever after, though tarnished, through hard work

   (E) that making one's own fortune and living happily ever after, through hard work, had become tarnished

17. Homer's *Odyssey* is often dramatized as a series of hairbreadth escapes from terrible monsters and vengeful gods, <u>and while those episodes are exciting and important literary achievements</u>, they stand apart from the poem's extensive attention to domestic life, to domestic values, and to a hero whose most important achievement is the reestablishment of his home and family.

   (A) and while those episodes are exciting and important literary achievements
   (B) and although in fact these episodes are exciting, important achievements in literature
   (C) and while an exciting and important literary achievement
   (D) and those episodes are exciting and important literary achievements
   (E) and with those episodes as exciting and important literary achievements

18. <u>Public enthusiasm that had been growing for airline travel, still in its infancy, when Amelia Earhart's plane disappeared in the 1930s, diminished for awhile</u>; however, today fear of flying is rare.

   (A) Public enthusiasm that had been growing for airline travel, still in its infancy, when Amelia Earhart's plane disappeared in the 1930s, diminished for awhile
   (B) Public enthusiasm that had been growing for airline travel, still in its infancy when Amelia Earhart's plane disappeared in the 1930s, diminished for awhile
   (C) Growing public enthusiasm for airline travel, still in its infancy, diminished for awhile after Amelia Earhart's plane disappeared in the 1930s
   (D) When Amelia Earhart's plane disappeared in the 1930s, growing public enthusiasm for airline travel, still in its infancy, diminished for awhile
   (E) After Amelia Earhart's plane disappeared in the 1930s, the enthusiasm that had been growing for airline travel in its infancy diminished for awhile

19. Much like Macbeth when he interprets the witches' prophecies all too literally, <u>the mysterious harpooner who Ahab takes aboard the *Pequod* has the captain accepting his strange prophecies without questioning their hidden meaning</u>.
    (A) the mysterious harpooner who Ahab takes aboard the *Pequod* has the captain accepting his strange prophecies without questioning their hidden meaning
    (B) the strange prophecies of the mysterious harpooner he has taken aboard the *Pequod* are accepted by Ahab without questioning their hidden meaning
    (C) the mysterious harpooner whom Ahab takes aboard the *Pequod* has the captain accepting his strange prophecies without questioning their hidden meaning
    (D) Ahab accepts the strange prophecy of the mysterious harpooner whom he has taken aboard the *Pequod,* without questioning their hidden meaning
    (E) Ahab accepts the strange prophecies of the mysterious harpooner he has taken aboard the *Pequod,* without questioning their hidden meaning

20. Golding's most famous novel concerns little boys, <u>once a well-behaved and civilized group, whose</u> resort to murder and savagery during their brief time on a tropical island without adult supervision.
    (A) once a well-behaved and civilized group, whose
    (B) once well-behaved and civilized, who
    (C) once a well-behaved and civilized herd, who
    (D) once civilized and well-behaved, whose
    (E) behaved and civilized, who

21. When reading some of the most rich and beautiful speeches in Shakespeare's *Romeo and Juliet,* when one stresses the singsong cadence of iambic pentameter, the lines take on an almost simpleminded, childish quality.

   (A) when one stresses the singsong cadence of iambic pentameter, the lines take on an almost simpleminded, childish quality

   (B) stressing the singsong cadence of iambic pentameter gives the lines an almost simpleminded, childish quality

   (C) if one stresses the singsong cadence of iambic pentameter, it gives the lines an almost simpleminded, childish quality

   (D) the simpleminded, childish quality of some lines results from the singsong cadence of iambic pentameter

   (E) the singsong cadence of iambic pentameter, sounds almost simpleminded and childish

22. The weather in San Diego, California, is temperate for most of the year, and although the air is not so clean as it used to be, it has remained virtually smog free through recent years of rapid industrial growth, unlike most urban areas in southern California.

   (A) unlike most urban areas in southern California

   (B) unlike the air in most southern California urban areas

   (C) unlike other southern California air

   (D) unlike southern California urban areas

   (E) in contrast to the smog condition elsewhere in urban southern California

23. Brokers who offer foreign cars on the "gray market," thus bypassing the car dealer by shipping directly from the manufacturer to the waiting consumer at the dock, claim that their purpose is not to cheat dealerships out of a profit, but rather to provide the consumer with the finest value for his or her dollar.
    (A) to provide the consumer with the finest value for his or her dollar
    (B) the provision of the finest value for the dollar
    (C) providing the finest values for consumer dollars
    (D) that they have an obligation to give consumers value for their dollars
    (E) to deliver value for the dollar

24. Two recent statements on the tenure of university professors offer conflicting points of view: those which say that lifetime tenure ensures academic freedom and those which say that lifetime tenure encourages professional laziness and irresponsibility.
    (A) those which say that lifetime tenure ensures academic freedom and those which say that lifetime tenure encourages professional laziness and irresponsibility
    (B) some declare that lifetime tenure ensures academic freedom, and others say that it encourages professional laziness and irresponsibility
    (C) saying that lifetime tenure either ensures academic freedom or encourages irresponsible laziness
    (D) one emphasizes the academic freedom that tenure ensures, and one stresses the professional laziness and irresponsibility it encourages
    (E) advocacies of academic freedom and warnings about professional laziness and irresponsibility

25. <u>With an explosive capacity that can devastate life and property for a radius of hundreds of miles, proponents of peace from several Western bloc countries met to discuss the continuing manufacture and deployment of nuclear warheads.</u>

(A) With an explosive capacity that can devastate life and property for a radius of hundreds of miles, proponents of peace from several Western bloc countries met to discuss the continuing manufacture and deployment of nuclear warheads.

(B) Proponents of peace from several Western bloc countries with an explosive capacity that can devastate life and property for a radius of hundreds of miles met to discuss the continuing manufacture and deployment of nuclear warheads.

(C) Meeting to discuss the continuing manufacture and deployment of nuclear warheads with an explosive capacity that can devastate life and property for a radius of hundreds of miles were several Western bloc countries.

(D) Proponents of peace from several Western bloc countries met to discuss the continuing manufacture and deployment of nuclear warheads that can devastate life and property with an explosive capacity for a radius of hundreds of miles.

(E) Proponents of peace from several Western bloc countries met to discuss the continuing manufacture and deployment of nuclear warheads with an explosive capacity that can devastate life and property for a radius of hundreds of miles.

26. During the French Revolution, especially the Reign of Terror, <u>citizens whom the government suspected of treasonous tendencies were eventually put to death</u> by Monsieur Sanson, the infamous executioner who supervised the killing of hundreds at the guillotine.

   (A) citizens whom the government suspected of treasonous tendencies were eventually put to death

   (B) citizens of which the government had suspicions were eventually put to death

   (C) suspicious citizens were eventually killed

   (D) citizens who the government suspected of treason were eventually put to death

   (E) the citizenry under suspicion were eventually put to death

27. <u>Irregardless of the "new modernism" in literature, which produces</u> novels which often read like the diaries of madmen, most readers still prefer a conventional plot and simple style.

   (A) Irregardless of the "new modernism" in literature, which produces

   (B) Irregardless of the "new modernism" in literature, which produced

   (C) Regardless, the "new modernism" in literature, which produces

   (D) Regardless of the "new modernism" in literature, which produces

   (E) Regardless of the "new modernism" in literature, which produce

28. During the last century, whaling voyages departed regularly from the New England states, <u>and because each voyage normally extends for years</u>, the hold was packed with supplies before a whaling ship set sail.

   (A) and because each voyage normally extends for years

   (B) and because each trip was long

   (C) and because each voyage normally extended for years

   (D) and while these were long trips

   (E) and because the voyage had lasted for years

29. As he looked out on an expanse that seemed empty of gods or goddesses, Odysseus must certainly have felt abandoned by the rulers on Olympus.
   (A) As he looked out on an expanse that seemed empty of gods or goddesses
   (B) As he looked out on an empty expanse of gods and goddesses
   (C) With no gods or goddesses as he looked out on the empty expanse
   (D) Facing the empty expanse of gods and goddesses
   (E) As he looked out on an expanse that seemed empty of either a god or a goddess

30. Arms talks from Geneva between China, the United States, the Soviet Union, and other nations may be even more effecting than many world leaders think they would be.
   (A) from Geneva between China, the United States, the Soviet Union, and other nations may be even more effecting than many world leaders think they would be
   (B) in Geneva between China, the United States, the Soviet Union, and other nations may be even more effective than many world leaders suppose
   (C) in Geneva between China, the United States, the Soviet Union, and other nations may be even more affecting than many world leaders think they will be
   (D) in Geneva among China, the United States, the Soviet Union, and other nations may be even more effective than many world leaders expect
   (E) between China, the United States, the Soviet Union, and other nations in Geneva may be even more effective than many world leaders believe

31. If Swift's *Gulliver's Travels* <u>attracts less of a readership than he did in the eighteenth century</u>, perhaps the reason is that modern readers do not know enough political history to appreciate the satire.

    (A) attracts less of a readership than he did in the eighteenth century
    (B) attracts less readers than the eighteenth century did
    (C) attracts fewer readers than it did in the eighteenth century
    (D) attracts fewer readers than he did in the eighteenth century
    (E) attracts less reading than it did in the eighteenth century

32. <u>Proposing that inordinate government spending was causative of the high deficit, the president presented a budget</u> that maintained relatively high defense expenditures while it reduced funding for certain social programs which, the administration argued, were receiving sufficient support from the private sector.

    (A) Proposing that inordinate government spending was causative of the high deficit, the president presented a budget
    (B) Proposing that government spending causes deficits, the president presented a budget
    (C) With a proposal that inordinate government spending was causative of the high deficit, the president presented a budget
    (D) The president presented a budget proposal that inordinate government spending was causative of the high deficit
    (E) Proposing that inordinate government spending caused the high deficit, the president presented a budget

33. Acknowledging in the volunteers' giving of a great deal of their time to canvas the neighborhood and collect donations from the neighbors, the chairman of the local United Way expressed his sincere gratitude.

   (A) Acknowledging the volunteers' giving of a great deal of their time to canvas the neighborhood and collect donations from the neighbors, the chairman of the local United Way expressed his sincere gratitude.

   (B) Acknowledging the time spent by neighborhood volunteers to canvas and to collect neighborhood donations, the chairman of the local United Way expressed his sincere gratitude.

   (C) With sincere gratitude, the chairman of the local United Way expressed his acknowledgment of the neighborhood donations canvased and collected on the volunteers' time.

   (D) The chairman of the local United Way offered sincere thanks to the volunteers who gave so much time to canvasing the neighborhood to collect donations.

   (E) The chairman of the local United Way thanked the neighborhood volunteers, sincerely.

34. A diagonal line connecting two corners of a rectangle is also the hypotenuse of each of two right triangles contained within the rectangle, which is longer than any of the sides.

   (A) which is longer than any of the sides
   (B) and the line is longer than any of the sides
   (C) which is longer than the sides
   (D) that is longer than any of the sides
   (E) that is longer than any of the other sides

Answers and Explanations

1. (E) Both *group* and *manifesto* are singular, so the singular pronoun *its* and the singular verb *addresses* must be used. The agreement is correct in choice (D), but *with that area in mind* is needlessly wordy.

2. **(B)** Choice (B) corrects the poor structure of the original wording. Choices (C), (D), and (E) change the meaning of the original expression slightly, (C) and (D) suggesting that the ring belongs to the *pushers,* not to the *drug dealer,* and (E) implying that the *pushers* were determined to destroy the ring.

3. **(C)** All choices are grammatically correct; however, choice (C) is the most direct expression of the original wording. Choices (D) and (E) change the meaning of the original, and choice (B) is awkward.

4. **(A)** The original is better than any of the alternatives.

5. **(E)** This is the most direct, clear, and economical choice that retains the essential meaning of the original underlined portion. Compared to choice (E), both (A) and (B) are wordy. Choice (C) is a sentence fragment, and (D) distorts the meaning.

6. **(D)** *To the behalf* is not idiomatic. Choice (D) corrects this error and does not make additional, unnecessary changes, as do the other choices.

7. **(A)** None of the alternate choices is more direct and clear than the original underlined portion. Since it is the *decrease* that has encouraged some economists, not the *rate,* choices (B), (C), (D), and (E) all change the meaning of the sentence.

8. **(D)** The use of *would have* and *could have* as the main verbs here does not clearly indicate that buying property twenty years ago is a much earlier action; the verb *had* makes clear the distinction between distant past and recent past. Choice (D) supplies the appropriate verb and eliminates the unnecessary *by.*

9. **(D)** *Majority* is a collective noun which may take either a singular or plural verb, depending on whether the group as a whole or the individuals are emphasized. But *lose* is a clearer and more economical expression than *become defeated.* Choices (B), (C), and (E) change the meaning of the sentence.

10. (E) *Focusing across* is idiomatically incorrect and also logically unsound (*focusing on* is better). The only choice that is both idiomatically correct and preserves the meaning of the original is (E).

11. (C) The error in the original is a diction error. *Effects* (results) is preferable to *affects*. Choices (D) and (E) are economical but change the meaning of the original significantly.

12. (C) Choice (C) best expresses the idea without changing the intent of the sentence as (E) does. The original and choices (B) and (D) are awkward.

13. (D) The verbs are the problem in the original underlined portion. The context supplied by the rest of the sentence suggests that the verbs should be simple past tense, both of them indicating what *was* true *in* the fourteenth century. As it stands, the underlined portion is internally contradictory. It states that Europe *had been* Catholic, implying that the region is no longer Catholic, but also states that Catholic influence *continued*. Choice (D) corrects this grammatical/logical problem while retaining the original intended meaning. Choices (B) and (E) are grammatically correct but omit information contained in the original sentence.

14. (A) Although choice (A) is perhaps not the best choice one can imagine, it is decidedly the best choice of the five offered here. "*Buntline Special*" should be placed as close to *gun* as possible. In choice (B), the opening phrase modifies *toy stores,* not *gun,* and the phrase *the 1950s* now modifies the *television series* instead of *sold.* Choice (C) also misplaces the phrase *in the 1950s.* Choices (D) and (E) are sentence fragments.

15. (A) The original underlined portion is the most clear and correct choice, resulting in a balanced sentence, with the structure of the second half (that is, the underlined portion) parallel to the structure of the first half: *the more* . . . subject . . . active verb. Choices (B), (C), and (D) omit *the more.* In choice (E), the verb is passive.

16. (C) The original version is confusing because the clause *which had become tarnished* is awkwardly separated from *dream* and the prepositional phrase *through hard work* is awkwardly separated from the verb it modifies, *earn.* In choices (B), (D), and (E), the prepositional phrase is misplaced.

17. (A) The original underlined portion is the best choice. Choice (B) is wordy, (C) introduces an agreement error, (D) introduces a comma error, and (E), by omitting the *while,* changes the meaning.

18. (C) The best choice here arranges the parts of the sentence in the most direct and clear way by keeping the modifiers as close as possible to the words they modify. In addition, choice (C) replaces *when* with a more appropriate and logical term, *after.*

19. (E) The underlined portion must name Ahab immediately in order to clarify the comparison between Ahab and Macbeth. It is Ahab, *not* the *harpooner,* choices (A) or (C), not the *prophecies,* choice (B), who is *much like Macbeth.* Choice (D) has the right structure but has an agreement error in *prophecy* and *their.*

20. (B) Choice (B) is grammatically correct and economical. In choice (C), *herd* introduces a meaning not in the original, while choice (E) omits details. Choices (A) and (D) are sentence fragments.

21. (B) Choice (B) is the most economical and clear version of the original. Choices (A) and (C) are wordy, containing the unnecessary phrases *when one* and *if one.* Choices (D) and (E) omit the notion of stressing and so change the meaning.

22. (B) The original underlined portion presents an illogical comparison, of *areas* to the topic of the first part of the sentence, *air.* Only choice (B) clarifies the air to air comparison, without the inappropriate wordiness of choice (E).

23. (A) The original underlined portion is the best choice. It maintains parallel structure with *to provide*. Each of the other choices makes unnecessary changes in grammar and syntax that do not improve the original.

24. (D) In the original underlined portion, *those* is incorrect. To express respectively two singular points of view, the noun or pronoun which refers to each must be singular; *those* is, of course, plural. Only choice (D) provides a clearly singular reference, *one*, for each viewpoint.

25. (E) The introductory phrase in the original (preceding the comma) properly modifies warheads. Only choice (E) makes this necessary change while retaining the intended meaning of the original.

26. (A) The original underlined portion is the best choice. *Whom* is used correctly, as the object of *suspected*. Each of the other choices omits or changes this correct pronoun unnecessarily or changes the meaning of the original.

27. (D) *Irregardless* is nonstandard usage. Apart from this error, the original underlined portion is correct and clear. To make sense, choice (C) would require the preposition *of*. Choice (E) contains an agreement error.

28. (C) The original underlined portion contains a verb tense error. *Extends* (A) and *has lasted* (E) are inconsistent with the past tense established through the rest of the sentence. Choice (C) supplies the simple past tense, *extended*, that agrees with the other verbs in the sentence. Choices (B) and (D), while grammatically correct, substitute the vaguer *long* for the phrase *for years*.

29. (A) It is an expanse, empty of gods, not an empty expanse of gods—choices (B) and (D). Choice (E) is needlessly wordy and (C) distorts the meaning.

30. (D) There are several errors in the original version that must be corrected: the preposition *in* for *from,* the adjective *effective* for *effecting,* and the preposition *among* for *between.*

31. (C) *Fewer readers* is more economical than choice (A). *Less* in choice (B) is incorrect when the noun (*readers*) can be numbered (for example: fewer gallons, less gasoline; fewer dollars, less money). Since the pronoun refers to the book, not to the author, *it,* not *he,* is correct. Choice (E) incorrectly uses the plural *attract*—*Gulliver's Travels* is the name of a book and is singular.

32. (E) *Caused* is better than the wordy and pretentious phrase *was causative of* in choices (A), (C), and (D). Choice (B) omits two adjectives and unnecessarily changes the tense in *causes.*

33. (D) The original underlined sentence as well as choices (B) and (C) are unnecessarily wordy. Choice (D) is an efficient, direct, and clear expression that retains the meaning of the original. Choice (E) leaves out essential information from the original.

34. (B) Though choice (B) requires more words, it is the only version that avoids the ambiguous pronouns—*which* in choices (A) and (C) and *that* in choices (D) and (E)—which seem at first to refer to *rectangle.*

INTRODUCTION TO CRITICAL REASONING

The Critical Reasoning section typically contains sixteen questions.

Ability Tested

This section tests your ability to read and understand the logic presented in brief passages or conversations.

Basic Skills Necessary

Candidates who read critically and understand simple logic and reasoning do well in this section. The ability to isolate the key issue and to identify irrelevant issues is important.

Directions

As you read the brief passage, you must follow the line of reasoning using only commonsense standards of logic. No knowledge of formal logic is required. Then you must choose the *best* answer, realizing that several choices may be possible, but only one will be best.

Analysis

Rely on common sense. No special expertise is necessary.

Use only what is presented or implied by the passage. Do not make leaps in logic to arrive at an answer choice. Don't read anything into the passage that isn't there.

Choose the *best* answer choice. The test makers strongly imply that there may be more than one good answer.

Suggested Approaches with a Sample

- **Preread the question following the passage.**

In most instances, each brief passage will be followed by one question. For these one-question passages, it may be time-effective to read the question before reading the passage. Many GMAT candidates have found that prereading the question eliminates having to read the passage a second time while searching for the answer, thus saving valuable minutes. Knowing what the question is *before* reading the passage enables you to focus on those elements of the passage essential to the question.

If you decide to read the question before reading the passage, *do not* preread the answer choices. Since four of the five choices are incorrect, scanning them introduces material eighty percent of which is irrelevant and/or inconsistent and therefore incorrect. Prereading the answer choices is a waste of time and energy.

Some candidates report that they can effectively preread several questions in those few instances where a passage is followed by two or more questions. Others find that it is difficult to keep more than one question in mind while reading the passage. Some candidates have found that given a lengthy question, prereading is not effective regardless of whether the passage is followed by one or several questions. Practice will help you determine when prereading is effective for you.

Try reading the *question* about the following passage first; then read the passage:

That seniors in the inner cities have inadequate health care available to them is intolerable. The medical facilities in the urban ghetto rarely contain basic medical supplies, and the technology in these hospitals is reflective of the 1960s, if that. Seniors living in the affluent suburbs, however, have available to them state-of-the-art technology and the latest in medical advances, drugs, and procedures.

Which of the following best expresses the primary point of the passage?

(A) Inner-city and suburban seniors should be cared for in hospitals equidistant from both.
(B) Inner-city seniors should be transported to suburban hospitals.
(C) Doctors should treat inner-city and suburban seniors equally.
(D) Better medical care and facilities should be provided for inner-city seniors.
(E) Inner-city seniors should have the same health care as that available to suburban seniors.

Prereading the question helps you to read the passage with a focus, that is, what is the author's point? The main point will be the overall thrust of the entire passage.

The major issue here is health care, and the author's point is that inner-city seniors should have health care better than that available to them now. The heavily charged word *intolerable* in the first sentence indicates that the author feels strongly that inadequate health care for inner-city seniors is not sufficient. Better care should be provided. Choice (D) is the best answer.

Notice that while a comparison is made to suburban seniors having superior health care, no direct argument is made that inner-city seniors should have the *same* health care as suburban seniors. The superior, *state-of-the-art* quality of suburban health care is presented in order to contrast with that of inner-city health care, and the contrast is used simply for that reason: to show how abysmal inner-city health care is in comparison. But nothing in the passage directly indicates that health care for inner-city seniors should necessarily be equivalent with that provided suburban seniors. Inferring this would be beyond the scope of the passage; choice (E) as the author's primary point is incorrect.

Choices (A) and (B) are incorrect because the issues of hospital relocation and transportation are never raised by the passage. And choice (C) not only raises the problematic issue of "equal" treatment (which, as stated previously, is not directly indicated in the passage) but also alters the focus simply to *doctors,* which in the context of a passage noting medical facilities, technology, supplies, etc., is far too narrow.

- **Read and analyze all the choices.**

Our analysis of this health care question critically assesses each of the answer choices. As you work the questions in the Critical Reasoning section, you should be assessing *all* the choices, eliminating (marking out) those that are off-topic, irrelevant, inconsistent, or beyond the scope of the passage and retaining (using question marks or circling the choice's letter) those that you think apply. As mentioned above, several choices frequently will appear to be correct. You are to choose the one that answers the question *best,* the one that is most directly relevant to the passage.

- **Know the Critical Reasoning question prototypes.**

Most of the Critical Reasoning questions fall into a small number of categories, or prototypes. You will find sixteen questions in a Critical Reasoning section but only about eight prototypes. These eight prototypes will be scrambled throughout the section, delivered in different ways. Knowing and anticipating these prototype questions and what they require in terms of an answer will be of great help, especially when a question appears to be long and confusing. Once you can identify the prototype, you can spend the bulk of your time understanding the passage and the answer choices.

PROTOTYPE 1: MAIN IDEA—The test may ask you to identify the main idea of a passage, and it may do this in a number of ways. As you can see in the health care passage, the main idea can be expressed as "the primary point of the passage" or "the author's primary point." Most of the time, the main idea will not be directly stated in the passage; you will have to derive it. Be careful to derive only what is most directly indicated by the passage. A jump of logic will take you beyond the scope of the passage (for example, in the previous passage, jumping from "providing better health care" to "providing health care equal to suburban care") and will be incorrect.

Some other ways (but not all the ways) that the main idea prototype can be asked are:

- Which of the following best expresses the point the author is attempting to make?

- The author's argument is best expressed as . . .

- Which of the following statements best expresses the author's central point in the passage above?

- In the passage above, the author argues that . . .

Sample Question

Whatever else might be said about American elections, they are already quite unlike Soviet elections in that Americans make choices. And one choice they can make in this free country is to stay home.

What is the author's point in the above passage?

(A) Americans who do decide to vote make more choices than those who do not.
(B) American elections embody many negative aspects, most of which are not embodied by Soviet elections.
(C) Choosing not to vote is the prerogative of a free citizen.
(D) All citizens vote in every Soviet election.
(E) Most American voters are not well informed enough to vote wisely.

Answer and explanation: (C) When considering the multiple choices, immediately eliminate those items which are (1) irrelevant to the question and/or the major issue of the passage and (2) not at all addressed by the passage. Consider the passage above. The author's point is necessarily connected with the major issue of the passage—in this case, free choice. The author stresses the free choice *not to vote*, by way of making the point. You may eliminate all choices which do not address the free choice not to vote: (A) is irrelevant because it addresses the number of choices rather than the freedom of choice; (B) raises issues scarcely addressed in the passage—that is, the negative aspects of elections. (D) doesn't address the issue of choosing not to vote; though it notes that all Soviet citizens must vote, it neglects the main point—that Americans don't have to; (E) is irrelevant to the issue of free choice, stressing instead voter information. The best choice is (C), which addresses the major issue, free choice, and also the author's specific point, the free choice not to vote.

PROTOTYPE 2: INFERENCE—The dictionary defines an inference as the act or process of deriving logical conclusions from a line of reasoning. For example, you can infer from the statement "only a minority of children under the age of six have visited a dentist" that a "majority of children under the age of six have not visited a dentist." This type of Critical Reasoning question will ask you to determine an inference or implication in a passage.

The distinction between the meanings of "infer" and "imply" is not very important in this section (although it may be in the Sentence Correction section). In actuality, they differ in meaning in the same way as "push" and "pull." A statement implies ("pushes out to you"); you infer ("pull from"). This grammatical distinction is not the operant element in this section; rather, you should be aware that "infers" or "implies" simply means the next logical step in an argument.

Other ways this prototype may be expressed are:

- Which of the following can be inferred from the passage?

- The author of the passage implies that . . .

- Which of the following inferences can be most reliably drawn from the passage?

- What can be validly inferred from the facts and premises expressed in the passage?

Sample Question

We doubt that the latest government report will scare Americans away from ham, bacon, sausages, hot dogs, bologna, and salami or that it will empty out the bars or cause a run on natural food supplies. If a diet were to be mandated from Washington, Americans probably would order the exact *opposite* course. Therefore the diet that does make sense is to eat a balanced and varied diet composed of foods from *all* food groups and containing a reasonable caloric intake.

Which of the following is (are) specifically implied by the passage?

  I. Vitamins are necessary to combat disease.
 II. A recent report warned of the risks of meat and alcoholic beverages.
III. Unorthodox suggestions for a more nutritional diet were recently made by the government.

(A) I only
(B) II only
(C) III only
(D) I and II only
(E) II and III only

Answer and explanation: (B) Since the author doubts that Americans will stop eating meats or visiting bars, one must conclude that the author is referring to the latest government report warning of the risks of meat and alcoholic beverages. Statement I concerning vitamins may be true but is not *specifically* implied other than in a very general sense (nutrition). Statement III is not true: there is nothing to suggest that the government report made "unorthodox" suggestions.

PROTOTYPE 3: ASSUMPTION—An assumption is an *unstated* notion on which a statement rests. For example, "I don't like people who continually interrupt me; therefore, you may conclude that I don't like Jack." For this argument to be logically valid, it must be assumed that Jack continually interrupts the author. In this type of question, you will be asked to determine what assumption lies behind the author's argument.

Other ways this prototype may be expressed are:

• Which of the following underlies the passage above?

• The author assumes that . . .

• The argument above logically depends on which of the following assumptions?

- What is the presupposition of the passage above?

- Necessary to the reasoning above is the assumption that . . .

Sample Question

In his first message to Congress, Harry Truman said, "The responsibility of the United States is to serve and not dominate the world."

Which of the following is one basic assumption underlying Truman's statement?

(A) The United States is capable of dominating the world.
(B) The United States chooses to serve rather than dominate the world.
(C) World domination is a virtue.
(D) One must be decisive when facing a legislative body for the first time.
(E) The United States, preceding Truman's administration, had been irresponsible.

Answer and explanation: (A) Truman's statement is not warranted unless one assumes the U.S. capability to dominate the world; that assumed capability makes the choice between serving and dominating possible and is thus a basic assumption.

PROTOTYPE 4: SUPPORT/WEAKEN—This question type asks for the answer choice that would support or weaken the passage. For example, the passage may state:

Research comparing children of cigarette-smoking parents in Virginia with children of nonsmoking parents in West Virginia found that children of smoking parents in Virginia have lower test scores than do children of nonsmokers in West Virginia. Therefore, secondhand cigarette smoke is a cause of the lower test scores.

Which of the following, if true, would weaken the conclusion above?

A correct answer would be: "Children in Virginia have lower test scores than children in West Virginia, regardless of whether their parents smoke or not." Notice that if children in Virginia have lower test scores than children in West Virginia, regardless of whether their parents smoke or not, then the cigarette-smoking parents cannot logically be claimed to be a cause of the lower test scores. This choice would weaken the conclusion. However, the question could have been:

Which of the following, if true, would strengthen the logic of the argument?

A correct answer would be: "A recent study indicates that, in general, children in any particular state tend to have similar test scores to children in any other state." Notice that this choice would strengthen the logic of the passage. If children in general have similar test scores state to state, then a subpopulation of children from smoking parents having lower test scores than a subpopulation of children from nonsmoking parents strengthens the conclusion that the smoking parents may have been the cause of the difference in scores.

Sometimes the question asks for what would be "relevant" to the reasoning. The choice that would either strengthen or weaken the logic would be the relevant choice.

Notice that this question type may contain the words "if true." That means accept all of the choices as being true: do not challenge their reasonableness or the possibility of their occurring. Rather, accept all the choices as being true and from there decide which would strengthen or weaken the argument, whatever the question requires.

Other ways this question type may be expressed are:

- Which of the following, if true, would support the argument?

- Which of the following, if true, would undermine the conclusion?

- Which of the following, if true, would challenge the logic of the reasoning of the passage?

- Which of the following would confirm the author's conclusion?

Sample Question

Experience shows that for every burglar shot by a homeowner there are many more fatal accidents involving small children, family slayings that could have been avoided but for the handy presence of a gun, and thefts of handguns by the criminals they are intended to protect against.

Which of the following facts, if true, would most seriously weaken the above contention?

(A) Criminals tend to sell the handguns they steal during the commission of a burglary.
(B) Burglars are also capable of causing fatal accidents.
(C) Every burglar shot by a homeowner is stopped from committing scores of further burglaries and injuring scores of other citizens.
(D) The number of burglars shot by homeowners is larger than the number of burglars shot by renters.
(E) Not all fatal accidents involve guns.

Answer and explanation: (C) This choice most directly addresses the argument of the passage. The passage argues that for every burglar shot, there are scores of slayings of the innocent; (C) argues that for every burglar shot, there are scores of prevented slayings.

PROTOTYPE 5: CONCLUSION—This prototype question asks for the conclusion which has not yet been stated in the passage. For example,

The county legislature has finally, after ten years of legal challenges, passed an antipollution ordinance. From a reading of the language of the legislation, it promises to be one of the most effective bills in the history of the state.

Which of the following can be deduced from the passage?

(A) The pollution problem will be eliminated in the county.
(B) The pollution problem will be reduced in the county.
(C) Pollution is not now a problem in the county.
(D) Pollution will be reduced in the state.
(E) The pollution problem will now be addressed through legislative action.

When you are selecting a conclusion for a passage, do not merely choose what may be possible. Usually several of the choices are possible. You are to select the one choice that may necessarily be concluded. So, in the above example, notice that while (A) and (B) are possible, they don't necessarily have to occur; the ordinance, after all, may not be effective despite its tough language. Choices (C) and (D) are even more remote. But of the five choices, (E) is the safest conclusion that can be drawn. When seeking a conclusion, choose the "safest" of the five choices.

Other ways this question type may be presented are:

- If the above passage is true, then which of the following must necessarily be true?

- Which of the following is the best deduction based upon the passage above?

- If the passage above is true, which of the following must logically follow?

- From the passage above, which of the following can reasonably be deduced?

- Based upon the passage above, the author would conclude . . .

Sample Question

Children learn about the ways of the society in which they are born from their playgroups. They will later transfer the experience gained in the primary group to the society at large. Very often, patterns of authority are consistent throughout a culture, from parental to political to spiritual.

Which of the following would be the most logical continuation of the passage above?

(A) Thus, one may learn relationships between primary groups.
(B) Thus, one cannot generalize from one group to the next.
(C) Thus, one may learn what is held to be of value in a society.
(D) Thus, one may determine the ways of society at a young age.
(E) Thus, one realizes that depriving children does not change their social behavior.

Answer and explanation: (D) The passage presumes that certain consistent patterns exist within a culture, from playgroup to society at large, from parental authority to political authority. In such a way, children are able to learn the ways of society. Choice (C) is not correct because the passage deals with authority, not with what is held to be of value.

PROTOTYPE 6: TECHNIQUE—This prototype question asks for the technique of reasoning used in the passage. For example, the passage may use a generalization to prove a specific point, or vice versa. Or it may use an analogy (a comparison) to further an argument. It may present a conclusion without adequately supporting it, or it may contradict its original premise within the passage. As you can see, a line of reasoning may be structured—or may be faulty—in many ways. Be aware that it usually does not matter whether you agree or disagree with the logic presented in the passage because in this case you are not being asked to determine the passage's validity. (That's another question type.) Rather, you need to identify in structural terms how the author has set up the argument.

Ways this prototype may be expressed are:

• The author makes her point primarily by . . .

• The author of the passage uses which of the following methods of persuasion?

• In the passage above, the author does which of the following?

• The author is using what line of reasoning to make the point?

Sample question

Tom's writing is always straightforward and honest. After all, whenever he writes a critique, he includes a special note that forewarns us that he will not mince words nor make any untruthful statements.

The statement above uses which of the following to support the argument?

(A) Generalization
(B) Circular reasoning
(C) Specific examples
(D) Deductive reasoning
(E) Formal logic

Answer and explanation: (B) The statement supports itself by saying it supports itself. This is circular reasoning.

PROTOTYPE 7: ERROR—This prototype asks you to find a logical mistake in the reasoning. As you read the passage, you should look for an inconsistency or flaw in logic. Typically the error will be so striking that, if you are not looking for it, it will cause you to stop in consternation, realizing that the logic of the passage has somehow broken. Prereading the question is effective for this prototype; once you know you're looking for an error, as soon as you reach it, instead of wondering why you're having trouble with the reasoning, you realize you have just discovered the flaw.

Ways that this prototype may be presented are:

• The conclusion above is unsound because the author . . .

• Which of the following inconsistencies seriously undermines the author's argument?

• The reasoning in the passage above is flawed because . . .

• Which of the following is an inherent error in logic in the passage above?

Sample Question

> *Speaker:*   One need not look very far to find abundant examples of incivility and brutality in the most genteel corners of American society.
>
> *Questioner:* Then why don't we step up law enforcement in the slums of our cities?

The question reveals which of the following misunderstandings?

(A) The misunderstanding that incivility and brutality have become more abundant
(B) The misunderstanding that law enforcement is related to the problems of incivility and brutality
(C) The misunderstanding of the speaker's position relative to incivility and brutality
(D) Misunderstanding of the meaning of the word *genteel*
(E) Misunderstanding of the meaning of the words *incivility* and *brutality*

Answer and explanation: (D) The questioner understands the speaker to be referring to a problem restricted to the slums and so does not understand that *genteel* refers to upper-class situations.

PROTOTYPE 8: PARALLEL—Here you are being asked not to identify how the author structures the line of reasoning or to identify an error in reasoning, but to "parallel" whatever line of reasoning is presented. That is to say, you must select the answer choice which uses either the same method of reasoning or the same type of error as the passage. Here again, whether or not the reasoning is faulty is not the important issue; paralleling the specific reasoning or error in the passage is your concern.

For example,

> Since all dogs are animals, and cats are animals, than all cats are dogs.

Which of the following parallels the reasoning in the passage above?

A correct answer would be: "All men are human beings, and children are human beings. Therefore all men are children." Notice how this choice is faulty in the same structural way as the original passage.

Other ways this prototype may be expressed are:

- Which of the following contains a logical flaw similar to the logical flaw in the passage above?

- The argument above exhibits the same principles of inference as which of the following arguments?

- Which of the following is logically most similar to the argument above?

- Which of the following supports its conclusion in the same way as the passage above?

Sample Question

Because cigarette smokers usually have a bad cough and Butch has a bad cough, it follows that Butch is probably a cigarette smoker.

Which of the following most closely parallels the reasoning used in the argument above?

(A) Because nonsmokers don't get emphysema and Bud doesn't have emphysema, it follows that Bud is probably not a smoker.
(B) Because weightlifters usually have large muscles and Bill is a weightlifter, it follows that Bill has large muscles.
(C) Because diamonds usually have little color and this gem has little color, it follows that this gem is probably a diamond.
(D) Because people with short hair usually get more haircuts and Al has short hair, it follows that Al recently got a haircut.
(E) Because coughing spreads germs and Sam is coughing, Sam is spreading germs.

Answer and explanation: (C) The direct connection between cigarette smoking and coughing made in the passage is not an *exclusive* connection which would warrant the conclusion that because Butch has a bad cough, he's probably a cigarette smoker. Butch could have a cold. In the same way, just because diamonds have little color, we cannot conclude that a gem with little color probably is a diamond (it could be clear glass). There is a presumption of exclusivity in both instances. Choice (C) is a stronger answer than (A) because the form of the argument is precisely the same in (C) and the original. Also, (A) is an absolute (*don't*), and (C) uses the word *usually* as does the original.

There may be several other question types in the Critical Reasoning section. The inclusion here of only eight prototypes does not mean that these are the only question types appearing in this section of the GMAT. However, your understanding and anticipation of these eight should help you more quickly identify what is being asked and therefore allow you to spend the bulk of your time reading and analyzing the passage and the answer choices.

A PATTERNED PLAN OF ATTACK

Critical Reasoning

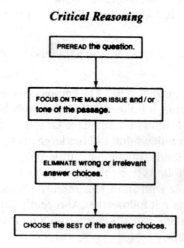

WARM-UP PROBLEMS

Without sign ordinances, everyone with the price of a can of spray paint can suddenly decide to publicly create their own personal Picassos, and soon the entire town would start to look like something out of *Alice in Wonderland*. Therefore we need sign ordinances.

1. The author makes which of the following basic assumptions?

    I. Spray paint is used for many signs.
    II. The entire town looking like *Alice in Wonderland* is undesirable.
    III. Sign ordinances are effective.

    (A) I only
    (B) II only
    (C) III only
    (D) I and III only
    (E) I, II, and III

Questions 2 and 3 are based on the following passage

In most economies, the government plays a role in the market system. Governments enforce the "rules of the game," impose taxes, and may control prices through price ceilings or price supports. These actions necessarily may create shortages or surpluses. In most developed and interdependent economies, the necessity of the government's playing some role in the economy seldom is disputed.

2. The final sentence in the passage suggests that
    (A) interdependence goes hand in hand with development
    (B) there are underdeveloped countries whose attitude toward government control may be hostile
    (C) disputes over government control usually come from an illiterate populace
    (D) price supports are necessary
    (E) economic success is a sophisticated achievement

3. The author of the passage would probably agree that
   (A) economic surpluses are always good
   (B) market shortages are a necessary evil
   (C) higher prices strengthen the economy
   (D) price ceilings add to the shortages
   (E) surpluses are not usually created intentionally

Questions 4 and 5 refer to the following passage

The new vehicle inspection program is needed to protect the quality of the state's air, for us and for our children. Auto exhausts are a leading contributor to coughing, wheezing, choking, and pollution. The state's long-term interests in the health of its citizens and in this area as a place to live, work, and conduct business depend on clean air.

4. Which of the following, if true, would most seriously weaken the argument above?
   (A) Since smog devices were made mandatory automotive equipment by the existing inspection program three years ago, pollution has decreased dramatically and continues to decrease.
   (B) Pollution problems are increasing in other states as well as in this one.
   (C) Sometimes coughing, wheezing, and choking are caused by phenomena other than pollution.
   (D) Vehicle inspectors are not always careful.
   (E) The state should not impose its interests upon the citizenry but should instead allow public health to be regulated by private enterprise.

5. Which of the following is an unstated assumption made by the author?
   (A) Working and conducting business may be different activities.
   (B) The state has been interested in the health of its citizens even before this inspection program was proposed.
   (C) Exhaust emissions contribute to pollution.
   (D) The new inspection program will be effective.
   (E) Our ancestors did not suffer from air pollution.

Questions 6 and 7 refer to the following passage

Voters on June 8 approved a $495 million bond issue for a state prison construction that is an obvious priority. Now the legislature has voted to put five more general obligation bond issues on the November ballot, adding another $1.5 billion to the state's long-term debt. Those on the November menu include $500 million for building and remodeling public schools, $450 million to extend the veterans home loan program, $200 million to subsidize low-interest mortgages for first-time home buyers, $85 million to acquire land for environmental protection, and $280 million to help counties expand or remodel their jails.

6. Which of the following statements is a point to which the author is most probably leading?
   (A) Two of these bond issues are certainly more important than the others.
   (B) We must face the obvious conclusion that prison construction is much less important than the improvement of public education and social programs for lawful citizens.
   (C) The cost of these bond issues is, on the face of it, negligible.
   (D) The voters cannot be expected to help make financial decisions for the state because most voters are suffering from their own severe financial problems.
   (E) These five bond proposals are quite enough, and between now and November voters will have to study them carefully to make sure that five are not too many.

7. Which of the following facts would most strongly weaken an argument for approval of the five new bond issues?
   (A) Environmental protection is not an overriding concern of the constituency.
   (B) The state's long-term debt cannot lawfully exceed $1.5 billion.
   (C) Improvements in education, the environment, criminal prosecution, and the real estate market are favored by the voters.
   (D) Similar bond proposals in other states have not been successful.
   (E) Two bills related to the housing of criminals are quite enough.

   Famous painter James Whistler said, "Industry in art is a necessity—not a virtue—and any evidence of the same, in the production, is a blemish, not a quality."

8. Whistler is arguing that
   (A) of necessity, art becomes industrialized
   (B) the qualities of art are its virtues
   (C) blemished paintings are the work of overindustrious artists
   (D) the product reflects the means of production
   (E) the artist must work hard, but the art should look easy

Deliberations of our governing bodies are held in public in order to allow public scrutiny of each body's actions and take to task those actions which citizens feel are not, for whatever reason, in their best interests.

9. With which of the following statements would the author of the above passage probably agree?
   (A) Deliberations of our governing bodies should be held in public.
   (B) Public scrutiny usually results in the criticism of our governing bodies.
   (C) The best interests of the public usually do not coincide with the motives of our governing bodies.
   (D) No government decisions ought to be kept from the public.
   (E) Citizens in other countries are not cared for by the government.

Questions 10 and 11 refer to the following passage

Recent studies indicate that more violent crimes are committed during hot weather than during cold weather. Thus, if we could control the weather, the violent crime rate would drop.

10. The argument above makes which of the following assumptions?

   I. The relationship between weather conditions and crime rate is merely coincidental.
   II. The relationship between weather conditions and crime rate is causal.
   III. The relationship between weather conditions and crime rate is controllable.

   (A) I only
   (B) II only
   (C) I and II only
   (D) II and III only
   (E) I, II, and III

11. The argument would be strengthened if it pointed out that
   (A) the annual crime statistics for New York are higher than those for Los Angeles
   (B) in laboratory tests, increased heat alone accounted for increased aggressive behavior between members of the test group
   (C) poor socioeconomic conditions, more uncomfortable in hot weather than in cold, are the direct causes of increased crime
   (D) weather control will be possible in the near future
   (E) more people leave their doors and windows open during hot weather

The state's empty $4 million governor's mansion on the banks of the Capitol River may be sort of a suburban Taj Mahal, as the governor once said. But why shouldn't the state unload it?

12. Which of the following is one of the author's basic assumptions?
   (A) The governor's mansion is out of place in the suburbs.
   (B) The reader is aware of the state's intention to "unload" the governor's mansion.
   (C) No one has yet lived in the governor's mansion.
   (D) The state is trying to sell the governor's mansion.
   (E) The governor was correct.

Questions 13 through 16 refer to the following passage

The older we get, the less sleep we should desire. This is because our advanced knowledge and capabilities are most enjoyable when used; therefore, "mindless" sleep becomes a waste of time.

13. Which of the following distinctions is *not* expressed or implied by the author?
   (A) Between sleep and wakefulness
   (B) Between youth and maturity
   (C) Between productivity and waste
   (D) Between a desire and a requirement
   (E) Between more sleep and less sleep

14. The author of this statement assumes that
    (A) less sleep is not desirable
    (B) sleep advances knowledge and capabilities
    (C) mindlessness coincides with wakefulness
    (D) knowledge and capabilities naturally improve with age
    (E) sleep is only for the young

15. This author's statement might be strengthened if he or she pointed out that
    (A) advanced knowledge is often manifested in creative dreams
    (B) the mind is quite active during sleep
    (C) few empirical studies have concluded that sleep is an intellectual stimulant
    (D) advanced capabilities are not necessarily mind-associated
    (E) dreams teach us how to use waking experiences more intelligently

16. The author's statement might be weakened by pointing out that
    (A) eight hours of sleep is a cultural, not a physical, requirement
    (B) the most capable people rarely sleep
    (C) rest is a positive contribution to knowledge and capability
    (D) young children enjoy themselves less than knowledgeable adults
    (E) people rarely waste time during their waking hours

By appropriating bailout money for the depressed housing industry, Congress is opening the door to a flood of special relief programs for other recession-affected businesses.

17. The author's attitude toward Congress's action is probably
    (A) neutral
    (B) disapproving
    (C) confused
    (D) happy
    (E) irate

The value of a close examination of the circumstances of an aircraft accident lies not only in fixing blame but in learning lessons.

18. The above statement fits most logically into which of the following types of passages?
    (A) A survey of the "scapegoat phenomenon" in modern society
    (B) An argument in favor of including specific details in any academic essay
    (C) An argument against the usefulness of the National Transportation Safety Board
    (D) A brief history of aeronautics
    (E) A description of the causes of a particular aircraft accident

Answers and Explanations

1. (E) All of the statements are assumptions of the author essential to the argument. The author assumes spray paint to be the medium that graffiti painters use and implicitly abhors the possibility of a town looking like *Alice in Wonderland*. In addition, his or her desire for sign ordinances assumes that they work and are effective in deterring spray painting.

2. (B) The last sentence says that it is *developed* or *interdependent* economies that acquiesce to the idea that government must control the economy to some extent. This leaves underdeveloped countries unspoken for and raises the possibility they might *not* acquiesce to government control.

3. (B) The paragraph states that government action *may create shortages* or *surpluses*.

4. (A) The argument for further supervision of vehicle use is most weakened by the statement that present safeguards are already doing the job. (C) and (D) slightly weaken the argument but do not address the overall position of the author.

5. (D) In order to argue for a new inspection program, the author must assume that that particular program, if enacted, will be effective. (C), the only other choice related to the points of the argument, expresses stated information rather than an unstated assumption.

6. (E) By listing high costs, the author is probably leading to the conclusion that the state's debt is being strained, a conclusion expressed in (E). (C) contradicts the author's emphasis on high costs. (A), (B), and (D) are neither expressed nor implied by the passage; their choice would rely on extraneous assumptions.

7. (B) This fact indicates that the passage of all the bond measures, which would take the debt over $1.5 billion, is illegal.

8. (E) Whistler is saying that constant effort (industry) is necessary but that the artwork (production) should not evidence that effort.

9. (A) By describing in very positive terms the effects of public deliberations, the author suggests the opinion that such deliberations *should* be public.

10. (B) The only correct choice is II; it is argued that hot weather *causes* crime. This is not mere coincidence, and the statement does not state that we *can* control the weather.

11. (B) The argument posits an exclusive relationship between hot weather and crime. (A), (C), and (E) contradict such an exclusive relationship. (D) is irrelevant to the relationship, and (B) provides evidence supporting and strengthening the heat-crime relationship.

12. (B) The author's final question necessarily rests on the assumption that the reader is aware of the state's intention; the author omits information expressing or explaining this intention.

13. (D) The author does not address the distinction between how much sleep we desire and how much our bodies require. Each of the other distinctions is addressed in the passage.

14. (D) In the passage, becoming older corresponds with "*advanced* knowledge and capabilities." Choices (A), (B), and (C) should be eliminated because each is contradicted by the assumptions of the passage (the passage suggests that *more* sleep is undesirable, knowledge and capabilities are connected with *wakefulness,* and mindlessness is connected with *sleep*). Choice (E) is a generalization not at all concerned with amount of sleep and therefore not relevant to the passage.

15. (C) Choices (A), (B), and (E) present information that supports the value of sleep, and (D) dissociates advanced capabilities from the mind, thus damaging the author's mind/mindlessness distinction.

16. (C) Only choice (C) asserts the positive value of sleep and thus weakens the author's stance in favor of decreased sleep.

17. (B) By describing the special relief programs as a *flood,* the author gives the programs a negative connotation and suggests disapproval.

18. (E) This choice is related most fully to the subject matter of the original statement.

Part III: Practice-Review-Analyze-Practice

Three Full-Length Practice Tests

This section contains three full-length practice simulation GMATs. The practice tests are followed by complete answers, explanations, and analysis techniques. The format, levels of difficulty, question structure, and number of questions are similar to those on the actual GMAT. The actual GMAT is copyrighted and may not be duplicated and these questions are not taken directly from the actual tests.

When taking these exams, try to simulate the test conditions by following the time allotments carefully.

PRACTICE TEST 1

Section I: Analytical Writing Assessment
               Essay 1—30 Minutes; 1 Essay Topic
               Essay 2—30 Minutes; 1 Essay Topic
Section II: Reading Comprehension—25 Minutes; 23 Questions
Section III: Problem Solving—25 Minutes; 16 Questions
Section IV: Sentence Correction —25 Minutes; 22 Questions
Section V: Data Sufficiency—25 Minutes; 20 Questions
Section VI: Critical Reasoning—25 Minutes; 16 Questions
Section VII: Problem Solving—25 Minutes; 16 Questions
Section VIII: Data Sufficiency—25 Minutes; 20 Questions

ANSWER SHEET FOR PRACTICE TEST 1
(Remove This Sheet and Use It to Mark Your Answers)

SECTION II	SECTION III	SECTION IV
1 Ⓐ Ⓑ Ⓒ Ⓓ Ⓔ	1 Ⓐ Ⓑ Ⓒ Ⓓ Ⓔ	1 Ⓐ Ⓑ Ⓒ Ⓓ Ⓔ
2 Ⓐ Ⓑ Ⓒ Ⓓ Ⓔ	2 Ⓐ Ⓑ Ⓒ Ⓓ Ⓔ	2 Ⓐ Ⓑ Ⓒ Ⓓ Ⓔ
3 Ⓐ Ⓑ Ⓒ Ⓓ Ⓔ	3 Ⓐ Ⓑ Ⓒ Ⓓ Ⓔ	3 Ⓐ Ⓑ Ⓒ Ⓓ Ⓔ
4 Ⓐ Ⓑ Ⓒ Ⓓ Ⓔ	4 Ⓐ Ⓑ Ⓒ Ⓓ Ⓔ	4 Ⓐ Ⓑ Ⓒ Ⓓ Ⓔ
5 Ⓐ Ⓑ Ⓒ Ⓓ Ⓔ	5 Ⓐ Ⓑ Ⓒ Ⓓ Ⓔ	5 Ⓐ Ⓑ Ⓒ Ⓓ Ⓔ
6 Ⓐ Ⓑ Ⓒ Ⓓ Ⓔ	6 Ⓐ Ⓑ Ⓒ Ⓓ Ⓔ	6 Ⓐ Ⓑ Ⓒ Ⓓ Ⓔ
7 Ⓐ Ⓑ Ⓒ Ⓓ Ⓔ	7 Ⓐ Ⓑ Ⓒ Ⓓ Ⓔ	7 Ⓐ Ⓑ Ⓒ Ⓓ Ⓔ
8 Ⓐ Ⓑ Ⓒ Ⓓ Ⓔ	8 Ⓐ Ⓑ Ⓒ Ⓓ Ⓔ	8 Ⓐ Ⓑ Ⓒ Ⓓ Ⓔ
9 Ⓐ Ⓑ Ⓒ Ⓓ Ⓔ	9 Ⓐ Ⓑ Ⓒ Ⓓ Ⓔ	9 Ⓐ Ⓑ Ⓒ Ⓓ Ⓔ
10 Ⓐ Ⓑ Ⓒ Ⓓ Ⓔ	10 Ⓐ Ⓑ Ⓒ Ⓓ Ⓔ	10 Ⓐ Ⓑ Ⓒ Ⓓ Ⓔ
11 Ⓐ Ⓑ Ⓒ Ⓓ Ⓔ	11 Ⓐ Ⓑ Ⓒ Ⓓ Ⓔ	11 Ⓐ Ⓑ Ⓒ Ⓓ Ⓔ
12 Ⓐ Ⓑ Ⓒ Ⓓ Ⓔ	12 Ⓐ Ⓑ Ⓒ Ⓓ Ⓔ	12 Ⓐ Ⓑ Ⓒ Ⓓ Ⓔ
13 Ⓐ Ⓑ Ⓒ Ⓓ Ⓔ	13 Ⓐ Ⓑ Ⓒ Ⓓ Ⓔ	13 Ⓐ Ⓑ Ⓒ Ⓓ Ⓔ
14 Ⓐ Ⓑ Ⓒ Ⓓ Ⓔ	14 Ⓐ Ⓑ Ⓒ Ⓓ Ⓔ	14 Ⓐ Ⓑ Ⓒ Ⓓ Ⓔ
15 Ⓐ Ⓑ Ⓒ Ⓓ Ⓔ	15 Ⓐ Ⓑ Ⓒ Ⓓ Ⓔ	15 Ⓐ Ⓑ Ⓒ Ⓓ Ⓔ
16 Ⓐ Ⓑ Ⓒ Ⓓ Ⓔ	16 Ⓐ Ⓑ Ⓒ Ⓓ Ⓔ	16 Ⓐ Ⓑ Ⓒ Ⓓ Ⓔ
17 Ⓐ Ⓑ Ⓒ Ⓓ Ⓔ		17 Ⓐ Ⓑ Ⓒ Ⓓ Ⓔ
18 Ⓐ Ⓑ Ⓒ Ⓓ Ⓔ		18 Ⓐ Ⓑ Ⓒ Ⓓ Ⓔ
19 Ⓐ Ⓑ Ⓒ Ⓓ Ⓔ		19 Ⓐ Ⓑ Ⓒ Ⓓ Ⓔ
20 Ⓐ Ⓑ Ⓒ Ⓓ Ⓔ		20 Ⓐ Ⓑ Ⓒ Ⓓ Ⓔ
21 Ⓐ Ⓑ Ⓒ Ⓓ Ⓔ		21 Ⓐ Ⓑ Ⓒ Ⓓ Ⓔ
22 Ⓐ Ⓑ Ⓒ Ⓓ Ⓔ		22 Ⓐ Ⓑ Ⓒ Ⓓ Ⓔ
23 Ⓐ Ⓑ Ⓒ Ⓓ Ⓔ		

CUT HERE

ANSWER SHEET FOR PRACTICE TEST 1
(Remove This Sheet and Use It to Mark Your Answers)

SECTION V	SECTION VI	SECTION VII	SECTION VIII
1 Ⓐ Ⓑ Ⓒ Ⓓ Ⓔ	1 Ⓐ Ⓑ Ⓒ Ⓓ Ⓔ	1 Ⓐ Ⓑ Ⓒ Ⓓ Ⓔ	1 Ⓐ Ⓑ Ⓒ Ⓓ Ⓔ
2 Ⓐ Ⓑ Ⓒ Ⓓ Ⓔ	2 Ⓐ Ⓑ Ⓒ Ⓓ Ⓔ	2 Ⓐ Ⓑ Ⓒ Ⓓ Ⓔ	2 Ⓐ Ⓑ Ⓒ Ⓓ Ⓔ
3 Ⓐ Ⓑ Ⓒ Ⓓ Ⓔ	3 Ⓐ Ⓑ Ⓒ Ⓓ Ⓔ	3 Ⓐ Ⓑ Ⓒ Ⓓ Ⓔ	3 Ⓐ Ⓑ Ⓒ Ⓓ Ⓔ
4 Ⓐ Ⓑ Ⓒ Ⓓ Ⓔ	4 Ⓐ Ⓑ Ⓒ Ⓓ Ⓔ	4 Ⓐ Ⓑ Ⓒ Ⓓ Ⓔ	4 Ⓐ Ⓑ Ⓒ Ⓓ Ⓔ
5 Ⓐ Ⓑ Ⓒ Ⓓ Ⓔ	5 Ⓐ Ⓑ Ⓒ Ⓓ Ⓔ	5 Ⓐ Ⓑ Ⓒ Ⓓ Ⓔ	5 Ⓐ Ⓑ Ⓒ Ⓓ Ⓔ
6 Ⓐ Ⓑ Ⓒ Ⓓ Ⓔ	6 Ⓐ Ⓑ Ⓒ Ⓓ Ⓔ	6 Ⓐ Ⓑ Ⓒ Ⓓ Ⓔ	6 Ⓐ Ⓑ Ⓒ Ⓓ Ⓔ
7 Ⓐ Ⓑ Ⓒ Ⓓ Ⓔ	7 Ⓐ Ⓑ Ⓒ Ⓓ Ⓔ	7 Ⓐ Ⓑ Ⓒ Ⓓ Ⓔ	7 Ⓐ Ⓑ Ⓒ Ⓓ Ⓔ
8 Ⓐ Ⓑ Ⓒ Ⓓ Ⓔ	8 Ⓐ Ⓑ Ⓒ Ⓓ Ⓔ	8 Ⓐ Ⓑ Ⓒ Ⓓ Ⓔ	8 Ⓐ Ⓑ Ⓒ Ⓓ Ⓔ
9 Ⓐ Ⓑ Ⓒ Ⓓ Ⓔ	9 Ⓐ Ⓑ Ⓒ Ⓓ Ⓔ	9 Ⓐ Ⓑ Ⓒ Ⓓ Ⓔ	9 Ⓐ Ⓑ Ⓒ Ⓓ Ⓔ
10 Ⓐ Ⓑ Ⓒ Ⓓ Ⓔ	10 Ⓐ Ⓑ Ⓒ Ⓓ Ⓔ	10 Ⓐ Ⓑ Ⓒ Ⓓ Ⓔ	10 Ⓐ Ⓑ Ⓒ Ⓓ Ⓔ
11 Ⓐ Ⓑ Ⓒ Ⓓ Ⓔ	11 Ⓐ Ⓑ Ⓒ Ⓓ Ⓔ	11 Ⓐ Ⓑ Ⓒ Ⓓ Ⓔ	11 Ⓐ Ⓑ Ⓒ Ⓓ Ⓔ
12 Ⓐ Ⓑ Ⓒ Ⓓ Ⓔ	12 Ⓐ Ⓑ Ⓒ Ⓓ Ⓔ	12 Ⓐ Ⓑ Ⓒ Ⓓ Ⓔ	12 Ⓐ Ⓑ Ⓒ Ⓓ Ⓔ
13 Ⓐ Ⓑ Ⓒ Ⓓ Ⓔ	13 Ⓐ Ⓑ Ⓒ Ⓓ Ⓔ	13 Ⓐ Ⓑ Ⓒ Ⓓ Ⓔ	13 Ⓐ Ⓑ Ⓒ Ⓓ Ⓔ
14 Ⓐ Ⓑ Ⓒ Ⓓ Ⓔ	14 Ⓐ Ⓑ Ⓒ Ⓓ Ⓔ	14 Ⓐ Ⓑ Ⓒ Ⓓ Ⓔ	14 Ⓐ Ⓑ Ⓒ Ⓓ Ⓔ
15 Ⓐ Ⓑ Ⓒ Ⓓ Ⓔ	15 Ⓐ Ⓑ Ⓒ Ⓓ Ⓔ	15 Ⓐ Ⓑ Ⓒ Ⓓ Ⓔ	15 Ⓐ Ⓑ Ⓒ Ⓓ Ⓔ
16 Ⓐ Ⓑ Ⓒ Ⓓ Ⓔ	16 Ⓐ Ⓑ Ⓒ Ⓓ Ⓔ	16 Ⓐ Ⓑ Ⓒ Ⓓ Ⓔ	16 Ⓐ Ⓑ Ⓒ Ⓓ Ⓔ
17 Ⓐ Ⓑ Ⓒ Ⓓ Ⓔ			17 Ⓐ Ⓑ Ⓒ Ⓓ Ⓔ
18 Ⓐ Ⓑ Ⓒ Ⓓ Ⓔ			18 Ⓐ Ⓑ Ⓒ Ⓓ Ⓔ
19 Ⓐ Ⓑ Ⓒ Ⓓ Ⓔ			19 Ⓐ Ⓑ Ⓒ Ⓓ Ⓔ
20 Ⓐ Ⓑ Ⓒ Ⓓ Ⓔ			20 Ⓐ Ⓑ Ⓒ Ⓓ Ⓔ

SECTION I: ANALYTICAL WRITING ASSESSMENT

GENERAL DIRECTIONS

In this section, you will have a total time of sixty minutes to plan and write two essays, one for each topic given. The specific time allotted for each essay is thirty minutes. For each essay, use three sides of 8½-by-11-inch lined paper.

Analysis of an Issue

Time: 30 Minutes

DIRECTIONS

This section will require you to analyze and explain your views on the issue given. Consider many points of view as you develop your own position on the issue. There is no right or wrong answer to the question.

Read the statement and directions carefully. Make any notes in your test booklet. Then write your response on the separate answer document. Be sure to use the answer document that goes with this writing task.

Some lawmakers have argued that the violence that results from the illegal sale of drugs can be eliminated if drugs are made legal. Addiction to drugs, they argue, is a disease, and drugs should be treated as we deal with alcohol and tobacco. But this is a solution to deal with drug violence and not with drug use. If drugs were legal, the use of drugs would only increase.

Which side of the issue do you find the more convincing, the case for or against drug legalization? Explain your position with specific support from your own experiences, observations, or readings.

Analysis of an Argument

Time: 30 Minutes

DIRECTIONS

This section will require you to critique the argument given. Questioning underlying assumptions, finding alternative explanations or counterexamples, and delineating evidence to strengthen or weaken an argument are some possible approaches.

Read the argument and directions carefully. Make any notes in your test booklet. Then write your response on the separate answer document. Be sure to use the answer document that goes with this writing task.

Several useless endangered species, like the spotted owl, the snail darter, or the gnatcatcher, are protected at great human expense. Thousands of workers in the lumber industry have lost their jobs because logging has been restricted. Construction jobs are lost because land that might be developed for human use is set aside for inedible fish and small birds.

Discuss this argument. Is it convincing? Does it use evidence well? How could it be made more persuasive? What would make its conclusion easier to evaluate?

SECTION II: READING COMPREHENSION

Time: 25 Minutes
23 Questions

DIRECTIONS

Each passage in this group is followed by questions based on its content. After reading a passage, choose the best answer to each question and blacken the corresponding space on the answer sheet. Answer all questions following a passage on the basis of what is *stated* or *implied* in that passage. You may refer back to the passage.

The railroads played a key role in the settlement of the West. They provided relatively easy access to the region for the first time, and they also actively recruited farmers to settle there (the Santa Fe Railroad, for example, brought 10,000 German Mennonites to Kansas). The railroads are criticized for their part in settling the West too rapidly, with its resultant economic unrest. (After the Civil War the vast Great Plains area was settled all at once.) Of course there were abuses connected with building and operating the railroads, but it must be pointed out that they performed a useful service in extending the frontier and helping to achieve national unity.

The real tragedy of the rapid settlement of the Great Plains was the shameful way in which the American Indians were treated. Threatened with the destruction of their whole mode of life, the Indians fought back savagely against the white man's final thrust. Justice was almost entirely on the Indians' side. The land was clearly theirs; frequently their title was legally certified by a treaty negotiated with the federal government. The Indians, however, lacked the military force and the political power to protect this right. Not only did white men encroach upon the Indians' hunting grounds, but they rapidly destroyed the Indians' principal means of subsistence—the buffalo. It has been estimated that some 15 million buffalo roamed the plain in the 1860s. By 1869, the railroads had cut the herd in half, and by 1875 the southern herd was all but eliminated.

By the middle of the 1880s, the northern herd was also a thing of the past. Particularly galling to the Indians was the fact that the white man frequently killed the buffalo merely for sport, leaving the valuable carcass to rot in the sun.

The plains Indians were considered different from the Indians encountered by the English colonists on the Atlantic coast. Mounted on horses descended from those brought by the Spanish to Mexico many years before, typical plains Indians were fierce warriors who could shoot arrows with surprising accuracy while galloping at top speed. Although they quickly adapted themselves to the use of the rifle, the Indians were not equal to the firepower of the United States Army and thus were doomed to defeat.

Theoretically, at least, the government tried to be fair to the Indians, but all too often the Indian agents were either too indifferent or corrupt to carry out the government's promises conscientiously. The army frequently ignored the Indian Bureau and failed to coordinate its policies with the civilians who were nominally in charge of Indian affairs. The settlers hated and feared the Indians and wanted them exterminated. This barbaric attitude is certainly not excusable, but it is understandable in the context of the times.

1. The author's attitude toward the treatment of American Indians by whites is one of
   (A) qualified regret
   (B) violent anger
   (C) strong disapproval
   (D) objective indifference
   (E) unfair bias

2. The author implied which of the following about the forces at work during the settlement of the Great Plains?
   (A) The federal government represented the moral use of law.
   (B) Justice was overcome by military firepower.
   (C) Attempts by the government to be fair were rejected by the Indians.
   (D) The settlers' hatred and fear was offset by the Indians' attempts at kindness.
   (E) The Indians and the white settlers shared a sporting interest in the hunting of buffalo.

3. Which of the following is concrete evidence that the white settlers did not need the buffalo for their own subsistence, as did the Indians?
   (A) More than half of the great buffalo herd had disappeared by 1869.
   (B) Nearly fifteen million buffalo were killed within twenty years.
   (C) Buffalo carcasses were left rotting in the sun by whites.
   (D) The railroad brought necessary food and supplies to the white settlers from the East.
   (E) The white settlers had their own hunting grounds separate from the Indians'.

4. What is the point of the comparison between plains Indians and the Indians encountered on the Atlantic coast?
   (A) The Atlantic coast Indians were not as abused by white settlers.
   (B) Because they were considerably better warriors than the Atlantic coast Indians, the plains Indians were a match for the United States military.
   (C) If Indians such as those on the Atlantic coast had populated the plains, there would have been no bloodshed of the white settlement.
   (D) The Indians encountered by English colonists posed no violent threat to the colonists.
   (E) The Atlantic coast Indians were unfamiliar with horses.

5. Which of the following characteristics of the passage suggests that the abuse of the Indians is a more significant topic for the author than the beneficial role of the railroads?
   (A) The statement that the railroads "are criticized for their part in settling the West too rapidly"
   (B) The amount of discussion devoted to the abuse of the Indians
   (C) The reliance on statistical details in both the first and second paragraphs
   (D) The very brief mention of the migration of German Mennonites
   (E) The perception that the achievement of national unity was one of the services that the railroad performed

6. The author of the passage would most likely disagree that
   (A) the United States government's policies toward the American Indians were shameful
   (B) the land that the Indians fought to retain belonged to them
   (C) numerous abuses were among the results of the railroads' rapid spread westward
   (D) some American Indian tribes used sophisticated weapons brought by settlers
   (E) the United States army could not be considered a friend of the American Indian

7. It can be inferred from the passage that the purpose of the Indian Bureau was to
   (A) try Indians who violated the laws of the new territory
   (B) establish reservations where the peaceful American Indians would live
   (C) assist with Indian affairs and policies of the government regarding the American Indian
   (D) bring to justice white settlers who treated the Indians in a savage or unlawful manner
   (E) assist the Indians in learning a new method of procuring food to rely less on buffalo meat

8. All of the following are presented as overt enemies of the Indians EXCEPT the
   (A) railroads
   (B) white hunters
   (C) army
   (D) Indian agents
   (E) Western settlers

When the new discipline of social psychology was born at the beginning of this century, its first experiments were essentially adaptations of the suggestion demonstration. The technique generally followed a simple plan. The subjects, usually college students, were asked to give their opinions or preferences concerning various matters; some time later they were again asked to state their choices, but now they were also informed of the opinions held by authorities or large groups of their peers on the same matters. (Often the alleged consensus was fictitious.) Most of these studies had substantially the same result: confronted with opinions contrary to their own, many subjects apparently shifted their judgments in the direction of the view of the majorities or the experts. The late psychologist Edward L. Thorndike reported that he had succeeded in modifying the aesthetic preferences of adults by this procedure. Other psychologists reported that people's evaluations of the merit of a literary passage could be raised or lowered by ascribing the passage to different authors. Apparently the sheer weight of numbers or authority sufficed to change opinions, even when no arguments for the opinions themselves were provided.

Now the very ease of success in these experiments arouses suspicion. Did the subjects actually change their opinions, or were the experimental victories scored only on paper? On grounds of common sense, one must question whether opinions are generally as watery as these studies indicate. There is some reason to wonder whether it was not the investigators who, in their enthusiasm for a theory, were suggestible, and whether the ostensibly gullible subjects were not providing answers which they thought good subjects were expected to give.

The investigations were guided by certain underlying assumptions, which today are common currency and account for much that is thought and said about the operations of propaganda and public opinion. The assumptions are that people submit uncritically and painlessly to external manipulation by suggestion or prestige, and that any given idea or value can be "sold" or "unsold" without reference to its merits. We should be skeptical, however, of the supposition that the power of social pressure necessarily implies uncritical submission to it; independence and the capacity to rise above group passion are also open to human beings. Further, one may question on psychological grounds whether it is possible as a rule to change a person's judgment of a situation or an object without first changing his or her knowledge or assumptions about it.

9. The first experiments in social psychology appeared to demonstrate all of the following EXCEPT that
    (A) many people will agree with what they believe to be the opinion held by the majority of their peers
    (B) many people will agree with what they believe to be the opinion of experts
    (C) many people change their opinions given good arguments for doing so
    (D) an individual's evaluation of a literary work can be altered by ascribing the work to a different writer
    (E) college students' opinions can be changed

10. According to the second paragraph, persons who first claimed to dislike a poem but changed their opinion when told the poem had been written by Shakespeare
    (A) may really like the poetry better because Shakespeare wrote it
    (B) may like the poetry better because Shakespeare is a highly regarded writer
    (C) are likely to be equally insecure in their evaluation of paintings or sculpture
    (D) may have changed their minds because they think the answer is expected
    (E) may be saying they have changed their minds though, in fact, they have no opinion

11. In the second paragraph of the passage, which of the following words or phrases most clearly suggests the author's skepticism about the early experiments?
    (A) "success"
    (B) "experimental victories"
    (C) "common sense"
    (D) "ostensibly gullible"
    (E) "answers"

12. The author cites the work of Edward L. Thorndike as an example of
    I. an alleged instance of the selling of an idea
    II. a pioneering social psychology study confirmed by the work of contemporary research
    III. the studies that demonstrated the willingness of subjects to change their views on matters of aesthetic preference

    (A) II only
    (B) I and II only
    (C) I and III only
    (D) II and III only
    (E) I, II, and III

13. The author implies that persons who altered their opinion on a controversial topic have most likely done so because they
    (A) have been influenced by overt social pressures
    (B) have been influenced by covert external manipulation
    (C) have learned more about the topic
    (D) have learned how experts judge the topic
    (E) are incapable of independent thought

14. The main point of the passage is to
    (A) question some assumptions about the influence of social pressures
    (B) show that a judgment of a situation cannot change without a change in the knowledge of the situation
    (C) demonstrate the gullibility of psychological investigators and their subjects
    (D) question the notion that any idea can be "sold" or "unsold"
    (E) support investigations into ideas of propaganda

15. With which of the following ideas would the author be most likely to agree?
    (A) Human beings can be programmed like machines.
    (B) Women are more likely to agree with men than with other women.
    (C) Women are more likely to agree with other women than with men.
    (D) Like women, men are capable of independent thought.
    (E) Like men, women submit uncritically to external manipulation.

16. Which of the following best describes how the passage is organized?
    (A) The ideas of the first paragraph are supported in the second and third paragraphs.
    (B) The ideas of the first paragraph are questioned in the second and third paragraphs.
    (C) The specific details of the first and second paragraphs are generalized in the third paragraph.
    (D) The first paragraph is concrete, while the second and third paragraphs are abstract.
    (E) Only the first paragraph uses figurative language.

In economics, demand implies something slightly different from the common meaning of the term. The layperson uses the term to mean the amount that is demanded of an item. Thus, if the price were to decrease and individuals wanted more of an item, it is commonly said that demand increases. To an economist, demand is a relationship between a series of prices and a series of corresponding quantities that are demanded at these prices. If one reads the previous sentence carefully, it should become apparent that there is a distinction between the quantity demanded and demand. This distinction is often a point of confusion. Demand is a relationship between price and quantities demanded, and therefore suggests the effect of one (e.g., price) on the other (e.g., quantity demanded). Therefore, knowlege of the demand for a product enables one to predict how much more of a good will be purchased if price decreases. But the increase in quantity demanded does not mean demand has increased, since the relationship between price and quantity demanded (i.e., the demand for the product) has not changed. Demand shifts when there is a change in income, expectations, taste, etc., such that a different quantity of the good is demanded at the same price.

In almost all cases, a consumer wants more of an item if the price decreases. This relationship between price and quantity demanded is so strong that it is referred to as the "law of demand." This "law" can be explained by the income and substitution effects. The income effect occurs because price increases reduce the purchasing power of the individual and, thus, the quantity demanded of goods must decrease. The substitution effect reflects the consumer's desire to get the "best buy." Accordingly, if the price of good A increases, the individual will tend to substitute another good and purchase less of good A. The negative correlation between price and quantity demanded is also explained by the law of diminishing marginal utility. According to this law, the additional utility the consumer gains from consuming a good decreases as successively more units of the good are consumed. Because the additional units yield less utility or satisfaction, the consumer is willing to purchase more only if the price of the good decreases.

Economists distinguish between individual and market demand. As the term implies, individual demand concerns the individual consumer and illustrates the quantities that individuals demand at different prices. Market demand includes the demand of all individuals for a particular good and is found by summing the quantities demanded by all individuals at the various prices.

17. Which of the following is an instance of a shift in demand as it is understood by economists?

    I. A market is selling two pounds of coffee for the price it usually charges for one pound; the *demand* for coffee has increased.

   II. The success of a television program featuring cartoon turtles has increased the *demand* for an oat cereal in turtle shapes.

  III. Because of the rail strike, California lettuce costs more in Chicago, and the *demand* for lettuce has fallen.

  (A) I only
  (B) II only
  (C) III only
  (D) I and III only
  (E) I, II, and III

18. Assume that as economists use the term, the demand for houses increases. Which of the following would most likely cause such a shift?
  (A) Prices are reduced on homes because of overbuilding.
  (B) The government predicts a large increase in the extent of unemployment.
  (C) A new government program provides jobs for a large number of workers.
  (D) A low-priced type of mobile home which is a good substitute for houses is announced.
  (E) The cost of lumber increases.

19. According to the passage, a change in demand, as economists use the term, would occur in which of the following situations?
  (A) The gasoline price increases, resulting in the increased sale of compact cars (whose price remains stable).
  (B) The gasoline price increases, resulting in the increased sale of compact cars (which go on sale in response to increased gas prices.)
  (C) The gasoline price decreases on the same day that a new 43-mpg car enters the market.
  (D) A federal order imposes a price ceiling on gasoline.
  (E) A federal order lifts price regulations for gasoline.

20. Assume that firms develop an orange-flavored breakfast drink high in vitamin C that is a good substitute for orange juice but sells for less. Based upon assertions in the passage, which of the following would occur with respect to the demand for orange juice?
    (A) Health food stores would resurrect the law of diminishing marginal utility.
    (B) Assuming that the price of fresh orange juice remained constant, more orange juice would be consumed.
    (C) The law of demand would prevail.
    (D) Assuming that the price of fresh orange juice remained constant, the demand would not change.
    (E) There is not enough information in the passage to answer this question.

21. For eleven months, the Acme food chopper led all others in sales. Though the price and the product have remained unchanged and no competitive product has been introduced, sales have fallen sharply. Economists would describe this phenomenon as
    (A) an increase in quantity demanded
    (B) the income effect
    (C) the substitution effect
    (D) the law of diminishing marginal utility
    (E) individual demand

22. According to the passage, a group of individuals will
    (A) derive increasingly less satisfaction from a product
    (B) exert individual demand under appropriate conditions
    (C) employ the boycott to lower prices
    (D) constitute a market
    (E) emphasize supply over demand

23. The purpose of the passage is to
    (A) introduce several important definitions
    (B) outline the theory of supply on demand
    (C) correct the layperson's economic misapprehensions about
        prices
    (D) introduce a student to a theory of marketing
    (E) question a popular misunderstanding of "demand"

STOP. IF YOU FINISH BEFORE TIME IS CALLED, CHECK
YOUR WORK ON THIS SECTION ONLY. DO NOT WORK
ON ANY OTHER SECTION IN THE TEST.

SECTION III: PROBLEM SOLVING

Time: 25 Minutes
16 Questions

DIRECTIONS

In this section solve each problem, using any available space on the page for scratchwork. Then indicate the *best* answer in the appropriate space on the answer sheet.

1. An astronaut weighing 207 pounds on Earth would weigh 182 pounds on Venus. The weight of the astronaut on Venus would be approximately what percent of his weight on Earth?
   (A) 50%
   (B) 60%
   (C) 70%
   (D) 80%
   (E) 90%

2. If it takes a machine ⅔ minute to produce one item, how many items will it produce in 2 hours?
   (A) ⅓
   (B) ⅘
   (C) 80
   (D) 120
   (E) 180

3. The closest approximation of $69.28 \times 0.004/0.03$ is
   (A) 0.092
   (B) 0.92
   (C) 9.2
   (D) 92
   (E) 920

Products	1960	1962	1964	1966	1968	1970
A	$4.20	$4.60	$5.00	$5.40	$5.80	$6.20
B	$6.30	$6.45	$6.60	$6.75	$6.90	$7.05

4. The chart above shows the prices of products A and B from 1960 to 1970. Using the chart, in what year will product A cost 40¢ more than product B?
   (A) 1974
   (B) 1976
   (C) 1977
   (D) 1978
   (E) 1980

5. The large square above consists of squares and isosceles right triangles. If the large square has side 4 cm, then the area of the shaded portion in square cm is
   (A) 2
   (B) 4
   (C) 6
   (D) 8
   (E) 12

6. The purchase price of an article is $48. In order to include 15% of cost for overhead and to provide $12 of net profit, the markup should be
   (A) 15%
   (B) 25%
   (C) 35%
   (D) 40%
   (E) 45%

7. Manny rides a bicycle 6 miles east, 5 miles north, 18 miles west, and 14 miles south, at a rate of 10 miles per hour. If Irv leaves at the same time and from the same place and walks directly to Manny's final destination at a rate of 5 miles per hour, he will
   (A) arrive at the same time as Manny
   (B) arrive before Manny
   (C) arrive after Manny
   (D) none of the above
   (E) cannot be determined from the information given

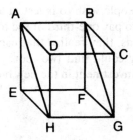

8. In the cube above, *AH* and *BG* are diagonals and the surface area of side *ABFE* is 16. What is the area of rectangle *ABGH*?
   (A) $4\sqrt{2}$
   (B) $16\sqrt{2}$
   (C) $16 + \sqrt{2}$
   (D) 16
   (E) $15\sqrt{3}$

9. If $x = y + y^2$, and y is a negative integer, when y decreases in value, then x
   (A) increases in value
   (B) fluctuates
   (C) decreases in value
   (D) remains the same
   (E) none of the above

10. A sporting goods store sold 64 Frisbees in one week, some for $3 and the rest for $4 each. If receipts from Frisbee sales for the week totaled $204, what is the fewest number of $4 Frisbees that could have been sold?
    (A) 24
    (B) 12
    (C) 8
    (D) 4
    (E) 2

11. Three business people wish to invest in a new company. Each person is willing to pay one-third of the total investment. After careful calculations, they realize that each of them would pay $7200 less if they could find two more equal investors. How much is the total investment in the new business?
    (A) $64,000
    (B) $54,000
    (C) $21,600
    (D) $5400
    (E) Cannot be determined

12. A man invested $1000, part at 5% and the rest at 6%. His total investment with interest at the end of the year was $1053. How much did he invest at 5%?
    (A) $500
    (B) $600
    (C) $700
    (D) $900
    (E) $950

13. A furniture store owner decided to drop the price of her recliners by 20% to spur business. By the end of the week she had sold 50% more recliners. What is the percentage increase of the gross?
    (A) 10%
    (B) 15%
    (C) 20%
    (D) 25%
    (E) 50%

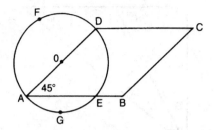

14. In the rhombus, $BC = 6, AE \cong 4$, and angle $DAE = 45°$. AD is the diameter of the circle. If a man started at C and followed around the outer edge of this figure to D, F, A, G, E, B, and back to C, approximately how far did he travel?
    (A) $14 + (^{27}/_4)\pi$
    (B) $14 + 6\pi$
    (C) $12 + 6\pi$
    (D) $14 + (^9/_2)\pi$
    (E) $12 + (^9/_2)\pi$

15. A bus leaves Burbank at 9:00 A.M., traveling east at 50 miles per hour. At 1:00 P.M. a plane leaves Burbank traveling east at 300 miles per hour. At what time will the plane overtake the bus?
    (A) 12:45 P.M.
    (B) 1:10 P.M.
    (C) 1:40 P.M.
    (D) 1:48 P.M.
    (E) 1:55 P.M.

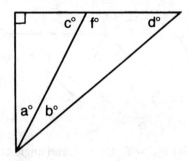

16. In the right triangle, $c = 2a$ and $d > 2b$; therefore which of the following must be true?

(A) $c > b + d$

(B) Angle a is greater than angle b.

(C) Angle a equals angle b.

(D) Angle b is greater than angle a.

(E) Angle d equals twice angle a.

STOP. IF YOU FINISH BEFORE TIME IS CALLED, CHECK YOUR WORK ON THIS SECTION ONLY. DO NOT WORK ON ANY OTHER SECTION IN THE TEST.

SECTION IV: SENTENCE CORRECTION

Time: 25 Minutes
22 Questions

DIRECTIONS

Some part of each sentence below is underlined; sometimes the whole sentence is underlined. Five choices for rephrasing the underlined part follow each sentence; the first choice (A) repeats the original, and the other four are different. If choice (A) seems better than the alternatives, choose answer (A); if not, choose one of the others.

For each sentence, consider the requirements of standard written English. Your choice should be a correct and effective expression, not awkward or ambiguous. Focus on grammar, word choice, sentence construction, and punctuation. If a choice changes the meaning of the original sentence, do not select it.

1. Ella was unable to attend her son's basketball games; because she worked the night shift, <u>arriving at 10 P.M. and leaving at 6 A.M.</u>
   (A) arriving at 10 P.M. and leaving at 6 A.M.
   (B) having arrived at 10 P.M. and leaving at 6 A.M.
   (C) she arrived at 10 P.M. and left at 6 A.M.
   (D) with an arrival at 6 and a departure at 10
   (E) from 10 P.M. to 6 A.M.

2. Although there was no contest for senator or governor and voters were expected to be apathetic, the referenda proved so controversial that 90% <u>of those registered showed up at the polls.</u>
   (A) of those registered showed up at the polls
   (B) of the registered showed up at the polls
   (C) of the registered voters showed up at the polls to vote
   (D) were registered to vote
   (E) who were not showed up at the polls

3. By leaving camp an hour before sunrise, the tourists in the Land Rover were able to catch sight of a lion and his mate <u>laying low in the tall jungle grass</u> waiting for the opportunity to capture an unwary antelope.
   (A) laying low in the tall jungle grass
   (B) the tall jungle grass concealing their low-lying bodies,
   (C) that laid low in the tall jungle grass
   (D) lying low in the tall jungle grass
   (E) was laying in the tall jungle grass

4. Every year the banker warned his borrowers that <u>planning a career in business is often easier than to pursue it.</u>
   (A) planning a career in business is often easier than to pursue it
   (B) to plan a career in business is often easier than pursuing it
   (C) planning a business career is often easier than pursuing it
   (D) the planning of a business career is often easier than its pursuit
   (E) a business career plan is often easier than a business career

5. With pennants waving and the band playing, <u>the huge crowd at the football game cheered the players making the touchdown from the stands.</u>
   (A) the huge crowd at the football game cheered the players making the touchdown from the stands
   (B) the huge crowd from the stands at the football game cheered the players making the touchdown
   (C) making the touchdown, the huge football game crowd cheered the players from the stands
   (D) the huge crowd at the football game cheered from the stands as the players made the touchdown
   (E) cheers arose from the stands as the football game players made the touchdown

6. According to the employers, the new union contract forbade working overtime past regular hours, and those who did not comply to this were severely censured.
    (A) working overtime past regular hours, and those who did not comply to this
    (B) working overtime, and those who did so
    (C) working after hours, and those not compliant
    (D) overtime, and those who did not comply with this
    (E) noncompliance with the antiovertime clause

7. Though the receptions at the embassy were usually formal and uneventful, to everyone's surprise a fight broke out when the foreign ambassador took a joke serious and punched the jokester hardly.
    (A) took a joke serious and punched the jokester hardly
    (B) took a joke seriously and hardly punched the jokester
    (C) hardly took a joke and seriously punched the jokester
    (D) took a joke seriously and punched the jokester hard
    (E) gave a hard punch to a serious jokester

8. Because Carla has always been careful to treat all her daycare children affectionately and she likes everyone as much as him, he does not feel special.
    (A) she likes everyone as much as him
    (B) she likes everyone as much as she
    (C) she has a liking for everyone equal to him
    (D) she has a liking for everyone equal to he
    (E) everyone she likes is equal to him

9. The public soon became outraged at the Cabinet member whom betrayed the public trust, and they demanded his ouster by the prime minister.
    (A) the Cabinet member whom betrayed the public trust
    (B) the untrustworthy Cabinet member
    (C) the Cabinet member with whom they betrayed the public trust
    (D) the Cabinet member who, after betraying the public trust
    (E) the Cabinet member who betrayed the public trust

10. Opinions about the ballot issue, of course, <u>varies according with the ethnic and economic status</u> of each voter, and for this reason, the poll of a small sample of voters is of no use.
    (A) varies according with the ethnic and economic status
    (B) varies according to ethnic and economic status
    (C) changes with ethnicity and the economy
    (D) vary according to the ethnic and economic status
    (E) vary according to ethnic and economical status

11. While declaring his support for a nuclear weapons freeze, <u>a small bomb exploded some distance from the Cabinet minister, who was startled but unharmed.</u>
    (A) a small bomb exploded some distance from the Cabinet minister, who was startled but unharmed
    (B) a small bomb startled the Cabinet minister, but did not harm him
    (C) a small bomb startled the Cabinet minister from a distance, but did not harm him
    (D) the Cabinet minister was startled by a bomb that exploded some distance from him, but unharmed
    (E) the Cabinet minister was startled but unharmed by a small bomb that exploded some distance from him

12. Having given up hope of influencing the vote, several disgruntled visitors had left the board meeting <u>before it had considered the new municipal tax cut.</u>
    (A) before it had considered the new municipal tax cut
    (B) before it considered the new municipal tax cut
    (C) before the members considered the new municipal tax cut
    (D) with the consideration of the new municipal tax cut yet to come
    (E) previous to the new municipal tax cut

13. Some Detroit car manufacturers promise to give rebates to new customers between June 1 and June 30, <u>granting the returned money during June but not thereafter</u>.
    (A) granting the returned money during June but not thereafter
    (B) during June but not thereafter
    (C) but not thereafter
    (D) no money after that
    (E) denying those who purchase before or after June

14. <u>After having read through the stack of bills laying on my desk</u>, I began wondering whether to file for bankruptcy or to try to consolidate my debts by a new loan.
    (A) After having read through the stack of bills laying on my desk
    (B) Having read through the stack of bills lying on my desk
    (C) Reading through the stack of bills littering my desk
    (D) The stack of bills lying on the desk, after I had read them
    (E) After having read through the stack of bills lying on my desk

15. Revisionist historians <u>have argued that the entry of the United States into</u> World War II was favored by the Chief Executive and his closest advisors.
    (A) have argued that the entry of the United States into
    (B) arguing about the United States entry into
    (C) entering an argument about the United States and
    (D) had been having an argument that the entry of the United States into
    (E) claim that the entry of the United States into

16. Gerrymandering <u>is when a voting area is unfairly divided</u> so that one political party gains advantage, and historically both the Democrats and Republicans have used the gerrymander.
    (A) is when a voting area is unfairly divided
    (B) divides a voting area unfairly
    (C) makes fair voting unfair
    (D) occurs when a voting area is unfairly divided
    (E) is when a voting area is divided unfairly

17. Frank Buck, "the great white hunter," was always portrayed on film as <u>fearless and having great skill in hunting dangerous animals</u>, such as lions, leopards, and Cape buffalo.
    - (A) fearless and having great skill in hunting dangerous animals
    - (B) fearless and very skillful in hunting dangerous animals
    - (C) having no fear and having great skill in hunting dangerous animals
    - (D) fearless and with skill in hunting dangerous animals
    - (E) hunting dangerous animals without fear and with skill

18. If a police officer were to mistake the citizen's friendly intentions, <u>and supposes her to be dangerous,</u> he might draw his revolver or call for backup assistance.
    - (A) and supposes her to be dangerous
    - (B) and supposed her to be dangerous
    - (C) and supposes danger from her
    - (D) and suspect her to be dangerous
    - (E) and suspected her to be dangerous

19. <u>After having finished the marathon,</u> both the winner and the losers felt proud of their having completed the course of more than twenty-six miles.
    - (A) After having finished the marathon
    - (B) Having finished the marathon
    - (C) Having been finished after the marathon
    - (D) Finishing the marathon
    - (E) The marathon finished

20. According to a report in the gossip columns, the actor, along with his butler, bodyguard, chauffeur, two maids, and four dogs, are on board the train bound for Cannes.

   (A) the actor, along with his butler, bodyguard, chauffeur, two maids, and four dogs, are on board

   (B) the actor and his butler and also his chauffeur, together with two maids and including four dogs, are on board

   (C) the actor, along with his butler, bodyguard, chauffeur, two maids, and four dogs, is on board

   (D) the actor, along with his butler, bodyguard, chauffeur, two maids, and four dogs, are climbing onto

   (E) the actor's butler, bodyguard, chauffeur, two maids, and four dogs are on board

21. Unaffected by both rising inflation and high interest rates were that type of enterprising American able to create a product adaptable to shifting public tastes.

   (A) were that type of enterprising American able to create a product

   (B) was that type of enterprising American able to create a products

   (C) were the productions of American enterprise

   (D) were enterprising Americans who were able to create products

   (E) enterprising Americans creating products

22. <u>Neither the director nor the investors in the second sequel predicts</u> that it will earn less money than the other two films, but they are disturbed by the box-office receipts on its opening weekend.

   (A) Neither the director nor the investors in the second sequel predicts
   (B) Neither the investors in the second sequel nor its director predicts
   (C) The director of the second sequel, along with its investors, predict
   (D) Neither the investors nor the directors of the second sequel predicts
   (E) About the second sequel, neither the director nor the investors predict

STOP. IF YOU FINISH BEFORE TIME IS CALLED, CHECK YOUR WORK ON THIS SECTION ONLY. DO NOT WORK ON ANY OTHER SECTION IN THE TEST.

SECTION V: DATA SUFFICIENCY

Time: 25 Minutes
20 Questions

DIRECTIONS

Each of the problems below consists of a question and two statements, labeled (1) and (2), in which certain data are given. You must decide whether the data given in the statements are *sufficient* to answer the question. Using the data given in the statements *plus* your knowledge of mathematics and everyday facts (such as the number of days in July or the meaning of *counterclockwise*), you are to blacken space

- (A) if statement (1) ALONE is sufficient, but statement (2) alone is not sufficient to answer the question asked;
- (B) if statement (2) ALONE is sufficient, but statement (1) alone is not sufficient to answer the question asked;
- (C) if BOTH statements (1) and (2) TOGETHER are sufficient to answer the question asked, but NEITHER statement ALONE is sufficient;
- (D) if EACH statement ALONE is sufficient to answer the question asked;
- (E) if statements (1) and (2) TOGETHER are NOT sufficient to answer the question asked, and additional data specific to the problem are needed.

1. How many rectangular tiles are required for the kitchen floor?
   (1) Each tile is 48 square inches.
   (2) The kitchen measures 10 feet by 7 feet.

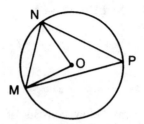

2. Within the circle with center O,
   how many degrees is angle MNO?
   (1) Angle $ONP = 31°$
   (2) Angle $NPM = 48°$

3. How much precipitation does Springfield need this month to attain its long-term average of 35 inches per year?
   (1) Over the last 11 months, the city has averaged 3 inches of precipitation per month.
   (2) Springfield has accumulated 94.3% of its mean annual precipitation during the last 11 months.

4. What is the range of a sports car on one tank of gasoline?
   (1) The tank holds 50 liters.
   (2) It consumes 8 liters of gasoline each 100 kilometers.

5. Five persons sat next to each other around a circular table to play cards. Did Grace sit next to Bill?
   (1) Dora sat next to Ethyl and Carl.
   (2) Grace sat next to Carl.

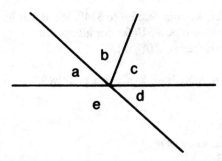

6. How many degrees is angle e?
   (1) $a + d = 82°$
   (2) $b + d = 111°$

7. What is Mary's age?
   (1) In two years, Mary will be twice as old as Beth is now.
   (2) Susan's age is the average of Mary's and Beth's ages.

8. What is the value of $\dfrac{14m^4}{s^6}$?
   (1) $m^2 = 3s^3$
   (2) $s^6 = 64$

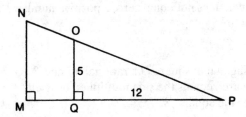

9. How long is MN?
   (1) $ON = 6\frac{1}{2}$
   (2) $MQ = 6$

10. A man's suit was discounted to $140. What was its list price?
    (1) There would be a $10 fee for alterations.
    (2) The sale was at "30% off."

11. In the expression $3x - 2y < z$, is y positive?
    (1) $x = 3$
    (2) $z = 17$

12. What is the value of p?
    (1) $2p + 3r = 11$
    (2) $p - r = 5$

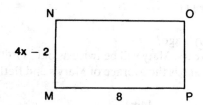

13. What is the width MN of rectangle $MNOP$?
    (1) $OP = x + 4$
    (2) The area is 48.

14. Is m, which does not equal zero, a positive number?
    (1) $m = m^2$
    (2) $m^2 = m^3$

15. Is the diagonal of square Q a rational number?
    (1) The area equals the side multiplied by itself.
    (2) The side equals $\sqrt{8}$.

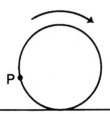

16. What is the diameter of the wheel above?
    (1) The wheel has rolled 36 feet.
    (2) Point P has touched the ground 5 times.

17. How long would it take Sue to paint the room?
    (1) Working with Bob, the project would last 2 hours.
    (2) Bob could accomplish the painting alone in $3\frac{1}{4}$ hours.

18. Is $x < 2$?
    (1) $x > x^2$
    (2) $(1/x) > 3$

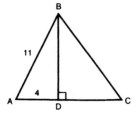

19. Given BD perpendicular to AC, what is the area of triangle BCD?
    (1) Angle $BAD = 69°$
    (2) $BD = CD$

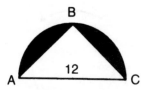

20. What is the area of the shaded portion of the half-circle?
    (1) *B* is the midpoint of $\overarc{AC}$.
    (2) Angle *ABC* is a right angle.

STOP. IF YOU FINISH BEFORE TIME IS CALLED, CHECK YOUR WORK ON THIS SECTION ONLY. DO NOT WORK ON ANY OTHER SECTION IN THE TEST.

SECTION VI: CRITICAL REASONING

Time: 25 Minutes
16 Questions

DIRECTIONS

You will be presented with brief passages or statements and will be required to evaluate their reasoning. In each case, select the best answer choice, even though more than one choice may present a possible answer. Choices which are unreasonable or incompatible with commonsense standards should be eliminated.

1. Which of the following most logically completes the passage at the blank below?

The English language, lacking the rigidity of most European tongues, has been bent and shaped in at least as many ways as there are countries or regions where it is spoken. Though purists often argue that "standard" English is spoken only in certain high-minded enclaves of the American northeast, the fact is that it is the most widely used language in the world and is not likely to yield that distinction for a very long time, if ever. Nevertheless, _____.

  (A) it remains one of the most widely spoken languages throughout the world
  (B) it can be understood in just about very corner of the globe
  (C) even making allowances for regional peculiarities, English as it is spoken has been much abused in recent times
  (D) though we may be proud of these facts, English remains one of the most difficult languages to master
  (E) English, as it is spoken, lacks the rigidity of the classical and more historic European languages

When President Lyndon Johnson signed the Voting Rights Act in 1965, he used fifty pens, handling them out as souvenirs to a joyous gathering in the President's Room of the Capitol, where Abraham Lincoln had signed the Emancipation Proclamation on January 1, 1863. When President Reagan signed an extension of the Voting Rights Act in 1982, he spoke affection- ately of "the right to vote," signed with a single pen, then concluded the four-minute ceremony by rising from his desk, announcing, "It's done."

2. If the passage above is true, which of the following is most probably true?
   (A) The Voting Rights Act did not require an extension.
   (B) The Voting Rights Act is not significantly related to the Emancipation Proclamation.
   (C) President Reagan saw himself as more like Lincoln than did Johnson.
   (D) President Reagan did not regard the extension of the act as an occasion for fanfare.
   (E) President Reagan objected strenuously to an extension of the Voting Rights Act.

3. *Senator:* Serving a few months as a Capitol page can be an exciting and enriching experience for high school students from around the country.
   Student: If the circumstances are right.

   The student's response suggests which of the following?
   (A) Belligerence
   (B) Acquiescence
   (C) Skepticism
   (D) Disbelief
   (E) Ignorance

   Money talks as never before in state and local elections, and the main cause is TV advertising. Thirty seconds can go as high as $2000. Political fundraising is one of the few growth industries left in America. The way to stop the waste might be for television to be paid by state and local government, at a standard rate, to provide air time to all candidates to debate the issues. This might be boring at first. But eventually candidates might actually brush up their debating skills and electrify the TV audience with content, not style.

4. Which of the following presuppositions is (are) necessary to the argument above?

    I. Candidates spend too much money on television advertising.

    II. Television can be used to educate and inform the public.

    III. The freedom of speech doesn't abridge the freedom to spend.

    (A) I only
    (B) II only
    (C) III only
    (D) I and II only
    (E) I, II, and III

Questions 5 and 6 refer to the following passage

According to a recent study by the National Academy of Public Administration, postal patrons are regularly affronted by out-of-order stamp vending machines, branch post office lobbies locked at night, and twenty-two-cent letters that take as long to get there as eight-cent letters did a decade ago.

5. Which of the following, if true, would weaken the implication of one of the writer's observations?

    (A) Most out-of-order vending machines are located in run-down neighborhoods.

    (B) Late-night vandalism has plagued post offices nationwide.

    (C) Postage rates rose 88 percent from 1971 to 1987, but the cost of first class mail is still cheaper in the U.S. than anywhere else.

    (D) As a public corporation, the Postal Service has increased its capital assets by $3 billion.

    (E) Ten years ago, most letters reached their destination within twenty-four hours.

6. Which of the following transitions probably begins a sentence critical of the argument in the passage?
   (A) However
   (B) In addition
   (C) Despite
   (D) In reality
   (E) Therefore

Of all the petty little pieces of bureaucratic arrogance, it's hard to imagine one smaller than that of the city schools in not admitting a British subject whose father is working—as a legal alien—for a nearby petrochemical company. Someone apparently decided that if the boy had been an illegal alien, a recent U.S. Supreme Court decision in a Texas case would have required the district to admit him, but since he is legal, there is no such requirement. That is nonsense.

7. Which of the following best expresses the point of the author's argument?
   (A) The city schools outside Texas should not base decisions on a precedent set in Texas.
   (B) The stability of a parent's job should have no bearing on the educational opportunity offered his or her child.
   (C) Bureaucratic arrogance has resulted in unsound legal interpretation.
   (D) Legal sense and nonsense are sometimes indistinguishable.
   (E) Both legal and illegal aliens should receive equal treatment.

Don't spend the night tossing and turning! Take Eezy-Z's for a sound, restful sleep . . . you'll wake up refreshed, energized, with no drugged-up hangover. Remember . . . Eezy-Z's when you need that sleep!

8. Which of the following is *not* a claim of Eezy-Z's?
   (A) A good night's sleep
   (B) Added energy
   (C) No aftereffects
   (D) Quickly falling asleep
   (E) A restful slumber

A researcher has concluded that women are just as capable as men in math but that their skills are not developed because society expects them to develop other and more diverse abilities.

9. Which of the following is a basic assumption of the researcher?
   (A) Ability in math is more important than ability in more diverse subjects.
   (B) Ability in math is less important than ability in more diverse subjects.
   (C) Women and men should be equally capable in math.
   (D) Women might be more capable than men in math.
   (E) Women tend to conform to social expectations.

Questions 10 and 11 refer to the following passage

Beginning this fall, Latino and Asian students will not be allowed to transfer out of bilingual classes (that is, a program in which courses are given in a student's native language) until they pass strict competency tests in math, reading, and writing—as well as spoken English. The board and its supporters say this will protect children from being pushed out of bilingual programs before they are ready. They have hailed this as a victory for bilingual education.

10. Which of the following, if true, is the strongest criticism of the position of the board?
    (A) A foreign student may be quite competent in math without being competent in English.
    (B) Some native students already in English-speaking classes are unable to pass the competency tests.
    (C) Most foreign students require many months of practice and instruction before mastering English skills.
    (D) Many students prefer to transfer out of bilingual classes before they have achieved competency in English.
    (E) Holding back students will double the number of students in bilingual classes—twice as many Latino and Asian children isolated from the English-speaking mainstream.

11. The argument above would be most strengthened if the author were to explain
    (A) how efficient the bilingual program is
    (B) how well staffed the bilingual program is
    (C) whether the community supports the bilingual program
    (D) whether any board members do not support the bilingual program
    (E) how the students feel about the bilingual program

The $464 million "reserve" in the 1987–88 budget adopted by the legislature in June turns out to have been based mainly on wishful thinking. Because of tax cuts approved by voters on the June ballot, along with the continuing recession and other events affecting income and expenses, the actual reserve in prospect may be as low as $7 million.

12. The author is probably leading to which of the following conclusions?
    (A) These facts warrant an investigation into who squandered $457 million.
    (B) A reserve in the budget is not so necessary as we might wish it to be.
    (C) The legislature would be wise not to add any new spending to the budget adopted in June.
    (D) The recession will probably not last much longer, but while it does the legislature must adjust the budget accordingly.
    (E) Legislative budgets are typically careless and unheeding of variable factors which may affect their accuracy.

Questions 13 and 14 refer to the following passage

"The sum of behavior is to retain a man's dignity without intruding upon the liberty of others," stated Sir Francis Bacon. If this is the case, then not intruding upon another's liberty is impossible.

13. The conclusion strongly implied by the author's arguments is that
    (A) retaining one's dignity is impossible without intruding upon another's liberty
    (B) retaining dignity never involves robbing others of liberty
    (C) dignity and liberty are mutually exclusive
    (D) there is always the possibility of a "dignified intrusion"
    (E) B. F. Skinner's *Beyond Freedom and Dignity* takes its cue from Bacon

14. The author's argument would be weakened if it were pointed out that

    I. Bacon's argument has been misinterpreted out of context
   II. neither liberty nor dignity can be discussed in absolute terms
  III. retaining dignity always involves a reduction of liberty

  (A) I only
  (B) III only
  (C) I and II only
  (D) II and III only
  (E) I, II, and III

15. Which of the following most logically completes the passage at the blank below?

In a civilized society, members of the community will often defer to others, even against their own better judgment. This situation may occur in public, in gatherings with strangers, or in the household with one's family or friends. It is a sign of a more sophisticated culture that one's immediate interests are thought to be secondary to those of another. On first examination this may seem to be selflessness, but _____.

  (A) actually it is not; it is just ignorance
  (B) rather it may take many names
  (C) actually it is
  (D) to some extent it does serve the ends of the individual concerned
  (E) sometimes it can harbor animosities and hostility

On a swimming team—
    All freestyle swimmers are Olympic winners.
    No blue-eyed swimmer is an Olympic winner.
    All Olympic winners go on to lucrative professional careers.

16. If it is determined that all of the above are true, then which of the following must also be true about the swimming team?
    (A) All those who go on to professional careers are freestyle swimmers.
    (B) Only freestyle swimmers go on to professional careers.
    (C) Some blue-eyed swimmers go on to lucrative professional careers.
    (D) No blue-eyed swimmer is a freestyle swimmer.
    (E) Only blue-eyed swimmers don't go on to lucrative careers.

STOP. IF YOU FINISH BEFORE TIME IS CALLED CHECK YOUR WORK ON THIS SECTION ONLY. DO NOT WORK ON ANY OTHER SECTION IN THE TEST.

SECTION VII: PROBLEM SOLVING

Time: 25 Minutes
16 Questions

DIRECTIONS

In this section solve each problem, using any available space on the page for scratchwork. Then indicate the *best* answer in the appropriate space on the answer sheet.

1. If $2/x = 4$ and if $2/y = 8$, then $x - y =$
   - (A) ⅛
   - (B) ¼
   - (C) ¾
   - (D) 4
   - (E) 24

2. What is the largest integer if the sum of three consecutive even integers is 318?
   - (A) 100
   - (B) 104
   - (C) 106
   - (D) 108
   - (E) 111

3. If the ratio of the side of Cube A to the side of Cube B is 2:1, then which of the following is the ratio of the surface areas?
   - (A) 1:2
   - (B) 2:1
   - (C) 3:1
   - (D) 4:1
   - (E) 8:1

4. The denominator of a fraction is 5 greater than the numerator. If the numerator and the denominator are increased by 2, the resulting fraction is equal to $\frac{7}{12}$. What is the value of the original fraction?
   (A) $\frac{5}{12}$
   (B) $\frac{1}{2}$
   (C) $\frac{9}{14}$
   (D) $\frac{2}{3}$
   (E) $\frac{12}{17}$

5. How much tea worth 93¢ per pound must be mixed with tea worth 75¢ per pound to produce 10 pounds worth 85¢ per pound?
   (A) $2\frac{2}{9}$
   (B) $3\frac{1}{2}$
   (C) $4\frac{4}{9}$
   (D) $5\frac{5}{9}$
   (E) $9\frac{1}{2}$

6. If 15 students in a class average 80% on an English exam and 10 students average 90% on the same exam, what is the average in percent for all 25 students?
   (A) 83%
   (B) 83½%
   (C) 84%
   (D) 85%
   (E) 86⅔%

7. Mr. Smitherly leaves Cedar Rapids at 8 A.M. and drives north on the highway at an average speed of 50 miles per hour. Mr. Dinkle leaves Cedar Rapids at 8:30 A.M. and drives north on the same highway at an average speed of 60 miles per hour. Mr. Dinkle will
   (A) overtake Mr. Smitherly at 9:30 A.M.
   (B) overtake Mr. Smitherly at 10:30 A.M.
   (C) overtake Mr. Smitherly at 11:00 A.M.
   (D) be 30 miles behind at 8:35 A.M.
   (E) never overtake Mr. Smitherly

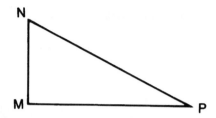

8. On △MNP, MN ⊥ MP, MP = 24, and NP = 26. What is the area of △MNP in square units?
   (A) 312
   (B) 240
   (C) 120
   (D) 60
   (E) Cannot be determined

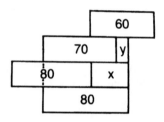

9. The horizontal length of each rectangle is marked within. What is the total horizontal length of x + y?
   (A) 40
   (B) 50
   (C) 80
   (D) 90
   (E) Cannot be determined

10. Tom has enough money to buy 45 bricks. If the bricks each cost 10 cents less, Tom could buy 5 more bricks. How much money does Tom have to spend on bricks?
   (A) $100
   (B) $50
   (C) $45
   (D) $40
   (E) $30

11. What is the total surface area in square meters of a rectangular solid whose length is 7 meters, width is 6 meters, and depth is 3 meters?
    (A)   32 m^2
    (B)   81 m^2
    (C) 126 m^2
    (D) 162 m^2
    (E) 252 m^2

12. The average of 9 numbers is 7 and the average of 7 other numbers is 9. What is the average of all 16 numbers?
    (A) 9
    (B) 8
    (C) 7⅞
    (D) 7½
    (E) 7¼

13. If the diameter of circle R is 30% of the diameter of circle S, the area of circle R is what percent of the area of circle S?
    (A)   9%
    (B) 15%
    (C) 30%
    (D) 60%
    (E) 90%

14. In a class of 200 students, 120 study Spanish and 100 study French. If a student must study at least one of these two languages, what percent of the students study French but not Spanish?
    (A) 80%
    (B) 40%
    (C) 30%
    (D) 20%
    (E) 10%

Toys	Cost to Manufacture	Profit per Toy
A	$2.5796	$2.4431
B	$2.5768	$2.4312

15. According to the chart above, how many of each toy would have to be manufactured so that the total price of toy A exceeds the total price of toy B by $147.00?
    (A)   100
    (B)   1000
    (C)   10,000
    (D)   100,000
    (E) 1,000,000

16. Which of the following cannot be weighed using a balance scale and these unit weights: 1, 4, 7, and 10?
    (A) 13
    (B) 15
    (C) 17
    (D) 19
    (E) 21

STOP. IF YOU FINISH BEFORE TIME IS CALLED, CHECK YOUR WORK ON THIS SECTION ONLY. DO NOT WORK ON ANY OTHER SECTION IN THE TEST.

SECTION VIII: DATA SUFFICIENCY

Time: 25 Minutes
20 Questions

DIRECTIONS

Each of the problems below consists of a question and two statements, labeled (1) and (2), in which certain data are given. You must decide whether the data given in the statements are *sufficient* to answer the question. Using the data given in the statements *plus* your knowledge of mathematics and everyday facts (such as the number of days in July or the meaning of *counterclockwise*), you are to blacken space

- (A) if statement (1) ALONE is sufficient, but statement (2) is not sufficient to answer the question asked;
- (B) if statement (2) ALONE is sufficient, but statement (1) alone is not sufficient to answer the question asked;
- (C) if BOTH statements (1) and (2) TOGETHER are sufficient to answer the question, but NEITHER statement ALONE is sufficient;
- (D) if EACH statement ALONE is sufficient to answer the question asked;
- (E) if statements (1) and (2) TOGETHER are NOT sufficient to answer the question asked, and additional data specific to the problem are needed.

1. What are the individual prices of three cameras?
   (1) The three cameras have an average price of $172.
   (2) Two are identical and sell for $332 together.

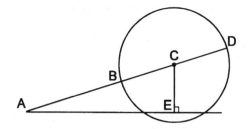

2. In the circle with center *C* above, what is the area of right triangle *ACE*?
   (1) *AE* equals 16 inches.
   (2) *BD* equals 12 inches.

3. How many black shoes were sold by Shepard's Shoe Emporium?
   (1) Three-quarters of the shoes sold were brown.
   (2) The Emporium sold 1284 left shoes.

4. A farmer wants to fence in a rectangular lot of 3000 square feet in which to raise pigs. Should he employ configuration X or configuration Y in order to minimize the cost of fencing?
   (1) Lot X would be 75 feet long and lot Y would be 50 feet wide.
   (2) Lot X would be 87½ percent longer than wide and lot Y would be 20 percent longer than wide.

5. Given three different integers, does the exponential quantity $(a - b)^c$ exceed zero?
   (1) $b < a$
   (2) $c = 2a$

6. Otto and his wife, Anna, leave home at 1 P.M. and bicycle in different directions. How far apart are they at 4 P.M.?
   (1) Otto rides at 12 mph westward for two hours and then stops.
   (2) Anna rides at 10 mph southward for one hour and then rides westward at the same speed for three hours.

7. How long would it take Joan to count the books in a small library?
   (1) She counts twice as fast as Emily.
   (2) Working together, Joan and Emily count the books in 26 hours.

8. What is the value of $x + y + z$?
   (1) $y + z = 2x$
   (2) $1/x + 1/y + 1/z = 4/9$

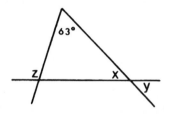

9. How many degrees is angle x?
   (1) $y = 47°$
   (2) $z = 110°$

10. One number is five more than half a second number, which is evenly divisible by a third number. What is the second number?
    (1) The first number is one less than the second.
    (2) The third number is two less than half the second.

11. Each of 200 electrical switches controls a separate light bulb. How many of the switches are in the OFF position?
    (1) 40 percent of the bulbs are glowing.
    (2) 5 percent of the bulbs are burnt out.

12. Beverage cans are manufactured of steel or aluminum. From the following graphs, what was the percentage change in number of beverage cans manufactured from 1975 to 1980?

(1)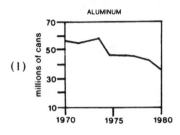

(2)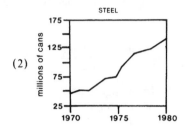

13. Is the product cd positive?
    (1) $3c = -8d^3$
    (2) $d > c + 4$

14. How much wallpaper is needed to cover the two largest walls of a narrow room which is 9 feet high?
    (1) The room is 10 feet wide.
    (2) The room is 24 feet long.

15. A savings account earned 1% interest compounded each month, credited on the last day of the month. One December 8 there was $1115.67 in the account. During which month did the account first exceed $1100?
    (1) $1000 was deposited on the previous December 31.
    (2) There were no deposits or withdrawals this year.

16. If $x < y$, is $(x - y) < yz$?
    (1) $y < 0$
    (2) $z < 0$

17. How many people are employed at a certain manufacturing plant with an annual payroll of $2,342,000?
    (1) Three-fourths of the employees are clerical, at an average salary of $16,020.
    (2) With 8 percent more employees, the payroll would equal $2,548,000.

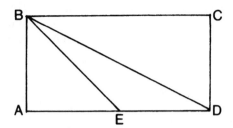

18. In the figure above, *ABCD* is a rectangle and *E* is the midpoint of one side. What is the area of triangle *BCD*?
    (1) *BE* = 5 inches
    (2) *CD* = 3 inches

19. Given that $m = n + 2$, what is the value of $m^2 - 4m + 4$?
    (1) $n = 20$
    (2) $n^2 = 400$

20. An ice-cream stand sells two sizes of cones, Generous and Colossal. How many Colossal cones were sold one day?
    (1) The total sales were $209.15.
    (2) Generous cones sold for 75¢ and Colossal cones sold for $1.25.

STOP. IF YOU FINISH BEFORE TIME IS CALLED, CHECK YOUR WORK ON THIS SECTION ONLY. DO NOT WORK ON ANY OTHER SECTION IN THE TEST.

ANSWER KEY FOR PRACTICE TEST 1
MULTIPLE-CHOICE SECTIONS

Section II Reading Comprehension	Section III Problem Solving	Section IV Sentence Correction	Section V Data Sufficiency
1. C	1. E	1. C	1. C
2. B	2. E	2. A	2. B
3. C	3. C	3. D	3. D
4. D	4. E	4. C	4. C
5. B	5. D	5. D	5. A
6. A	6. D	6. B	6. A
7. C	7. B	7. D	7. E
8. A	8. B	8. A	8. A
9. C	9. A	9. E	9. D
10. D	10. B	10. D	10. B
11. D	11. B	11. E	11. E
12. C	12. C	12. C	12. C
13. C	13. C	13. C	13. D
14. A	14. D	14. B	14. D
15. D	15. D	15. A	15. B
16. B	16. B	16. B	16. E
17. B		17. B	17. C
18. C		18. D	18. D
19. A		19. B	19. B
20. C		20. C	20. A
21. D		21. D	
22. D		22. B	
23. A			

Section VI Critical Reasoning	Section VII Problem Solving	Section VIII Data Sufficiency
1. C	1. B	1. C
2. D	2. D	2. E
3. C	3. D	3. E
4. D	4. B	4. D
5. E	5. D	5. D
6. A	6. C	6. C
7. C	7. C	7. C
8. D	8. C	8. E
9. E	9. E	9. D
10. E	10. C	10. A
11. A	11. D	11. E
12. C	12. C	12. C
13. A	13. A	13. A
14. C	14. B	14. B
15. D	15. C	15. B
16. D	16. D	16. C
		17. E
		18. C
		19. D
		20. E

HOW TO SCORE YOUR ESSAYS

Have someone knowledgeable in the writing process evaluate your essays using the following checklist and grading scale. Remember, because the essays must be written in a limited time period, minor errors of grammar or mechanics will not affect your scores.

Analysis of an Issue	Yes, completely	Yes, partially	No
1. Does the essay focus on the assigned topic and cover all of the tasks?			
2. Does the essay show an understanding of the complexity of the issue?			
3. Does the essay show cogent reasoning and logical position development?			
4. Are there sufficient relevant persuasive supporting details?			
5. Is the essay well organized?			
6. Does the essay show a command of standard written English?			

Analysis of an Argument	**Yes, completely**	**Yes, partially**	**No**
1. Does the essay focus on the assigned topic and cover all of the tasks?			
2. Does the essay carefully analyze the important features of the argument?			
3. Does the essay show cogent reasoning and logical development?			
4. Are there sufficient relevant supporting details of the critique?			
5. Is the essay well organized?			
6. Does the essay show a command of standard written English?			

HOW TO SCORE YOUR MULTIPLE-CHOICE QUESTIONS

1. Add the total number of correct responses for each secton.
2. Add the total number of incorrect responses (only those attempted or marked in) for each section.
3. The total number of incorrect responses should be divided by 4, giving the adjustment factor.
4. Subtract this adjustment factor from the total number of correct responses to obtain a corrected raw score.
5. This score is then scaled from 200 to 800.

Example:
A. If the total number of correct answers was 80 out of a possible 113.
B. And 24 problems were attempted but missed.
C. Dividing the 24 by 4 gives an adjustment factor of 6.
D. Subtracting this adjustment factor of 6 from the original 80 correct gives a corrected raw score of 74.
E. This corrected raw score is then scaled to a range of 200 to 800.

SCORE RANGE APPROXIMATORS

The following chart is designed to give you an approximate score range only, not an exact score. When you take the GMAT, you will have questions that are similar to those in this book; however, some questions may be slightly easier or more difficult. Needless to say, this may affect your scoring range.

Because one section of the GMAT is experimental (it doesn't count toward your score), for the purposes of this approximation, do not count Section VIII. Remember, on the actual test the experimental section could appear anywhere on your test.

Corrected Raw Score	Approximate Score Range
97–113	700–800
81–96	610–690
64–80	530–600
48–63	440–520
30–47	350–430
14–29	260–340
0–13	200–250

Keep in mind that this is just an approximate score range. An average score on the GMAT is approximately 480.

ANALYZING YOUR TEST RESULTS

The charts on the following pages should be used to carefully analyze your results and spot your strengths and weaknesses. The complete process of evaluating your essays and analyzing individual problems in each subject area should be completed for each Practice Test. These results should then be reexamined for trends in types of errors (repeated errors) or poor results in specific subject areas. THIS REEXAMINATION AND ANALYSIS IS OF TREMENDOUS IMPORTANCE IN HELPING YOU MAXIMIZE YOUR SCORE.

ANALYSIS SHEET FOR
MULTIPLE-CHOICE SECTIONS

	Possible	Completed	Right	Wrong
Section II: Reading Comprehension	23			
Section III: Problem Solving	16			
Section IV: Sentence Correction	22			
Section V: Data Sufficiency	20			
Section VI: Critical Reasoning	16			
Section VII: Problem Solving	16			
Section VIII: Data Sufficiency	20			
OVERALL TOTALS	133			

WHY???????????????????????????????

ANALYSIS SHEET FOR MULTIPLE-CHOICE PROBLEMS MISSED

One of the most important parts of test preparation is analyzing WHY! you missed a problem so that you can reduce the number of mistakes. Now that you have taken the practice test and corrected your answers, carefully tally your mistakes by marking them in the proper column.

REASON FOR MISTAKE

	Total Missed	Simple Mistake	Misread Problem	Lack of Knowledge
Section II: Reading Comprehension				
Section III: Problem Solving				
Section IV: Sentence Correction				
Section V: Data Sufficiency				
Section VI: Critical Reasoning				
Section VII: Problem Solving				
Section VIII: Data Sufficiency				
OVERALL TOTALS				

Reviewing the above data should help you determine WHY you are missing certain problems. Now that you have pinpointed the type of error, take the next practice test focusing on avoiding your most common type.

COMPLETE ANSWERS AND EXPLANATIONS FOR PRACTICE TEST 1 MULTIPLE-CHOICE SECTIONS

SECTION II: READING COMPREHENSION

1. (C) Although the author does not express violent anger, the characterization of the treatment of the Indians as a *tragedy* and the pronouncement that the whites' behavior was *barbaric* certainly express strong disapproval.

2. (B) Although justice was on the Indians' side (second paragraph), *the Indians were not equal to the firepower of the United States Army.* Each of the other choices contradicts information in the passage.

3. (C) This is evidence that the whites killed buffalo for sport rather than for subsistence. The disappearance of the buffalo herd is not, of itself, evidence that the buffalo did not provide subsistence to the whites.

4. (D) The point of comparison is that the Atlantic coast Indians were not fierce warriors like the plains Indians. Thus they did not pose any kind of violent threat.

5. (B) Three of the four paragraphs of the passage are devoted to discussing the abuse of the plains Indians. The "weight" which the author gives to this topic suggests its significance.

6. (A) The author states that the government itself *tried to be fair,* but that the *agents'* indifference or corruption failed the American Indians.

7. (C) According to the final paragraph of the passage, *the Indian agents were either too indifferent or corrupt to carry out the government's promises conscientiously. The army frequently ignored the Indian Bureau and failed to coordinate its policies with the civilians who were nominally in charge of Indian affairs.* Choices (B) and (D) may be historically correct but cannot specifically be inferred from the passage.

8. (A) Though the passage criticizes the railroads, it does not present them as overt enemies of the Indians, while the last paragraph cites the agents, the army, and the settlers.

9. (C) The first paragraph supports answers (A), (B), (D), and (E). One of the points of the experiments described is to show that people will change their opinions *without* being given good reasons to do so.

10. (D) The second paragraph (and the third) questions the validity of the conclusions of the experiments described in the first paragraph.

11. (D) By calling the subjects *ostensibly gullible,* the author suggests that what was ostensible may not have been true.

12. (C) Thorndike's claims to have altered his subjects' aesthetic preferences are instances of selling an idea and studies of change of aesthetic preference, but the passage does not assert that contemporary research confirms these claims.

13. (C) The passage concludes that a change of judgment is likely to be based on a change of knowledge or assumptions about the topic.

14. (A) Though the passage refers to ideas in choices (B), (C), and (D), only (A) is the main point of the *whole* passage.

15. (D) The passage gives us no information on the author's views of men as opposed to women. Answer (D), referring to both men and women, is clearly implied by the last paragraph.

16. (B) The first paragraph (the claims of early social psychologists) presents ideas that are questioned in the second and third paragraphs.

17. (B) Demand, as economists use the word, requires the relationship between price and the quantity demanded to remain unchanged. In both I and III the price has changed, rising in III and falling in I.

18. (C) The passage says the *demand shifts when there is a change in income, expectations, taste, etc., such that a different quantity of the good is demanded at the same price.* (A), (D), and (E) all involve a changing price, and (B) would reduce income so that demand would decrease.

19. (A) Initially, the passage emphasizes a distinction between *demand* and *quantity demanded,* concluding that *demand shifts when there is a change in income, expectations, taste, etc., such that a different quantity of the good is demanded at the same price.* This statement fits (A) precisely. All other choices include or allow for a changing price.

20. (C) This situation establishes a relationship between price and quantity which parallels the paragraph's explanation of the *law of demand.* This section discusses *the consumer's desire to get the "best buy"* and goes on to say that *if the price of good A increases, the individual will tend to substitute another good and purchase less of good A.* Since the appearance of a lower-priced breakfast drink makes orange juice more "expensive" in relation, the law of demand as so described would prevail.

21. (D) According to the law of diminishing marginal utility, as more units of a good are consumed, there is less utility or consumer satisfaction (paragraph 3).

22. (D) The third paragraph distinguishes between *individual demand* and *market demand;* the former is exercised by a single person, whereas the latter is exerted by a group of individuals. With this distinction in mind, we may conclude that a group of individuals constitutes a market.

23. (A) The passage defines a number of important economic
terms. Though it does question a popular misunderstanding
(E), it does so only in the first paragraph. The passage does not
deal with supply, (B), or marketing, (D).

SECTION III: PROBLEM SOLVING

1. (E) Since this is an approximation, round off

$$\frac{\text{Venus weight of } 182}{\text{Earth weight of } 207} \text{ to } \frac{180}{200} \text{ which is } 90\%$$

2. (E) First change 2 hours into 120 minutes.
   (Always get a common unit of measurement.)

   Then dividing 120 by $\frac{2}{3}$ gives

   $$^{60}\cancel{120} \times \frac{3}{\cancel{2}_1} = 180$$

   The correct answer is (E), 180 items. Notice choices (A) and (B) are ridiculous answers.

3. (C) This problem is most easily completed by rearranging and approximating as follows:

   $$\frac{69.28 \times 0.004}{0.03} \cong 69 \times \frac{0.004}{0.03} \cong 69 \times 0.1 = 6.9$$

   which is the only reasonably close answer to 9.2

4. (E) Simply continue the chart as follows, adding 40¢ for each two years to Product A and 15¢ for each two years to Product B:

Products	1972	1974	1976	1978	1980
A	$6.60	$7.00	$7.40	$7.80	$8.20
B	$7.20	$7.35	$7.50	$7.65	$7.80

It is evident that the correct answer is 1980.

5. **(D)** Since the large square has side 4 cm, then its area must be 16. By careful grouping of areas, you will see that there are 4 unshaded smaller squares, and 4 shaded smaller squares (match the shaded parts to four squares) therefore ½ of the area is shaded, or 8 sq cm.

6. **(D)** The net profit is 25% since $12 is 25% of $48. Now add in 15% for overhead and you have 25% + 15% = 40%.

7. **(B)** The following diagram shows Manny's bicycling path and Irv's walking path.

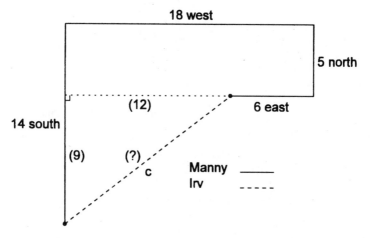

Manny traveled 43 miles at 10 miles per hour, so it took him 4.3 hours. The distance Irv travels is calculated by subtracting travel in opposite directions and using the Pythagorean theorem. 6 east and 18 west leaves 12 west, while 5 north and 14 south leaves 9 south. The right triangle has legs of 9 and 12. Therefore the hypotenuse must be 15 (3:4:5 ratio) or using the theorem,

$$a^2 + b^2 = c^2$$

$$9^2 + 12^2 = c^2$$

$$81 + 144 = c^2$$

$$225 = c^2$$

$$15 = c$$

Irv must travel 15 miles at 5 miles per hour, or 3 hours. Since they both start at the same time, Irv arrives much earlier than Manny.

8. (B) Since the surface area of side *ABFE* is 16, then each side is 4. Now use the Pythagorean theorem to find the length of the diagonal that is also the length of the rectangle.

$$4^2 + 4^2 = AH^2$$
$$16 + 16 = AH^2$$
$$32 = AH^2$$
$$\sqrt{32} = AH$$

Simplifying

$$\sqrt{32} = \sqrt{16 \times 2} = \sqrt{16} \times \sqrt{2} = 4\sqrt{2}$$

Now multiplying length times width gives

$$4 \times 4\sqrt{2} = 16\sqrt{2}$$

Notice you may have recognized the ratio of a 45°:45°:90° triangle as 1:1:$\sqrt{2}$ and found the diagonal quickly using 4:4:4$\sqrt{2}$.

9. (A) Substituting small negative integers is the most effective method for this problem.

Let $y = -1$

then $x = -1 + (-1)^2$
$x = -1 + 1$
$x = 0$

Now let $y = -2$

then $x = -2 + (-2)^2$
$x = -2 + 4$
$x = 2$

Therefore x increases in value.

10. (B) Let x be the number of $4 Frisbees, then $64 - x$ is the number of $3 Frisbees. This gives the equation $3(64 - x) + 4(x) = 204$. Solving gives

$$192 - 3x + 4x = 204$$
$$192 + x = 204$$
$$x = 12$$

Therefore, the fewest number of $4 Frisbees is 12. Note that you could have worked from the answers by substituting in each possibility.

11. (B) If each could save $7200, then all 3 could save $21,600. Let x stand for the amount each of the five business people invests, then the difference between the five and three investments would be

$$5x - 3x = 21,600$$
$$\text{or} \qquad 2x = 21,600$$
$$x = 10,800$$

Hence each of the five invests $10,800, therefore the total investment is $5 \times 10,800$ or $54,000.

Note that answers (C), (D), and (E) were not reasonable. Another method could have used one of the original investor's savings and worked from the equation $1/3x - 1/5x = 7200$.

12. (C) Let x be the amount invested at 5%, then $1000 - x$ is the amount invested at 6%. This gives the equation $5(x) + 6(1000 - x) = 5300$. Solving gives

$$5x + 6000 - 6x = 5300$$
$$6000 - x = 5300$$
$$-x = -700$$
$$x = 700$$

Therefore $700 was invested at 5%.

Note that answers (A), (D), and (E) were not reasonable.

13. **(C)** The best way to solve this problem is by using simple numbers. If the recliners originally sold at $100 each, then a 20% reduction would leave a price of $80 each. If the owner sold 50% more recliners, it would be the same as $40 more for each original sale. This would be $120, ($80 + $40), which is 20% more than $100 per recliner.

An alternate method would be to let 3/2 represent a 50% increase, then 3/2 times 80% = 120%, which is a 20% increase over the original 100%.

14. **(D)** Since *ABCD* is a rhombus, all sides are equal, therefore *BC* = *CD* = 6, and *BC* + *CD* = 12. *AB* = 6, minus *AE* ≅ 4 leaves 6 − 4 ≅ 2, which is the approximate length of *BE*. Adding 12 + 2 = 14, gives the distance around the rhombus that will be traveled. Now using the formula for circumference of a circle = 2π*r* or π*D* leaves 6π as the circumference of the complete circle. Because the inscribed angle is 45°, arc *DE* is 90° (inscribed angle is half of the arc it intercepts). This 90° will not be traveled as it is in the interior of the figure, therefore only 270° of the 360° in the complete circle will be traveled, or ¾ of the circle. ¾ × 6π = 9π/2. This added to the original 14 gives answer (D) 14 + (9π/2), or 14 + (9/2)π.

15. **(D)** Set up the equation as follows:

Let *t* be the length of time it will take the plane to overtake the bus, then *t* + 4 is the time that the bus has traveled before the plane starts. The distance that the bus has traveled by 1 P.M. is 50(*t* + 4), since distance equals rate times time (*d* = *rt*). The distance the plane will travel is 300*t*. Now setting these two equal to each other (they will have to travel the same distance for one to overtake the other) gives 50(*t* + 4) = 300*t*. Solve the equation as follows:

$$50(t + 4) = 300t$$
$$50t + 200 = 300t$$
$$200 = 250t$$

Therefore $$⅘ = t$$

⅘ of an hour (⅘ × 60) is 48 minutes. Hence it will take 48 minutes for the plane to overtake the bus and since the plane is starting at 1 P.M. it will overtake the bus at 1:48 P.M.

16. (B) In the right triangle, if $c = 2a$, then angle $a = 30°$ and $c = 60°$. Since angle f is supplementary to angle c, angle f must be 120°. If angle f is 120°, then there are 60° left to be divided between angles d and b (remember there are 180° in a triangle). Since $d > 2b$, then b must be less than 30°, therefore the correct answer is (B) angle a (30°) is greater than angle b (less than 30°).

Notice the way you should have marked the diagram to assist you.

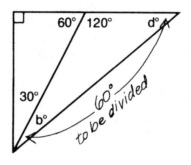

SECTION IV: SENTENCE CORRECTION

1. (C) With the semicolon, the second part of the original sentence is a fragment; so are choices (B), (D), and (E).

2. (A) The original is better than any of the alternatives.

3. (D) The verb *lying* (resting—lie, lay, lain) is correct here; *laying* (placing—lay, laid, laid) takes an object.

4. (C) The original is flawed by faulty parallelism. *Planning* is not parallel to *to pursue* (the former a gerund, the latter an infinitive). Choice (C) corrects this problem; *planning* is parallel to *pursuing*.

5. (D) *From the stands,* in the original, is a misplaced modifier suggesting that the players made the touchdown from the stands, which is highly impossible. Choice (E) leaves *crowd* out of the sentence (a significant omission), and all other choices except (D) contain misplaced modifiers.

6. (B) The original contains two important errors. *Overtime* and *past regular hours* are repetitious and *comply to this* is both vague and nonidiomatic. Choice (B) corrects both of these weaknesses. (D) is a correct expression but retains the vague pronoun *this,* which possibly refers to either the contract or the overtime.

7. (D) Both errors in the original result from a confusion of adjectives and adverbs. *Seriously,* an adverb, correctly modifies the verb *took;* and *hard,* used as an adverb meaning *with strength,* correctly modifies *punched.* Choices (B), (C), and (E) significantly change the meaning of the original.

8. (A) The original is correct. The sentence abbreviates "She likes everyone as much as *she likes* him." All other choices are either ungrammatical or change the meaning of the sentence.

9. (E) The correct pronoun in this case is *who,* the subject of *betrayed.*

10. (D) The original contains two errors. *Varies* does not agree with the plural subject, *opinions;* and *according with* is not idiomatic. (C) is a correct phrase but changes and obscures the meaning of the sentence.

11. (E) The introductory phrase is a dangling modifier, corrected by following *freeze* with *the Cabinet minister* to make clear to whom the introductory phrase refers. Choice (D) is not best because *but unharmed* is left in an awkward position.

12. (C) The original contains two errors. *It* suggests that the meeting, not the members, does the considering, and *had considered* is a verb tense simultaneous with *had left* and does not indicate that considering the tax cut occurred after the visitors had left. Choice (D) is unnecessarily wordy and leaves unsaid who did the considering.

13. (C) *Granting the returned money during June* is repetitious, and of the choices offered, (C) is the clearest and most economical expression.

14. (B) The original contains two errors. *After having read* is redundant (*having read* already contains the *after* meaning), and *laying* (which means *putting*) is incorrect (*lying* is correct).

15. (A) The original is better than any of the alternatives.

16. (B) *Is when* is not acceptable because *gerrymandering* is not a time; choice (E) repeats this error. (D) is not best because it leaves vague whether gerrymandering is synonymous with unfair division. (C) is very general and vague.

17. (B) The original is flawed by faulty parallelism. *Fearless* is not parallel to *having great skill.* Choice (B) corrects this problem. *Fearless* is parallel to *skillful.* (C) and (E) are both unnecessarily wordy.

18. (D) *Supposes* is not the correct verb tense; in order to be parallel with *to mistake,* the verb in the underlined portion must also connect idiomatically with *to. Suspect* is the only possible choice.

19. (B) *Having finished* expresses the past tense by itself, so *after* is repetitious (its meaning is already implied in *having finished*). None of the other choices expresses the past tense both economically and clearly.

20. (C) The verb in this sentence should be *is* (not *are*) to agree with the singular subject, *actor.* A parenthetical phrase enclosed by commas and beginning with words such as *along with, including,* and *as well as* changes the number of neither the subject nor the verb. Choice (B) correctly uses *are* because the subject in this sentence has been made plural; however, the construction is awkward and wordy. Choice (D) retains the incorrect *are* and changes the meaning of the sentence. (E) leaves out the fact that the actor is on the train.

21. (D) In the original, the verb *were* does not agree with the subject, *type.* (B) is incorrect because it uses the plural *products* with *a.* (E) is incorrect because it results in a sentence fragment. (D) is an economical and clear choice that retains the meaning of the original.

22. (B) When subjects are connected with *nor* or *or,* the verb is governed by the subject closest to it; in (A) and (D) the closer subject does not agree with the verb. (E) is awkward. In (B), the subject, *director,* agrees with the verb, *predicts.*

SECTION V: DATA SUFFICIENCY

1. (C) The number of tiles would equal the area of the kitchen divided by the area of one tile, or $(120 \times 84)/48 = 210$ tiles.

2. (B) The central angle MON must be 96°, twice the inscribed angle NPM. Further, the triangle MNO has two radii as sides, so it is isosceles, and angle OMN = MNO. Therefore 2(MNO) + 96° = 180°, and one may solve for MNO = 42°.

3. (D) Either statement allows us to calculate the required precipitation, P.

$$(1) \ P = 35 - 33$$
$$(2) \ P = 35(1 - 0.943)$$

4. (C) The question asks how far the car can travel, and the answer would be $\frac{50}{8} \times 100 = 625$ kilometers. It is essential to realize that liters measure volume and kilometers measure distance.

5. (A) Since Ethyl, Dora, and Carl are consecutive, Grace and Bill must be in the remaining adjacent seats.

6. (A) Because vertical angles are equal, $a = d$. From statement (1) we can find that angle $a = 41°$. In the figure, angles a and e are supplementary, so angle $e = 180 - 41 = 139°$.

7. (E) The two statements may be translated into the equations

$$(1) \ M + 2 = 2B$$
$$(2) \ S = (M + B)/2$$

As two equations are insufficient to determine three variables, Mary's age is indeterminate.

8. (A) From the first statement, $m^2/s^3 = 3$, and squaring each side, $m^4/s^6 = 9$. Substituting into the original expression, $14(m^4/s^6) = 14 \times 9 = 126$.

9. (D) Either statement suffices to determine MN to be $7\frac{1}{2}$. Because of similar triangles, $MN{:}OQ = MP{:}QP = NP{:}OP$. From the Pythagorean theorem, $OP = 13$. By addition, $NP = ON + OP = 6\frac{1}{2} + 13 = 19\frac{1}{2}$; also $MP = 18$. Therefore $MN{:}5 = 18{:}12 = 19\frac{1}{2}{:}13$ and we can solve for MN.

10. (B) The sale price equaled the list price L minus 30%. So $\$140 = 0.7L$, and $L = 140/0.7 = \$200$.

11. (E) Making substitutions from both statements yields the expression $9 - 2y < 17$. To solve for y, we first subtract 9 from both sides and then divide by -2; the latter operation reverses the sense of the inequality. The solution $y > -4$ records that y may be positive, zero, or negative (between 0 and -4).

12. (C) Since there are two unknowns, we need two equations to solve for p and r. From (2), $p = r + 5$. Substituting that for p in (1) yields $2r + 10 + 3r = 11$, or $r = \frac{1}{5}$. Since $p = r + 5$, $p = \frac{1}{5} + 5 = \frac{26}{5}$.

13. (D) From the first statement, $x + 4 = 4x - 2$, because opposite sides of a rectangle are equal. So $x = 2$ and the width $x + 4 = 6$. Or we can use the area of the second statement, as width $=$ area/length $= \frac{48}{8} = 6$.

14. (D) The sole solution is $m = 1 = 1 \times 1 = 1 \times 1 \times 1$ and so m is positive. Note that $-1 \neq (-1)(-1) \neq (-1)(-1)(-1)$.

15. (B) Necessarily the diagonal equals the side times $\sqrt{2}$, so from the second statement, $d = \sqrt{8} \times \sqrt{2} = \sqrt{16} = 4$, a rational number.

16. (E) Since P is not now touching the ground, all we know is that the wheel has traveled more than 5 circumferences but less than $5\frac{1}{4}$. So, $5\pi d < 36 < 5\frac{1}{4}\pi d$. Hence the diameter is uncertain, somewhere in the range 2.18 to 2.29 feet.

17. (C) Remember that rate = 1/time, so Sue's rate = $1/s$ where s is the time for her to paint the room. Since

$$\text{Sue's rate} + \text{Bob's rate} = \text{joint rate}$$
$$1/s \quad + \quad 1/3\frac{1}{4} \quad = \quad \frac{1}{2}$$

which can be solved for

$$s = 5.2 \text{ hours}$$

18. (D) The first statement implies that x is a positive number but less than 1. The second statement yields $x < \frac{1}{3}$. Either statement answers the question that, yes, x is less than 2.

19. (B) From the Pythagorean theorem we know that $AD^2 + BD^2 = AB^2$, so $BD^2 = 16 + 121$, and $BD = \sqrt{137}$. The second statement tells us that the base and height of the triangle are equal, so $A = \frac{1}{2}bh = \frac{1}{2}\sqrt{137} \times \sqrt{137} = {}^{137}\!/_2$.

20. (A) Angle ABC, inscribed on a diameter, is necessarily 90°, so the second statement adds nothing new. But the first statement implies the triangle has an altitude equal to the circle's radius, 6. So the shaded area equals the area of the semicircle, ($\frac{1}{2} \times \pi \times 6^2$) minus the area of the triangle ($\frac{1}{2}bh = \frac{1}{2} \times 12 \times 6 = 36$).

SECTION VI: CRITICAL REASONING

1. (C) The transitional word *nevertheless* establishes a juxtaposition of the phrases immediately before and after it. Therefore (A) and (B) are incorrect. Choice (D) may be a good answer, but (C) is better, as it addresses a concern initially introduced in the paragraph and brings the passage full circle.

2. (D) Choices (B) and (E) are contradicted by the passage, and the passage does not support the probability of (A) or (C). Choice (D) is reasonable, plausible, and probable, given the information in the passage.

3. (C) The student's qualification shows that he or she doubts whether the Senator's statement is absolutely true, but the response is not so pronounced as to suggest any of the other choices.

4. (D) The argument presupposes both that candidates are spending too much on television advertising ("the waste") and that television can be used to inform the public ("provide air time to all candidates to debate the issues"). Statement III is irrelevant to the argument.

5. (E) This choice weakens the point made by the final observation. Each of the other choices either strengthen points made by the observation or are irrelevant.

6. (A) Only this choice necessarily introduces a contrasting statement, one which would probably take issue with the points of the argument. (C) and (D) might possibly begin critical, contrasting statements but may have other uses as well.

7. (C) Geographic location and employment status are irrelevant issues, so (A) and (B) should be eliminated. (D) and (E) are too general and vague. Only (C) makes explicit the point of the author's argument, that interpretation of the Texas law is arrogant and unsound.

8. (D) The commercial either explicitly states or implies all but (D). It makes no reference to how long it will take to fall asleep or how quickly the drug works. It does, however, claim to provide a restful, good night's sleep, with added energy and no aftereffects the next morning.

9. (E) The researcher concluded that women could be just as capable as men in math but that they develop other abilities because of social pressures. Thus, the researcher assumes that women do conform to social expectations.

10. (E) Choices (A) and (B) are irrelevant to the argument, and (D) is an illogical criticism. (E) is a logical conclusion that poses a significant problem.

11. (A) All of the other choices are much less relevant than the issue of how efficiently and effectively the program helps students to achieve competency.

12. (C) Each of the other choices requires assumptions and conclusions not supported or implied by the argument. The stress in the argument on reduced funds leads logically to the conclusion that further spending is unwise.

13. (A) Bacon advocates retaining dignity without intruding upon liberty. The author implies that retaining dignity is impossible without intruding upon another's liberty by stating that not intruding upon liberty is impossible. (B), (C), and (D) contradict the author's argument, and (E) presents an irrelevant issue.

14. (C) I and II only. The author both relies on an interpretation of Bacon's statement and discusses liberty and dignity in absolute terms; I and II subvert such reliance. III supports, reiterates in fact, the author's argument.

15. (D) The passage sets up the thesis that sometimes individuals yield to others' interests. Choices (A) and (E) are unsubstantiated or not mentioned in the passage; (C) does not fit the structure of the sentence; (B) could possibly be the correct answer, but (D) more nearly completes the thought of the passage and is neatly juxtaposed with the first part of the incomplete sentence.

16. (D) Since no blue-eyed swimmer is an Olympic winner, then no blue-eyed swimmer may be a freestyle swimmer, since *all* freestyle swimmers are Olympic winners. (B) and (E) are false because they exclude other possibilities which may, in fact, exist.

SECTION VII: PROBLEM SOLVING

1. (B) Solving the first equation for x

$$\frac{2}{x} = 4$$

$$2 = 4x$$

$$\frac{2}{4} = x$$

Therefore $\frac{1}{2} = x$

Now solving the second equation for y

$$\frac{2}{y} = 8$$

$$2 = 8y$$

$$\frac{2}{8} = y$$

Therefore $\frac{1}{4} = y$

Substituting these values for $x - y$ gives $\frac{1}{2} - \frac{1}{4} = \frac{2}{4} - \frac{1}{4} = \frac{1}{4}$

Therefore $x - y = \frac{1}{4}$, and the correct answer is (B).

2. (D) This problem is most easily answered by dividing 318 by 3 to get 106 which must be the middle number; therefore the largest is 108. You could have used the equation

$$\underset{(2x)}{\text{Smallest}} \quad + \underset{(2x + 2)}{\text{Middle}} + \underset{(2x + 4)}{\text{Largest}} = 318$$

and worked from there.

3. (D) If cube A has side 2, then the surface area is 24 square units since the area of one face is 2×2, or 4, and there are 6 equal faces to a cube. If cube B has side 1, then the surface area is 6 square units since the area of one face is 1×1, or 1, and there are 6 faces. Therefore the ratio could be 24:6, or 4:1.

4. (B) Set up the problem as follows

$$\frac{x + (2)}{x + 5 + (2)} = \frac{7}{12}, \text{ or } \frac{x + 2}{x + 7} = \frac{7}{12}$$

By observation $x = 5$ since $\frac{5 + 2}{5 + 7} = \frac{7}{12}$

Substituting into the original fraction $\frac{x}{x + 5}$ gives

$$\frac{5}{5 + 5} = \frac{5}{10} = \frac{1}{2}$$

A longer method would have been to solve $\frac{x + 2}{x + 7} = \frac{7}{12}$ as follows:

Cross multiplying gives

$$12x + 24 = 7x + 49$$
$$5x = 25$$
$$x = 5$$

and then substitute in $\frac{x}{x + 5}$

5. (D) The only reasonable answer is 5⅝ since 85¢ per pound is slightly closer to 93¢ per pound than 75¢ per pound. Then slightly more than half of the 10 pounds must be 93¢ per pound.

Algebraically, let x stand for the pounds of 93¢ tea, then $10 - x$ is the 75¢ tea. This leads to the equation

$$0.93x + 0.75(10 - x) = 0.85(10)$$

Solving gives $93x + 750 - 75x = 850$

$$18x = 100$$

$$x = \frac{100}{18}$$

Therefore $x = 5⅝$

6. (C) In this type of problem (weighted average) you must multiply the number of students times their respective scores and divide this total by the number of students as follows:

$$15 \times 80\% = 1200$$
$$\frac{10 \times 90\% = \ \ 900}{25 \qquad\quad 2100}$$

Now divide 25 into 2100. This gives an average of 84%, therefore the correct answer is (C).

7. (C) Let x be the length of time Mr. Dinkle travels, then $x + \frac{1}{2}$ is the time Mr. Smitherly travels. This gives the equation $50(x + \frac{1}{2}) = 60x$, to see when they will meet. Solving gives

$$50x + 25 = 60x$$
$$25 = 10x$$
$$2.5 = x$$

Therefore, it will take Mr. Dinkle $2\frac{1}{2}$ hours to overtake Mr. Smitherly. Since Mr. Dinkle starts at 8:30 A.M., he will overtake Mr. Smitherly at 11:00 A.M.

Note that answers (A), (D), and (E) are not reasonable.

8. (C) The area of $\triangle MNP = \frac{1}{2}bh = \frac{1}{2}(MP)(MN)$.
   Since $\triangle MNP$ is a right triangle the Pythagorean theorem says

$$c^2 = a^2 + b^2$$
$$(NP)^2 = (MP)^2 + (MN)^2$$
$$26^2 = 24^2 + (MN)^2$$
$$676 = 576 + (MN)^2$$
$$(MN)^2 = 100$$
$$MN = \sqrt{100} = 10$$

Hence the area of MNP $= \frac{1}{2}(MN)(MP)$

$$= \frac{1}{2}(10)(24)$$
$$= 120$$

9. (E) The horizontal length of x cannot be determined because there is no indication of the overlapping length of the rectangle to the left of x. If x cannot be determined, then $x + y$ cannot be determined.

10. (C) Let c = cost of each brick. Let M = total money. Thus $M = 45c$ and $M = 50(c - 10)$.

Therefore $45c = 50(c - 10)$

$$45c = 50c - 500$$
$$500 = 5c$$
$$100 = c$$

Thus $M = 4500$ cents, or \$45.00.

11. (D) A rectangular solid consists of six rectangular faces. This one in particular has two 7×6, two 6×3, and two 7×3 rectangles with areas of 42, 18, and 21, respectively. Hence the total surface area will be $2(42) + 2(18) + 2(21) = 84 + 36 + 42 = 162$ square meters.

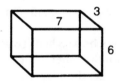

12. (C) If the average of 9 numbers is 7, then the sum of these numbers must be 9×7, or 63.

If the average of 7 numbers is 9, then the sum of these numbers must be 7×9, or 63.

The sum of all 16 numbers must be $63 + 63$, or 126.

Hence the average of all 16 numbers must be

$$126 \div 16 = \frac{126}{16} = 7\frac{14}{16} = 7\frac{7}{8}$$

Notice answers (A) and (E) are not reasonable.

13. (A) Ratio of diameters = ratio of radii

$$\frac{d_1}{d_2} = \frac{r_1}{r_2} = \frac{30}{100} = 3/10$$

Ratio of area = (ratio of radii)^2

$$\frac{A_1}{A_2} = \left(\frac{r_1}{r_2}\right)^2$$

$$\frac{A_1}{A_2} = 9/100$$

Hence the area of circle R is 9/100, or 9%, of the area of circle S.

14. (B) Since 100 plus 120 is 220, there must be 20 students that study both languages. Thus, of the 100 who study French, 80 do not study Spanish. 80 is 40% of the total of 200.

15. (C) The total price of toy A is $5.0227 [$2.5796 + $2.4431], and the total price of toy B is $5.0080 [$2.5768 + $2.4312]. Toy A exceeds toy B by $0.0147; therefore 10,000 of each must be manufactured to have a $147.00 difference.

16. (D) Only the 19 cannot be weighed. To get 13, place 10 and 4 on one side and the 1 on the other. To get the 15, place the 10, 4, and 1 on one side. To get the 17, place the 10 and 7 on one side. To get the 21, place the 10, 7, and 4 on one side.

SECTION VIII: DATA SUFFICIENCY

1. (C) Statement (1) implies that the three cameras sell for a total price of 3 × $172 = $516. Statement (2) implies that two of the cameras each sell for ½($332) = $166. The third camera must sell for $516 − $332 = $184.

2. (E) The area of the right triangle equals half the product of the two legs, AE and CE. The length of AE is given (1). But point E is not on the circle, so CE is less than ½(BD), the diameter (2). Lacking the length of CE, one cannot calculate the area.

3. (E) The second statement means that the Emporium sold a total of 2568 shoes. You cannot assume from the first statement that one-quarter of those shoes were black, because some shoes are neither black nor brown.

4. (D) This problem may be solved swiftly with knowledge of the principle that for quadrilaterals of equal area, the square has the shortest perimeter. Then the farmer would need less fencing for the stubbier configuration, approaching a square. Statement (2) yields that information immediately. Since the area of 3000 equals the length times the width, statement (1) implies that lot X would be 75 × 40 and lot Y would be 60 × 50. From either statement, lot Y would have the shorter perimeter.

5. (D) If $b < a$, statement (1), then $(a - b) > 0$ and, for any c, $(a - b)^c$ is positive. Incidentally, if $c = 0$, the entire exponential quantity equals 1, by definition. Also, if $c = 2a$, statement (2), then c is an even integer and the entire exponential quantity is positive, even if $(a - b)$ is negative.

6. (C) Since the compass directions are at right angles, the distance can be computed from the Pythagorean theorem, providing Otto's and Anna's positions at 4 P.M. are known. Otto will be 24 miles west of the origin. Anna will be 10 miles south and 20 miles west of the origin. Relative to Otto, Anna is 10 miles south and 4 miles east at 4 P.M. It is helpful to sketch a map in a problem involving positions.

7. **(C)** The problem may be solved utilizing both statements. Emily and Joan's joint rate of counting is 1/26 of the books per hour. If y is Emily's rate, then Joan's rate is $2y$, twice as fast. The individual rates sum to the joint rate:

$$2y + y = \tfrac{1}{26}$$

$$y = \tfrac{1}{78} \qquad \text{Emily's rate}$$
$$2y = \tfrac{1}{39} \qquad \text{Joan's rate}$$

Because rates are the reciprocals of the times, *and conversely,* it would take Joan 39 hours (the reciprocal of her rate) to tally the books alone.

8. **(E)** Neither statement permits the calculation of $x + y + z$. Especially, the second statement cannot be inverted to obtain 9/4, for the summation of fractions requires a common denominator:

$$\frac{yz + xz + xy}{xyz} = \frac{4}{9}$$

9. **(D)** From the first statement, $x = y = 47°$, for vertical angles are equal. From the second statement, the interior angle adjacent to z is 70°, because that angle and z sum to a straight angle. Since the interior angles of a triangle add to 180°, you can write the equation $x + 63° + 70° = 180°$, permitting the determination of x.

10. **(A)** Let's symbolize the first number as f and the second as s. The main clause of the first sentence of the question yields the equation $f = 5 + \tfrac{1}{2}s$, and statement (1) is the equation $f = s - 1$. Those two linear equations with two unknowns can be solved for both the first number ($f = 11$) and the second number ($s = 12$).

11. **(E)** The question cannot be answered, even with both statements, because any burnt-out bulb could have its switch either ON or OFF.

12. (C) To solve the problem, it is necessary to know the *total* number of beverage cans manufactured in both 1975 and 1980. Graph (1) has the data for aluminum cans and graph (2) has the data for steel cans. The data from the two graphs must be added together.

13. (A) From statement (1), $3c$ and $8d^3$ have opposite signs. Hence c and d^3 have opposite signs. With the odd exponent, the sign of d will be the same as d^3. So statement (1) is sufficient to answer the question, even though the answer is "no."

14. (B) The amount of wallpaper can be measured in square feet, the area of the two largest walls. Each large wall has an area equal to the length of the room times the height of the room. The total amount of wallpaper required is $2 \times 24 \times 9 = 432$ square feet.

15. (B) The month is uniquely determined only if there were no deposits or withdrawals from the account, else any month is possible. With the restriction, the account exceeded $1100 first on October 31st, when the interest credited brought the account up to $1104.62.

16. (C) The question can be answered with both pieces of information. With $x < y$ and $y < 0$, then $(x - y)$ is negative. With $y < 0$ and $z < 0$, then the product yz is positive. Given both statements, $(x - y)$ is less than yz.

17. (E) The information is insufficient to determine the number of workers at the plant. Statement (1) is inadequate without the average salary of the remaining workers. Statement (2) is inadequate because the extra employees may not earn the same average salary as the original employees.

18. (C) In the rectangle, $BA = CD = 3$ inches. So two sides of right triangle BAE are known and the length of side AE can be found with the Pythagorean theorem to be 4 inches. As point E is the midpoint of AD, the length of the rectangle is twice AE, or 8 inches. The area of the right triangle BCD is half the product of the sides adjacent to the right angle:

$$A = \tfrac{1}{2}bh = \tfrac{1}{2}(8)(3) = 12 \text{ in}^2$$

19. (D) Substituting $n = 20$ into the equation $m = n + 2$, it is found that $m = 22$. That value can be substituted into the quadratic expression:

$$m^2 - 4m + 4 = (22)^2 - 4(22) + 4 = 400$$

Statement (2) gives two values for m ($+22$, -18), each of which when substituted into the expression $m^2 - 4m + 4$ yields 400, so either statement (1) or (2) alone is sufficient.

20. (E) The question is indeterminate because many different combinations of the two cone prices can sum to $209.15. The question could be answered if you also knew *either* the number of Generous cones *or* the number of all cones.

PRACTICE TEST 2

ANSWER SHEET FOR PRACTICE TEST 2
(Remove This Sheet and Use It to Mark Your Answers)

SECTION II	SECTION III	SECTION IV

SECTION II

1 Ⓐ Ⓑ Ⓒ Ⓓ Ⓔ
2 Ⓐ Ⓑ Ⓒ Ⓓ Ⓔ
3 Ⓐ Ⓑ Ⓒ Ⓓ Ⓔ
4 Ⓐ Ⓑ Ⓒ Ⓓ Ⓔ
5 Ⓐ Ⓑ Ⓒ Ⓓ Ⓔ

6 Ⓐ Ⓑ Ⓒ Ⓓ Ⓔ
7 Ⓐ Ⓑ Ⓒ Ⓓ Ⓔ
8 Ⓐ Ⓑ Ⓒ Ⓓ Ⓔ
9 Ⓐ Ⓑ Ⓒ Ⓓ Ⓔ
10 Ⓐ Ⓑ Ⓒ Ⓓ Ⓔ

11 Ⓐ Ⓑ Ⓒ Ⓓ Ⓔ
12 Ⓐ Ⓑ Ⓒ Ⓓ Ⓔ
13 Ⓐ Ⓑ Ⓒ Ⓓ Ⓔ
14 Ⓐ Ⓑ Ⓒ Ⓓ Ⓔ
15 Ⓐ Ⓑ Ⓒ Ⓓ Ⓔ

16 Ⓐ Ⓑ Ⓒ Ⓓ Ⓔ
17 Ⓐ Ⓑ Ⓒ Ⓓ Ⓔ
18 Ⓐ Ⓑ Ⓒ Ⓓ Ⓔ
19 Ⓐ Ⓑ Ⓒ Ⓓ Ⓔ
20 Ⓐ Ⓑ Ⓒ Ⓓ Ⓔ

21 Ⓐ Ⓑ Ⓒ Ⓓ Ⓔ
22 Ⓐ Ⓑ Ⓒ Ⓓ Ⓔ
23 Ⓐ Ⓑ Ⓒ Ⓓ Ⓔ

SECTION III

1 Ⓐ Ⓑ Ⓒ Ⓓ Ⓔ
2 Ⓐ Ⓑ Ⓒ Ⓓ Ⓔ
3 Ⓐ Ⓑ Ⓒ Ⓓ Ⓔ
4 Ⓐ Ⓑ Ⓒ Ⓓ Ⓔ
5 Ⓐ Ⓑ Ⓒ Ⓓ Ⓔ

6 Ⓐ Ⓑ Ⓒ Ⓓ Ⓔ
7 Ⓐ Ⓑ Ⓒ Ⓓ Ⓔ
8 Ⓐ Ⓑ Ⓒ Ⓓ Ⓔ
9 Ⓐ Ⓑ Ⓒ Ⓓ Ⓔ
10 Ⓐ Ⓑ Ⓒ Ⓓ Ⓔ

11 Ⓐ Ⓑ Ⓒ Ⓓ Ⓔ
12 Ⓐ Ⓑ Ⓒ Ⓓ Ⓔ
13 Ⓐ Ⓑ Ⓒ Ⓓ Ⓔ
14 Ⓐ Ⓑ Ⓒ Ⓓ Ⓔ
15 Ⓐ Ⓑ Ⓒ Ⓓ Ⓔ

16 Ⓐ Ⓑ Ⓒ Ⓓ Ⓔ

SECTION IV

1 Ⓐ Ⓑ Ⓒ Ⓓ Ⓔ
2 Ⓐ Ⓑ Ⓒ Ⓓ Ⓔ
3 Ⓐ Ⓑ Ⓒ Ⓓ Ⓔ
4 Ⓐ Ⓑ Ⓒ Ⓓ Ⓔ
5 Ⓐ Ⓑ Ⓒ Ⓓ Ⓔ

6 Ⓐ Ⓑ Ⓒ Ⓓ Ⓔ
7 Ⓐ Ⓑ Ⓒ Ⓓ Ⓔ
8 Ⓐ Ⓑ Ⓒ Ⓓ Ⓔ
9 Ⓐ Ⓑ Ⓒ Ⓓ Ⓔ
10 Ⓐ Ⓑ Ⓒ Ⓓ Ⓔ

11 Ⓐ Ⓑ Ⓒ Ⓓ Ⓔ
12 Ⓐ Ⓑ Ⓒ Ⓓ Ⓔ
13 Ⓐ Ⓑ Ⓒ Ⓓ Ⓔ
14 Ⓐ Ⓑ Ⓒ Ⓓ Ⓔ
15 Ⓐ Ⓑ Ⓒ Ⓓ Ⓔ

16 Ⓐ Ⓑ Ⓒ Ⓓ Ⓔ
17 Ⓐ Ⓑ Ⓒ Ⓓ Ⓔ
18 Ⓐ Ⓑ Ⓒ Ⓓ Ⓔ
19 Ⓐ Ⓑ Ⓒ Ⓓ Ⓔ
20 Ⓐ Ⓑ Ⓒ Ⓓ Ⓔ

ANSWER SHEET FOR PRACTICE TEST 2
(Remove This Sheet and Use It to Mark Your Answers)

SECTION V	SECTION VI	SECTION VII	SECTION VIII
1 Ⓐ Ⓑ Ⓒ Ⓓ Ⓔ	1 Ⓐ Ⓑ Ⓒ Ⓓ Ⓔ	1 Ⓐ Ⓑ Ⓒ Ⓓ Ⓔ	1 Ⓐ Ⓑ Ⓒ Ⓓ Ⓔ
2 Ⓐ Ⓑ Ⓒ Ⓓ Ⓔ	2 Ⓐ Ⓑ Ⓒ Ⓓ Ⓔ	2 Ⓐ Ⓑ Ⓒ Ⓓ Ⓔ	2 Ⓐ Ⓑ Ⓒ Ⓓ Ⓔ
3 Ⓐ Ⓑ Ⓒ Ⓓ Ⓔ	3 Ⓐ Ⓑ Ⓒ Ⓓ Ⓔ	3 Ⓐ Ⓑ Ⓒ Ⓓ Ⓔ	3 Ⓐ Ⓑ Ⓒ Ⓓ Ⓔ
4 Ⓐ Ⓑ Ⓒ Ⓓ Ⓔ	4 Ⓐ Ⓑ Ⓒ Ⓓ Ⓔ	4 Ⓐ Ⓑ Ⓒ Ⓓ Ⓔ	4 Ⓐ Ⓑ Ⓒ Ⓓ Ⓔ
5 Ⓐ Ⓑ Ⓒ Ⓓ Ⓔ	5 Ⓐ Ⓑ Ⓒ Ⓓ Ⓔ	5 Ⓐ Ⓑ Ⓒ Ⓓ Ⓔ	5 Ⓐ Ⓑ Ⓒ Ⓓ Ⓔ
6 Ⓐ Ⓑ Ⓒ Ⓓ Ⓔ	6 Ⓐ Ⓑ Ⓒ Ⓓ Ⓔ	6 Ⓐ Ⓑ Ⓒ Ⓓ Ⓔ	6 Ⓐ Ⓑ Ⓒ Ⓓ Ⓔ
7 Ⓐ Ⓑ Ⓒ Ⓓ Ⓔ	7 Ⓐ Ⓑ Ⓒ Ⓓ Ⓔ	7 Ⓐ Ⓑ Ⓒ Ⓓ Ⓔ	7 Ⓐ Ⓑ Ⓒ Ⓓ Ⓔ
8 Ⓐ Ⓑ Ⓒ Ⓓ Ⓔ	8 Ⓐ Ⓑ Ⓒ Ⓓ Ⓔ	8 Ⓐ Ⓑ Ⓒ Ⓓ Ⓔ	8 Ⓐ Ⓑ Ⓒ Ⓓ Ⓔ
9 Ⓐ Ⓑ Ⓒ Ⓓ Ⓔ	9 Ⓐ Ⓑ Ⓒ Ⓓ Ⓔ	9 Ⓐ Ⓑ Ⓒ Ⓓ Ⓔ	9 Ⓐ Ⓑ Ⓒ Ⓓ Ⓔ
10 Ⓐ Ⓑ Ⓒ Ⓓ Ⓔ	10 Ⓐ Ⓑ Ⓒ Ⓓ Ⓔ	10 Ⓐ Ⓑ Ⓒ Ⓓ Ⓔ	10 Ⓐ Ⓑ Ⓒ Ⓓ Ⓔ
11 Ⓐ Ⓑ Ⓒ Ⓓ Ⓔ	11 Ⓐ Ⓑ Ⓒ Ⓓ Ⓔ	11 Ⓐ Ⓑ Ⓒ Ⓓ Ⓔ	11 Ⓐ Ⓑ Ⓒ Ⓓ Ⓔ
12 Ⓐ Ⓑ Ⓒ Ⓓ Ⓔ	12 Ⓐ Ⓑ Ⓒ Ⓓ Ⓔ	12 Ⓐ Ⓑ Ⓒ Ⓓ Ⓔ	12 Ⓐ Ⓑ Ⓒ Ⓓ Ⓔ
13 Ⓐ Ⓑ Ⓒ Ⓓ Ⓔ	13 Ⓐ Ⓑ Ⓒ Ⓓ Ⓔ	13 Ⓐ Ⓑ Ⓒ Ⓓ Ⓔ	13 Ⓐ Ⓑ Ⓒ Ⓓ Ⓔ
14 Ⓐ Ⓑ Ⓒ Ⓓ Ⓔ	14 Ⓐ Ⓑ Ⓒ Ⓓ Ⓔ	14 Ⓐ Ⓑ Ⓒ Ⓓ Ⓔ	14 Ⓐ Ⓑ Ⓒ Ⓓ Ⓔ
15 Ⓐ Ⓑ Ⓒ Ⓓ Ⓔ	15 Ⓐ Ⓑ Ⓒ Ⓓ Ⓔ	15 Ⓐ Ⓑ Ⓒ Ⓓ Ⓔ	15 Ⓐ Ⓑ Ⓒ Ⓓ Ⓔ
16 Ⓐ Ⓑ Ⓒ Ⓓ Ⓔ	16 Ⓐ Ⓑ Ⓒ Ⓓ Ⓔ	16 Ⓐ Ⓑ Ⓒ Ⓓ Ⓔ	16 Ⓐ Ⓑ Ⓒ Ⓓ Ⓔ
17 Ⓐ Ⓑ Ⓒ Ⓓ Ⓔ			17 Ⓐ Ⓑ Ⓒ Ⓓ Ⓔ
18 Ⓐ Ⓑ Ⓒ Ⓓ Ⓔ			18 Ⓐ Ⓑ Ⓒ Ⓓ Ⓔ
19 Ⓐ Ⓑ Ⓒ Ⓓ Ⓔ			19 Ⓐ Ⓑ Ⓒ Ⓓ Ⓔ
20 Ⓐ Ⓑ Ⓒ Ⓓ Ⓔ			20 Ⓐ Ⓑ Ⓒ Ⓓ Ⓔ
21 Ⓐ Ⓑ Ⓒ Ⓓ Ⓔ			21 Ⓐ Ⓑ Ⓒ Ⓓ Ⓔ
22 Ⓐ Ⓑ Ⓒ Ⓓ Ⓔ			22 Ⓐ Ⓑ Ⓒ Ⓓ Ⓔ

SECTION I: ANALYTICAL WRITING ASSESSMENT

GENERAL DIRECTIONS

In this section, you will have a total time of sixty minutes to plan and write two essays, one for each topic given. The specific time allotted for each essay is thirty minutes. For each essay, use three sides of 8½-by-11-inch lined paper.

Analysis of an Issue

Time: 30 Minutes

DIRECTIONS

This section will require you to analyze and explain your views on the issue given. Consider many points of view as you develop your own position on the issue. There is no right or wrong answer to the question.

Read the statement and directions carefully. Make any notes in your test booklet. Then write your response on the separate answer document. Be sure to use the answer document that goes with this writing task.

Motorcyclists by the thousands have protested the law which requires them to wear helmets at all times. They object to the high cost of the helmets, the fact that the helmets obscure their view, and, above all, the loss of personal freedom to dress as they please. Authorities, on the other hand, argue that motorcycle deaths are fifteen percent lower and hospital costs for injured bikers forty percent lower in states with helmet laws.

Which position do you find more convincing, that of the motorcyclists or of the government? Explain your reasoning and support your case with additional detail.

Analysis of an Argument

Time: 30 Minutes

DIRECTIONS

This section will require you to critique the argument given. Questioning underlying assumptions, finding alternative explanations or counterexamples, and delineating evidence to strengthen or weaken an argument are some possible approaches.

Read the argument and directions carefully. Make any notes in your test booklet. Then write your response on the separate answer document. Be sure to use the answer document that goes with this writing task.

A city short of revenue cannot afford to ban cigarette smoking in all of its bars and restaurants. The direct loss of revenue to these businesses, to other businesses directly related to them, and to other businesses in the city will be huge, since smokers will simply go to unrestricted restaurants and bars in the cities and towns nearby. Ultimately, the revenue loss to the city will be very large.

Write an essay in which you discuss the validity of this argument. Analyze its line of reasoning and its use of evidence. What change would you make to create a more convincing argument?

SECTION II: READING COMPREHENSION

Time: 25 Minutes
23 Questions

DIRECTIONS

Each passage in this group is followed by questions based on its content. After reading a passage, choose the best answer to each question and blacken the corresponding space on the answer sheet. Answer all questions following a passage on the basis of what is *stated* or *implied* in that passage. You may refer back to the passage.

Many people seem to think that science fiction is typified by the covers of some of the old pulp magazines; the Bug-Eyed Monster, embodying every trait and feature that most people find repulsive, is about to grab, and presumably ravish, a sweet, blonde, curvaceous, scantily-clad Earth girl. This is unfortunate because it demeans and degrades a worthwhile and even important literary endeavor. In contrast to this unwarranted stereotype, science fiction rarely emphasizes sex, and when it does, it is more discreet than other contemporary fiction. Instead, the basic interest of science fiction lies in the relation between man and his technology and between man and the universe. Science fiction is a literature of change and a literature of the future, and while it would be foolish to claim that science fiction is a major literary genre at this time, the aspects of human life that it considers make it well worth reading and studying—for no other literary form does quite the same things.

What is science fiction? To begin, the following definition should be helpful: science fiction is a literary sub-genre which postulates a change (for human beings) from conditions as we know them and follows the implications of these changes to a conclusion. Although this definition will necessarily be modified and expanded, it covers much of the basic groundwork and provides a point of departure.

The first point—that science fiction is a literary sub-genre—is a very important one, but one which is often overlooked or ignored in most discussions of science fiction. Specifically, science fiction is either a short story or a novel. There are only a few dramas which could be called science fiction, with Karel Capek's *RUR* (Rossum's Universal Robots) being the only one that is well known; the body of poetry that might be labeled science fiction is only slightly larger. To say that science fiction is a sub-genre of prose fiction is to say that it has all the basic characteristics and serves the same basic functions in much the same way as prose fiction in general—that is, it shares a great deal with all other novels and short stories.

Everything that can be said about prose fiction, in general, applies to science fiction. Every piece of science fiction, whether short story or novel, must have a narrator, a story, a plot, a setting, characters, language, and theme. And like any prose, the themes of science fiction are concerned with interpreting man's nature and experience in relation to the world around him. Themes in science fiction are constructed and presented in exactly the same ways that themes are dealt with in any other kind of fiction. They are the result of a particular combination of narrator, story, plot, character, setting, and language. In short, the reasons for reading and enjoying science fiction, and the ways of studying and analyzing it, are basically the same as they would be for any other story or novel.

1. Although few examples of science fiction written before 1900 exist, we can infer that it has been most popular in the twentieth century because
   (A) with the growth of literacy, the size of the reading public has increased
   (B) competition from television and film has created a demand for more exciting fiction
   (C) science fiction is easier to understand than other kinds of fiction
   (D) the increased importance of technology in our lives has given science fiction an increased relevance
   (E) other media have captured the large audience that read novels in the nineteenth century

2. According to the definition in the passage, a fictional work that places human beings in a prehistoric world inhabited by dinosaurs
   (A) cannot properly be called science fiction because it does not deal with the future
   (B) cannot properly be called science fiction because it does not deal with technology
   (C) can properly be called science fiction because it is prose fiction
   (D) can properly be called science fiction because it places people in an environment different from the one we know
   (E) can properly be called science fiction because it deals with man's relation to the world around him

3. Science fiction is called a literary sub-genre because
   (A) it is not important enough to be a literary genre
   (B) it cannot be made into dramatic presentation
   (C) it has its limits
   (D) it shares characteristics with other types of prose fiction
   (E) to call it a "genre" would subject it to literary jargon

4. From the passage, we can infer that science fiction films based upon ideas that have originally appeared in other media are chiefly adaptations of
   (A) short stories
   (B) plays
   (C) novels
   (D) poems
   (E) folk tales

5. The author believes that, when compared to other literary genres, science fiction is
   (A) deficient in its use of narrators
   (B) unable to be adapted to drama
   (C) a minor but worthwhile kind of fiction
   (D) more concerned with plot than with theme
   (E) in need of a unique literary approach if it is to be properly understood

6. The emphasis on theme in the final paragraph of the passage suggests that the author regards which of the following as an especially important reason for reading science fiction?
   (A) The discovery of meaning
   (B) The display of character
   (C) The beauty of language
   (D) The psychological complexity
   (E) The interest of setting

7. One implication of the final sentence in the passage is that
   (A) the reader should turn next to commentaries on general fiction
   (B) there is no reason for any reader not to like science fiction
   (C) the reader should compare other novels and stories to science fiction
   (D) there are reasons for enjoying science fiction
   (E) those who can appreciate prose fiction can appreciate science fiction

8. An appropriate title for this passage would be
   (A) On the Inaccuracies of Pulp Magazines
   (B) Man and the Universe
   (C) Toward a Definition of Science Fiction
   (D) A Type of Prose Fiction
   (E) Beyond the Bug-Eyed Monster

Let us take the terms "subjective" and "objective" and see if we can make up our minds what we mean by them in some such statement as this: "Philosophers and artists are subjective; scientists, objective." First of all we must point out that the two terms make up a semantic pair. The one has no meaning without the other. We may define each by antonym with the other. We may define them by synonym by translating the last syllable and say that "subjective" pertains to a subject, and "objective" pertains to an object. By operation analysis we may say that subjects perceive or conceive objects in the process of knowing. The word "knowing" reminds us that we are talking about the central nervous system and should waste no time in examining our terms for their sensory, affective, and logical components. It is easy to see from the following discussion that no particular sensory mechanism is necessarily involved and that although the sentence might be uttered with some considerable emotional content, it is used here entirely without feelings of praise or blame. The terms are primarily logical. What, then, is the basic logical relation that establishes whatever meaning they have? What goes on in the world when a poet is being subjective, and how does it differ from what goes on when a scientist is being objective?

When the poet sings "Drink to me only with thine eyes," he is responding immediately or in retrospect to an object, his beloved, outside himself; but he is fundamentally concerned with the sensations and emotions which that object stimulates in him; and whether the object justifies his praise in the opinion of others, or indeed whether there actually is such an object, is quite irrelevant to his purpose, which is the weaving of a beautiful pattern of sound and imagery into a richly affective concept of feminine loveliness. This it is to be subjective.

Now the scientist is primarily concerned with the identity and continuity of the external object that stimulates his response. Scientists characteristically have been rather unphilosophic about these objects that they observe so objectively, and philosophers have been characteristically unscientific about them. It need not seem absurd to locate the Eiffel Tower, or Everest, or the Grand Canyon, for that matter, in the mind because it is so perfectly obvious that they can exist as the Eiffel Tower, Everest, or the Grand Canyon nowhere else. Perhaps we can take a step toward clarification of this puzzling state of affairs and move a little closer to our definition of "objective" by suggesting a distinction between an object and thing. Let us define object as the external cause of a thing. Whether objects "exist" is obviously not discussable, for the word "object" as used here must necessarily stand not for a thing but for a hypothesis. There is, for example, no way of telling whether objects are singular or plural, whether one should say the stimulus of the Eiffel Tower experience or the stimuli of the Eiffel Tower experience. If, then, it is impossible even for the scientist to escape the essential subjectivity of his sensations, generalizations, and deductions, what do we mean by calling him objective?

9. The sentence examined by the author in the first paragraph would have an affective component if
    (A) "artists" were changed to "painters"
    (B) "philosophers" were changed to "logical positivists"
    (C) the physical characteristics of philosophers, artists, and scientists were vividly described
    (D) "subjective" and "objective" were changed, respectively, to "irrational" and "rational"
    (E) "subjective" and "objective" were changed, respectively, to "lunatic" and "trustworthy"

10. Which of the following is not a semantic pair?
    (A) Chaos/order
    (B) Fact/fiction
    (C) Sitting/standing
    (D) Light/darkness
    (E) Virtue/vice

11. Which of the following pairs best exemplifies the subjective/objective opposition as defined by the passage?
    (A) Art/philosophy
    (B) Knower/known
    (C) Object/thing
    (D) Stimulus/stimuli
    (E) Emotion/sensation

12. The passage refers to "Drink to me only with thine eyes" primarily in order to
    (A) suggest the affective powers of sound and imagery
    (B) exemplify the objective
    (C) exemplify the subjective
    (D) demonstrate how art can convey universal significance on an object
    (E) illustrate the difference between literal and metaphorical language

13. Given the content of the first and second paragraphs, the reader expects that the third paragraph will
    (A) explain how the scientist is objective
    (B) define the identity and conformity of external objects
    (C) analyze what it is to be subjective
    (D) discriminate between an object and a thing
    (E) explore the implications of objectivity

14. According to the passage, "objectivity" depends on the assumption that
    (A) discrete objects exist external to the mind
    (B) one's vocation in life should be logical
    (C) subjectivity is a cognitive weakness
    (D) science is a viable discipline
    (E) the Eiffel Tower is a singular stimulus, not a diffuse experience

15. Faced with this statement, "What you see is just in your head," the author of the passage would be likely to
    (A) strongly disagree
    (B) agree that the statement is probably true
    (C) argue against the appropriateness of the word "just"
    (D) assume that the person making the statement is not a scientist
    (E) argue that what is seen cannot be located outside of or inside the mind

16. According to the definitions of the third paragraph, which of the following are true of an object?

    I. The reality of an object is hypothetical.
    II. Whether objects are plural or singular is uncertain.
    III. An object is the external cause of a thing.

    (A) III only
    (B) I and II only
    (C) I and III only
    (D) II and III only
    (E) I, II, and III

Each method of counting bacteria has advantages and disadvantages; none is 100 percent accurate. Cell counts may be made with a counting chamber, a slide marked with a grid to facilitate counting of cells and to determine the volume of liquid in the area counted. Counts are made under a microscope and calculations made to determine the number of cells per ml of the original culture. Electronic cell counters can be used to count cells suspended in a liquid medium which passes through a hole small enough to allow the passage of only one bacterial cell at a time. The counter actually measures the rise in electric resistance of the liquid each time a cell passes through the hole. Smear counts are similar to cell counts: a known volume of culture is spread over a known area (1 cm^2) of a slide and then stained. Counts are made from several microscope fields, and calculations are made. In membrane filter counts a known volume of a culture is passed through a filter, which is then examined microscopically for cells. The advantage of cell counts, smear counts, and membrane filter counts is that they are quickly accomplished with little complicated equipment; however, both living and dead cells are counted.

The serial-dilution method involves the making of a series of dilutions, usually by a factor of 10, into a nutrient medium. The highest dilution producing growth gives a rough indication of the population of the original culture; for example, if the highest dilution to produce growth is the 1:100 dilution, the original culture had between 100 and 1000 cells per ml.

Plate counts are made by making serial dilutions (usually in sterile tap water or an isotonic solution) of the original culture. Samples of known volume of the dilutions are transferred to petri dishes and mixed with nutrient agar. After a suitable incubation period the colonies on the plates with between 30 and 300 colonies are counted. Because each colony is assumed to have arisen from a single cell, calculations can be made to determine the original population size. Plate counts have the advantage of not including dead cells, and they can be used when the population is so low as to make other methods impractical, but they require more time than direct counts, and they detect only those organisms that can grow under the conditions of incubation; the development of one colony from more than one cell is also a source of error. In connection with this technique a modification of the membrane filter count can be used. After filtration, the filter is placed on a pad soaked in nutrient media and allowed to incubate; resulting colonies are counted and appropriate calculations made.

A colorimeter or spectrophotometer is used in turbidimetric methods; the instrument measures the amount of light transmitted by test tubes with and without cultures; the difference represents the light absorbed or scattered by the bacterial cells and gives an indication of their concentration.

The total cell volume in a sample can be determined by centrifuging the sample in a calibrated centrifuge tube. From the known volume of a single cell and volume of the sample cells, the original population size can be calculated.

17. The author's primary purpose in this passage is to
    (A) argue for the development of a fully accurate counting method
    (B) discuss the advantages of several methods of counting cells
    (C) show that new counting methods have surpassed those used in the past
    (D) give instruction in the performance of cell counts
    (E) describe a variety of methods of counting bacteria

18. We can infer that no method of bacteria counting is wholly accurate because
    I. the number of cells is likely to be so large
    II. the cells are microscopic in size
    III. both living and dead cells are counted

    (A) II only
    (B) I and II only
    (C) I and III only
    (D) II and III only
    (E) I, II, and III

19. If we know the total bacteria cell volume in a sample, to determine the bacteria cell count we must also know

    I. the volume of a single cell
    II. the volume of the nutrient culture
    III. the volume of the calibrated centrifuge tube

    (A) I only
    (B) II only
    (C) III only
    (D) I and II only
    (E) II and III only

20. If the serial dilution method is used and the highest dilution to produce growth is the 1:10,000 dilution, the original culture contained
    (A) exactly 1000 cells per ml
    (B) between 100 and 1000 cells per ml
    (C) between 1000 and 10,000 cells per ml
    (D) between 10,000 and 100,000 cells per ml
    (E) between 100,000 and 1,000,000 cells per ml

21. One method of counting bacteria that does not suffer from a major disadvantage is a
    (A) plate count
    (B) smear count
    (C) counting chamber count
    (D) serial dilution count
    (E) membrane filter count

22. The passage contains information that answers which of the following questions?

   I. Why do researchers prefer to use smear counts instead of plate counts or membrane filter counts?
   II. When the population of bacteria is extremely low, which is the most practical counting method?
   III. What advantages does the colorimeter have over the spectrophotometer?

   (A) I only
   (B) II only
   (C) III only
   (D) I and II only
   (E) I, II, and III

23. Which of the following best describes the audience to which this passage is probably addressed?
   (A) Advanced students in microbiology
   (B) Casual readers of a scientific magazine
   (C) Elementary school students
   (D) Introductory college biology students
   (E) High school mathematics students

STOP. IF YOU FINISH BEFORE TIME IS CALLED, CHECK YOUR WORK ON THIS SECTION ONLY. DO NOT WORK ON ANY OTHER SECTION IN THE TEST.

SECTION III: PROBLEM SOLVING

Time: 25 Minutes
16 Questions

DIRECTIONS

In this section solve each problem, using any available space on the page for scratchwork. Then indicate the *best* answer in the appropriate space on the answer sheet.

1. During one season, a tennis team won 21 matches and lost 30% of their matches. What was the number of matches that the team lost?
   (A) 70
   (B) 30
   (C) 9
   (D) 7
   (E) 5

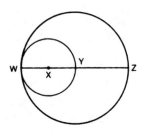

2. In the figure, X and Y are the centers of the two circles. If the area of the larger circle is 144π, what is the area of the smaller circle?
   (A) 72π
   (B) 36π
   (C) 24π
   (D) 12π
   (E) Cannot be determined

3. There are 36 students in a certain geometry class. If two-thirds of the students are boys and three-fourths of the boys are under six feet tall, how many boys in the class are under six feet tall?
   (A) 6
   (B) 12
   (C) 18
   (D) 24
   (E) 27

4. If m and n are integers and $\sqrt{mn} = 10$, which of the following cannot be a value of $m + n$?
   (A) 25
   (B) 29
   (C) 50
   (D) 52
   (E) 101

Houses Sold in One Year

Age	Number
1–2	1200
3–4	1570
5–6	1630
7–8	1440
9–10	1520

5. According to the chart, how many more houses from 5 to 10 years old were sold than those 4 to 8 years old?
   (A) 2455
   (B) 1570
   (C) 150
   (D) 130
   (E) Cannot be determined

6. If $x, y,$ and z are consecutive positive integers greater than 1, not necessarily in that order, then which of the following is (are) true?

I. $x > z$
II. $x + y > z$
III. $yz > xz$
IV. $xy > y + z$

(A) I only
(B) II only
(C) II and III only
(D) II and IV only
(E) III and IV only

7. If electricity costs x cents per kilowatt hour for the first 30 kilowatt hours and y cents per kilowatt hour for each additional kilowatt hour, what is the cost of z kilowatt hours $(z > 30)$?
(A) $30(x - y) + yz$
(B) $30y - 30x + yz$
(C) $30(x - y + z)$
(D) $(z - 30)x + 30y$
(E) $30x + (y - 30)z$

8. A man walks from B to C, a distance of x miles, at 8 miles per hour and returns at 12 miles per hour. What is his average speed?
(A) 10 mph
(B) 9.6 mph
(C) 8.8 mph
(D) 8.4 mph
(E) Cannot be determined from the information given

9. If a 32-inch chord is drawn in a circle of radius 20 inches, how far is the chord from the center of the circle?
(A) 4 inches
(B) 6 inches
(C) 8 inches
(D) 10 inches
(E) 12 inches

10. A drawer contains red socks, black socks, and white socks. What is the least number of socks that must be taken out of the drawer to be sure of having 4 pairs of socks? (A pair is two socks of the same color.)
    (A) 8
    (B) 10
    (C) 12
    (D) 14
    (E) 16

11. The product of x and y is a constant. If the value of x is increased by 50%, by what percentage must the value of y be decreased?
    (A) 50%
    (B) 40%
    (C) 33⅓%
    (D) 25%
    (E) None of these

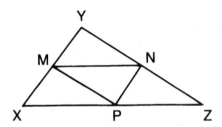

12. In $\triangle XYZ$, points M, N, and P are midpoints. If $XY = 10$, $YZ = 15$, and $XZ = 17$, what is the perimeter of $\triangle MNP$?
    (A) 10⅔
    (B) 14
    (C) 16
    (D) 21
    (E) Cannot be determined

13. If 20% of a class averages 80% on a test, 50% of the class averages 60% on the test, and the remainder of the class averages 40% on the test, what is the overall class average?
    (A) 80%
    (B) 74%
    (C) 58%
    (D) 56%
    (E) None of these

14. The current in a river is 4 mph. A boat can travel 20 mph in still water. How far up the river can the boat travel if the round trip is to take 10 hours?
    (A)   69 miles
    (B)   88 miles
    (C)   96 miles
    (D) 100 miles
    (E) 112 miles

15. In a triangle, the ratio of two angles is 5:2, and the third angle is equal to the difference between the other two. What is the number of degrees in the smallest angle?
    (A) 18
    (B) 25²⁄₇
    (C) 25⁵⁄₇
    (D) 36
    (E) Cannot be determined

16. Macey is three times as old as Mike. In 8 years, she will be twice as old as Mike. How old was Macey 3 years ago?
    (A)   5
    (B)   8
    (C) 21
    (D) 24
    (E) 30

STOP. IF YOU FINISH BEFORE TIME IS CALLED, CHECK YOUR WORK ON THIS SECTION ONLY. DO NOT WORK ON ANY OTHER SECTION IN THE TEST.

SECTION IV: DATA SUFFICIENCY

Time: 25 Minutes
20 Questions

DIRECTIONS

Each of the problems below consists of a question and two statements, labeled (1) and (2), in which certain data are given. You must decide whether the data given in the statements are *sufficient* to answer the question. Using the data given in the statements *plus* your knowledge of mathematics and everyday facts (such as the number of days in July or the meaning of *counterclockwise*), you are to blacken space

- (A) if statement (1) ALONE is sufficient, but statement (2) alone is not sufficient to answer the question asked;
- (B) if statement (2) ALONE is sufficient, but statement (1) alone is not sufficient to answer the question asked;
- (C) if BOTH statements (1) and (2) TOGETHER are sufficient to answer the question asked, but NEITHER statement ALONE is sufficient;
- (D) if EACH statement ALONE is sufficient to answer the question asked;
- (E) if statements (1) and (2) TOGETHER are NOT sufficient to answer the question asked, and additional data specific to the problem are needed.

1. Assuming that neither m nor n is zero, is the product m^2n positive?
   (1) $m > 0$
   (2) $n > 0$

267

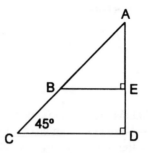

2. What is the ratio of the area of quadrilateral *BCDE* to the area of triangle *ABE*?
   (1) $BC = \frac{1}{2}AC$
   (2) Angle $CBE = 135°$

3. Where is the center of a circle on the *xy* plane?
   (1) The circle passes through both the origin and (0,7).
   (2) The diameter equals 10.

4. What is the average of ten numbers?
   (1) Nine of the numbers sum to 45.
   (2) One of the numbers is 15.

5. What is the area of a rectangular field?
   (1) The diagonal is twice the width.
   (2) The length is 173 feet.

6. Given $2m^2 + n^2 = 27$, what is the value of *m*?
   (1) *n* is positive.
   (2) $m = n$

7. How far is Sacramento from Los Angeles?
   (1) A car that obtains 28 miles per gallon drove the distance on exactly one tank of gasoline.
   (2) Another car averaged 50 miles per hour and arrived in 8 hours.

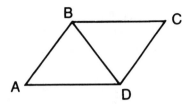

8. In rhombus *ABCD*, what is angle *BCD*?
   (1) *BC = BD*
   (2) Angle *BDA* = 60°

9. Is the product *xy* > 27?
   (1) 2 < *x* < 5
   (2) 6 > *y*

10. Three spies Ex, Why, and Zee together know 19 different secrets. There is no overlap of information. How many secrets does Why know?
    (1) Ex knows one more than Why and twice as many as Zee.
    (2) Why knows three more secrets than Zee.

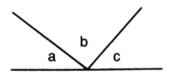

11. How many degrees is angle *c*?
    (1) *b* is a right angle.
    (2) *a* + *b* = 131°

12. The positive integer *C* is a perfect cube; what is its value?
    (1) 30 < *C* < 100
    (2) *C* is an even number.

13. How much gross profit did White Store make during its Great Refrigerator Sale?
    (1) The store sold 112 refrigerators for $33,060.
    (2) The refrigerators cost White an average of $186.

14. What is the volume of a cylindrical can?
    (1) The radius of the can is 3 inches.
    (2) The area of the bottom is 9π square inches.

15. What is the value of $x^3 - 2x^2 + 7$?
    (1) $3x^3 - x = 2$
    (2) $x^5 = 1$

16. What is Toni's typing speed in words per minute?
    (1) She completed a report of 3150 words in one hour.
    (2) The report had 7 pages, each averaging 450 words.

17. Which is greater, cf or fg?
    (1) $c > g$
    (2) $f^2 = cg$

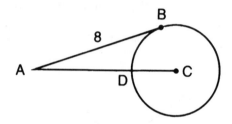

18. Given that AB is tangent to the circle with center C, what is the
    length of the circle's radius?
    (1) $AD = 4$
    (2) $AC = 10$

19. If gasoline costs $1.09 per gallon and alcohol costs $1.81, what
    fraction of each would be used to make Gasohol 99?
    (1) The mixture is predominantly gasoline.
    (2) A gallon of Gasohol 99 costs $1.22.

20. What is the value of $(u + v)$?
    (1) $2w - 7 = 0$
    (2) $u + v - 3w = 11$

STOP. IF YOU FINISH BEFORE TIME IS CALLED, CHECK YOUR WORK ON THIS SECTION ONLY. DO NOT WORK ON ANY OTHER SECTION IN THE TEST.

SECTION V: SENTENCE CORRECTION

Time: 25 Minutes
22 Questions

DIRECTIONS

Some part of each sentence below is underlined; sometimes the whole sentence is underlined. Five choices for rephrasing the underlined part follow each sentence; the first choice (A) repeats the original, and the other four are different. If choice (A) seems better than the alternatives, choose answer (A); if not, choose one of the others.

For each sentence, consider the requirements of standard written English. Your choice should be a correct and effective expression, not awkward or ambiguous. Focus on grammar, word choice, sentence construction, and punctuation. If a choice changes the meaning of the original sentence, do not select it.

1. <u>To enjoy exploring marine life in general, and so that they could learn in particular about the ways in which certain sea animals possess "human" traits</u>, the university's school of oceanography offered supervised summer field trips for the elementary school children in the area.
    (A) To enjoy exploring marine life in general, and so that they could learn in particular about the ways in which certain sea animals possess "human" traits
    (B) To stress the enjoyment of marine life in general, and particularly the ways in which certain sea animals are "human"
    (C) In order to teach young people about the "human" traits of certain sea animals, and to provide them an opportunity to enjoy marine exploration in general
    (D) Because marine life in general shares certain "human" traits
    (E) From general marine life to the specifically "human" possessions of sea animals

2. Success in school, according to many of the more cynical critics of public education, is like playing marbles: distinguished achievement depends not upon talent but upon luck.

   (A) Success in school, according to many of the more cynical critics of public education, is like playing marbles:
   (B) Criticizing success in public education cynically, may compare successful schooling to a successful marble game:
   (C) School is a game of marbles, according to many of the more cynical critics of public education
   (D) The more cynical critics of public education say that success in school is like playing marbles:
   (E) Many of the more cynical critics of public education say that succeeding in school is like playing marbles:

3. The defendant's refusal to discuss his whereabouts completely convinced the jury of his guilt, even though so many other facts surrounding the crime indicated not only that he was entirely innocent but also that he had been "framed" by members of a local syndicate.

   (A) The defendant's refusal to discuss his whereabouts completely convinced the jury of his guilt
   (B) Refusing to completely discuss the defendant's whereabouts, the jury was completely convinced of his guilt
   (C) The defendant's refusal to complete a discussion of his whereabouts convinced the jury of his guilt
   (D) The defendant's refusal to discuss his complete whereabouts convinced the jury that he was guilty
   (E) Guilty in the eyes of the jury because his whereabouts had not been completely discussed

4. <u>By composing at the typewriter, the poetry of this century often illustrates a more purposeful alignment of lines and letters made possible by the typewriter itself.</u>
   - (A) By composing at the typewriter, the poetry of this century often illustrates a more purposeful alignment of lines and letters made possible by the typewriter itself.
   - (B) The poets of this century who compose at the typewriter often take advantage of that machine to arrange lines and letters more purposefully.
   - (C) The typewriters of the poets of this century align lines and letters more purposefully.
   - (D) With the typewriter as their means of composition, the poets of this century often align lines and letters more purposefully than the poets before the typewriter.
   - (E) With the more purposeful alignment of lines and letters, the poets of this century rely on the typewriter often.

5. <u>Because nuclear weapons have been scorned by so many liberal activists with the power to destroy the world</u>, both of the superpowers have begun to consider both the limitation and the reduction of their arsenals.
   - (A) Because nuclear weapons have been scorned by so many liberal activists with the power to destroy the world
   - (B) World-destroying nuclear weapons have been scorned by many liberal activists
   - (C) With the power to destroy the world, liberal activists have scorned nuclear weapons
   - (D) Because nuclear weapons with the power to destroy the world have been scorned by so many liberal activists
   - (E) Liberal activists scorning nuclear weapons

6. The typical holiday shopper, although seduced by row upon row of novelty gifts, tend to purchase more practical items these days because he or she realizes that frivolous gadgets are often cheaply made.

(A) The typical holiday shopper, although seduced by row upon row of novelty gifts, tend to purchase more practical

(B) As a typical holiday shopper, the tendency to purchase row upon row of novelty gifts is won over by the purchase of more practical

(C) Typically, the holiday shopper who is attracted to novelty gifts tends to remain practical with

(D) The typical holiday shopper, although seduced by row upon row of novelty gifts, tends to purchase more practical

(E) The typical holiday shopper, although seduced by row upon row of novelty gifts, tends to purchase the most practical

7. The most recent National Conference of Mathematics Teachers addressed the problem of convincing students who rely on calculators that the ability to calculate mentally or with pencil and paper is important.

(A) The most recent National Conference of Mathematics Teachers addressed the problem of convincing students who

(B) The most recent problem faced by the National Conference of Mathematics Teachers was convincing students who

(C) The most recent National Conference of Mathematics Teachers addressed the problem of convincing students whom

(D) Most recently, the National Conference of Mathematics Teachers addressed the problem of convincing students who

(E) The most recent National Conference of Mathematics Teachers addressed those students who

8. <u>Understanding the droning lecturer with comprehension re-quired the intense concentration of the class members present in the lecture hall, all of whom were students.</u>

   (A) Understanding the droning lecturer with comprehension required the intense concentration of the class members present in the lecture hall, all of whom were students.
   (B) Comprehending the droning lecturer with the intense concentration of the class members present.
   (C) To understand the droning lecturer, the students had to concentrate intensely.
   (D) As the lecturer droned on, the students found themselves required to concentrate in order to understand.
   (E) The students listening to the lecturer, who was droning, increased their comprehension by concentrating.

9. Though the chief appeal of their program is their disagreement, <u>movie critics Gene Siskel and Roger Ebert often praise distinguished performances even when they are new to the screen.</u>

   (A) movie critics Gene Siskel and Roger Ebert often praise distinguished performances even when they are new to the screen
   (B) movie critics Gene Siskel and Roger Ebert, praising distinguished performances that are new to the screen
   (C) even distinguished performances that are new to the screen are praised by movie critics Gene Siskel and Roger Ebert
   (D) movie critics Gene Siskel and Roger Ebert often praise distinguished performances, even those by actors new to the screen
   (E) with distinguished performances in mind, movie critics Gene Siskel and Roger Ebert often praise even new screen actors

10. In *Charlotte's Web,* Wilbur is awarded a blue ribbon not because his appearance is superior to the other pigs but also with reference to the belief that he possesses some sort of "supernatural" power.

    (A) his appearance is superior to the other pigs but also with reference to the belief that he possesses

    (B) he looked better than the other pigs but because he was thought to possess

    (C) of his superior appearance but as far as the belief that he possessed

    (D) he looks better than that of the other pigs but because of a belief in supernatural power

    (E) he looks better than the other pigs but because he is thought to possess

11. Clarity and brilliance, in addition to enjoying the beauty: these are the qualities of a beautiful diamond and along with it a beautiful painting.

    (A) Clarity and brilliance, in addition to enjoying the beauty: these are the qualities of a beautiful diamond and along with it a beautiful painting.

    (B) Clarity, brilliance, and beauty: these are the qualities of a beautiful diamond as well as a beautiful painting.

    (C) To be clear, brilliant and beautiful is to be either a beautiful diamond or a beautiful painting.

    (D) Diamonds and paintings give out clarity, brilliance, and beauty.

    (E) Where there are clarity and brilliance and beauty there are the qualities of not only a beautiful diamond but also a beautiful painting.

12. <u>According to legend, while working as an engineer, a train collided with Casey Jones and killed him</u>, but he remains with us as part of a rich American folk history of songs and legends.
   (A) According to legend, while working as an engineer, a train collided with Casey Jones and killed him
   (B) The legendary engineer Casey Jones experienced a collision with another train on the job that killed him
   (C) Engineer Casey Jones was killed when his train collided with another
   (D) Driving the engine, another train killed Casey Jones
   (E) An engineer's work brought Casey Jones to his death when he was hit by a train while working

13. With the advent of sound, many stars of silent films found themselves unable to adapt to the "talkies" <u>because their speaking voices were either unattractive or their acting consisted of only exaggerated pantomime.</u>
   (A) because their speaking voices were either unattractive or their acting consisted of only exaggerated pantomime
   (B) because of their voices either being unattractive or their acting being exaggerated pantomime
   (C) with their unattractive voices and exaggerated pantomime
   (D) because of their unattractive voices or exaggerated pantomime that didn't require sound
   (E) because either their voices were unattractive or their acting was only exaggerated pantomime

14. According to statistics, one in every two marriages ends in divorce, most often involving married couples not wealthy enough to "buy" each other's love.

(A) According to statistics, one in every two marriages ends in divorce, most often involving married couples not wealthy enough to "buy" each other's love.

(B) Statistically, fifty percent of marriages are divorces, often caused by people not wealthy enough to "buy" each other's love.

(C) According to statistics, half of all marriages end in divorce, often because the partners are not wealthy enough to "buy" each other's love.

(D) Statistics tell half of all marriages that they will end in divorce, often because the partners are not wealthy enough to "buy" each other's love.

(E) Those who cannot "buy" each other's love are destined for divorce in at least half the cases, according to statistics.

15. The All-Star Game signals the middle of the baseball season and reminds the losing teams that the time for them to improve their playing is running out.

(A) The All-Star Game signals the middle of the baseball season

(B) With double significance, the All-Star Game occurs midway through

(C) The baseball season is divided in half by the All-Star Game

(D) The baseball All-Star Game signals the middle of the season

(E) With the All-Star Game, half the season is over

16. <u>Not gaining sufficient legislative approval, thousands of women vowed to keep the Equal Rights Amendment alive by continuing their protests.</u>

(A) Not gaining sufficient legislative approval, thousands of women vowed to keep the Equal Rights Amendment alive by continuing their protests.

(B) Not gaining sufficient legislative approval, the Equal Rights Amendment had thousands of women vowing to keep it alive with their protests.

(C) Thousands of women vowed to keep the Equal Rights Amendment alive in spite of failure to gain legislative approval.

(D) After the Equal Rights Amendment did not gain sufficient legislative approval, thousands of women vowed to keep it alive by continuing their protests.

(E) Not gaining sufficient legislative approval, protests continued by women who vowed to keep the Equal Rights Amendment alive.

17. <u>Recounting a painful childhood experience, the woman remembered that her father was very angry when she failed the fifth grade because she could see him shaking with anger.</u>

(A) Recounting a painful childhood experience, the woman remembered that her father was very angry when she failed the fifth grade because she could see him shaking with anger.

(B) Recounting a painful childhood experience, the woman recounted that her father was shaking with anger when she failed the fifth grade.

(C) Painfully, the woman remembered when she failed the fifth grade and when her father was shaking with anger.

(D) The failure of the fifth grade and her father's anger were painful for the woman recounting the experience.

(E) The woman described her father's shaking with anger when he learned that she had failed the fifth grade.

18. Though the Foreign Office claimed the troops were sent to protect innocent civilians, <u>the principle reason for the British invasion was because</u> the sovereignty of British territory had been challenged.
    (A) the principle reason for the British invasion was because
    (B) the principle reason for the British invasion was that
    (C) the principal reason for the British invasion was that
    (D) the British invaded because
    (E) principally, the British staged an invasion because

19. <u>The governor understood that if she did not sign the new budget quick, the state</u> might begin the new fiscal year not only with a significant deficit but also with no budgetary guidelines for lessening that deficit.
    (A) The governor understood that if she did not sign the state budget quick, the state
    (B) Not signing the new state budget quickly, the governor knew that the state
    (C) Without a quick signing, the governor new that as far as the budget was concerned, the state
    (D) The governor understood that if she did not sign the new budget quickly, the state
    (E) The governor understood that if she did not sign the budget and sign it quickly, that the effects of that action might cause the state to

20. Most television is escapist, but <u>reading modern novels continually reminds many people</u> that we live in an age of lost faith and growing anxiety.
    (A) reading modern novels continually reminds many people
    (B) reading modern novels frequently reminds many people
    (C) those who read modern novels continually realize
    (D) those who continually read modern novels realize
    (E) the reading of modern novels is what continually reminds many people

21. Most citizens of nineteenth-century London believed that remaining respectable was more important and more difficult than to question the virtues of the age.
    (A) to question
    (B) questioning
    (C) the question of
    (D) a question over
    (E) all

22. If all the local candidates would have participated in the debate, the voters would have a better understanding of the contending points of view.
    (A) If all the local candidates would have participated in the debate
    (B) If all the candidates had engaged in local debate
    (C) If all the local candidates had participated in the debate
    (D) Debating as they should have
    (E) After a debate

STOP. IF YOU FINISH BEFORE TIME IS CALLED, CHECK YOUR WORK ON THIS SECTION ONLY. DO NOT WORK ON ANY OTHER SECTION IN THE TEST.

SECTION VI: PROBLEM SOLVING

Time: 25 Minutes
16 Questions

DIRECTIONS

In this section solve each problem, using any available space on the page for scratchwork. Then indicate the *best* answer in the appropriate space on the answer sheet.

1. A small college reduced its faculty by approximately 13 percent to 195 professors. What was the original number of faculty members?
   (A) 182
   (B) 208
   (C) 224
   (D) 254
   (E) 302

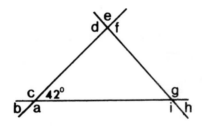

2. In the figure above, what is the sum of the nine angles labeled with letters?
   (A) 138°
   (B) 378°
   (C) 678°
   (D) 900°
   (E) Cannot be determined

283

3. Three factories of Conglomerate Corporation are capable of manufacturing hubcaps. Two of the factories can each produce 100,000 hubcaps in 15 days. The third factory can produce hubcaps 30% faster. How many days would it take to produce a million hubcaps with all three factories working simultaneously?
   (A) 38
   (B) 42
   (C) 46
   (D) 50
   (E) 54

4. The three digits of a number add up to 11. The number is divisible by 5. The left most digit is double the middle digit. What is the product of the three digits?
   (A)   40
   (B)   72
   (C)   78
   (D)   88
   (E) 125

5. Which of the five choices is equivalent to the expression

   $$\frac{x - 4}{2x^2 - 10x + 8} ?$$

   (A) $\dfrac{1}{2x^2 - 9x}$

   (B) $\dfrac{1}{2x^2 - 9x + 4}$

   (C) $\dfrac{1}{2x + 4}$

   (D) $\dfrac{1}{2x}$

   (E) $\dfrac{1}{2x - 2}$

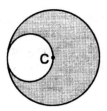

6. In the figure above, point C is the center of the larger circle. What is the ratio of the area of the shaded crescent to the area of the small circle?
   (A) 2
   (B) 2.4
   (C) 3
   (D) 3.25
   (E) 4

7. A woman has three blouses of different colors, three skirts of different colors, and two different pairs of shoes. She refuses to wear her pink blouse with her green skirt. How many different blouse-skirt-shoe combinations could she wear?
   (A) 8
   (B) 12
   (C) 16
   (D) 17
   (E) 18

8. Given the two equations $3r + s = 17$ and $r + 2s = 9$, by how much does r exceed s?
   (A) 3
   (B) 4
   (C) 5
   (D) 6
   (E) 7

9. A couple who own an appliance store discover that if they advertise a sales discount of 10% on every item in the store, at the end of one month the number of total items sold increases 20%. Their gross income from sales for one month increases by what percent?
   - (A) 2%
   - (B) 4%
   - (C) 5%
   - (D) 8%
   - (E) 12%

10. The first five numbers in a regular sequence are 4, 10, 22, 46, and 94. What is the next number in the sequence?
    - (A) 142
    - (B) 154
    - (C) 176
    - (D) 182
    - (E) 190

11. Approximately how many cubic feet of water are needed to fill a circular swimming pool that is 50 feet across and 8 feet deep?
    - (A)   400
    - (B)   6000
    - (C) 16,000
    - (D) 20,000
    - (E) 42,000

12. An incredible punch is composed of buttermilk, orange juice, and brandy. How many pints of orange juice are required to make 7½ gallons of punch containing twice as much buttermilk as orange juice and three times as much orange juice as brandy?
    - (A) 16
    - (B) 18
    - (C) 20
    - (D) 22
    - (E) 24

13. If $x = 6$ and $y = -2$, what is the value of $(x - 2y)^y$?
    (A) -100
    (B)   0.01
    (C)   0.25
    (D)   4
    (E)   8

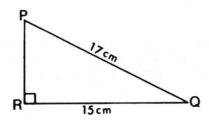

14. What is the perimeter of right triangle PQR?
    (A) 39 cm
    (B) 40 cm
    (C) 41 cm
    (D) 42 cm
    (E) 43 cm

15. A ferry can transport 78 tons of vehicles. Automobiles range in weight from 1800 to 3200 pounds. What is the greatest number of automobiles that can be loaded onto the ferry?
    (A) 23
    (B) 41
    (C) 48
    (D) 62
    (E) 86

16. Given the exponential quantities $m = 8^5$ and $n = 2^{12}$, what is the quotient m/n?
    (A) 6^{-7}
    (B) 7^{-6}
    (C) 6
    (D) 8
    (E) 16

STOP. IF YOU FINISH BEFORE TIME IS CALLED, CHECK YOUR WORK ON THIS SECTION ONLY. DO NOT WORK ON ANY OTHER SECTION IN THE TEST.

SECTION VII: PROBLEM SOLVING

Time: 25 Minutes
16 Questions

DIRECTIONS

In this section solve each problem, using any available space on the page for scratchwork. Then indicate the *best* answer in the appropriate space on the answer sheet.

1. A bookseller sells his books at a 20% markup in price. If he sells a book for $12.00, how much did he pay for it?
   (A) $14.40
   (B) $14.00
   (C) $10.00
   (D) $9.60
   (E) $5.00

2. Five A's and two B's exactly balance six B's and five C's. One A and four C's exactly balance two A's and four B's. What is the weight of A in terms of C?
   (A) $(3/2) C$
   (B) $(6/5) C$
   (C) $(5/6) C$
   (D) $(2/3) C$
   (E) $(1/2) C$

3. If paint costs $3.20 per quart, and a quart covers 20 square feet, how much will it cost to paint the outside of a cube 10 feet on each edge?
   (A) $1.60
   (B) $16.00
   (C) $96.00
   (D) $108.00
   (E) None of these

4. Simplify: $2 + \dfrac{1}{2 + \dfrac{1}{2 + \frac{1}{2}}}$

(A) 29/12

(B) 12/5

(C) 70/29

(D) 19/8

(E) 12/29

5. If $x = \dfrac{1 + y}{y}$, then $y =$

(A) $\dfrac{1}{x - 1}$

(B) $\dfrac{1}{x + 1}$

(C) $\dfrac{1 + x}{x}$

(D) $\dfrac{1 - x}{x}$

(E) x

6. Machine A can do a certain job in 8 hours. Machine B can do the same job in 10 hours. Machine C can do the same job in 12 hours. All three machines start the job at 9:00 A.M. Machine A breaks down at 11:00 A.M., and the other two machines finish the job. Approximately what time will the job be finished?
   (A) Noon
   (B) 12:30 P.M.
   (C)   1:00 P.M.
   (D)   1:30 P.M.
   (E)   2:00 P.M.

Questions 7–8 refer to the chart.

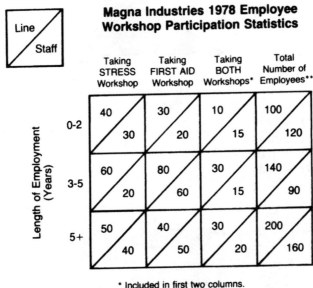

Magna Industries 1978 Employee Workshop Participation Statistics

Line / Staff	Taking STRESS Workshop	Taking FIRST AID Workshop	Taking BOTH Workshops*	Total Number of Employees**
0-2	40 / 30	30 / 20	10 / 15	100 / 120
3-5	60 / 20	80 / 60	30 / 15	140 / 90
5+	50 / 40	40 / 50	30 / 20	200 / 160

Length of Employment (Years)

* Included in first two columns.
** Including nonparticipants in workshop.

7. What is the number of line employees with 3 to 5 years of employment not taking the First Aid workshop?
   (A) 20
   (B) 60
   (C) 80
   (D) 140
   (E) 190

8. Approximately what percent of the employees with 5 or more years employment are not taking either workshop?
   (A) 86%
   (B) 64%
   (C) 50%
   (D) 14%
   (E) 7%

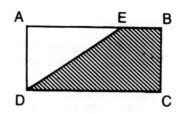

9. What is the area of the shaded portion of this rectangle, given that $AD = 6$, $CD = 8$, and $AE = x$?
   (A) $48 - 3x$
   (B) $48 + 3x$
   (C) $3x + 16$
   (D) $24 - 3x$
   (E) $24 + 3x$

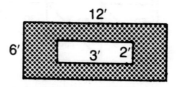

10. How many 2-inch by 3-inch rectangular tiles are required to tile this shaded region?
    (A) Less than 10
    (B) 10–100
    (C) 101–1000
    (D) 1001–1500
    (E) 1500+

11. If the radius of a circle is decreased 20%, what happens to the area?
    (A) 10% decrease
    (B) 20% decrease
    (C) 36% decrease
    (D) 40% decrease
    (E) None of these

12. Two quarts containing ⅔ water and ⅓ formula are mixed with three quarts containing ⅜ water and ⅝ formula. Approximately what percent of the combined five quart mixture is water?
    (A) 40%
    (B) 45%
    (C) 50%
    (D) 55%
    (E) 60%

13. Three consecutive traffic signals each show either red or green. How many different arrangements of the three signals are possible? (Note: "Red–red–green" is different from "green–red–red.")
    (A) 10
    (B) 9
    (C) 8
    (D) 7
    (E) 6

14. An empty fuel tank is filled with brand Z gasoline. When the tank is half empty, it is filled with brand Y gasoline. When the tank is half empty again, it is filled with brand Z gasoline. When the tank is half empty again, it is filled with brand Y gasoline. At this time, what percent of the gasoline in the tank is brand Z?
    (A) 50%
    (B) 40%
    (C) 37.5%
    (D) 33⅓%
    (E) 25%

15. To rent an office, each member of a club must pay n dollars. If two more members join the club, the per-member payment would be reduced by two dollars. Which of the following could be the number of members currently in the club?

   I. 16
  II. 17
 III. 18

(A) I only
(B) II only
(C) I and III only
(D) II and III only
(E) I, II, and III

16. What is the area of a square that has a diagonal of length $\sqrt{10}$?
(A) 5
(B) 10
(C) 20
(D) 40
(E) None of these

STOP. IF YOU FINISH BEFORE TIME IS CALLED, CHECK YOUR WORK ON THIS SECTION ONLY. DO NOT WORK ON ANY OTHER SECTION IN THE TEST.

SECTION VIII: CRITICAL REASONING

Time: 25 Minutes
16 Questions

DIRECTIONS

You will be presented with brief passages or statements and will
be required to evaluate their reasoning. In each case, select the best
answer choice, even though more than one choice may present a
possible answer. Choices which are unreasonable or incompatible
with commonsense standards should be eliminated.

The water quality of Lake Tahoe—the largest, deepest, high
mountain lake in North America—is steadily diminishing. Protect-
ing its delicate ecological balance is essential.

1. Which of the following arguments most closely resembles the
   argument above?
   (A) The ability of many famous artists of the 1930s is steadily
       diminishing. Encouraging their continued productivity is
       essential.
   (B) Erosion has taken its toll on Mt. Rushmore, defacing the
       historical monument. Appropriating money for its repair
       and restoration must be given priority.
   (C) The quality of life in our older cities has ceased to be a
       concern to many legislators.
   (D) The water quality of Lake Erie has been a diminishing
       concern of both Americans and Canadians over the past
       decade.
   (E) The Grand Canyon, a deep natural excavation and a
       national monument, has steadily diminished in its appeal
       to tourists. Protecting its waning popularity is essential.

In parts of the world where the life spans are short, forty may be
regarded as an advanced age. People who live longer are believed to
possess special powers. These elders are sometimes treated with a
deference based on fear rather than love.

2. The final statement in the passage is based on which of the following assumptions?
   (A) Deference is normally accorded based on love.
   (B) Few elders are treated with deference.
   (C) People who live shorter lives have no special powers.
   (D) People with special powers are not loved.
   (E) A deference based on fear is stronger than one based on love.

The fish *Alpha splendes* usually lives in a lake where there are dissolved alkalies. Lake Huron contains the dissolved alkalies soda and potash. There are no *Alpha splendes* in Lake Huron.

3. Which of the following could logically complete an argument with the premises given above?

   I. Therefore, *Alpha splendes* needs alkalies other than soda and potash.
   II. Therefore, there may not be sufficient dissolved alkalies in the lake.
   III. Therefore, there will be no *Alpha splendes* living in this lake.

   (A) I only
   (B) II only
   (C) III only
   (D) I and II only
   (E) II and III only

The evolution of the various forms of life from biochemical mass must not be considered a linear progression. Rather, the fossil record suggests an analogy between evolution and a bush whose branches go every which way. Like branches, some evolutionary lines simply end, and others branch again. Many biologists believe the pattern to have been as follows: bacteria emerged first and from them branched viruses, red algae, blue-green algae, and green flagellates. From the latter branched green algae, from which higher plants evolved, and colorless rhizoflagellates, from which diatoms, molds, sponges, and protozoa evolved. From ciliated protozoa (ciliophora) evolved multinucleate (syncytial) flatworms. These branched into five lines, one of which leads to the echinoderms and chordates. The remaining lines lead to most of the other phyla of the animal kingdom.

4. Which of the following best expresses the analogy between evolution and a bush?
   (A) Species is to evolution as bush is to branching.
   (B) Species is to branching as bush is to evolution.
   (C) Evolution is to species as bush is to branch viruses.
   (D) Evolution is to species as bush is to branches.
   (E) Evolution is to species as branches is to bush.

The term "articulation disorder" refers to the difficulty an individual has when he uses the speech sounds of the language spoken around him. No communication dysfunction is more familiar to the speech pathologist than the problem of misarticulation. Articulation disorders represent over two-thirds of the speech clinician's caseload; a rather sizeable percentage when one considers that voice, rhythm, and language disorders also fall under this professional's review.

5. The passage implies that one of the factors contributing to the importance of articulation disorders is
   (A) the speech clinician's practice of treating nonserious disorders
   (B) the lack of organic causes of such disorders
   (C) the tendency of many children to "outgrow" the disorder
   (D) the high incidence of such disorders
   (E) the stress placed on such disorders by hospital administrators

Questions 6 and 7 are based on the following passage

It is evident that the methods of science have been highly successful. Psychologist B.F. Skinner believes that the methods of science should be applied to the field of human affairs. We are all controlled by the world, part of which is constructed by man. Is this control to occur by accident, by tyrants, or by ourselves? A scientific society should reject accidental manipulation. He asserts that a specific plan is needed to promote fully the development of human beings and society. We cannot make wise decisions if we continue to pretend that we are not controlled.

As Skinner points out, the possibility of behavioral control is offensive to many people. We have traditionally regarded man as a free agent whose behavior occurs by virtue of spontaneous inner changes. We are reluctant to abandon the internal "will" which makes prediction and control of behavior impossible.

6. According to the passage, Skinner would probably agree with each of the following statements EXCEPT:
   (A) Rats and pigeons are appropriate animals for behavioristic study.
   (B) These behaviors we normally exhibit are not the only ones we are capable of.
   (C) The concept of behavioral control has popular appeal.
   (D) Inner causes of behavior are more difficult to observe than outer ones.
   (E) Positive reinforcement will affect learning in school.

7. The author implies that Skinner feels that the scientific procedure he advocates might be effective as
   (A) a means of enhancing our future
   (B) an explanation of the causes of dictatorships
   (C) a means for replacing teachers with computers
   (D) a way of identifying characteristics common to rats, pigeons, and humans
   (E) a way to understand the human mind

Questions 8 and 9 are based on the following passage

Every speech intended to persuade either argues for a proposition or argues against a proposition. Any speech which argues for a proposition either presents all of the facts or presents a few of the facts, and any speech which argues against a proposition either presents all of the facts or presents a few of the facts. No speech which presents either all of the facts, a few of the facts, or just one fact is uninformative.

8. If the statements made in the passage above are true, it follows that
   (A) every speech presents either all of the facts or a few of the facts
   (B) every speech intended to persuade presents many of the facts of the argument
   (C) every uninformative speech presents none of the facts
   (D) some uninformative speeches present either all of the facts or a few of the facts
   (E) some speeches intended to persuade present neither all of the facts nor a few of the facts

9. Which of the following statements represent a valid conclusion based upon the passage above?
   (A) No speech intended to persuade presents some of the facts.
   (B) No informative speech both intends to persuade and contains a few of the facts.
   (C) No informative speech both argues against a proposition and contains all of the facts.
   (D) No informative speech is intended to persuade.
   (E) No speech is both intended to persuade and uninformative.

Voltaire once said, "Common sense is not so common."

10. Which of the following most nearly parallels Voltaire's statement?
    (A) God must have loved the common man; he certainly made enough of them.
    (B) The common good is not necessarily best for everyone.
    (C) Jumbo shrimp may not actually be very big.
    (D) Good people may not necessarily have good sense.
    (E) Truth serum cannot contain the truth.

The dance tonight is a ball, and my child's toy is a ball. Therefore, in addition to the fact that they are called by the same name, there is a way in which the dance and my child's toy are like each other.

11. Which of the following statements would explain why the conclusion of the argument does not follow from the premises?

    I. The dance tonight may not be a ball.
    II. Something which is neither a dance nor a toy may be a ball.
    III. The dance tonight and my child's toy are not each a ball in the same sense of the word.
    IV. A ball cannot be anything except a dance or a toy.

    (A) II only
    (B) III only
    (C) I and II only
    (D) II and IV only
    (E) I, II, and IV only

Socrates believed that virtue is the outcome of knowledge and that evil is fundamentally ignorance. This is an early instance of the belief that the intellectual or rational is dominant in man and morally superior.

12. Socrates' point of view, as described in the passage, implies which of the following conclusions about evil people?
    (A) They are ignorant.
    (B) They are unable to achieve complete self-knowledge.
    (C) They are inherently virtuous but incapable of showing it.
    (D) They are often either ignorant or irrational.
    (E) They often dominate those who are morally superior.

Questions 13 and 14 are based on the following passage

Skinner established himself as one of the country's leading behaviorists with the publication of his *Behavior of Organisms* in 1938. Although obviously influenced by Watson's behaviorism, Skinner's system appears to follow primarily from the work of Pavlov and Thorndike. Unlike some other followers of Watson, who studied behavior in order to understand the "workings of the mind," Skinner restricted himself to the study of overt or measurable behavior. Without denying either mental or physiological processes, he finds that a study of behavior does not depend on conclusions about what is going on _____.

13. The best completion for the final sentence in the passage above is
    (A) outside the organism
    (B) outside the brain
    (C) inside the organism
    (D) inside the nervous system
    (E) outside the nervous system

14. Which of the following can be concluded from the information given in the passage above?
    (A) Some followers of Watson's behaviorism seek to understand the "workings of the mind."
    (B) Followers of Pavlov seek to understand the "workings of the mind."
    (C) The work of Thorndike varies from the work of Pavlov.
    (D) The work of Pavlov and Watson varies from the work of Thorndike.
    (E) Watson's behaviorism did not influence Skinner.

Questions 15 and 16 are based on the following passage

All acts have consequences. Given this fact, we may wish to play it safe by never doing anything.

15. The speaker implies that
    (A) we may prefer to live safely
    (B) all acts have consequences
    (C) consequentiality is not safe
    (D) doing nothing has lesser consequences
    (E) not doing anything is not an act

16. What conclusion about consequences must we accept if we accept the speaker's statement?
    (A) Consequences are significant only for active people.
    (B) All consequences are dangerous.
    (C) There are some acts that do not produce consequences.
    (D) Consequences have moral force.
    (E) Inaction has moral force.

STOP. IF YOU FINISH BEFORE TIME IS CALLED, CHECK YOUR WORK ON THIS SECTION ONLY. DO NOT WORK ON ANY OTHER SECTION IN THE TEST.

ANSWER KEY FOR PRACTICE TEST 2
MULTIPLE-CHOICE SECTIONS

Section II Reading Comprehension	Section III Problem Solving	Section IV Data Sufficiency	Section V Sentence Correction
1. D	1. C	1. B	1. C
2. D	2. B	2. A	2. E
3. D	3. C	3. E	3. A
4. C	4. C	4. E	4. B
5. C	5. E	5. C	5. D
6. A	6. B	6. C	6. D
7. E	7. A	7. B	7. A
8. C	8. B	8. D	8. C
9. E	9. E	9. E	9. D
10. C	10. B	10. A	10. E
11. B	11. C	11. B	11. B
12. C	12. D	12. A	12. C
13. A	13. C	13. C	13. E
14. A	14. C	14. E	14. C
15. C	15. D	15. B	15. A
16. E	16. C	16. A	16. D
17. E		17. E	17. E
18. B		18. D	18. C
19. A		19. B	19. D
20. D		20. C	20. D
21. A			21. B
22. B			22. C
23. D			

Section VI Problem Solving	Section VII Problem Solving	Section VIII Critical Reasoning
1. C	1. C	1. B
2. D	2. A	2. A
3. C	3. C	3. B
4. A	4. A	4. D
5. E	5. A	5. D
6. C	6. C	6. C
7. C	7. B	7. A
8. A	8. B	8. C
9. D	9. A	9. E
10. E	10. E	10. C
11. C	11. C	11. B
12. B	12. C	12. A
13. B	13. C	13. C
14. B	14. C	14. A
15. E	15. E	15. E
16. D	16. A	16. B

HOW TO SCORE YOUR ESSAYS

Have someone knowledgeable in the writing process evaluate your essays using the following checklist and grading scale. Remember, because the essays must be written in a limited time period, minor errors of grammar or mechanics will not affect your scores.

Analysis of an Issue	Yes, completely	Yes, partially	No
1. Does the essay focus on the assigned topic and cover all of the tasks?			
2. Does the essay show an understanding of the complexity of the issue?			
3. Does the essay show cogent reasoning and logical position development?			
4. Are there sufficient relevant persuasive supporting details?			
5. Is the essay well organized?			
6. Does the essay show a command of standard written English?			

Analysis of an Argument

	Yes, completely	Yes, partially	No
1. Does the essay focus on the assigned topic and cover all of the tasks?			
2. Does the essay carefully analyze the important features of the argument?			
3. Does the essay show cogent reasoning and logical development?			
4. Are there sufficient relevant supporting details of the critique?			
5. Is the essay well organized?			
6. Does the essay show a command of standard written English?			

HOW TO SCORE YOUR MULTIPLE-CHOICE QUESTIONS

1. Add the total number of correct responses for each section.
2. Add the total number of incorrect responses (only those attempted or marked in) for each section.
3. The total number of incorrect responses should be divided by 4, giving the adjustment factor.
4. Subtract this adjustment factor from the total number of correct responses to obtain a corrected raw score.
5. This score is then scaled from 200 to 800.

Example:
A. If the total number of correct answers was 80 out of a possible 113.
B. And 24 problems were attempted but missed.
C. Dividing the 24 by 4 gives an adjustment factor of 6.
D. Subtracting this adjustment factor of 6 from the original 80 correct gives a corrected raw score of 74.
E. This corrected raw score is then scaled to a range of 200 to 800.

SCORE RANGE APPROXIMATORS

The following chart is designed to give you an approximate score range only, not an exact score. When you take the GMAT, you will have questions that are similar to those in this book; however, some questions may be slightly easier or more difficult. Needless to say, this may affect your scoring range.

Because one section of the GMAT is experimental (it doesn't count toward your score), for the purposes of this approximation, do not count Section VII. Remember, on the actual test the experimental section could appear anywhere on your test.

Corrected Raw Score	Approximate Score Range
97–113	700–800
81–96	610–690
64–80	530–600
48–63	440–520
30–47	350–430
14–29	260–340
0–13	200–250

Keep in mind that this is just an approximate score range. An average score on the GMAT is approximately 480.

ANALYZING YOUR TEST RESULTS

The charts on the following pages should be used to carefully analyze your results and spot your strengths and weaknesses. The complete process of evaluating your essays and analyzing individual problems in each subject area should be completed for each Practice Test. These results should then be reexamined for trends in types of errors (repeated errors) or poor results in specific subject areas. THIS REEXAMINATION AND ANALYSIS IS OF TREMENDOUS IMPORTANCE IN HELPING YOU MAXIMIZE YOUR SCORE.

ANALYSIS SHEET FOR
MULTIPLE-CHOICE SECTIONS

	Possible	Completed	Right	Wrong
Section II: Reading Comprehension	23			
Section III: Problem Solving	16			
Section IV: Data Sufficiency	20			
Section V: Sentence Correction	22			
Section VI: Problem Solving	16			
Section VII: Problem Solving	16			
Section VIII: Critical Reasoning	16			
OVERALL TOTALS	129			

WHY??????????????????????????????????

ANALYSIS SHEET FOR
MULTIPLE-CHOICE PROBLEMS MISSED

One of the most important parts of test preparation is analyzing WHY! you missed a problem so that you can reduce the number of mistakes. Now that you have taken the practice test and corrected your answers, carefully tally your mistakes by marking them in the proper column.

REASON FOR MISTAKE

	Total Missed	Simple Mistake	Misread Problem	Lack of Knowl- edge
Section II: Reading Comprehension				
Section III: Problem Solving				
Section IV: Data Sufficiency				
Section V: Sentence Correction				
Section VI: Problem Solving				
Section VII: Problem Solving				
Section VIII: Critical Reasoning				
OVERALL TOTALS				

Reviewing the above data should help you determine WHY you are missing certain problems. Now that you have pinpointed the type of error, take the next practice test focusing on avoiding your most common type.

COMPLETE ANSWERS AND EXPLANATIONS FOR PRACTICE TEST 2 MULTIPLE-CHOICE SECTIONS

SECTION II: READING COMPREHENSION

1. (D) Choices (A), (B), and (E) do not apply to science fiction as opposed to other fiction genres. Choice (C) may or may not be true. Since science fiction is concerned with the *relation between man and his technology,* it follows that as technology becomes more important, the fiction of technology would become more popular.

2. (D) Paragraph two defines science fiction as postulating a change from known to unknown conditions.

3. (D) The last sentence of the third paragraph explains why science fiction is called a sub-genre of fiction.

4. (C) Though short stories are a possible source, it is more probable that the longer novel is the source of science fiction films. The passage alludes to the scarcity of science fiction works in poetry or drama.

5. (C) The first paragraph says science fiction is not *a major literary genre,* but *well worth reading and studying.*

6. (A) The theme is the controlling idea or meaning of a work of literature.

7. (E) The final sentence presents a general comparison between *any other story or novel* and science fiction, emphasizing their similarities, and thus suggesting that the sub-genre of science fiction should be read as one reads fiction in general.

8. (C) The first paragraph leads up to the central question—*What is science fiction?* All of the passage is an attempt to answer that question. Choices (A) and (D) are too specific; (B) is too general; and (E) does not fit the tone of the passage.

9. (E) The author makes the point that this sentence does not have affective (emotional) content because *it is used here entirely without feelings of praise or blame.* Choice (E) changes the force of the sentence by substituting terms which are always associated with praise or blame. (D) is a possibility along these lines, but *irrational* and *rational* are not as emotionally charged as *lunatic* and *trustworthy.*

10. (C) Early in the passage we are told that in a semantic pair *the one* (term) *has no meaning without the other. We may define each by antonym with the other.* In short, semantic pairs are pairs of direct opposites. Only (C) is not such a pair.

11. (B) The first paragraph says *subjects perceive or conceive objects in the process of knowing.* The pair that may best be substituted in that is *knower* and *known.*

12. (C) The passage uses *Drink to me only with thine eyes* to show that the poet is fundamentally concerned with sensations and emotions. Using this quote is an example of the subjective. In fact, the author finishes the paragraph by saying *This it is to be subjective.*

13. (A) Since the passage begins with the idea that the artist is subjective and the scientist objective, and the second paragraph deals with the subjectivity of the artist, we expect the third paragraph to be about the objectivity of the scientist.

14. (A) The author tells us that scientists, who he defines as *objective,* are *primarily concerned with the identity and continuity of the external object that stimulates* (their) *response.* That is, to be objective one must believe that the world is a collection of stable objects, each of which always looks the same. (E) is a single example consistent with this assumption, but is not itself broad enough to support the question of objectivity in general. (D) is also too broad to be the best answer. (C) is not an assumption allowed by the passage.

15. (C) The author concludes by saying that *it is impossible even for the scientist to escape the essential subjectivity of his sensations, generalizations, and deductions.* Since everything is subjective, since different people each see the same thing a bit differently, one is seeming to devalue this case by saying that *what you say you see is just in your head. In your head* is not an unimportant place; according to the passage, it is the only place.

16. (E) The third paragraph defines an *object* as the *external cause of a thing*—a *hypothesis,* with its singularity or plurality indeterminable. This is a definition peculiar to this passage.

17. (E) Though the passage alludes to the advantage of one method, the excerpt as a whole is concerned with describing several methods used to count bacteria.

18. (B) Though some methods count both living and dead cells, one method that is described counts only living cells.

19. (A) If we know the total volume of the bacteria cells and the volume of one cell, we can divide the former by the latter to determine the total number of cells.

20. (D) In the second paragraph, the example says a 1:100 dilution indicates a total of 100 to 1000 cells per ml. Multiplying these figures by one hundred, the answer will be between 10,000 and 100,000.

21. (A) The plate count method does not count dead cells.

22. (B) The third paragraph asserts that plate counts can be used when the population is so low as to make other methods impractical. The first question is untrue; the fourth paragraph does not distinguish between a colorimeter and a spectrophotometer.

23. (D) The passage is too advanced for options (B) or (C), but not so technical as we would expect for advanced students (A). The subject of the passage is not mathematics (E).

SECTION III: PROBLEM SOLVING

1. **(C)** Since 21 is 70% of the total, the total must be 30. Thus the team lost 9 matches.

   $21 = 70\%$ of x
   $21 = 0.7x$
   $\frac{21}{0.7} = x$
   $30 = x$
   $30 - 21 = 9$

   Notice answers (A) and (B) are not reasonable.

2. **(B)** Area of larger circle $= 144\pi$

   Since area $= \pi r^2$, then

   $\pi r^2 = 144\pi$
   $r^2 = 144$
   $r = 12$

   Radius of larger circle $= 12$
   Diameter of smaller circle $= 12$
   Radius of smaller circle $= 6$

   Area of smaller circle $= \pi r^2$
   $ = \pi(6)^2$
   $ = 36\pi$

3. **(C)** Since two-thirds of the students are boys, we have $\frac{2}{3}(36) = 24$ boys in the class.
   Out of the 24 boys in the class, three-fourths of them are under six feet tall or $\frac{3}{4}(24) = 18$ boys under six feet tall.

4. **(C)** Since $\sqrt{mn} = 10$, $mn = 100$, and the possible values for m and n would be: 1 and 100, 2 and 50, 4 and 25, 5 and 20, 10 and 10. Since none of these combinations yield $m + n = 50$, choice (C) is correct.

5. **(E)** Since the chart does not distinguish how many houses are 3 years old or 4 years old, the answer cannot be determined.

6. (B) Adding any two of three consecutive positive integers greater than 1, will always be greater than the other integer, therefore II is true. The others cannot be determined, as they depend on values and/or the order of $x, y,$ and z.

7. (A) From the given information, it costs $30x$ for the first 30 kilowatt hours. Thus $z - 30$ kilowatt hours remain at y cents per kilowatt hour. Thus $30x + (z - 30)y = (30x) - (30y) + yz = 30(x - y) + yz$.

8. (B) Average speed is total distance/total time. The total distance is $2x$. Time going is $x/8$. Time coming back is $x/12$. Thus average speed is

$$\frac{2x}{x/8 + x/12} = \frac{2x}{3x/24 + 2x/24}$$

$$= \frac{2x}{5x/24} = \frac{2x}{1} \cdot \frac{24}{5x} = \frac{48}{5} = 9.6$$

Notice answers (C), (D), and (E) were not reasonable.

9. (E) From the figure, we use the Pythagorean theorem and find the missing side, x, is 12 inches. Thus, (E) is correct.

$a^2 + b^2 = c^2$

$16^2 + x^2 = 20^2$

$256 + x^2 = 400$

$x^2 = 400 - 256$

$x^2 = 144$

$x = 12$

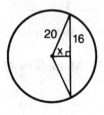

10. (B) If only 9 were picked out, it is possible to get 3 of each color. Thus the 10th is necessary to be sure of 4 pairs.

11. **(C)** If x is increased by 50%, we can represent it by $\frac{3}{2}x$. We must multiply this by $\frac{2}{3}y$ in order to keep the product equal to xy. Since $\frac{2}{3}$ is a $\frac{1}{3}$ reduction, answer (C) is the correct response. You could have also tried using some values for x and y.

12. **(D)** Perimeter of $\triangle MNP$ = $\frac{1}{2}$(perimeter of $\triangle XYZ$)

$$= \frac{1}{2}(XY + YZ + XZ)$$
$$= \frac{1}{2}(10 + 15 + 17)$$
$$= \frac{1}{2}(42)$$

Perimeter of $\triangle MNP = 21$

13. **(C)** We look at total percentage points.

$(20)(80) + (50)(60) + (30)(40) = 5800 = 58\%$

Notice answers (A) and (B) are not reasonable.

14. **(C)** We can set up the following chart

	D	$=$	R	$\times$	T
Up	D		16		$\dfrac{D}{16}$
Down	D		24		$\dfrac{D}{24}$

Since the time is 10 hours for the whole trip,

$\dfrac{D}{16} + \dfrac{D}{24} = 10$ Multiply by 48, $3D + 2D = 480$

$$5D = 480$$
$$D = 96$$

15. (D) Let

$5x$ = first angle
$2x$ = second angle
$5x - 2x = 3x$ = third angle

Since the sum of the angles in any triangle is 180°, we have

$5x + 2x + 3x = 180°$
$10x = 180°$
$x = 18°$

Hence $5x = 90°$
$2x = 36°$
$3x = 54°$

The smallest angle will have a measure of 36°.

16. (C) Let x be Mike's age. Thus, $3x$ is Macey's age. Thus $3x + 8 = 2(x + 8)$, $3x + 8 = 2x + 16$. Thus $x = 8$. Therefore, $3x = 24$. Thus Macey is 24 and three years ago was 21.
Notice you could have worked from the answers.

SECTION IV: DATA SUFFICIENCY

1. **(B)** Whether m is positive or negative, m^2 must be positive. So the sign of n determines the sign of the product.

2. **(A)** Area *BCDE* equals triangle *ACD* minus triangle *ABE*. From the sketch it is clear that the two triangles are similar, as their respective sides are parallel. From (1) we see that the base and height of *ABE* are half those of *ACD*, hence the area of *ABE* is one-quarter that of *ACD*. Consequently, the area *BCDE* is three times the area of *ABE*.

3. **(E)** The first statement lists two points through which the circle passes, but many circles could pass through any two points. Knowing the diameter would still not yield a unique circle.

4. **(E)** To calculate the average, we require the sum of the ten numbers. Statement (1) offers the sum of nine. We do not know whether the number cited in (2) is one of those nine.

5. **(C)** The first statement implies that the diagonal divides the field into two 30°–60° right triangles, with sides in the ratio $1:2:\sqrt{3}$. Employing that ratio to find the width with a length of 173 feet, the width equals 100 feet. Then the area equals 17,300 square feet.

6. **(C)** From the second statement, $3m^2 = 27$, $m^2 = 9$, and $m = \pm 3$. But from both statements, since n is positive, so must be m.

7. **(B)** Statement (1) lacks the capacity of the tank. But from (2) and the formula $d = rt$ you can compute the distance to be 400 miles.

8. **(D)** The definition of a rhombus stipulates the equality of its four sides. The first statement reveals that the two triangles are equilateral, so all the angles must be $60°$. From the second statement, $CBD = 60°$ (by alternate interior angles); triangle BCD is isosceles with $BC = CD$ (from the definition of a rhombus), so angle $BDC = CBD = 60°$; subtracting those angles from $180°$ leaves $60°$ for angle BCD.

9. **(E)** From (1), $x < 5$, and from (2), $y < 6$, so $xy < 30$. Hence the product may or may not exceed 27.

10. **(A)** The first statement translates to $Y = X - 1$ and $Z = \frac{1}{2}X$. Given that $X + Y + Z = 19$, substitution yields $X + X - 1 + \frac{1}{2}X = 19$, so $X = 8$. From (1), $Y = 7$ and $Z = 4$.

11. **(B)** Since the three angles sum to a straight angle, $c = 180° - 131° = 49°$.

12. **(A)** The first five perfect cubes are 1, 8, 27, 64, and 125. Therefore $C = 64$.

13. **(C)** From the second statement, the refrigerators cost $112 \times \$186 = \$20,832$. Subtraction from the sale revenue in (1) leaves a gross profit of $12,228.

14. **(E)** Volume is the product of three dimensions. For the can, volume equals its base area (two dimensional) times its height; but the height is not stated.

15. **(B)** We cannot solve the first equation by elementary methods. The second equation implies $x = 1$. Hence $x^3 - 2x^2 + 7 = 6$.

16. **(A)** From (1), Toni types $3150/60 = 52\frac{1}{2}$ words per minute.

17. **(E)** From (2), the product cg is positive, hence c and g have the same sign: f could be either positive or negative. Assume all three numbers are positive, and from (1) $cf > cg$. However, if we assume c and g are positive but f is negative, then from (1) $cf < cg$. The contradiction makes the problem indeterminate.

18. **(D)** The radius BC must be perpendicular to the tangent AB so ABC is a right triangle. The second statement implies it is a 6-8-10 right triangle, so the radius is 6. We can solve from the first statement with the Pythagorean theorem:

$$(AC)^2 = (AB)^2 + (BC)^2$$

$$(4 + r)^2 = 8^2 + r^2$$

$$16 + 8r + r^2 = 64 + r^2$$

$$r = {}^{48}\!/_8 = 6$$

19. **(B)** Let g be the fraction of gasoline. Then the fraction of alcohol is $1 - g$. So for the mixture, $1.09g + 1.81(1 - g) = 1.22$, and we can solve for $g = 0.82$. Gasohol 99 is 82% gasoline and 18% alcohol.

20. **(C)** From the first statement, $w = 3\frac{1}{2}$. Substituting that into (2) yields $u + v - 3 \cdot 3\frac{1}{2} = 11$, which can be solved for $(u + v) = 21\frac{1}{2}$.

SECTION V: SENTENCE CORRECTION

1. (C) Along with having inconsistent verb tense and wordiness problems, the original sentence illustrates a long dangling modifier. The underlined portion seems to modify *the university's school of oceanography* and thereby seems to say that the *school* is enjoying *exploring marine life,* etc. Only (C) offers an introductory phrase that is both correct and unambiguous. (B) and (D), although gramatically correct, significantly change the intended meaning of the original sentence.

2. (E) The original sentence contains a subtle error in faulty parallelism. The items compared—*success in school* and *playing marbles*—become parallel if *success* is changed to *succeeding.* (E) makes this necessary change and also brings the compared items closer together in order to further clarify their relationship.

3. (A) Choice (B) is a dangling phrase. Choice (C) is wordy and changes the meaning. Choice (D) has a misplaced modifier (*complete*) and choice (E) has no grammatical subject.

4. (B) The introductory phrase is a dangling modifier and makes the sentence seem to say that the poetry is composing at the typewriter. Choice (B) makes it clear that the poets do the composing and does so without significantly altering the meaning of the original.

5. (D) A misplaced modifier here makes it seem that liberal activists have *the power to destroy the world.* Choice (D) logically links nuclear weapons with the power to destroy the world. Although choice (B) is somewhat clearer than the original, it creats a clause incompatible with the rest of the sentence.

6. (D) In the original, the subject, *shopper,* does not agree with the verb, *tend.* Choice (D) corrects this error without making additional, unnecessary changes.

323

7. (A) The original is more correct, clear, and logical than any of the other choices.

8. (C) The original is extremely wordy, filled with repetitious phrases (for instance, *understanding . . . with comprehension* and *class members . . . were students*). All choices except (C) retain some of the original wordiness or are grammatically unacceptable.

9. (D) The pronoun *they* is not used clearly in the original; it is illogical to conclude that *they* refers to *distinguished performances* because all performances are *new to the screen*. (Each performance is done only once even though it may be shown many times.) New *performers* (as opposed to veteran actors) may be new to the screen, however, and the use of *actors* in choice (D) provides this clear, logical reference.

10. (E) The conventions of standard written English dictate that *but also* be preceded by *not only*, which is not the case in the original here. Additionally, the underlined portion illogically compares *appearance* to *other pigs* and relies on a vague, wordy phrase, *with reference to the belief*. Choice (E) remedies all of these problems by simplifying the structure and clarifying the diction. (B) is not a good choice because it employs the past tense. The original is in present tense, and there is no reason to change it because present tense is appropriate when one discusses "timeless" works of art and literature.

11. (B) Two major errors weaken the original. (1) Faulty parallelism—*enjoying the beauty* is not parallel in structure with *clarity* and *brilliance*. (2) Vague wordiness—*and along with it* might suggest that the diamond and the painting are being perceived together, but the more logical meaning is that they are phenomena that are generally similar to one another. (B) is syntactically and logically correct and retains the intended meaning of the original.

12. (C) The original is constructed so that *a train* seems to be *working as an engineer*. Also, the phrase *according to legend* repeats information supplied later in the sentence. Choice (C) is both economical and clearly constructed.

13. (E) *Either* is misplaced in the original so that it does not refer to *voices* as well as *acting*. (E) corrects this error, eliminates the repetitious term *speaking*, and changes *consisted of* to *was* to produce a more economical, parallel structure.

14. (C) The original is not the best choice here because it is not as economical and clear as (C). Each of the other choices is either too wordy, vague, or illogical.

15. (A) The original is perfectly clear and correct, and none of the other choices is an improvement.

16. (D) The introductory phrase is a dangling modifier, making it seem as if the *women* did not gain legislative approval. Only choice (D) both clarifies the relationship between the Equal Rights Amendment and legislative approval and indicates that the failure of the amendment precedes the protests logically and chronologically.

17. (E) The original suggests that she failed the fifth grade possibly because of her father's shaking. (B) is clearer in this respect but repetitious with its use of both *recounting* and *recounted*. Choice (E) is the clearest and most economical of the choices. The fact that such an experience would be painful is obvious, and since the experience happened in fifth grade, it is clearly a childhood experience. The sentence is not harmed by the lack of these details.

18. (C) The original contains two errors: *principle* (fundamental truth) is incorrect usage, and *reason ... was because* is a redundant phrase. Only choice (C) corrects both of these errors and retains the full meaning of the original.

19. (D) In the original sentence, the adjective *quick* is used incorrectly to modify an *action,* signing. Actions are modified by adverbs—in this case, *quickly.* This is the only necessary change.

20. (D) *Continually* is a squinting modifier, unclear because it may refer to either *reading* or *reminds.* Choice (D) clarifies its reference. Choice (E) is vague and wordy.

21. (B) *To question* is not parallel with *remaining;* only (B) corrects this problem.

22. (C) In order to indicate that participation in the debate precedes voter understanding, the verb *had* must replace *would have.* None of the other choices retains the original meaning clearly and fully.

SECTION VI: PROBLEM SOLVING

1. **(C)** Since the reduction was approximately 13 percent, the 195 professors are 87 percent of the original number.

$$195 = 0.87n$$

$$n = \frac{195}{0.87} \cong 224$$

2. **(D)** The four angles around each point of intersection sum to 360°, a complete revolution. The twelve angles in the figure must sum to $3 \times 360° = 1080°$. Three of the angles are the interior angles of a triangle, so the nine lettered angles equal $1080° - 180° = 900°$. The 42° angle was merely a distraction.

3. **(C)** Let's calculate the rates of production per day. Two of the factories each make $100,000/15 \cong 6667$ hubcaps per day. The third plant makes $1.3 \times 6667 \cong 8667$ hubcaps per day. The total production rate is $8667 + 2(6667) = 22,001$ hubcaps per day. At that rate it would take 45.5 days to produce a million hubcaps.

4. **(A)** Since the number is divisible by 5, it must end with a 0 or 5. Because the first digit is double the second, the first two digits of the number must be 21, 42, 63, or 84. The only combination that adds to 11 is 425. The product of those digits is $4 \times 2 \times 5 = 40$.

5. **(E)** Since the five choices all have a numerator of 1, the denominator of the correct choice times $(x - 4)$ will equal $(2x^2 - 10x + 8)$. That denominator may be found by dividing polynomials:

$$
\begin{array}{r}
2x - 2 \quad\quad\quad \leftarrow \textit{denominator of answer} \\
x - 4 \overline{\smash{\big)}\ 2x^2 - 10x + 8} \\
\underline{2x^2 - 8x \quad\quad\quad} \\
-2x + 8 \\
\underline{-2x + 8}
\end{array}
$$

327

6. (C) The radius of the large circle equals the diameter of the small circle, so the radius of the large circle is twice the radius of the small circle. Area is proportional to the square of the radius, so the large circle has an area $2^2 = 4$ times that of the small circle. If the small circle is ¼ of the large circle, then the crescent area is ¾ of the large circle. The crescent and small circle are in the ratio $(¾)(¼) = 3$.

7. (C) The maximum number of dress combinations is $3 \times 3 \times 2 = 18$. However, because the woman won't wear her pink blouse and green skirt with either of the two pairs of shoes, two of the combinations are excluded. She could wear $18 - 2 = 16$ different combinations.

8. (A) You must solve the two simultaneous linear equations for both variables.

$$3r + s = 17 \quad \text{The first equation}$$
$$\underline{-3r - 6s = -27} \quad \text{The second equation times } -3$$
$$-5s = -10 \quad \text{Adding two equations}$$
$$s = 2 \quad \text{Solution for s}$$

$$3r + 2 = 17 \quad \text{Substituting into the first equation}$$
$$3r = 15$$
$$r = 5 \quad \text{Solution for r}$$

So r exceeds s by 3.

9. (D) Begin with an arbitrary number of items sold, say 10, for a gross income of $1000. By reducing the price 10% to $90, the owners sell 20% more items, or now 12. Now their gross income is $12 \times \$90 = \$1080$. The percent increase is 80/1000 or 8%.

10. (E) The given sequence more than doubles at each step, so it is fundamentally a geometric (multiplicative) sequence rather than an arithmetic (additive) sequence. Each term is two more than double the preceding term. The next number in the sequence would be $2 + 2(94) = 190$.

11. (C) The volume of the swimming pool equals its area times its depth. The circular area has a radius of 25 feet.

$$V = \pi r^2 h = 3.14(25)^2(8) = 15,700$$

That volume is closest to choice (C).

12. (B) Since there are 8 pints per gallon, the volume of punch is 60 pints. If we call the amount of orange juice J, then the amount of buttermilk is $2J$ and the amount of brandy is $J/3$. All the ingredients add to 60 pints.

$$J + 2J + J/3 = 60$$

$$\frac{3J + 6J + J}{3} = 60$$

$$3J + 6J + J = 180$$

$$10J = 180$$

$$J = 18 \text{ pints of orange juice}$$

13. (B) Substituting for x and y, the expression is

$$(6 - 2(-2))^{-2}$$

$$= (6 + 4)^{-2} = (10)^{-2}$$

$$= \frac{1}{(10)^2} = \frac{1}{100} = 0.01$$

14. (B) The third side of the right triangle can be found using the Pythagorean theorem.

$$a^2 + b^2 = c^2$$

$$a^2 + (15)^2 = (17)^2$$

$$a^2 + 225 = 289$$

$$a^2 = 64$$

$$a = 8$$

The perimeter is the sum of the three sides of the triangle.

$$8 + 15 + 17 = 40 \text{ cm}$$

15. (E) The ferry can transport the maximum number of cars when they are all the minimum weight, 1800 pounds. Each of those cars weighs $1800/2000 = 0.9$ tons. The number of those automobiles that can be transported by the ferry is its capacity divided by the weight of one car: $78/0.9 = 86.67$ automobiles.

16. (D) Exponential quantities can be readily divided (or multiplied) if they have the same base. To convert m from base-8 to base-2, consider that $8 = 2^3$. Therefore, $m = 8^5 = (2^3)^5 = 2^{15}$.

$$\frac{m}{n} = \frac{2^{15}}{2^{12}} = 2^3 = 8$$

If two exponential quantities have the same base, they may be divided by subtracting the exponent of the denominator from the exponent of the numerator.

SECTION VII: PROBLEM SOLVING

1. (C) If x represents the cost of the book, then we have the following equation:

$$x + 0.20x = \$12.00$$
$$1.2x = \$12.00$$
$$x = \$10.00$$

2. (A) Set up two equations.

$$5A + 2B = 6B + 5C \quad 1A + 4C = 2A + 4B$$
$$5A = 4B + 5C \qquad 4C = A + 4B$$
$$4C - A = 4B$$

Substitute $4C - A$ for $4B$ in the other equation.

$$5A = 4C - A + 5C$$

$$6A = 9C$$

$$A = (9/6)C$$

$$= (3/2)C$$

3. (C) The six faces of the cube each have an area of $10 \times 10 = 100$ square feet. That is a total of 600 square feet. Since it takes one quart for each 20 square feet, you need 30 quarts. Take $30 \times \$3.20 = \$96.00$

4. (A) Start at the lower right, add the whole number 2 with the fraction. Change to an improper fraction, invert, and continue.

5. (A) We solve for y as follows:

$$x = \frac{1 + y}{y}$$

$$xy = 1 + y$$

$$xy - y = 1$$

$$y(x - 1) = 1$$

$$y = \frac{1}{x - 1}$$

6. **(C)** Since machine A worked for 2 hours and could do the entire job in 8 hours, machine A must have done ¼ of the job. We have the following formula in which the value of x represents the time actually worked.

$$\overset{A}{2/8} + \overset{B}{x/10} + \overset{C}{x/12} = 1$$

$$x/10 + x/12 = 3/4$$

$$6x + 5x = 45$$

$$11x = 45$$

$$x = 4\tfrac{1}{11}$$

9:00 A.M. + $4\tfrac{1}{11}$ hours $\cong$ 1:00 P.M.

7. **(B)** There are 140 line employees with 3 to 5 years of employment. There are 80 of them taking the First Aid workshop. Thus, $140 - 80 = 60$.

8. **(B)** For the line employees, there are 30 taking both workshops, 20 taking only the Stress workshop, and 10 taking only the First Aid workshop. For the staff employees, there are 20 taking both, 20 taking only the Stress workshop, and 30 taking only the First Aid workshop. Thus, 130 are taking at least one workshop. Therefore 230 out of 360 are not taking a workshop, or 64%.

9. **(A)** The shaded area is the difference between the entire rectangle (with an area of $6 \times 8 = 48$) and the white triangle (with an area of $(6 \times x)/2 = 3x$). Thus, $48 - 3x$.

10. (E) First find the area of the shaded region. The difference of the outer rectangle $(6 \times 12 = 72)$ and the inner rectangle $(2 \times 3 = 6)$ is 66 square feet. Since it takes 24 2-inch by 3-inch tiles to cover one square foot, the correct answer is $24 \times 66 = 1584$.

11. (C) If the radius of a circle is 1, and it is reduced by 20%, it becomes 0.8. Since the area formula squares the radius, the original factor remains 1, but the new factor becomes 0.64, which is a 36% decrease.

12. (C) Looking at the water, we have ⅔ of 2 quarts = 4/3 quarts, and ⅜ of 3 quarts = 9/8 quarts. These add together to give 2¹¹⁄₂₄ which is very close to 50% of 5 quarts.

13. (C) There are 8 different arrangements, as follows:

red-red-red	green-green-red
green-green-green	green-red-red
red-green-green	red-green-red
green-red-green	red-red-green

14. (C) We can tabulate the data:

	part of tank brand Z	part of tank brand Y
after first fill up	1	0
before second fill up	½	0
after second fill up	½	½
before third fill up	¼	¼
after third fill up	¾	¼
before fourth fill up	⅜	⅛
after fourth fill up	⅜	⅝

Since the tank is now full, ⅜, or 37.5% is brand Z.

15. (E) Any number of members is possible as long as the number of dollars per member is two more than the number of members.

16. (A) From the relationship that exists in a right triangle, we see that the sides of the square must equal the square root of 5. Thus the area of the square is 5.

SECTION VIII: CRITICAL REASONING

1. (B) The argument mentions the reduced quality of a nationally prominent outdoor attraction and advocates its protection. Only (B) makes a similar argument about a similar phenomenon.

2. (A) The final statement that elders believed to possess special powers are *sometimes treated with a deference based on fear rather than love* assumes that deference is normally accorded based on love.

3. (B) II only. The only reasonable completion of the argument would be that the alkalies in Lake Huron may be insufficient to support *Alpha splendes*.

4. (D) *Evolution* is to *species* in the same way as *bush* is to *branches*. Just as the branches of a bush reach out every which way in varying lengths, the results of evolution (forms of life, species) have developed in irregular "branches." This is the main point of the paragraph.

5. (D) The paragraph implies the importance of articulation disorders by mentioning how heavily they contribute to a clinician's caseload.

6. (C) In the second paragraph, we read of his recognition that behaviorism is offensive to many people—that it does *not* have popular appeal.

7. (A) The passage discusses the possible application of Skinner's theory to the field of human affairs and in promoting the development of humankind.

8. (C) If no speech which presents one or more facts is uninformative, any and every uninformative speech must present no facts.

9. (E) Since all speeches intended to persuade contain few or all facts, such a speech cannot be uninformative, since an uninformative speech is *factless*.

10. (C) Voltaire's statement shows the irony that the descriptive word used (*common*) may not, in reality, be so. Likewise, the adjective describing the shrimp (*jumbo*) indicates that the shrimp are large; this may not be the case.

11. (B) III only. The same word may have more than one meaning, each of which may be completely different from the others. In this case, the word *ball* means two different things.

12. (A) This question draws from a simple, explicit statement: *Socrates believed . . . that evil is fundamentally ignorance.* Each of the other choices is an unwarranted complication or extension of this statement.

13. (C) As the passage states, Skinner cared about only *overt* or measurable behavior, not any response only *within* the organism.

14. (A) The passage explicitly states that some followers of Watson studied behavior to understand the *workings of the mind*.

15. (E) Choices (A) and (B) are not implied; they are explicitly stated. (C) is vague; the meaning of *consequentiality* is not clear. (D) is incorrect because the author is arguing that doing nothing has no consequences. Choice (E) is correct. This author says that doing nothing keeps us safe from consequences; this could be true only in light of the implication that doing nothing is not an act.

16. (B) According to the author, the alternative to experiencing consequences is playing it *safe*. This can mean only that consequences are dangerous.

PRACTICE TEST 3

ANSWER SHEET FOR PRACTICE TEST 3
(Remove This Sheet and Use It to Mark Your Answers)

SECTION II	SECTION III	SECTION IV
1 Ⓐ Ⓑ Ⓒ Ⓓ Ⓔ	1 Ⓐ Ⓑ Ⓒ Ⓓ Ⓔ	1 Ⓐ Ⓑ Ⓒ Ⓓ Ⓔ
2 Ⓐ Ⓑ Ⓒ Ⓓ Ⓔ	2 Ⓐ Ⓑ Ⓒ Ⓓ Ⓔ	2 Ⓐ Ⓑ Ⓒ Ⓓ Ⓔ
3 Ⓐ Ⓑ Ⓒ Ⓓ Ⓔ	3 Ⓐ Ⓑ Ⓒ Ⓓ Ⓔ	3 Ⓐ Ⓑ Ⓒ Ⓓ Ⓔ
4 Ⓐ Ⓑ Ⓒ Ⓓ Ⓔ	4 Ⓐ Ⓑ Ⓒ Ⓓ Ⓔ	4 Ⓐ Ⓑ Ⓒ Ⓓ Ⓔ
5 Ⓐ Ⓑ Ⓒ Ⓓ Ⓔ	5 Ⓐ Ⓑ Ⓒ Ⓓ Ⓔ	5 Ⓐ Ⓑ Ⓒ Ⓓ Ⓔ
6 Ⓐ Ⓑ Ⓒ Ⓓ Ⓔ	6 Ⓐ Ⓑ Ⓒ Ⓓ Ⓔ	6 Ⓐ Ⓑ Ⓒ Ⓓ Ⓔ
7 Ⓐ Ⓑ Ⓒ Ⓓ Ⓔ	7 Ⓐ Ⓑ Ⓒ Ⓓ Ⓔ	7 Ⓐ Ⓑ Ⓒ Ⓓ Ⓔ
8 Ⓐ Ⓑ Ⓒ Ⓓ Ⓔ	8 Ⓐ Ⓑ Ⓒ Ⓓ Ⓔ	8 Ⓐ Ⓑ Ⓒ Ⓓ Ⓔ
9 Ⓐ Ⓑ Ⓒ Ⓓ Ⓔ	9 Ⓐ Ⓑ Ⓒ Ⓓ Ⓔ	9 Ⓐ Ⓑ Ⓒ Ⓓ Ⓔ
10 Ⓐ Ⓑ Ⓒ Ⓓ Ⓔ	10 Ⓐ Ⓑ Ⓒ Ⓓ Ⓔ	10 Ⓐ Ⓑ Ⓒ Ⓓ Ⓔ
11 Ⓐ Ⓑ Ⓒ Ⓓ Ⓔ	11 Ⓐ Ⓑ Ⓒ Ⓓ Ⓔ	11 Ⓐ Ⓑ Ⓒ Ⓓ Ⓔ
12 Ⓐ Ⓑ Ⓒ Ⓓ Ⓔ	12 Ⓐ Ⓑ Ⓒ Ⓓ Ⓔ	12 Ⓐ Ⓑ Ⓒ Ⓓ Ⓔ
13 Ⓐ Ⓑ Ⓒ Ⓓ Ⓔ	13 Ⓐ Ⓑ Ⓒ Ⓓ Ⓔ	13 Ⓐ Ⓑ Ⓒ Ⓓ Ⓔ
14 Ⓐ Ⓑ Ⓒ Ⓓ Ⓔ	14 Ⓐ Ⓑ Ⓒ Ⓓ Ⓔ	14 Ⓐ Ⓑ Ⓒ Ⓓ Ⓔ
15 Ⓐ Ⓑ Ⓒ Ⓓ Ⓔ	15 Ⓐ Ⓑ Ⓒ Ⓓ Ⓔ	15 Ⓐ Ⓑ Ⓒ Ⓓ Ⓔ
16 Ⓐ Ⓑ Ⓒ Ⓓ Ⓔ	16 Ⓐ Ⓑ Ⓒ Ⓓ Ⓔ	16 Ⓐ Ⓑ Ⓒ Ⓓ Ⓔ
		17 Ⓐ Ⓑ Ⓒ Ⓓ Ⓔ
		18 Ⓐ Ⓑ Ⓒ Ⓓ Ⓔ
		19 Ⓐ Ⓑ Ⓒ Ⓓ Ⓔ
		20 Ⓐ Ⓑ Ⓒ Ⓓ Ⓔ

CUT HERE

ANSWER SHEET FOR PRACTICE TEST 3
(Remove This Sheet and Use It to Mark Your Answers)

SECTION V

1 Ⓐ Ⓑ Ⓒ Ⓓ Ⓔ
2 Ⓐ Ⓑ Ⓒ Ⓓ Ⓔ
3 Ⓐ Ⓑ Ⓒ Ⓓ Ⓔ
4 Ⓐ Ⓑ Ⓒ Ⓓ Ⓔ
5 Ⓐ Ⓑ Ⓒ Ⓓ Ⓔ

6 Ⓐ Ⓑ Ⓒ Ⓓ Ⓔ
7 Ⓐ Ⓑ Ⓒ Ⓓ Ⓔ
8 Ⓐ Ⓑ Ⓒ Ⓓ Ⓔ
9 Ⓐ Ⓑ Ⓒ Ⓓ Ⓔ
10 Ⓐ Ⓑ Ⓒ Ⓓ Ⓔ

11 Ⓐ Ⓑ Ⓒ Ⓓ Ⓔ
12 Ⓐ Ⓑ Ⓒ Ⓓ Ⓔ
13 Ⓐ Ⓑ Ⓒ Ⓓ Ⓔ
14 Ⓐ Ⓑ Ⓒ Ⓓ Ⓔ
15 Ⓐ Ⓑ Ⓒ Ⓓ Ⓔ

16 Ⓐ Ⓑ Ⓒ Ⓓ Ⓔ
17 Ⓐ Ⓑ Ⓒ Ⓓ Ⓔ
18 Ⓐ Ⓑ Ⓒ Ⓓ Ⓔ
19 Ⓐ Ⓑ Ⓒ Ⓓ Ⓔ
20 Ⓐ Ⓑ Ⓒ Ⓓ Ⓔ

21 Ⓐ Ⓑ Ⓒ Ⓓ Ⓔ
22 Ⓐ Ⓑ Ⓒ Ⓓ Ⓔ

SECTION VI

1 Ⓐ Ⓑ Ⓒ Ⓓ Ⓔ
2 Ⓐ Ⓑ Ⓒ Ⓓ Ⓔ
3 Ⓐ Ⓑ Ⓒ Ⓓ Ⓔ
4 Ⓐ Ⓑ Ⓒ Ⓓ Ⓔ
5 Ⓐ Ⓑ Ⓒ Ⓓ Ⓔ

6 Ⓐ Ⓑ Ⓒ Ⓓ Ⓔ
7 Ⓐ Ⓑ Ⓒ Ⓓ Ⓔ
8 Ⓐ Ⓑ Ⓒ Ⓓ Ⓔ
9 Ⓐ Ⓑ Ⓒ Ⓓ Ⓔ
10 Ⓐ Ⓑ Ⓒ Ⓓ Ⓔ

11 Ⓐ Ⓑ Ⓒ Ⓓ Ⓔ
12 Ⓐ Ⓑ Ⓒ Ⓓ Ⓔ
13 Ⓐ Ⓑ Ⓒ Ⓓ Ⓔ
14 Ⓐ Ⓑ Ⓒ Ⓓ Ⓔ
15 Ⓐ Ⓑ Ⓒ Ⓓ Ⓔ

16 Ⓐ Ⓑ Ⓒ Ⓓ Ⓔ

SECTION VII

1 Ⓐ Ⓑ Ⓒ Ⓓ Ⓔ
2 Ⓐ Ⓑ Ⓒ Ⓓ Ⓔ
3 Ⓐ Ⓑ Ⓒ Ⓓ Ⓔ
4 Ⓐ Ⓑ Ⓒ Ⓓ Ⓔ
5 Ⓐ Ⓑ Ⓒ Ⓓ Ⓔ

6 Ⓐ Ⓑ Ⓒ Ⓓ Ⓔ
7 Ⓐ Ⓑ Ⓒ Ⓓ Ⓔ
8 Ⓐ Ⓑ Ⓒ Ⓓ Ⓔ
9 Ⓐ Ⓑ Ⓒ Ⓓ Ⓔ
10 Ⓐ Ⓑ Ⓒ Ⓓ Ⓔ

11 Ⓐ Ⓑ Ⓒ Ⓓ Ⓔ
12 Ⓐ Ⓑ Ⓒ Ⓓ Ⓔ
13 Ⓐ Ⓑ Ⓒ Ⓓ Ⓔ
14 Ⓐ Ⓑ Ⓒ Ⓓ Ⓔ
15 Ⓐ Ⓑ Ⓒ Ⓓ Ⓔ

16 Ⓐ Ⓑ Ⓒ Ⓓ Ⓔ
17 Ⓐ Ⓑ Ⓒ Ⓓ Ⓔ
18 Ⓐ Ⓑ Ⓒ Ⓓ Ⓔ
19 Ⓐ Ⓑ Ⓒ Ⓓ Ⓔ
20 Ⓐ Ⓑ Ⓒ Ⓓ Ⓔ

21 Ⓐ Ⓑ Ⓒ Ⓓ Ⓔ
22 Ⓐ Ⓑ Ⓒ Ⓓ Ⓔ
23 Ⓐ Ⓑ Ⓒ Ⓓ Ⓔ

SECTION VIII

1 Ⓐ Ⓑ Ⓒ Ⓓ Ⓔ
2 Ⓐ Ⓑ Ⓒ Ⓓ Ⓔ
3 Ⓐ Ⓑ Ⓒ Ⓓ Ⓔ
4 Ⓐ Ⓑ Ⓒ Ⓓ Ⓔ
5 Ⓐ Ⓑ Ⓒ Ⓓ Ⓔ

6 Ⓐ Ⓑ Ⓒ Ⓓ Ⓔ
7 Ⓐ Ⓑ Ⓒ Ⓓ Ⓔ
8 Ⓐ Ⓑ Ⓒ Ⓓ Ⓔ
9 Ⓐ Ⓑ Ⓒ Ⓓ Ⓔ
10 Ⓐ Ⓑ Ⓒ Ⓓ Ⓔ

11 Ⓐ Ⓑ Ⓒ Ⓓ Ⓔ
12 Ⓐ Ⓑ Ⓒ Ⓓ Ⓔ
13 Ⓐ Ⓑ Ⓒ Ⓓ Ⓔ
14 Ⓐ Ⓑ Ⓒ Ⓓ Ⓔ
15 Ⓐ Ⓑ Ⓒ Ⓓ Ⓔ

16 Ⓐ Ⓑ Ⓒ Ⓓ Ⓔ

SECTION I: ANALYTICAL WRITING ASSESSMENT

GENERAL DIRECTIONS

In this section, you will have a total time of sixty minutes to plan and write two essays, one for each topic given. The specific time allotted for each essay is thirty minutes. For each essay, use three sides of 8½-by-11-inch lined paper.

Analysis of an Issue

Time: 30 Minutes

DIRECTIONS

This section will require you to analyze and explain your views on the issue given. Consider many points of view as you develop your own position on the issue. There is no right or wrong answer to the question.

Read the statement and directions carefully. Make any notes in your test booklet. Then write your response on the separate answer document. Be sure to use the answer document that goes with this writing task.

There comes a point in athletic competition when the less intelligence a player has, the greater will be his or her success. It is better to be not very bright if you wish to be a successful athlete. The thinkers harm their performance by worry or by distracting their concentration from the game. An athlete need not be stupid, but it is better to be dull than bright.

Write an essay in which you support or refute this notion. Briefly consider what could be said on the other side, and support your premise with specific details drawn from your observations or readings.

Analysis of an Argument

Time: 30 Minutes

DIRECTIONS

This section will require you to critique the argument given. Questioning underlying assumptions, finding alternative explanations or counterexamples, and delineating evidence to strengthen or weaken an argument are some possible approaches.

Read the argument and directions carefully. Make any notes in your test booklet. Then write your response on the separate answer document. Be sure to use the answer document that goes with this writing task.

The passage of new laws to lengthen the required prison sentences for violent crimes will not reduce the crime rates. Since no one commits a crime with the expectation of being caught and sent to prison, increasing the sentences for a criminal act can have no deterrent effect. A recently captured kidnapper confessed he had killed his kidnapped victim because he feared he would be apprehended and imprisoned for the kidnapping.

Write an essay in which you evaluate this argument. What purpose is served by the specific evidence used? What are the strengths and/or the weaknesses of this paragraph?

SECTION II: CRITICAL REASONING

Time: 25 Minutes
16 Questions

DIRECTIONS

You will be presented with brief passages or statements and will be required to evaluate their reasoning. In each case, select the best answer choice, even though more than one choice may present a possible answer. Choices which are unreasonable or incompatible with commonsense standards should be eliminated.

Aristotle said that art represents "general truths" about human nature. Our city councilman is arguing in favor of the artistry—a giant mural in front of a Jeep dealership, portraying a variety of four-wheel-drive vehicles. He cites Aristotle's conception of art as his support.

1. The passage above raises which of the following questions?
   (A) Can a city councilman understand Aristotle?
   (B) Which general truths about human nature does a four-wheel-drive mural *not* represent?
   (C) Could Aristotle have predicted a modern society filled with sophisticated machines?
   (D) To what extent are four-wheel-drive vehicles representative of a general advance in modern technology?
   (E) What "general truth" about human nature does a mural of four-wheel-drive vehicles represent?

2. *Speaker 1:* The holy passion of friendship is of so sweet and steady and loyal and enduring a nature that it will last through a whole lifetime.

   Speaker 2: If not asked to lend money.

The two speakers represent which of the following contrasting attitudes?
(A) Faith and despair
(B) Idealism and cynicism
(C) Idealism and optimism
(D) Socialism and capitalism
(E) Friendship and enmity

   Unfortunately, only 11 percent of the driving public uses regular seat belts. Automatic restraints are the answer, and the quicker they are required, the sooner highways deaths will be reduced.

3. The author's conclusion is based upon which of the following assumptions?
(A) Only 11 percent of the driving public cares about passengers' lives.
(B) The use of restraints reduces highway deaths.
(C) Regular seat belts are inadequate safety devices.
(D) It is unfortunate that 89 percent of the driving public does not use regular seat belts.
(E) Highway deaths occur often enough so that reducing them is a necessity.

   The heart and soul of our business is credibility. We get that credibility and respect, and the power that goes with it, only by being a socially and professionally responsible agent for the public. In some ways we journalists have to have the same attitude to news as an employee of a bank has to money—it isn't ours. We're handling it on behalf of other people, so it cannot be converted to our own use. If we do, it's embezzlement.

4. Which of the following criticisms would most weaken the comparison between journalists and bank employees?
   (A) Different newspapers print different news, just as different banks hold assets from various sources.
   (B) Journalists are necessarily more creative individuals than bank employees.
   (C) The heart and soul of the banking business is money, not credibility.
   (D) A bank teller need not be credible, just responsible.
   (E) Embezzlement is properly a crime against the bank, not against the depositors.

Consumers are not so easily manipulated as they are often painted. They may know what they want, and what they want may be greatly different from what other people believe they need.

5. Which of the following statements, if true, most weakens the above argument?
   (A) Most people continue to buy the same brand of a product year after year.
   (B) Companies that advertise the most sell the most products.
   (C) Store shelves packed with a variety of different brands have the potential to confuse the consumer.
   (D) Most consumers know which brand they are going to buy before entering a store.
   (E) People who shop with others rarely argue with their companions.

Questions 6 and 7 refer to the following passage

The last census showed a sharp rise during the 1970s in the number of Americans living together as unmarried couples, but a more recent increase in the marriage rate in 1981 suggests that matrimony will make a comeback in the 1980s.

6. Which of the following best refutes the argument above?
   (A) One of the causes of more marriages is that the large population resulting from a baby boom is just now reaching marriageable age.
   (B) Although information about the 1981 marriage rate is not complete, most analysts consider it to be reliable.
   (C) Many of those marrying in 1981 were couples who had lived together during the 1970s.
   (D) The number of Americans living together did not rise at a consistent rate during the 1970s.
   (E) The marriage rate increased dramatically in 1971 and fell even more dramatically in following years.

7. With which of the following would the author be likely to agree?
   (A) Americans should not live together as unmarried couples.
   (B) Matrimony is preferable to living together.
   (C) Economic circumstances have made matrimony attractive as a way of paying less income tax.
   (D) The attitudes of young people in the 1980s are altogether different from the attitudes of young people in the 1970s.
   (E) Prevailing attitudes toward marriage tend to persist for more than one year.

The shortsightedness of our government and our scientists has virtually nullified all of their great discoveries because of their failure to consider the environmental impact. The situation is far from hopeless, but our government agencies must become better watchdogs.

8. This argument fails to place any blame on

   I. consumers who prefer new technology to clean air
  II. the ability of government to actually police industry
 III. legal loopholes which allow industry abuse of government regulations

  (A) I only
  (B) II only
  (C) III only
  (D) I and III only
  (E) I, II, and III

Questions 9 and 10 refer to the following passage

The department store owned by my competitor sells green necklaces that glow in the dark. Only those customers of mine wearing those necklaces must be giving business to the competition.

9. The conclusion could best be strengthened by
  (A) deleting "that glow in the dark"
  (B) changing "sells" to "has sold"
  (C) changing "the competition" to "my competitor"
  (D) inserting "only" as the first word in sentence one
  (E) changing "wearing" to "owning"

10. The author foolishly assumes that
  (A) the customers might find the necklaces attractive
  (B) customers are not buying other products from the competition
  (C) customers will wear the necklaces in daylight
  (D) a department store should not sell necklaces
  (E) the competition is outselling the author

11. Which of the following most logically completes this passage?

   Several of the survivors discussed their dilemma. They could remain on the island and attempt to survive as best they knew how. Or they could attempt to escape, using the resources available to them. None of the group wished to venture away from their uncertain sanctuary, but all of them knew that help would be a long time coming. Their discussions were thus _____.

   (A) futile, arbitrary, and capricious
   (B) limited by their imagination and resolve
   (C) dampened by a sense of impending doom
   (D) possible, but by no means successful
   (E) courageous and honorable

Questions 12 and 13 refer to the following letter

To the Chair:

   At the October 7th meeting it was decided that no two officers would hold positions on the same committee. It has recently come to my attention that both Charles S. Smith and Arnold Krunkle will be serving in some capacity on the Building and Maintenance Committee, and both have been nominated for officer status. As you know, this is in direct disregard for the rules as voted by the membership last October 7th. I would hope that sufficient action be taken by the Disciplinary Committee (on which committee both of the above are members) so that this problem will be remedied.

                                        Sincerely,
                                        Irving H. Fortnash

12. Which of the following is the essential flaw that the writer of the letter fails to notice?
    (A) Smith and Krunkle are already serving together on the Disciplinary Committee.
    (B) The Chairman has no power in the matter.
    (C) The membership cannot pass rules limiting members.
    (D) Smith and Krunkle are not yet officers.
    (E) Building and Maintenance is actually two committees.

13. Which of the following most completely and reasonably describes actions that may occur in the near future?
    (A) Fortnash resigns his membership.
    (B) Either Smith or Krunkle resigns his membership.
    (C) Krunkle resigns his committee post on the Building and Maintenance Committee.
    (D) Smith resigns his position on the Building and Maintenance Committee.
    (E) One of the two (Smith or Krunkle) resigns his position on the Building and Maintenance Committee, and the other resigns his position on the Disciplinary Committee.

Flamo Lighters when you need them! Always reliable, always dependable. In all weather, with ten-year guarantee. Don't get caught without a light—keep a Flamo in your pocket wherever you go!

14. All of the following are claims made or implied by Flamo Lighters EXCEPT
    (A) convenience
    (B) dependability
    (C) longevity
    (D) winter-proof
    (E) all-purpose

All race-car lovers enjoy classical music.
No backgammon players enjoy classical music.
All those who enjoy classical music also enjoy fine wine.

15. If each of the above statements is true, which of the following must also be true?
    (A) Everyone who plays backgammon enjoys fine wine.
    (B) No one who enjoys fine wine plays backgammon.
    (C) No backgammon players are race-car lovers.
    (D) No backgammon players enjoy fine wine.
    (E) No race-car lover enjoys fine wine.

It has been proven that the "lie detector" can be fooled. If one is truly unaware that one is lying, when in fact one is, then the "lie detector" is worthless.

16. Without contradicting his or her own statements, the author might present which of the following arguments as a strong point in favor of the lie detector?
    (A) The methodology used by investigative critics of the lie detector is itself highly flawed.
    (B) Law-enforcement agencies have purchased too many detectors to abandon them now.
    (C) Circumstantial evidence might be more useful in a criminal case than is personal testimony.
    (D) The very threat of a lie-detector test has led a significant number of criminals to confess.
    (E) People are never "truly aware" that they are lying.

STOP. IF YOU FINISH BEFORE TIME IS CALLED. CHECK YOUR WORK ON THIS SECTION ONLY. DO NOT WORK ON ANY OTHER SECTION IN THE TEST.

SECTION III: PROBLEM SOLVING

Time: 25 Minutes
16 Questions

DIRECTIONS

In this section solve each problem, using any available space on the page for scratchwork. Then indicate the *best* answer in the appropriate space on the answer sheet.

1. ¼ of ⅗ is what percent of ¾?
    (A) 15%
    (B) 20%
    (C) 33⅓%
    (D) 75%
    (E) 80%

2. A $74.95 lawn chair was sold for $59.95 at a special sale. By approximately what percent was the price decreased?
    (A) 15%
    (B) 20%
    (C) 25%
    (D) 60%
    (E) 80%

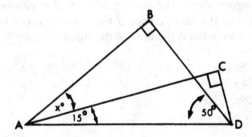

3. In the figure above, $x =$
    (A) 15
    (B) 25
    (C) 35
    (D) 45
    (E) 55

351

4. If x is a positive even number, then each of the following is odd except
   (A) $(x + 3)(x + 5)$
   (B) $x^2 + 5$
   (C) $x^2 + 6x + 9$
   (D) $3x^2 + 4$
   (E) $5(x + 3)$

5. The length of a rectangle is decreased by 15% and its width is increased by 40%. Does the area of the rectangle decrease or increase and by what percent?
   (A) Decreases by 19%
   (B) Decreases by 25%
   (C) Increases by 6%
   (D) Increases by 19%
   (E) Increases by 25%

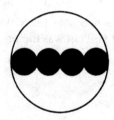

6. In the figure above, the centers of 4 equal circles lie along the diameter of the large circle. If the circumference of the large circle is 64π, what is the area of the shaded region?
   (A) 16π
   (B) 32π
   (C) 64π
   (D) 128π
   (E) 256π

7. What number times $(\frac{1}{3})^2$ will give the value of 3^3?
   - (A)   3
   - (B)   9
   - (C)   27
   - (D) 108
   - (E) 243

8. If one root of the equation is $x^2 - 5x + m = 0$ is 10, what is the value of $m + 3$?
   - (A)   50
   - (B)   10
   - (C)   −5
   - (D) −47
   - (E) −50

9. If $x > 0$, which of the following is equal to $\sqrt{72x^5}$?
   - (A) $36\sqrt{2x^5}$
   - (B) $36x\sqrt{2x}$
   - (C) $18x^2\sqrt{2x}$
   - (D) $6x^2\sqrt{2x}$
   - (E) $6x\sqrt{2x^2}$

10. Thirty percent of the girls in a college class are science majors, and the non-science majors comprise 80% of the class. What percentage of the boys are science majors if 40% of the class are boys?
    - (A)   2%
    - (B)   5%
    - (C) 28%
    - (D) 30%
    - (E) 45%

11. How many two-digit numbers are there whose remainder when divided by 10 is 1, and whose remainder when divided by 6 is 5?
    - (A) 3
    - (B) 4
    - (C) 5
    - (D) 6
    - (E) 7

12. Which is closest to 1?

(A) $\dfrac{3}{3 + 0.03}$

(B) $\dfrac{3}{(3 + 0.03)^2}$

(C) $\dfrac{3}{3 + 0.3}$

(D) $\dfrac{3}{3 + (0.03)^2}$

(E) $\dfrac{3}{(3 + 0.3)^2}$

13. $2000 is deposited in a savings account which pays 6% annual interest compounded semiannually. To the nearest dollar, how much is in the account at the end of the year?
   (A) $2060
   (B) $2120
   (C) $2122
   (D) $2247
   (E) $2258

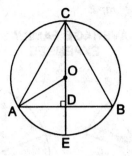

14. Equilateral triangle *ABC* is inscribed in a circle with center *O*, as shown. If the radius of the circle is 2, what is the area of triangle *ABC*?
    (A) 3
    (B) $2\sqrt{3}$
    (C) $3\sqrt{2}$
    (D) $3\sqrt{3}$
    (E) $4\sqrt{2}$

Question 15 refers to the graphs.

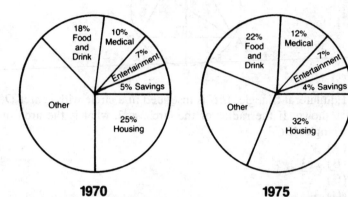

**AVERAGE FAMILY'S
EXPENSES**

**1970
Average Income $12,000**

**1975
Average Income $16,000**

15. What was the percent increase from 1970 to 1975 in the percentage spent on food and drink?
    (A) 4%
    (B) 18%
    (C) 22%
    (D) 40%
    (E) 50%

16. If *a*, *b*, and *c* are consecutive positive odd integers, not necessarily in that order, which of the following must be true?

   I. $a + b > c$
  II. $bc > a$
 III. $(a + c)^2 > b$

   (A) I only
   (B) II only
   (C) III only
   (D) I and II only
   (E) II and III only

STOP. IF YOU FINISH BEFORE TIME IS CALLED, CHECK YOUR WORK ON THIS SECTION ONLY. DO NOT WORK ON ANY OTHER SECTION IN THE TEST.

SECTION IV: DATA SUFFICIENCY

Time: 25 Minutes
20 Questions

DIRECTIONS

Each of the problems below consists of a question and two statements, labeled (1) and (2), in which certain data are given. You must decide whether the data given in the statements are *sufficient* to answer the question. Using the data given in the statements *plus* your knowledge of mathematics and everyday facts (such as the number of days in July or the meaning of *counterclockwise*), you are to blacken space

- (A) if statement (1) ALONE is sufficient, but statement (2) alone is not sufficient to answer the question asked;
- (B) if statement (2) ALONE is sufficient, but statement (1) alone is not sufficient to answer the question asked;
- (C) if BOTH statements (1) and (2) TOGETHER are sufficient to answer the question asked, but NEITHER statement ALONE is sufficient;
- (D) If EACH statement ALONE is sufficient to answer the question asked;
- (E) if statements (1) and (2) TOGETHER are NOT sufficient to answer the question asked, and additional data specific to the problem are needed.

1. What is the volume of a certain box?
   (1) One side of the box has an area of 16 square inches.
   (2) The box is cubical.

2. Given that $x = y + z$, where the three values are different positive integers, is x a prime number?
   (1) y and z are odd.
   (2) $z = 3y$

3. What is the distance from Chicago to Miami?
   (1) A 550 mph turbojet takes $3\frac{1}{4}$ hours for the flight.
   (2) The jet consumes 3 gallons of fuel per mile.

358

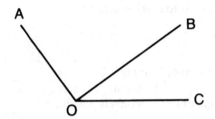

4. How many degrees is angle *AOB*?
   (1) Angle is *BOC* = 35.
   (2) $\overline{AO}$ is perpendicular to $\overline{OB}$.

5. Is a tick longer in duration than a tock?
   (1) There are 48 tocks each day.
   (2) A tick is longer than a minute.

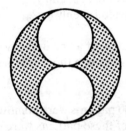

6. The centers of the 3 circles lie on one line (the circles intersect as shown). What is the area of the shaded part of the figure?
   (1) Each of the small circles has a diameter of 5.
   (2) The large circle has a radius of 5.

7. What is the value of *m*?
   (1) $4m - 5 = 7$
   (2) $m^2 + 9 = 6m$

8. How much ethylene glycol antifreeze must be mixed with water to fill a car radiator?
   (1) The radiator has a capacity of 3 gallons.
   (2) The solution must be 40% water.

9. If a is to b as b is to c, is c positive?
   (1) $c = 2a$
   (2) $b^2 = 32$

10. What is the sum of 5 numbers?
   (1) The average of the numbers is zero.
   (2) Only one of the numbers is positive.

11. Does $x = y$?

   (1) $4x - 2y = 80$

   (2) $x = \dfrac{40 + y}{2}$

12. Is the number N an integer?
   (1) The factors of N are 3, 5, and 7.
   (2) N cannot be divided evenly by 2.

13. What is the orientation of a line in the xy plane?
   (1) The line passes through the point $(5, a)$.
   (2) $a = -3$

14. During 1990, 17,500 patients were admitted to Warehall Hospital, and exactly $\frac{1}{6}$ of these patients were discharged within one day. Of those patients discharged within one hour, $\frac{1}{4}$ were seen by only one doctor. How many patients during 1990 were seen by only one doctor?
   (1) Of the total number of patients admitted to Warehall Hospital in 1990, $\frac{1}{9}$ were discharged within one hour.
   (2) Exactly 11,050 patients were discharged after three days.

15. So far this year, Mr. and Mrs. Dufaa have paid what percent of their annual home expenses?
    (1) So far the Dufaas have paid ½ of their annual electricity bill, ½ of their annual gas bill, ¼ of their annual water bill, and ¾ of their annual trash bill.
    (2) The Dufaas' annual home expenses include four items: electricity, gas, water, and trash removal.

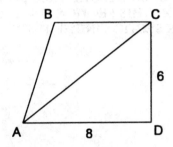

16. In the trapezoid *ABCD*, what is the area of triangle *ABC*?
    (1) $AC = 10$
    (2) $BC = 7$

17. How much principal and interest are still owed on a home originally sold for $179,000?
    (1) The interest rate when the home was purchased was 9%.
    (2) The owner has yet to make 84 payments of $1124 each.

18. A school play requires 24 actors to be cast among boys, girls, and adults. If no actors may take two roles, how many adult actors are needed?
    (1) The ratio of boys needed to girls is 2 to 1.
    (2) The ratio of children needed to adults is 3 to 1.

19. How many years old is Anne?
    (1) Next year, Anne will be half as old as her mother.
    (2) In five years, Anne will be twice as old as a decade ago.

20. Students took a test and received either A's, B's, C's, D's, or F's. If 30% of the class got A's or B's, and 50% got C's or D's, how many students got F's?
    (1) 10 students received B's.
    (2) There were a total of 40 students in the class.

STOP. IF YOU FINISH BEFORE TIME IS CALLED, CHECK YOUR WORK ON THIS SECTION ONLY. DO NOT WORK ON ANY OTHER SECTION IN THE TEST.

SECTION V: SENTENCE CORRECTION

Time: 25 Minutes
22 Questions

DIRECTIONS

Some part of each sentence below is underlined; sometimes the whole sentence is underlined. Five choices for rephrasing the underlined part follow each sentence; the first choice (A) repeats the original, and the other four are different. If choice (A) seems better than the alternatives, choose answer (A); if not, choose one of the others.

For each sentence, consider the requirements of standard written English. Your choice should be a correct and effective expression, not awkward or ambiguous. Focus on grammar, word choice, sentence construction, and punctuation. If a choice changes the meaning of the original sentence, do not select it.

1. The vice president of the local bank spoke <u>for a half an hour and told his colleague that he, his colleague, must consider finding a new job,</u> or accept a reduction in salary.
    - (A) for a half an hour and told his colleague that he, his colleague, must consider finding a new job
    - (B) for a half hour and told his colleague that he must consider to find a new job
    - (C) for half an hour and told his colleague that the colleague must get employed by a new bank
    - (D) for half an hour telling his colleague that he must find a new job
    - (E) for a half hour and told his colleague to consider finding a new job

363

2. That she neglected the children, that the house remained dirty and cluttered, and poor personal hygiene were reasons for firing the housekeeper.

(A) That she neglected the children, that the house remained dirty and cluttered, and poor personal hygiene were reasons for firing the housekeeper.

(B) That she neglected the children, house dirt and clutter, and poor personal hygiene were reasons for firing the housekeeper.

(C) That she neglected the children, dirty and cluttered house, and not good personal hygiene were reasons for firing the housekeeper.

(D) Neglect of the children, poor housecleaning, and that she had poor personal hygiene were reasons for firing the housekeeper.

(E) The housekeeper's neglect of the children, poor housecleaning, and lack of good personal hygiene were reasons for her firing.

3. Because they refuse to follow the conventional dress code, neither Barbara nor her friends is invited to pledge the local sorority.

(A) is invited to pledge the local sorority

(B) are invited to pledge the local sorority

(C) is pledging the local sorority

(D) are pledging the local sorority

(E) will pledge

4. The statement <u>that the consequences of smoking marijuana are no greater than drinking alcohol</u> is an argument often given for legalizing the use of marijuana.

   (A) that the consequences of smoking marijuana are no greater than drinking alcohol

   (B) that the consequences of marijuana are no greater than the consequences of alcohol

   (C) that the consequences of drinking alcohol are as great as the consequences of smoking marijuana

   (D) that the consequences of smoking marijuana are no greater than those of drinking alcohol

   (E) that the consequences of smoking marijuana are as great as drinking alcohol are great

5. As the shrill, piercing sound of the sirens <u>approached, several of my neighbors' dogs start</u> to howl, waking up every household in the neighborhood.

   (A) approached, several of my neighbors' dogs start

   (B) approached, several of my neighbors' dogs started

   (C) approach, several of my neighbors' dogs starts

   (D) approach, several of my neighbors' dogs start

   (E) approach, several dogs of my neighbor started

6. After reconsidering my original judgments, I feel obliged to reread <u>the book I maligned and which initially seemed so inconsequential</u>.

   (A) the book I maligned and which initially seemed so inconsequential

   (B) the book in which I maligned what first seemed so inconsequential

   (C) the maligned book which I initially deemed inconsequential

   (D) the book I malign initially and inconsequentially

   (E) the book I will malign because of its initial inconsequentiality

7. <u>On arriving at Dulles International Airport, his friends met him and took him immediately to his speaking engagement</u> in Springfield.
   - (A) On arriving at Dulles International Airport, his friends met him and took him immediately to his speaking engagement
   - (B) Arriving at Dulles International Airport, his friends who met him immediately took him to his speaking engagement
   - (C) When he arrived at Dulles International Airport, his friends met him and took him immediately to his speaking engagement
   - (D) When he arrived at Dulles International Airport, he was taken immediately to his speaking engagement
   - (E) After arriving at Dulles International Airport, he was immediately taken to his speaking engagement

8. Among the members of the legal profession there are <u>many who try to keep their clients out of court</u> and save their clients' money.
   - (A) many who try to keep their clients out of court
   - (B) ones who try to keep their clients out of court
   - (C) they who try to keep their clients out of court
   - (D) many of whom try to keep their clients out of court
   - (E) a few who try to keep their clients out of court

9. As the rising toll of victims at Chernobyl makes clear, <u>neither the scientists nor the ecologists knows</u> how to deal with the lethal effects of nuclear power plant accidents.
   - (A) neither the scientists nor the ecologists knows
   - (B) neither the scientists nor the ecologists know
   - (C) neither the scientists or the ecologists know
   - (D) neither the scientists together with the ecologists knows
   - (E) not the scientists or the ecologists know

10. None of the applicants could file all of the forms in time because the job application did not state <u>to whom to be sent the personal references.</u>

   (A) to whom to be sent the personal references
   (B) to who the personal references should be sent
   (C) to whom to send the personal references
   (D) to whom the personal references will be sent
   (E) to whom to send the personal references to

11. I'll never forget the tranquil desert resort <u>where having golfed, while I vacationed, in winter, when I was younger.</u>

   (A) where having golfed, while I vacationed, in winter, when I was younger
   (B) where I golfed, while having had vacationed in winter when I was younger
   (C) where I golfed while wintering, when I was younger
   (D) where I having had golf, while I vacationed in winter when I was younger
   (E) where I golfed while I vacationed in winter when I was younger

12. <u>We who graduated from high school in the United States in the early 60's were</u> caught in the middle of the crisis in education created by the Soviet Union's "Sputnik" success.

   (A) We who graduated from high school in the United States in the early 60's were
   (B) We, who graduated from high school in the United States in the early 60's, were
   (C) We who then graduated high school in the United States in the early 60's were
   (D) Those of us who then graduated from high school in the United States in the early 60's were
   (E) We high school graduates who were in the United States in the early 60's were

13. I will not object to him joining the fraternity if he is willing to accept its social and academic obligations, to pay his fees on time, and to play on house athletic teams.
    (A) I will not object to him joining the fraternity
    (B) I do not object to his joining the fraternity
    (C) I will make no objection to him joining the fraternity
    (D) I do not object to him joining the fraternity
    (E) I will not object to his joining the fraternity

14. After battling hypertension for years, Marvin Murphy was relieved by the results of his doctor's annual physical examination, which indicated his blood pressure was normal.
    (A) his doctor's annual physical examination, which
    (B) his annual physical examination by which it was
    (C) his annual physical examination, which
    (D) an annual physical examination by his doctor, which
    (E) his doctor's annual physical examination that

15. No matter what experience you have had with forest fires, if you would have witnessed the fire roaring down through the canyon, you would have been terrified.
    (A) if you would have witnessed
    (B) if you witnessed
    (C) if you could witness
    (D) if you had witnessed
    (E) when you witnessed

16. When the Republican Party was the minority party, <u>its ability to win a presidential election was determined by the number of Democratic and independent voters it attracts</u>.

   (A) its ability to win a presidential election was determined by the number of Democratic and independent voters it attracts

   (B) its ability to win a presidential election is determined by the number of Democratic and independent voters it attracts

   (C) its ability to win a presidential election has been determined by the number of Democratic and independent voters it attracts

   (D) the number of Democratic and independent voters it attracts determines its ability to win a presidential election

   (E) the number of Democratic and independent voters it attracted determined its ability to win a presidential election

17. The boundaries of the Pleasant Valley School District <u>have and will continue to include</u> the small cities of Millerton, Cedarville, Granite, and Homersfield.

   (A) have and will continue to include

   (B) have included and will continue to include

   (C) has included and will continue to include

   (D) has and will continue to include

   (E) include and will include

18. <u>Irregardless of her physical beauty</u>, the judges did not vote for her to represent their state in the Miss America Pageant, but chose the candidate with superior musical abilities.

   (A) Irregardless of her physical beauty

   (B) In spite of her physical beauty

   (C) While her physical beauty was superb

   (D) No matter how extraordinary her physical appearance

   (E) Regardless how beautiful her physical appearance

19. Contrary to the popularly held opinion, painting is a multifaceted, versatile, and a field in which a great deal of artistic diversity is possible.
    (A) multifaceted, versatile, and a field in which a great deal of artistic diversity is possible
    (B) field in which a lot of multifaceted, versatile artistry is possible
    (C) multifaceted field with versatility and diversity also possible
    (D) multifaceted, versatile, and artistically diversified field
    (E) field of multifaceted versatility and diversified artistry

20. One question haunted the swindled, penniless investor: What should his fortune have been if he had not been lured into that last, fateful investment?
    (A) What should his fortune have been if he had not been lured into that last, fateful investment
    (B) What will his fortune have been if he were not lured into that last, fateful investment
    (C) What would his fortune have been if he had not been lured into that last, fateful investment
    (D) What could his fortune have been had not he been lured into that last, fateful investment
    (E) What would his fortune be if he had only resisted the lure of that last fateful investment

21. The desert canyon, which in spring had appeared lush with scrub oak and blooming cacti, but grew brown and sere as the hot August winds continued.
    (A) canyon, which in spring had appeared lush with scrub oak and blooming cacti, but grew
    (B) canyon had appeared lush with scrub oak and blooming cacti and grew
    (C) canyon which in spring had appeared lush with scrub oak and blooming cacti grows
    (D) canyon in the spring appeared lush with scrub oak and blooming cacti, but has grown
    (E) canyon, which in spring had appeared lush with scrub oak and blooming cacti, grew

22. Arthur was sorry he had agreed to employ his cousin's law firm, because at first meeting with the lawyer, the lawyer seemed indecisive.
    (A) at first meeting with the lawyer, the lawyer seemed indecisive
    (B) at first meeting, the lawyer seemed indecisive
    (C) at first meeting the lawyer seems indecisive
    (D) at first meeting, he seemed an indecisive lawyer
    (E) at first meeting the lawyer, he seems indecisive

STOP. IF YOU FINISH BEFORE TIME IS CALLED, CHECK YOUR WORK ON THIS SECTION ONLY. DO NOT WORK ON ANY OTHER SECTION IN THE TEST.

SECTION VI: PROBLEM SOLVING

Time: 25 Minutes
16 Questions

DIRECTIONS

In this section solve each problem, using any available space on the page for scratchwork. Then indicate the *best* answer in the appropriate space on the answer sheet.

1. Dividing by $\frac{3}{8}$ and then multiplying by $\frac{5}{6}$ is the same as dividing by what number?
   (A) $3\frac{1}{5}$
   (B) $\frac{16}{5}$
   (C) $\frac{20}{9}$
   (D) $\frac{9}{20}$
   (E) $\frac{5}{16}$

2. How many different three-person committees can be formed from six people?
   (A)   2
   (B) 18
   (C) 20
   (D) 36
   (E) 108

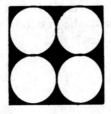

3. In the figure above, 4 equal circles are drawn within a square whose perimeter is 32. What is the area of the shaded region?
   (A) $32 - 16\pi$
   (B) $64 - 16\pi$
   (C) $64 - 32\pi$
   (D) $32\pi - 32$
   (E) $64\pi - 64$

4. Harriet planned to complete a certain task on Wednesday, January 1, but because of illness the completion date was postponed 48 days. On which day of the week in February was the task completed?
   (A) Monday
   (B) Tuesday
   (C) Wednesday
   (D) Thursday
   (E) Friday

5. Given positive integer y, which of the following CANNOT be evenly divisible by y?
   (A) $y + 1$
   (B) $y + 2$
   (C) $2y + 1$
   (D) $y - 1$
   (E) $y + \frac{1}{2}$

6. If the numerator of a fraction is tripled, and the denominator of a fraction is doubled, the resulting fraction will reflect an increase of what percent?

(A) $16\frac{1}{6}\%$
(B) 25%
(C) $33\frac{1}{3}\%$
(D) 50%
(E) $66\frac{2}{3}\%$

7. How many positive two-digit numbers, *ab*, are possible such that *ab* is divisible by 8 and the sum of *a* and *b* is divisible by 8?

(A) 0
(B) 1
(C) 2
(D) 3
(E) 4

8. A corporation triples its annual bonus to 50 of its employees. What percent of the employees' new bonus is the increase?

(A) 50%
(B) $66\frac{2}{3}\%$
(C) 100%
(D) 200%
(E) 300%

9. Felix earned 30% more per month than Oscar. If Felix's salary is decreased 10% and Oscar's salary is increased 10%, then Felix would be earning what percent more than Oscar?

(A) 10%
(B) 9.09%
(C) 7%
(D) 6.36%
(E) Cannot be determined

10. How much water must be added to 10 gallons of 10% brine solution to decrease the concentration to 7%?
    (A) 0–1.5 gal
    (B) 1.5–3 gal
    (C) 3–4.5 gal
    (D) 4.5–6 gal
    (E) 6+ gal

11. The smallest of three consecutive even integers is 40 less than three times the largest. What is the largest of these integers?
    (A) 14
    (B) 17
    (C) 18
    (D) 19
    (E) 20

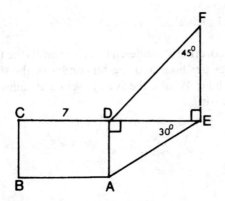

12. In the figure above, rectangle *ABCD* has perimeter 22; the length of *DC* is 7. What is the area of △*DEF*?
    (A) 12
    (B) $8\sqrt{3}$
    (C) 24
    (D) 32
    (E) 64

13. Dan can do a job alone in 15 hours. Fred, working alone, can do the same job in just 10 hours. If Dan works alone for 9 hours and then stops, how many hours will it take Fred, working alone, to complete the job?
    (A) 4
    (B) 5
    (C) 6
    (D) 12
    (E) 12.5

14. In a circle, a 10-inch chord is drawn at a distance of 12 inches from the center. What is the radius of the circle?
    (A) $2\sqrt{61}$ inches
    (B) 26 inches
    (C) $5\sqrt{3}$ inches
    (D) 13 inches
    (E) $2\sqrt{11}$ inches

15. On a trip covering 360 miles, a bicyclist travels the first 150 miles at 30 miles per hour and the remainder of the distance at 35 miles per hour. What is the average speed, in miles per hour, for the entire trip?
    (A) 28
    (B) 32½
    (C) 32⁸⁄₁₁
    (D) 46⁴⁄₁₁
    (E) 65

16. If $\dfrac{x^2 + 5x + 6}{x^2 - 4} = \dfrac{3}{2}$, then the value of x is

    (A) -12
    (B) $-2\frac{2}{5}$
    (C) -2
    (D) 2
    (E) 12

STOP. IF YOU FINISH BEFORE TIME IS CALLED, CHECK YOUR WORK ON THIS SECTION ONLY. DO NOT WORK ON ANY OTHER SECTION IN THE TEST.

SECTION VII: READING COMPREHENSION

Time: 25 Minutes
23 Questions

DIRECTIONS

Each passage in this group is followed by questions based on its content. After reading a passage, choose the best answer to each question and blacken the corresponding space on the answer sheet. Answer all questions following a passage on the basis of what is *stated* or *implied* in that passage. You may refer back to the passage.

If you make a marked increase in the amount of light falling upon the normal eye, you observe an immediate adjustment of the iris to reduce the size of the pupil. This is called an unconditioned response, and the increased light is called an unconditioned stimulus. Now, if you make numerous trials taking care to sound a buzzer whenever the light is increased, the iris can be "taught," that is to say, conditioned, to reduce the pupil at the sound of the buzzer alone. This learned response is called a conditioned response and the sound of the buzzer, a conditioned stimulus.

Now symbols are our most important conditioned stimuli, and successful communication depends upon complementary conditioning, or complementary experience. Just as we find ourselves shouting at listeners who do not speak our language, so by a similar irrational impulse we assume that those with whom we attempt to communicate are equipped with complementary sets of conditioned responses to our own common stock of symbols. It is easy to see the stupidity of expecting one who does not speak English to converse with you in English. It is not so easy to realize that one who does speak English may not have been conditioned to operate with the same set of senses for the familiar terms common to your vocabulary and his.

Let us consider a hypothetical pair of communicants, utterer and interpreter, from the operation point of view. We shall assume that our utterer has six hats: red, blue, yellow, black, gray, and white. If

378

the rods and cones (the tiny end organs packed together on what corresponds to the sensitive films in the stereoscopic or double-lens camera) of the retinae of his eyes are not defective, he will be able to see that the six hats differ even though they are of the same shape and material. If we reduce the light so that he can barely see, the white and the yellow will seem to be the same. But as the light grows stronger he will be able to see that the red, blue, and yellow affect him differently from black, gray, and white. He now has sufficient experience (remember, this is all grossly oversimplified) to conceive of color and shade. But he can also distinguish the red hat from the blue and yellow hats, the yellow from the blue and red, and so forth. He is thus ready for the concepts red, blue, and yellow if, for example, we provide him with a red feather, a blue feather, and a yellow feather. Indeed, he may have the human impulse to decorate the hat with the corresponding feather. And if the feathers seem to have more in common with the white hat than the other hats have in common with the white hat, he can see that his concept of shade will determine the difference between the two reds, the two blues, or the two yellows, and he will have need of the concepts of light and dark. And as we increase the number of shades he will require relation concepts like those expressed in the suffixes -er and -est. By repeating the conventional symbols "hat" and "red" with the red hat, he conditions the sound of the words to the sight of the hat. If he sees that the relation of each feather to its hat is similar to the other two, he has need of a relation concept like the one expressed by the preposition "in," and he is thus prepared to say to himself "light red feather in dark red hat." Now in the dark he is not able to tell one hat or one feather from another; but in the middle of a moonless night he is able to think "red feather in red hat" simply by uttering the appropriate symbols to himself. And with his human impulse to try new combinations, he can even think "yellow feather in blue hat" without ever having seen them thus combined.

1. The primary purpose of the passage is to
   (A) define an aspect of a topic
   (B) reconcile differing theories
   (C) propose a topic for investigation
   (D) solve a puzzle
   (E) analyze a phenomenon

2. Which of the following may be best described as an uncondi-
   tioned stimulus?
   (A) An unanswered telephone ringing in an empty office
   (B) A whistle that blows at five o'clock every week day
   (C) A shoelace that breaks in two
   (D) A match that burns the finger of a careless pipe smoker
   (E) An alarm clock that rings at midnight

3. Applying information from the passage, we may conclude that a
   child who begins feeling hungry as the school lunch bell rings
   each day may be exhibiting
   (A) an awareness of time
   (B) a complementary structure
   (C) a conditioned response
   (D) an unconditioned stimulus
   (E) a conditioned appetite

4. The passage suggests that a person who speaks English attempt-
   ing to communicate with a person who does not speak English is
   (A) bound to fail completely
   (B) still dependent upon complementary responses to com-
       mon symbols
   (C) likely to be more successful if he raises his voice
   (D) likely to be able to communicate where there are familiar
       words common to both speakers' vocabularies
   (E) subject to the limitations of third party translations

5. In the last paragraph of the passage, by discussing the different
   effects of reduced and increased light, the author is

   I. pointing to a limitation in the dependence of perception by
      sight
   II. preparing to discuss the concepts of light and dark
   III. laying the ground for the distinction between what can be
        seen and what can be thought

   (A) III only
   (B) I and II only
   (C) I and III only
   (D) II and III only
   (E) I, II, and III

6. Of the following, the most plausible criticism that could be directed at the "hats" example is that it is
    (A) too difficult to follow
    (B) irrelevant
    (C) too hypothetical
    (D) too dependent on the esoteric language
    (E) unreasonable

7. According to the passage, the acquisition of symbols allows us not only to communicate, but also to
    (A) argue logically
    (B) imagine
    (C) respond to unconditioned stimuli
    (D) respond to conditioned stimuli
    (E) decorate hats

8. The passage is most relevant to which of the following areas of study?
    (A) Aesthetics of logic
    (B) Literature and history
    (C) Sociology
    (D) Linguistics and psychology
    (E) Anthropology

Because sharks are such ancient life forms, for many years scientists considered them primitive. But a growing body of research on sharks and their relatives portrays these creatures as behaving in ways far more sophisticated and complex than was thought possible. Scientists are documenting elaborate social behaviors among these fish, including never-before-witnessed mating rituals that seem to be based on electrical signals.

Compared to other fishes, sharks have huge brains. Their brain-to-bodyweight ratio is more comparable to that found in birds and mammals than to other fishes. But because sharks are so difficult to study—they are dangerous, far-ranging, and usually inhabit murky waters—scientists only recently have accumulated enough data to even hint at their behavioral and sensory complexity. In one of the most surprising findings, a researcher discovered a new sense organ, located on top of certain sharks' heads. The organ is a sort of light-gathering "third eye," known in some prehistoric fishes, the lantern fishes, and at least one living reptile, the tuatara of New Zealand. Its precise function in the six-gilled shark is still uncertain, though sensing light at the deep depths to which they dive is most likely.

Sharks are literally covered in sense organs. Over the last two decades, researchers have found chemical receptor cells embedded inside sharks' teeth, in their throats, around the heads, and in pore-like openings on the skin. With no fewer than four separate sensory systems to detect chemicals in the water, sharks are able to detect amino acids in concentrations as low as one part per billion. Past researchers have documented that sharks also have good vision and can see in color; they have directional hearing, and although they cannot hear notes much above middle C, they can hear sounds below the threshold of human hearing.

But perhaps the most astounding sense possessed by sharks is their ability to sense electric fields. Sharks, skates, and rays—a group of closely related fishes collectively known as elasmobranchs— can detect fields so weak they cannot be measured by standard laboratory equipment. All live organisms, immersed in water, have a weak bioelectric field, a current generated between biological membranes and the surrounding water. Elasmobranch fishes use electroreception to locate prey. Some scientists suspect that sharks, skates, and rays, sensing and interpreting the much larger voltage potentials created by salt-water currents moving through the earth's magnetic field, use this information to navigate.

Now it appears that electroreception may also play a key role in the mating system of sharks and the one thousand other fishes in the same taxonomic group. The females use electroreception for some sort of social cues. Receptive females may be advertising their availability by congregating in large, highly visible, unburied piles; but unreceptive females, perhaps already pregnant, may use electro-reception to locate other buried females to hide from amorous males in buried aggregation. Sharks and rays might purposely vary the information content of their electric fields to send different messages to one another. Field strength intensifies when the fishes open their mouths. Literally, "heavy breathing" could enhance a female's attraction.

9. The author refers to the shark's reputation as a primitive animal in order to
   (A) stress the evolutionary progress of the modern shark
   (B) question this opinion in the light of modern research
   (C) support an argument for the increased funding of scientific study of the shark
   (D) introduce the thesis of the passage
   (E) indirectly support the conclusion of earlier shark researchers

10. The complexity of the shark has been underestimated for which of the following reasons?

    I. Sharks are a very ancient life form.
    II. Sharks are dangerous.
    III. Sharks rarely live in clear waters.

    (A) II only
    (B) I and II only
    (C) I and III only
    (D) II and III only
    (E) I, II, and III

11. The passage compares the shark to all of the following EXCEPT
    (A) skates
    (B) a reptile
    (C) birds
    (D) rays
    (E) a dolphin

12. The passage implies that, compared to other fishes, sharks are more
    (A) voracious
    (B) prolific
    (C) sensitive to sound
    (D) intelligent
    (E) able to endure lower depths

13. It can be inferred from the passage that female sharks hiding in groups from male sharks
   (A) could not be found if they were buried in the sand
   (B) could be discovered by a male shark using his "third eye"
   (C) would emit no bioelectrical signals
   (D) would be easier to detect by electroreception than a female shark hiding alone
   (E) would open their mouths as often as possible

14. According to the passage, sharks may use their electroreceptive ability for all of the following EXCEPT to
   (A) locate prey
   (B) navigate
   (C) gather light
   (D) locate other sharks
   (E) locate breeding partners

15. Which of the following is most relevant to the research described in the passage?
   (A) Certain birds communicate by emitting cries pitched two octaves above middle C.
   (B) Certain migrating birds determine their location by detecting variations in the strength of the earth's magnetic field.
   (C) Migrating herds of wildebeest can reach their destination in spite of major changes in a landscape from one year to the next.
   (D) Some migrating birds and insects appear to arrive at the same place on exactly the same day year after year.
   (E) Dogs are capable of hearing sounds at pitches inaudible to human ears.

16. The author of the passage employs all of the following EXCEPT
   (A) personal opinion
   (B) questioning prior opinion
   (C) generalization
   (D) double meaning
   (E) comparison

Economic growth involves both benefits and costs. The desirability of increasing production has frequently been challenged in recent years, and some have even maintained that economic growth is merely a quantitative enlargement that has no human meaning or value. However, economic growth is an increase in the capacity to produce goods and services that people want. Since the product of economic growth can be measured by its value to someone, it is important to ask whose standard of valuation counts.

In the United States, the value of a product is what purchasers pay for it. This is determined by the purchasers' preferences combined with conditions of supply, which in turn reflect various other factors, such as natural and technological circumstances at any given time and the preferences of those who supply capital and labor. The value by which we measure a product synthesizes all these factors. Gross National Product (GNP) is the market value of the nation's total output of goods and services.

Gross National Product is not a perfect measure of all the activities involved in economic output. It does not account for deteriorations or improvements in the environment, even when they are incidental results of the production process. On the other hand, it does not count as "product" many benefits provided as side effects of the economic process; it does not include productive but unpaid work (such as that done by a housewife); and it does not reckon with such other factors as the burdensomeness of work, the length of the work week, and so forth.

Nonetheless, the GNP concept makes an important contribution to our understanding of how the economy is working. While it is not a complete measure of economic productivity and even less so of "welfare," the level and rate of increase of the GNP are clearly and positively associated with what most people throughout the world see as an improvement in the quality of life.

Although there has been much soul-searching about the role of increasing material affluence in the good life, it seems quite certain that most Americans prefer a rapidly growing GNP and its consequences. This does not mean that growth of the GNP is an absolute that must be furthered at all costs. Growth of the GNP has its costs, and beyond a certain point they are not worth paying. Moreover, people want things that are not measured in the GNP. Still, while human values and conditions of life change, and might conceivably make the social cost of a rising GNP seem too high, it is likely that we would still be concerned about the growth of our nation's GNP.

In any case, since there is little evidence of a decline in the value assigned to economic output as a whole, the factors that influence our capacity to produce remain of great importance. In the long run, the same factors result in a growing GNP and in other social benefits: size and competence of population, state of knowledge, amount of capital, and the effectiveness with which these are combined and utilized.

17. The main purpose of the passage is to
    (A) define the limitations of using GNP to measure the nation's well-being
    (B) contrast the American and the European GNPs
    (C) argue for the value of increased economic output
    (D) explain the disadvantages of measuring the quality of life using a scale of material affluence
    (E) define Gross National Product

18. Those who decide the value of a product are
    (A) the GNP
    (B) economic theorists
    (C) its advertisers
    (D) its patent holders
    (E) its purchasers

19. The rhetorical purpose of the third paragraph of the passage is to

    I. anticipate objections to what the GNP fails to take into account
    II. cite examples of "products" the GNP ought to include
    III. develop the definition of paragraph two with specific details

    (A) I only
    (B) II only
    (C) III only
    (D) I and II only
    (E) I, II, and III

20. We can infer from the passage that of the following, the factor that does not influence the growth of the GNP is
    (A) the condition of the population
    (B) a dependence on spiritual values
    (C) the capital available in the country
    (D) knowledge related to production of goods and services
    (E) the efficiency of the production process

21. A critic of the limitations of the measurements of the GNP might cite its failure to consider all of the following EXCEPT
    (A) the steady increase in American workers' leisure time
    (B) cooperative baby-sitting projects among parents with young children
    (C) the widespread existence of chemicals in American rivers
    (D) the value of the time a salaried stock broker spends on research
    (E) the valuation of family household management

22. As it is used in the fourth paragraph of the passage, the word "welfare" can be best defined as
    (A) a measure of economic productivity
    (B) the quality of life of the public as a whole
    (C) government-supported payments to the indigent
    (D) public payments for unpaid production work such as child care
    (E) state-supported income supplements

23. We might assume that the author favors the continuing growth of the GNP because
    (A) although he mentions that the GNP has its costs, he does not examine those costs carefully
    (B) it does not include such factors as the burdensomeness of work
    (C) he wishes to represent a minority opinion
    (D) he does not believe in perfect measures of economic growth
    (E) he believes that human values and the conditions of life are subject to change

STOP. IF YOU FINISH BEFORE TIME IS CALLED, CHECK YOUR WORK ON THIS SECTION ONLY. DO NOT WORK ON ANY OTHER SECTION IN THE TEST.

SECTION VIII: PROBLEM SOLVING

Time: 25 Minutes
16 Questions

DIRECTIONS

In this section solve each problem, using any available space on the page for scratchwork. Then indicate the *best* answer in the appropriate space on the answer sheet.

1. $\dfrac{\dfrac{7}{10} \times 14 \times 5 \times \dfrac{1}{28}}{\dfrac{10}{17} \times \dfrac{3}{5} \times \dfrac{1}{6} \times 17} =$

    (A) $\dfrac{4}{7}$

    (B) 1

    (C) $\dfrac{7}{4}$

    (D) 2

    (E) $\dfrac{17}{4}$

2. N is a positive integer. When $N + 1$ is divided by 5, the remainder is 4. What is the remainder when N is divided by 5?
    (A) 6
    (B) 5
    (C) 4
    (D) 3
    (E) 2

3. Mary spent ⅖ of her money on new clothes and then deposited ½ of what remained into her savings account. If she then had $21 left, how much did she have at the start?
   - (A) $30
   - (B) $35
   - (C) $70
   - (D) $105
   - (E) $210

Station-to-Station and Credit Card	Person-to-Person	Each Additional Minute		
first three minutes	first three minutes	8:00 A.M. to 5:00 P.M. Mon.–Fri.	5:00 P.M. to 11:00 P.M. Mon.–Sat.	11:00 P.M. to 8:00 A.M. Sun.–Fri.
$2.75	$4.35	$0.46	$0.30	$0.19

4. Listed above are the rates for operator-assisted telephone calls from San Diego to New York City. On a Friday at 4:17 P.M., Mr. Talbot made a person-to-person phone call from San Diego to New York City. When he received his monthly phone bill, Mr. Talbot noted that this call cost $14.09. To the nearest minute, how long did this call last?
   - (A) 23
   - (B) 24
   - (C) 25
   - (D) 26
   - (E) 27

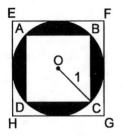

5. Square *ABCD* is inscribed in circle *O*, which is inscribed in larger square *EFGH*, as shown in the diagram above. If the radius of circle *O* is 1, then the shaded area is approximately what percent of the area of square *EFGH*?
   (A) 3%
   (B) 4%
   (C) 25%
   (D) 50%
   (E) 75%

6. A salesman receives a salary of $150 per week and earns a commission of 15% on all sales he makes. How many dollars worth of sales does he need to make in order to bring his total weekly income to $600?
   (A) $3000
   (B) $3150
   (C) $4000
   (D) $4150
   (E) $5000

7. If $(x + 1)$ times $(2x + 1)$ is an odd integer, then x must be
   (A) an odd integer
   (B) an even integer
   (C) a prime number
   (D) a composite number
   (E) a negative integer

8. $6x - 12 = -6y$
   $5y + 5x = 15$

   Which of the following is the number of solutions to the system of equations shown above?
   (A) More than three
   (B) Exactly three
   (C) Exactly two
   (D) Exactly one
   (E) None

9. Forty percent of the employees of Company A are females, and 60% of Company B are females. If 30 female employees move from Company B to Company A, make the percent of female employees between the two companies equal, and if the total number of employees in each company are equal, how many total male employees are there in Companies A and B together?
   (A) 400
   (B) 300
   (C) 200
   (D) 100
   (E) 50

18. If $x^2 + y^2 = 14$ and $xy = 3$, then $(x - y)^2 =$
   (A) 8
   (B) 11
   (C) 14
   (D) 17
   (E) 20

11. If @ is a binary operation defined as the difference between an integer n and the product of n and 5, then what is the largest positive integer n such that the outcome of the binary operation @ of n is less than 10?
   (A) 1
   (B) 2
   (C) 3
   (D) 4
   (E) 5

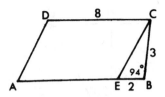

12. The area of parallelogram *AECD*
    (A) is greater than 24 square units
    (B) is less than 24 square units
    (C) is equal to 24 square units
    (D) is equal to 40 square units
    (E) cannot be determined from the information given

13. Gasoline varies in cost from $0.96 to $1.12 per gallon. If a car's mileage varies from 16 to 24 miles per gallon, what is the difference between the most and least that the gasoline for a 480-mile trip will cost?
    (A) $5.12
    (B) $7.04
    (C) $11.52
    (D) $14.40
    (E) $52.80

14. A prize of $600 is to be distributed among 20 winners, each of whom must be awarded at least $20. If ⅖ of the prize will be distributed to ⅗ of the winners, what is the greatest possible individual reward?
    (A) $20
    (B) $25
    (C) $200
    (D) $220
    (E) $300

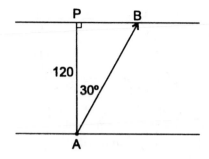

15. A boat leaves point *A* heading directly across the river to point *P*, 120 yards away. A swift current immediately changes the boat's direction, causing it to land instead at point *B*. How many yards is point *B* from the intended destination, *P*?

    (A) 40
    (B) 45
    (C) 60
    (D) $40\sqrt{3}$
    (E) $60\sqrt{3}$

16. In 1991, the Johnsons spent $800 on the family's water bills. Anticipating that water rates would increase in 1992 by 50%, the Johnsons cut back their water usage. By how much must the Johnsons have reduced their 1992 water usage to pay exactly the same amount in 1992 as they paid in 1991?

    (A)   33⅓%
    (B)   40%
    (C)   50%
    (D)   66⅔%
    (E) 100%

STOP. IF YOU FINISH BEFORE TIME IS CALLED, CHECK YOUR WORK ON THIS SECTION ONLY. DO NOT WORK ON ANY OTHER SECTION IN THE TEST.

ANSWER KEY FOR PRACTICE TEST 3
MULTIPLE-CHOICE SECTIONS

Section II Critical Reasoning	Section III Problem Solving	Section IV Data Sufficiency	Section V Sentence Correction
1. E	1. B	1. C	1. E
2. B	2. B	2. D	2. E
3. B	3. B	3. A	3. B
4. E	4. D	4. B	4. D
5. B	5. D	5. E	5. B
6. E	6. E	6. A	6. A
7. E	7. E	7. D	7. C
8. D	8. D	8. C	8. A
9. D	9. D	9. E	9. B
10. B	10. B	10. A	10. C
11. C	11. A	11. E	11. E
12. D	12. D	12. A	12. A
13. E	13. C	13. E	13. E
14. E	14. D	14. E	14. D
15. C	15. C	15. E	15. D
16. D	16. C	16. C	16. E
		17. B	17. B
		18. B	18. B
		19. B	19. D
		20. B	20. C
			21. E
			22. B

Section VI Problem Solving	Section VII Reading Comprehension	Section VIII Problem Solving
1. D	1. A	1. C
2. C	2. D	2. D
3. B	3. C	3. C
4. B	4. B	4. B
5. E	5. C	5. C
6. D	6. C	6. A
7. C	7. B	7. B
8. B	8. D	8. E
9. D	9. B	9. B
10. C	10. D	10. A
11. C	11. E	11. B
12. C	12. D	12. B
13. A	13. D	13. D
14. D	14. C	14. D
15. C	15. B	15. D
16. E	16. A	16. A
	17. E	
	18. E	
	19. A	
	20. B	
	21. D	
	22. B	
	23. A	

HOW TO SCORE YOUR ESSAYS

Have someone knowledgeable in the writing process evaluate your essays using the following checklist and grading scale. Remember, because the essays must be written in a limited time period, minor errors of grammar or mechanics will not affect your scores.

Analysis of an Issue	Yes, completely	Yes, partially	No
1. Does the essay focus on the assigned topic and cover all of the tasks?			
2. Does the essay show an understanding of the complexity of the issue?			
3. Does the essay show cogent reasoning and logical position development?			
4. Are there sufficient relevant persuasive supporting details?			
5. Is the essay well organized?			
6. Does the essay show a command of standard written English?			

Analysis of an Argument

	Yes, completely	Yes, partially	No
1. Does the essay focus on the assigned topic and cover all of the tasks?			
2. Does the essay carefully analyze the important features of the argument?			
3. Does the essay show cogent reasoning and logical development?			
4. Are there sufficient relevant supporting details of the critique?			
5. Is the essay well organized?			
6. Does the essay show a command of standard written English?			

HOW TO SCORE YOUR MULTIPLE-CHOICE QUESTIONS

1. Add the total number of correct responses for each section.
2. Add the total number of incorrect responses (only those attempted or marked in) for each section.
3. The total number of incorrect responses should be divided by 4, giving the adjustment factor.
4. Subtract this adjustment factor from the total number of correct responses to obtain a corrected raw score.
5. This score is then scaled from 200 to 800.

Example:

A. If the total number of correct answers was 80 out of a possible 113.
B. And 24 problems were attempted but missed.
C. Dividing the 24 by 4 gives an adjustment factor of 6.
D. Subtracting this adjustment factor of 6 from the original 80 correct gives a corrected raw score of 74.
E. This corrected raw score is then scaled to a range of 200 to 800.

SCORE RANGE APPROXIMATORS

The following chart is designed to give you an approximate score range only, not an exact score. When you take the GMAT, you will have questions that are similar to those in this book; however, some questions may be slightly easier or more difficult. Needless to say, this may affect your scoring range.

Because one section of the GMAT is experimental (it doesn't count toward your score), for the purposes of this approximation, do not count Section VIII. Remember, on the actual test the experimental section could appear anywhere on your test.

Corrected Raw Score	Approximate Score Range
97–113	700–800
81–96	610–690
64–80	530–600
48–63	440–520
30–47	350–430
14–29	260–340
0–13	200–250

Keep in mind that this is just an approximate score range. An average score on the GMAT is approximately 480.

ANALYZING YOUR TEST RESULTS

The charts on the following pages should be used to carefully analyze your results and spot your strengths and weaknesses. The complete process of evaluating your essays and analyzing individual problems in each subject area should be completed for each Practice Test. These results should then be reexamined for trends in types of errors (repeated errors) or poor results in specific subject areas. THIS REEXAMINATION AND ANALYSIS IS OF TREMENDOUS IMPORTANCE IN HELPING YOU MAXIMIZE YOUR SCORE.

ANALYSIS SHEET FOR
MULTIPLE-CHOICE SECTIONS

	Possible	Completed	Right	Wrong
Section II: Critical Reasoning	16			
Section III: Problem Solving	16			
Section IV: Data Sufficiency	20			
Section V: Sentence Correction	22			
Section VI: Problem Solving	16			
Section VII: Reading Comprehension	23			
Section VIII: Problem Solving	16			
OVERALL TOTALS	129			

WHY??????????????????????????????

ANALYSIS SHEET FOR
MULTIPLE-CHOICE PROBLEMS MISSED

One of the most important parts of test preparation is analyzing WHY! you missed a problem so that you can reduce the number of mistakes. Now that you have taken the practice test and corrected your answers, carefully tally your mistakes by marking them in the proper column.

REASON FOR MISTAKE

	Total Missed	Simple Mistake	Misread Problem	Lack of Knowl- edge
Section II: Critical Reasoning				
Section III: Problem Solving				
Section IV: Data Sufficiency				
Section V: Sentence Correction				
Section VI: Problem Solving				
Section VII: Reading Comprehension				
Section VIII: Problem Solving				
OVERALL TOTALS				

Reviewing the above data should help you determine WHY you are missing certain problems. Now that you have pinpointed the type of error, take the next practice test focusing on avoiding your most common type.

COMPLETE ANSWERS AND EXPLANATIONS FOR
PRACTICE TEST 3
MULTIPLE-CHOICE SECTIONS

SECTION II: CRITICAL REASONING

1. (E) This choice raises the question relevant to establishing the mural as art in Aristotelian terms.

2. (B) The first speaker puts forth a "perfect" view of friendship (idealistic), and the second questions the endurance of friendship (cynicism).

3. (B) The conclusion that highway deaths will be reduced with the advent of automatic restraints is necessarily based upon the assumption that such restraints reduce highway deaths. None of the other choices focuses on the conclusion; (E) is an assumption which could motivate the passage as a whole, rather than just the conclusion.

4. (E) Choices (C) and (D) do not address the comparison between journalists and bank employees; and (A) and (B) use the comparison in statements irrelevant to the points in the passage. (E) criticizes the term that links bad journalists with bad bank employees—embezzlement—by pointing out that bank embezzlement does not so directly affect the customers of a bank in the same way as biased or false journalism affects the customers (readers) of a newspaper.

5. (B) This suggests that exterior forces, such as advertising, influence consumer choices and undercuts the contention that consumers know what they want. Each of the other choices is either irrelevant or strengthens rather than weakens the argument.

6. (E) Choices (A), (C), and (D) are irrelevant to the argument, and (B) actually strengthens the argument. (E) suggests that the evidence from one year cannot reliably predict a long-term trend.

7. (E) This is implied in the final sentence. Each of the other choices requires assumptions or beliefs extraneous to the passage.

8. (D) I and III. Neither consumers nor legal loopholes are mentioned in the statement.

9. (D) Making *only* the first word of sentence 1 does not solve all of the logical problems in the passage, but it does strengthen the passage by indicating that customers with green necklaces must have bought them from the competition.

10. (B) The author does not realize that customers not wearing green necklaces may have bought other items from the competition.

11. (C) The passage establishes that the survivors were caught in a life and death "survival" situation. While (B) may be a possible choice, answer (C) logically follows the sense of their dilemma, clouded by uncertainty and the possibility of death.

12. (D) The letter fails to note that the decision concerns *officers,* and Smith and Krunkle have been merely nominated to be officers and are not yet such. The other choices are either not stated in the letter or are not essential to the argument.

13. (E) Answers (B), (C), and (D) are only partial descriptions and, although may be correct, are not as complete a description of possible future action as answer (E). Nothing in the letter would imply the action stated in (A).

14. (E) Flamo Lighters claim to be convenient ("in your pocket wherever you go"), have longevity ("ten-year guarantee"), winter-proof ("all-weather"), and dependable ("always reliable, always dependable"). They do not profess to be all-purpose, however.

15. (C) All race-car lovers enjoy classical music. Since there are no backgammon players who enjoy classical music, then none of the backgammon players are race-car lovers. (D) is false because statement 3 does not necessarily exclude those who don't enjoy classical music from enjoying fine wine.

16. (D) Only this choice both represents a *strong* point *and* is not contradictory. (A), (C), and (E) contradict the argument, and (B) is not a relatively strong point.

SECTION III: PROBLEM SOLVING

1. (B) First, note that ¼ of ⅗ = ³⁄₂₀. We then have: ³⁄₂₀ is what percent of ¾?

$$\frac{\text{is number}}{\text{of number}} = \frac{\text{percent}}{100}$$

$$\frac{3/20}{3/4} = \frac{P}{100}$$

Cross multiplying gives

$$\frac{3}{4}P = \frac{3}{\cancel{20}_1}(\cancel{100}^5)$$

$$\frac{3}{4}P = 15$$

$$P = \frac{4}{\cancel{3}_1}(\cancel{15}^5)$$

$$P = 20$$

Thus, (B) 20% is the correct answer.

2. (B) Percent change is found by using the formula

$$\text{percent decrease or increase} = \frac{\text{change}}{\text{starting point}}$$

The change was $75 - 60 = 15$. (Notice that rounding off is possible.) The starting point was 75. Thus, ¹⁵⁄₇₅ = ⅕ = 20%.

3. (B) In $\triangle ABD$, the sum of $\angle A$, $\angle B$, and $\angle BDA$ is $180°$. If $\angle B = 90°$ and $\angle BDA = 50°$, then $\angle A = 40°$. Since $\angle A = x° + 15°$, we have

$$40° = x° + 15°$$

$$25° = x°$$

Therefore $\qquad x = 25$

4. (D) Let us examine each choice.

(A): $(x + 3)(x + 5)$ Since x is even, both $x + 3$ and $x + 5$ are odd; then (odd)(odd) = odd.

(B): $x^2 + 5$ Since x is even, x^2 is even, and $x^2 + 5$ is odd.

(C): $x^2 + 6x + 9$ Since x is even, x^2 is even and $6x$ is even; then (even) + (even) + (odd) = odd.

(D): $3x^2 + 4$ Since x is even, $3x^2$ is even; then (even) + (even) = *even*.

(E): $5(x + 3)$ Since x is even, $x + 3$ is odd; then (odd)(odd) = odd.

5. (D) Let $85\%L$ represent a 15% decrease in length. Then $140\%W$ represents a 40% increase in width. The new rectangle will have

$$\text{area} = (\text{new length})(\text{new width})$$

$$= (85\%L)(140\%W)$$

$$= \frac{\overset{17}{\cancel{85}}}{\underset{20}{\cancel{100}}} L \cdot \frac{\overset{7}{\cancel{140}}}{\underset{5}{\cancel{100}}} W$$

$$= \frac{119}{100} LW$$

$$= 119\%LW$$

The old rectangle has area $100\%LW$. Thus, the new rectangle has area *19% greater* than the original 100%.

6. **(E)** The circumference of the large circle is 64π.

$$\text{Since circumference} = 2\pi r$$

$$64\pi = 2\pi r$$

$$32 = r$$

Radius of large circle = 32

Diameter of 2 small circles = 32
So diameter of 1 small circle = 16
Radius of small circle = 8

$$\text{Area of small circle} = \pi r^2$$

$$= \pi \times 8^2$$

$$= 64\pi$$

So area of 4 small circles = 4 × (area of 1 small circle)

$$= 4(64\pi)$$

$$= 256\pi$$

7. **(E)** First simplify 3^3, which is $3 \times 3 \times 3 = 27$. Then simplify $(\frac{1}{3})^2$, which is $\frac{1}{3} \times \frac{1}{3} = \frac{1}{9}$. Now divide 27 by $\frac{1}{9}$, which is the same as $27 \times \frac{9}{1} = 243$.

8. **(D)** If one root of the equation is 10, then the factored form of $x^2 - 5x + m = 0$ is $(x - 10)(x + ?) = 0$. Since the middle term of the quadratic is $-5x$, then ? must be 5. So the factored version is $(x - 10)(x + 5)$. To check this, multiply the means and extremes together and add them.

$$+5x$$
$$-10x$$
$$(x - 10)(x + 5)$$

Therefore, m would have the value of -10×5, or -50. But the problem asks for $m + 3$, which is $-50 + 3$ or -47.

9. (D) Simplify the problem as follows:

$$\sqrt{72x^5} = \sqrt{36 \cdot 2 \cdot x^4 \cdot x}$$

Since the $\sqrt{36}$ is 6, and $\sqrt{x^4}$ is x^2, then

$$\sqrt{36 \cdot 2 \cdot x^4 \cdot x} = 6x^2\sqrt{2x}$$

You could also have worked from the answers.

10. (B) Begin by using an arbitrary number, say 100, for the total number of students in the class. Therefore, there are 40 boys and 60 girls. Of the 60 girls, 30%, or 18, are science majors. Since non-science majors comprise 80% of the class, then there are 80 non-science majors and 20 science majors. We already know that 18 science majors are girls, so the remaining 2 science majors must be boys. Among the 40 boys there are 2 science majors, so 5% of the boys are science majors.

11. (A) The two-digit numbers whose remainder is 1 when divided by 10 are: 11, 21, 31, 41, 51, 61, 71, 81, and 91. When divided by 6, the remainder is 5 for the numbers 11, 41, and 71. Therefore, 3 numbers satisfy the conditions of the problem.

12. (D) Note that choices (B) and (E) are approximately equal to $3/(3)^2$ or $1/3$. For the remaining choices, the fraction closest to 1 will be the fraction whose denominator has the *least* value added to 3. Choice (D) has the smallest value, 0.0009, added to 3. Note: $(0.03)^2 = 0.0009$.

13. (C) A 6% annual interest rate, compounded semiannually (every half year) is the same as a 3% semiannual interest rate. At the end of first half of year: Interest on $2000 at 3% = $2000 × 0.03 = $60. New balance at end of first half year = $2000 + $60 = $2060. At the end of first full year: Interest on $2060 at 3% = $2060 × 0.03 = $61.80 ≅ $62. New balance at end of first full year = $2060 + $62 = $2122.

14. **(D)** Since arc *AC* is 120°, then arc *AE* equals 60°. Therefore, $\angle AOE$ is 60° and $\triangle AOD$ is a 30°-60°-90° triangle and its sides are in the proportion 1-$\sqrt{3}$-2. Since *AO* is 2, *AD* equals $\sqrt{3}$, and *OD* is 1. So the base of $\triangle ABC$ is $2\sqrt{3}$, and its height is $1 + 2 = 3$. So the area of *ABC* $= \frac{1}{2}bh = \frac{1}{2}(2\sqrt{3})(3) = 3\sqrt{3}$.

15. **(C)** There was an increase from 18% to 22%. That is a 4% increase. Therefore a 4% increase from 18% is a 22% increase in the percent spent on food and drink.

16. **(C)** The positive odd integers *a*, *b*, and *c* could be 1, 3, and 5. Option I is not necessarily true: $1 + 3$ is not greater than 5. Option II is not necessarily true: 1×3 is not greater than 5. Only option III must be true: the square of the sum of any two integers will be greater than the third integer.

SECTION IV: DATA SUFFICIENCY

1. (C) If the box is cubical, then each side is square. An edge of the box would be the square root of the side, or 4 inches. The volume equals the edge cubed, or 64 cubic inches.

2. (D) No, x is not prime. From the first statement we know that x is even, or divisible by two. From the second statement we deduce that $x = y + 3y = 4y$, so 4 is a factor of x.

3. (A) Distance equals rate times time. Statement (1) tells us the rate and time. Multiplying 550 by 3¼ yields a distance of 1788 miles.

4. (B) Since $\overline{AO}$ is perpendicular to $\overline{OB}$, AOB is a right angle.

5. (E) The first statement implies that a tock equals 30 minutes, but the duration of a tick is indefinite.

6. (A) The shaded part equals the area of the large circle minus the areas of the two small circles. For any circle, $A = \pi r^2$ and we can ascertain the radii of the circles from statement (1) alone. The small circles are of equal size, with radii of 2½. Because the small circles are equal, their diameter is the radius of the large circle. Shaded area $= 25\pi - 2(25/4)\pi = (25/2)\pi$.

7. (D) To solve the first expression, we add 5 to both sides and divide by 4. The second expression is solved by collecting terms on the left, $m^2 - 6m + 9 = 0$, and factoring, $(m - 3)^2 = 0$. From either expression, $m = 3$.

8. (C) The radiator requires 60% antifreeze in its 3 gallons, or 1.8 gallons antifreeze.

9. (E) The first statement reveals only that c and a have the same sign. From the initial proportion and the second statement, $ac = b^2 = 32$, but the sign of c is indeterminate.

413

10. (A) Because the average is the sum divided by 5, the sum must be the average times 5. Therefore the sum is zero.

11. (E) No relationship can be determined between x and y, since the two equations are the same. (Multiply the second equation by 4.)

12. (A) The product of the factors is 105. N must be an integer that is an odd multiple of 105. The very mention of factors in (1) implies that N is an integer.

13. (E) Combining both statements, all we know is that the line passes through the point $(5, -3)$, and the orientation is unspecified.

14. (E) We have no information concerning the number of patients who stayed more than one day and were seen by only one doctor.

15. (E) No exact dollar amounts are given for the individual bills. Had the Dufaas paid ½ of each of the bills, 50% would be the answer, but since they paid different fractional amounts of some of the bills, with each bill potentially a different dollar amount, the percent paid of the total amount can differ, depending upon the relative amounts of the different bills. (For example, if the Dufaas' annual trash bill was significantly larger than the other bills, the total percent paid on all the bills would be closer to 75% than 25%).

16. (C) In the trapezoid, $\overline{BC}$ is evidently parallel to $\overline{AD}$. The first statement reveals that triangle ACD is a 6-8-10 right triangle, with angle $ADC = 90°$. Because $\overline{BC}$ is parallel to $\overline{AD}$, angle BCD must also equal 90°. Consider triangle ABC with base $\overline{BC}$. The altitude to vertex A equals $\overline{CD}$, because $\overline{CD}$ is perpendicular to $\overline{BC}$. Then the area $= \frac{1}{2}bh = \frac{1}{2}(\overline{BC})(\overline{CD}) = \frac{1}{2} \times 7 \times 6 = 21$.

17. (B) Statement (2) is sufficient. Since 84 payments of $1124 each are still to be paid, simply multiply 84 times 1124 to find the principal and interest still owed.

18. (B) From statement (2), let x equal the number of adults and $3x$ equal the number of children.

$$3x + x = 24$$

$$4x = 24$$

$$x = 6 = \text{number of adults needed}$$

Statement (1) gives a ratio between boys and girls, but no exact numbers can be determined, so the number of adults cannot be determined.

19. (B) The first statement translates to the equation $A + 1 = \frac{1}{2}(M + 1)$ which has two unknowns and cannot be solved for A. But the second statement means $A + 5 = 2(A - 10)$ and we can solve for Anne's age, 25 years.

20. (B) Since a total of 80% received A's, B's, C's, and D's, then 20% received F's. 20% of 40 (the total given in statement 2) = 8 students. The first statement does not help because we don't know how many students received A's.

SECTION V: SENTENCE CORRECTION

1. (E) Choice (E) best simplifies the awkward wording of the original sentence. Choices (C) and (D) change the meaning slightly by eliminating the notion of *consider,* and choice (B) is not idiomatic.

2. (E) Choice (E) best expresses the parallel form called for in this sentence (*neglect, housecleaning, lack*—all nouns). The other choices contain the same "unparallel" structure of the original wording.

3. (B) Choice (B) contains the correct verb form *are* for the *neither . . . nor* construction. The verb in this case should be plural to match *friends,* which is the closer of the two subjects to the verb. Choice (D) correctly uses *are* but changes the meaning of the original.

4. (D) Choice (D) correctly states the comparison by adding *those.* The alternative wordings do not clearly express the comparison. Choice (B) is wordy and imprecise, and (C) changes the meaning of the original sentence.

5. (B) Choice (B) corrects the verb agreement problem in the original wording. The verbs must both be past tense or both be present tense. No other choice uses proper tense without introducing a subject-verb agreement error.

6. (A) The original is better than any of the alternatives. All other choices are less direct, create ambiguities, or change the meaning of the original.

7. (C) Choice (C) clarifies the ambiguous wording of the original sentence. It is clear in (C) who is arriving and who is doing the meeting.

8. (A) The original wording is the best expression of this idea. Choice (E) changes the meaning slightly. The other choices are either stylistically awkward or ungrammatical.

9. (B) Choice (B) correctly supplies the plural *know,* which agrees with *ecologists.* The subject closest to the verb determines the number of the verb in this case. Choice (B) also retains the necessary *neither . . . nor.*

10. (C) Choice (C) best corrects the awkward wording in the original sentence. Choice (D), although grammatically correct, changes the meaning of the original.

11. (E) Choice (E) corrects the "disjointed" wording of the original sentence.

12. (A) Of the choices given, the original is the best phrasing. The commas in choice (B) change the meaning of the original by making the phrase nonrestrictive. In (C), *graduated high school* is not acceptable standard written English. Choice (D) is awkward and (E) changes the meaning of the sentence.

13. (E) Choice (E) correctly states *his joining.* The possessive *his* is called for here before the *-ing* verb form *joining.* Choice (D), while grammatically correct, slightly alters the meaning of the original sentence.

14. (D) Choice (D) clarifies whose physical examination is in question—Marvin's or the doctor's. Choice (C) is straightforward and concise, also leaving no doubt as to whose examination it is; however, the *doctor* is not mentioned, and because one cannot assume that all physical examinations are administered by a doctor, this information must be included.

15. (D) Choice (D) supplies the correct verb form *had witnessed* called for by the original sentence.

16. (E) Choice (E) is the most direct, concise wording of the original sentence. The verbs in these answer choices are the problem areas. Choice (B), for example, is incorrect because of the present tense *is* and *attracts.*

17. (B) Choice (B) corrects the verb problem in the original sentence. *Have and will continue to include* is better expressed as *have included and will continue to include.*

18. (B) Choice (B) eliminates the *irregardless* of the original wording. *Irregardless* is incorrect in standard written English. Choices (C) and (D) change the original meaning slightly and are therefore wrong. Choice (E) is not idiomatic.

19. (D) Choice (D) provides the parallel structure needed in this sentence for the three ideas stated in a series. The other choices are structurally wrong or alter the original meaning.

20. (C) Choice (C) supplies the correct verb for this sentence, *would.* The other choices either introduce additional errors or change the original meaning.

21. (E) Choice (E) eliminates the *but* in the original wording and supplies the correct punctuation for the *which* clause, needing commas to set it off from the rest of this sentence.

22. (B) Choice (B) is correct because it is both concise and clear. The other choices are ambiguous or unnecessarily change the past tense of the original to the present tense. Choice (D) is a less direct, more wordy way to express what choice (B) does more concisely.

SECTION VI: PROBLEM SOLVING

1. (D) Dividing by a number is the same as multiplying by its inverse, and vice versa. Thus multiplying by 5/6 is the same as dividing by 6/5. Thus the answer is $(3/8)(6/5) = 18/40 = 9/20$.

2. (C) The following are the possible combinations: 123, 124, 125, 126, 134, 135, 136, 145, 146, 156, 234, 235, 236, 245, 246, 256, 345, 346, 356, 456. Thus there are 20 combinations. Using the formula,

$$\binom{6}{3} = \frac{6}{3!(3!)} = \frac{6 \times 5 \times 4 \times 3 \times 2 \times 1}{3 \times 2 \times 1 \times 3 \times 2 \times 1} = 20$$

$$\text{The formula is } \binom{n}{r} = \frac{n!}{r!(n-r)!}$$

3. (B) Since the perimeter of the square is 32, each side of the square is 8.

Area of square $= 8^2 = 64$

Note that $\quad 4r = 8 \text{ or } r = 2$

Area of *1* circle $\quad = \pi r^2$
$\qquad\qquad\qquad = \pi \times 2^2$
$\qquad\qquad\qquad = 4\pi$

Area of *4* circles $\quad = 4 \times (\text{area of 1 circle})$
$\qquad\qquad\qquad = 4(4\pi)$
$\qquad\qquad\qquad = 16\pi$

Then shaded area $= (\text{area of square}) - (\text{area of 4 circles})$
$\qquad\qquad\qquad = 64 - 16\pi$

4. (B) Forty-eight days late is one day shy of exactly 7 weeks. (7 weeks $\times$ 7 days/week $=$ 49 days.) If the job were finished in 49 days, then it would have been completed on the same day, Wednesday. But since 48 is one day less than 7 weeks, it was completed one day earlier than Wednesday: Tuesday.

419

5. **(E)** If y is a positive integer, y could be 1. Choices (A), (B), (C), and (D) are all evenly divisible by 1. Only choice (E), $1\frac{1}{2}$, is not divisible by 1.

6. **(D)** Begin by choosing a simple fraction, say 100/100. If the numerator is tripled and the denominator is doubled, the resulting fraction will be 300/200, or $1\frac{1}{2}$. So the new fraction represents a 50% increase over the original fraction.

7. **(C)** Two 2-digit numbers, 80 and 88, are each divisible by 8, and the sums of their digits are divisible by 8.

8. **(B)** If the annual bonus were normally $100, tripled it would be $300. Therefore, the increase ($200) is $\frac{2}{3}$ of the new bonus ($300). Two-thirds is $66\frac{2}{3}\%$.

9. **(D)** Since Felix earns 30% more than Oscar, let x = Oscar's salary and $1.3x$ = Felix's salary. If Felix's salary is reduced by 10%, he is now earning $1.3x - 0.13x = 1.17x$. If Oscar's salary is increased 10% he is now earning $1x + 0.1x = 1.1x$. Felix is now earning $(0.07x/1.1x) = 6.36\%$ more than Oscar.

10. **(C)** Set up an equation for the amount of salt.

10% of 10	plus	0% of x	equals	7% of $(10 + x)$
1.0	+	0	=	$(0.7 + 0.07x)$

$$1 = 0.7 + 0.07x$$

$$0.3 = 0.07x$$

$$\frac{0.3}{0.07} = x$$

Solving for x, we get $4\frac{2}{7}$.

11. **(C)** Set the three consecutive even integers equal to $x, x + 2$, and $x + 4$. The equation: $x = 3(x + 4) - 40, x = 3x + 12 - 40$, $-2x = -28$. Thus $x = 14$. But that is the smallest of the three integers. Thus 18 is the largest.

12. (C) Since the perimeter of rectangle *ABCD* is 22 and *DC* = 7, we have

$$22 = 2(AD) + 2(7)$$
$$22 = 2(AD) + 14$$
$$8 = 2(AD)$$
$$4 = AD$$

Next note that $\triangle ADE$ is a 30°-60°-90° triangle with side ratios $1:\sqrt{3}:2$. Since the side across from 30° is 4, the side across from 60° is $4\sqrt{3}$. Thus $DE = 4\sqrt{3}$. Also note that $\triangle DEF$ is a 45°-45°-90° triangle with side ratios $1:1:\sqrt{2}$. Since $DE = 4\sqrt{3}$, then $EF = 4\sqrt{3}$. Then the area of *DEF*

$$= \tfrac{1}{2}(EF)(DE)$$
$$= \tfrac{1}{2}(4\sqrt{3})(4\sqrt{3})$$
$$= \tfrac{1}{2} \times 16 \times 3$$
$$= 24$$

13. (A) Since it takes Dan 15 hours to complete the job, then in 9 hours he will be able to do only $\tfrac{9}{15}$, or $\tfrac{3}{5}$, of the job. This leaves $\tfrac{2}{5}$ of the job to be finished by Fred. Since Fred takes 10 hours to do the *whole* job by himself, to do only $\tfrac{2}{5}$ of the job, it would take Fred $\tfrac{2}{5} \times 10 = 4$ hours.

14. (D) From the figure and using the Pythagorean theorem, we find the radius is 13 inches.

$$5^2 + 12^2 = r^2$$
$$25 + 144 = r^2$$
$$169 = r^2$$
$$13 = r$$

Alternate method: If you recognized the 5-12-13 right triangle, you could quickly find *r* to be 13.

15. (C) Average speed is (total distance)/(total time). The total distance is 360 miles. Time for the first 150 miles is $150/30 = 5$ hours. The time for the remaining 210 miles is $210/35 = 6$ hours. Thus average speed is $360/(5 + 6) = 360/11 = 32\frac{8}{11}$ mph.

16. (E) Factoring both numerator and denominator of the left side gives

$$\frac{\overset{1}{\cancel{(x+2)}}(x + 3)}{\underset{1}{\cancel{(x+2)}}(x - 2)} = \frac{3}{2}$$

Thus

$$\frac{x + 3}{x - 2} = \frac{3}{2}$$

Cross multiplying gives

$$2(x + 3) = 3(x - 2)$$
$$2x + 6 = 3x - 6$$
$$6 = x - 6$$
$$12 = x$$

SECTION VII: READING COMPREHENSION

1. (A) Though (C) is a possible response, the best option here is (A). The subject of the passage is the role of symbols in communication. Starting with that answer, choice (A) is better than (C) or the others.

2. (D) An unconditioned stimulus will be unprepared for and lead to an unconditioned response—in this case, no doubt, the holder crying out and dropping the match.

3. (C) The bell conditions the child's response, just as the buzzer conditions the eye's response in the example in the passage. That is, after many days of associating the bell with lunch, the child has been "taught" to feel hungry when the bell rings.

4. (B) The passage suggests that complementary responses to common symbols are crucial in communication, even when there is no common language.

5. (C) The discussion shows how perception by sight is determined by the availability of light and looks ahead to the conclusion that the imagination can work in darkness.

6. (C) This answer might be arrived at by considering that the "hats" example is reasonable, relevant, pointed, and simply written; therefore, all choices except (C) are eliminated. But it may also be argued that the example does not describe a "real" situation.

7. (B) This is the passage's final point, that one can think *yellow feather in a blue hat,* without seeing or having seen the items together.

8. (D) The passage is most clearly relevant to linguistics (the science of language) and to psychology (the science dealing with the mind and mental processes).

9. (B) The purpose of the passage is to describe the complexity of the shark revealed by modern researchers.

10. (D) Shark study has been slowed because the sharks are so dangerous and live in murky waters.

11. (E) All of the comparisons except to a dolphin occur in the passage.

12. (D) The second paragraph refers to the much larger brain that sharks possess.

13. (D) All organisms have a bioelectric field, so the male shark would be able to find many sharks more easily than one. They congregate to make it more difficult for the male to grasp one, not to make detection more difficult.

14. (C) The *third eye* is the light-gathering organ.

15. (B) The sharks' sensing the voltage created by currents moving through the earth's magnetic field is at least tangentially relevant to choice (B).

16. (A) The passage is objective. It uses the other techniques, including the double meaning in *heavy breathing*.

17. (E) Though parts of the passage would support the ideas of (A), (C), or (D), the best answer here is (E). In questions about the "purpose" of a passage, the best answers will apply to almost all of the excerpt, not to just one paragraph.

18. (E) The second paragraph says that *the value of a product is what purchasers pay for it.* The other factors which may help determine value are not listed as choices.

19. (A) The rhetorical purpose is its function in the development of the argument. Though some feel the GNP ought to include the work described in the third paragraph, the author takes no stand. In any case, II is not a rhetorical purpose. III is inaccurate.

20. (B) Choices (A), (C), (D), and (E) are all listed or implied as growth factors in the passage (paragraph 6).

21. (D) The GNP does not include *productive but unpaid work.* But a salaried stock broker would be paid for time spent doing research.

22. (B) The context of the passage makes it clear that the word *welfare* refers to the public well-being. The sentence is citing an area that the GNP does not measure that is parallel to *economic productivity.*

23. (A) In the fifth paragraph the author states, *Growth of the GNP has its costs,* but without emphasizing those costs he soon concludes that *while. . . the social cost of a rising GNP seem*(s) *too high, it is likely that we would still be concerned about the growth of the nation's GNP.* In other words, he deemphasizes the negative effects of a growing GNP in order to emphasize people's general appreciation of such growth. Choices (B), (D), and (E) are true, but they do not support a belief in the growth of the GNP.

SECTION VIII: PROBLEM SOLVING

1. (C) $\dfrac{\dfrac{\overset{1}{\cancel{7}}}{\cancel{10}_{2}} \times \dfrac{14}{1} \times \dfrac{\overset{1}{\cancel{5}}}{1} \times \dfrac{1}{\cancel{28}_{4}}}{\dfrac{\cancel{10}^{2}}{\cancel{17}_{1}} \times \dfrac{\cancel{3}^{1}}{\cancel{5}_{1}} \times \dfrac{1}{\cancel{6}_{2}} \times \dfrac{\cancel{17}}{1}} = \dfrac{\dfrac{14}{8}}{\dfrac{2}{2}} = \dfrac{\dfrac{7}{4}}{1} = \dfrac{7}{4}$

2. (D) When $N + 1$ is divided by 5, the remainder is 4. When N (which is one less than $N + 1$) is divided by 5, the remainder should be 3 (which is one less than 4).

3. (C) Having spent 2/5 of her money on clothes, Mary has 3/5 of her money left. Then 1/2 of 3/5, or 3/10, is placed in her savings account. She has now spent $2/5 + 3/10 = 7/10$ of her money. Thus, she has 3/10 remaining. If m is the money she started with, and she has only \$21 left, we have the equation

$$(3/10)m = 21$$

$$m = 21(10/3)$$

$$m = 70$$

4. (B)

Mr. Talbot's charge for the call	\$14.09
Cost of first 3 minutes of a person-to-person call	−\$4.35
Cost of additional minutes	\$9.74

$\dfrac{\text{Cost of additional minutes}}{\text{Cost of each additional minute}} \quad \dfrac{\$9.74}{\$0.46} \cong 21 \text{ minutes}$

Total length of call = first 3 minutes + additional minutes
= 3 + 21 = 24 minutes

5. (C) The area of any square equals one-half the product of its diagonals. Thus, the area of square $ABCD = \frac{1}{2}(2)(2) = 2$. The area of circle O equals $\pi r^2 \cong 3 \times 1 = 3$. The shaded area = the area of circle O minus the area of square $ABCD$, or $3 - 2 = 1$. Notice that to find the area of square $EFGH$, you may move the radius as follows:

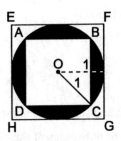

Thus the sides of square $EFGH$ are each 2, so its area is $2 \times 2 = 4$. Therefore the shaded area is approximately 1 out of 4, or 25% of square $EFGH$. You may also have simply eliminated answer choices (A), (B), (D), and (E) by inspection. Every choice except (C) is ridiculous. Be aware that this type of elimination by inspection is possible only if the diagram is drawn close to scale and if the answer choices are far enough apart to allow approximating.

6. (A) The desired weekly income is $600. $600 − $150 (weekly salary) = $450 (amount to be made up from commission). Let x = number of dollars in sales for one week. Since the salesman earns 15% on all sales, this gives the equation

$$0.15x = 450$$

$$x = 450/0.15$$

$$x = 3000$$

Therefore the salesman must make sales totaling $3000.

7. (B) Solve this problem by plugging in simple numbers. Start with 1, an odd integer.

$$(1 + 1) \text{ times } (2 \cdot 1) + 1 =$$
$$(2) \quad \text{times} \quad (2 + 1) \quad =$$
$$2 \quad \times \quad 3 \quad = 6 \quad \text{Not odd.}$$

Now try 2, an even integer.

$$(2 + 1) \text{ times } (2 \cdot 2) + 1 =$$
$$(3) \quad \text{times} \quad (4 + 1) \quad =$$
$$3 \quad \times \quad 5 \quad = 15 \quad \text{Odd.}$$

8. (E) First rearrange and simplify the first equation as follows:

Add $+12$ and $+6y$ to both sides of the equation $6x - 12 = -6y$ and you get

$$\begin{array}{rcl} 6x - 12 & = & -6y \\ + 12 + 6y & = & +6y + 12 \\ \hline 6x \quad + 6y & = & 12 \end{array}$$

Now dividing through by 6 leaves $x + y = 2$.

Next, rearrange and simplify the second equation as follows:

$5y + 5x = 15$ is the same as $5x + 5y = 15$. Dividing through by 5 leaves $x + y = 3$.

The equations $x + y = 2$ and $x + y = 3$ have no solutions in common because you can't add the same two numbers and get two different answers.

9. (B) Try a simple number of total employees and see what happens. If the total employees for Company A is 100, then 40 are female and 60 are male. Then Company B has 60 females and 40 males. If 30 female employees move from Company B to A, then there are 70 in A and 30 in B. They are not equal. Next try 200. Then Company A has 80 females and 120 males, while Company B has 120 females and Company B, 90 females. Try 300. If A has 300, then 120 are female, and 180 are male, and B has 180 female and 120 male. If 30 females from Company B

join Company A, then each company has 150 females, so each company must have 150 males for a total of 300.

10. (A) Note that $(x - y)^2 = x^2 - 2xy + y^2$

$$= \underbrace{x^2 + y^2} - \underbrace{2xy}$$

$$= \quad 14 \quad - 2(3)$$

$$= 14 - 6$$

$$= 8$$

11. (B) The @ of 2 = (2)(5) − 2 = 8. So 2 is the largest positive integer n such that @ of n will be less than 10.

12. (B) Notice that in triangle BCE the angle at B equals 94°. Therefore any perpendicular dropped from C to line AB must be less than 3 (see diagram below). Since the area of a parallelogram = base × height, then the area of parallelogram $AECD = 8 ×$ (a height less than 3) = an area less than 24.

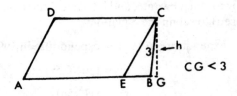

13. (D) The most the trip will cost is when gas costs $1.12 and the mileage is 16 mph. Thus $1.12 × (480/16) = $33.60. The least would be $0.96 × (480/24) = $19.20. The difference is $14.40.

14. (D) If 2/5 of the prize (2/5 of $600 = $240) is distributed to 3/5 of the winners (3/5 of 20 is 12 winners), this indicates that each of those 12 winners will receive the minimum of $20. That leaves $360 to be divided among 8 remaining winners. If 7 of those winners receive the minimum $20 (total $140), then the eighth winner would receive all the remaining prize money, $360 − $140 = $220.

15. (D) Points A, B, and P form a 30°-60°-90° triangle, the sides of which are in a 1-$\sqrt{3}$-2 relationship. A proportion can therefore be established:

$$\frac{120}{\sqrt{3}} = \frac{?}{1}$$

Solving:

$$\frac{120}{\sqrt{3}} = \frac{x}{1}$$

$$x = \frac{120}{\sqrt{3}}$$

$$x = \frac{120}{\sqrt{3}} \cdot \frac{\sqrt{3}}{\sqrt{3}} = \frac{120\sqrt{3}}{3} = 40\sqrt{3}$$

16. (A) Let x equal 1991's amount used; let y equal 1991's rate. Therefore, xy = 1991's water expenditure. For 1992, instead of y, use 1.5y for the new rate, and let p equal the new fraction of x (water used) to set up the equation:

expenditure in 1991 = expenditure in 1992

$$xy = (px)(1.5y)$$

$$xy = xy(1.5p)$$

$$1 = 1.5p$$

$$1/1.5 = p$$

$$0.66\tfrac{2}{3} = p$$

Since for 1992, the Johnsons must use only 66⅔% of 1991's amount, they must reduce their 1991 usage by 33⅓%.

FINAL PREPARATION: "The Final Touches"

1. Make sure that you are familiar with the testing center location and nearby parking facilities.
2. The last week of preparation should be spent primarily on reviewing strategies, techniques, and directions for each area.
3. Don't *cram* the night before the exam. It's a waste of time!
4. Remember to bring the proper materials to the test—identification, admission ticket, three or four sharpened Number 2 pencils, a watch, and a good eraser.
5. Start off crisply, working the ones you know first, and then coming back and trying the others.
6. If you can eliminate one or more of the choices, make an educated guess.
7. Mark in reading passages, underline key words, write out information, make notations on diagrams, take advantage of being permitted to write in the test booklet.
8. Make sure that you are answering "what is being asked" and that your answer is reasonable.
9. Using the SUCCESSFUL OVERALL APPROACH (p. 7) is the key to getting the ones right that you should get right—resulting in a good score on the GMAT.

Holy Ways of Wales

Jim Green

First impression: 2000

© Jim Green and Y Lolfa

Photographs by the author, CADW and Wales Tourist Board
Cover design by Ceri Jones

ISBN: 086243 519 6

Printed, published and bound in Wales by:
Y Lolfa Cyf., Talybont, Ceredigion SY24 5AP
e-bost ylolfa@ylolfa.com
y we www.ylolfa.com
ffôn (01970) 832 304
ffacs 832 782
isdn 832 813

Contents

Ynys Môn
(Anglesey)

Bangor

Caernarfon

Treffynnon
(Holywell)

CAER
(CHESTER)

Aberdaron

Harlech

Ynys Enlli
(Bardsley Island)

Dolgellau

Tywyn

Machynlleth

Aberystwyth

Ystrad-fflur
(Strata Florida)

Aberteifi
(Cardigan)

HENFFORDD
(HEREFORD)

Llanbedr Pont Steffan
(Lampeter)

Tyddewi (St David's)

Caerfyrddin
(Carmarthen)

Y Fenni
(Abergavenny)

Hwlffordd
(Haverfordwest)

Castell-nedd
(Neath)

Abertawe
(Swansea)

CAERDYDD
(CARDIFF)

INTRODUCTION

If Wales cannot claim to be a holy land it can certainly claim to be a land of holy places. So many of its place names declare its long history of faith. 'Llan', which begins the name of so many towns, villages and hamlets, is often interpreted as meaning 'church'. However, 'llan' probably meant the small enclosure that surrounded the dwelling of a missionary monk. This holy place was often the site of any church that was subsequently built and whatever follows is often the name of the 'saint' associated with the original settlement. So Llanaelhaearn is the church of Aelhaearn and Llandudno, with a slight change, is the church of Tudno. Wales is also a land of holy wells. Many of these holy wells may have been sacred places in pre-Christian times and when the missionary monks of the 5th and 6th centuries arrived bringing Christianity the wells were taken over and christianised.

These missionary monks were the 'saints' whose names are scattered across Wales, but they were not the first Christians. There would have been Christians among the Romano-British community but when the Roman legions withdrew that Christian presence would have remained probably only in the south east where the Roman presence had been most settled. The Christianity which took such a deep and fierce hold of the Welsh people was Celtic Christianity. It came from Ireland, Scotland and Brittany and was strenuously taken up by home grown missionaries of Wales. This was a different tradition from the Roman Christianity brought by Augustine to the pagan southern English on the orders of Pope Gregory the Great. The Celtic Church was predominantly monastic rather than governed by

bishops and influenced by the Desert Fathers who lived as hermits. It set great store on learning and where monasteries were set up many became great centres of scholarship. The Celtic monks were enthusiastic missionaries and from the Celtic lands they set out to win Europe for Christ. When the Celtic tradition eventually met the Roman tradition, in England, they would clash, Rome would be triumphant and what Augustine began the Normans would complete. But what Celtic Christianity achieved in its missionary work was, by the standards of any age, amazing. These were giants whose seven league boots of faith and scholarship took them across the wild Celtic lands and seas establishing places of worship and learning.

Though many of the names left to us today are little more than names, some of the Celtic saints, by their holiness, scholarship and the wonder of what they were able to achieve, became icons of later ages. St. David became the most famous of the Welsh saints, the Patron of Wales, and his resting place, the cathedral at Tyddewi (St.David's), a place of great pilgrimage. Yet, even within the realms of academic scholarship, little for certain is known about St. David. The number of places that bear his name is a monument to the scale and success of his work. He left many religious foundations but the one at Tyddewi (St. David's) has been called a 'veritable nursery of saints'. However, nothing was written down about St. David until 1090. The then bishop of Tyddewi (St. David's), Rhygyfarch, was involved in the power struggle in the British Church. The Normans favoured unity under Canterbury and the Celtic Church was fighting to save its identity. The story of St.David written down by Rhygyfarch was, alas, as much propaganda as history. Like other Lives of the Welsh Saints,

his story, coming so long after his death and in such different times, contained much of wonder and miracles but considerably less of hard fact.

However, the story served to fuel the widespread popular piety of the Middle Ages. The Normans built in stone; they meant their work to last. They built, both to their own glory and to the glory of God, castles and cathedrals. People travelled and pilgrimage became not only an act of popular piety, it became an industry. From the highest in the land to the lowest, divine intervention in the affairs of life was sought. The holiest places became the places of greatest pilgrimage: first the Holy Land, next Rome. After Rome, Santiago de Compostella, the resting place of the Apostle James, and, alongside Santiago de Compostella, Tyddewi (St. David's) and Ynys Enlli (Bardsey)! The pilgrims today still flock to the great shrine of St. James in Spain. But it is hard to imagine quiet, remote Tyddewi (St. David's) as its equal and impossible to imagine forgotten Ynys Enlli (Bardsey) as a rival. Yet they were. Pope Callistus II in 1190 declared two pilgrimages to Tyddewi (St. David's) as equal to one pilgrimage to Rome, just the same as Santiago de Compostella. And Ynys Enlli (Bardsey) held the same status. It was a place of ancient holiness and the burial place of so many saints – great and small – that the number could not be counted. From the 12th to the 15th century pilgrimage flourished. In Wales there were many pilgrimage sites but four stand out as of particular importance: Tyddewi (St. David's), Ynys Enlli (Bardsey), Treffynnon (Holywell) and a remote abbey, Ystrad-fflur (Strata Florida), the valley of flowers. Tyddewi (St. David's) had the great saint. Treffynnon (Holywell) had the revered St. Winifride, Ynys Enlli (Bardsey) had so

many saints buried on it everyone had lost count and Ystrad-fflur (Strata Florida) had a secret relic so holy that its identity was known only to a few and guessed at by everybody else. It was said to be the cup used by Christ at the Last Supper.

This was the age of popular piety, relics and pilgrimage. The great pilgrimage route was based, where possible, on what had been left of the old Roman ways and went from the South Wales/English border around Hereford along the coast to Tyddewi (St. David's). From there it went north to Ystrad-fflur (Strata Florida) Abbey in mid West Wales and then either to the Llŷn Peninsula down to Ynys Enlli (Bardsey) or up to the north east to Treffynnon (Holywell). Another route ran from Treffynnon (Holywell) across North Wales, via Bangor, down to Ynys Enlli (Bardsey). In 1415 King Henry V made the pilgrimage on foot from Shrewsbury, where St. Winifride's remains had been taken, to her shrine at Treffynnon (Holywell) to give thanks for his victory at Agincourt. Travellers, rich and poor, relied on religious hospitality and paid for it. Places like Dinas Basing (Basingwerk Abbey), next to Treffynnon (Holywell), became rich but almost everything ceased with the Reformation and the dissolution of the monasteries. The pilgrim ways declined and finally ceased although local customs survived an amazingly long time in some parts. Tyddewi (St. David's) became a backwater, Ynys Enlli (Bardsey) was almost forgotten, Ystrad-fflur (Strata Florida) became a ruin. Treffynnon (Holywell) survived, just, but only as a shadow of its once great glory.

Then, slowly and recently, a revival started. It is still in its infancy and may die away once more. But the holy places of Wales are being rediscovered, not just as sites of interest, but as places with a tradition

of holiness which remain accessible even to the modern traveller. Where so many feet have trodden in faith, passing slowly from holy place to holy place, the travellers are returning. Now it is often by car along fast roads or winding lanes. But they are not always idle tourists just interested in the rural and the remote or the ancient and interesting. They are looking at places of faith and reflecting on their own place in the landscape of belief. Quite what it is they look for and what they find may be unclear to them and to others, but just the travelling, looking and reflecting makes them pilgrims. Pilgrimage has been described as two journeys in one, the outer journey which takes the body from one place to another and the inner journey which takes the soul, spirit or inner person onwards. The outer journey, when ended, usually finds the pilgrim back home where the journey started. But if the inner journey has been made with an open mind and a willing heart the person who returns home from the pilgrimage is changed and will have moved on in the greater pilgrimage that is life itself.

FROM TREFFYNNON (HOLYWELL) TO YNYS ENLLI (BARDSEY)

Treffynnon (Holywell) to Llanelwy (St. Asaph)

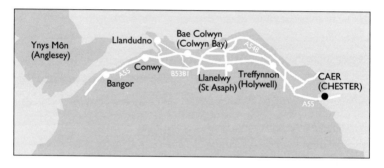

St. Winifride's Well, Treffynnon (Holywell)

Treffynnon (Holywell) is situated in an area of the Welsh–English border country, the Marches, where the savage violence and the deep piety of the Middle Ages seemed able to exist side by side. Although of no special interest the town has good parking, local shops and places of refreshment. Treffynnon (Holywell) lies between the A55 and the A548. The shrine's links with those two great border fortress towns, Chester and Shrewsbury, are ancient and travel today from those centres is, as it always has been, very good. The coast road may suit those who do not appreciate the motorway-like A55. The armies have gone and the pilgrims are fewer but many of the holy places remain, often changed and in changed surroundings, but still holy and not

15

gone nor forgotten.
The beautiful well of
Winifride or
Gwenffrewi lies just
below the town of
Treffynnon
(Holywell) on the
road down to Maes-
glas (Greenfield), on the
coast. To one side of the

St. Winifride's Chapel

shrine is the Pilgrims' Rest, a functional building providing rest and
refreshment rather than architectural beauty. Below the shrine is an
old, defunct, textile mill. Above the shrine stands the parish church of
St. James with its imposing tower. Entrance to the shrine is through a
gate beside the gate house where the small entrance fee is collected.
The shrine's shop is well stocked and there are toilet facilities.

The story of St. Winifride is very ancient and, like most ancient
traditions, was handed down by word of mouth before being written
down. St. Winifride lived in the 7th century but her story, as we have
it today, was not preserved in a written form until the 12th century.
William Caxton chose to print the 'Life of St. Winifride' in 1485
which indicates the status afforded to the saint in the 15th century.

The story tells of a princess of the family of Tewyth, a local prince
in the province of Tegeingl (Delyn), niece of Beuno, a monk who was
to become one of the greatest of the Welsh saints. Beuno's church
stood near Winifride's home. The house was visited one day by a band
of armed young men led by Prince Caradog of Penarlâg whilst

Winifride's parents were at Mass. She offered the band hospitality and Caradog set about trying to seduce her. She ran to find safety in her uncle's church but, on reaching the doorway, Caradog, who had followed her, cut off her head with a single blow from his sword. Beuno came out of the church and took the severed head and restored it to the body praying that God would grant a return of life to Winifride. Life was restored, Caradog was swallowed up by the earth where he stood and a spring arose where the head had fallen! Winifride was restored with only a thin white scar around her neck.

Those elements of the story, the great miracle of restored life, the awful punishment of Caradog and the mystical creation of a spring, are astonishing if believed to be true. However, there are other important elements less clear in their significance to the modern mind than they would have been to the people of that time. T. Charles Edwards in his pamphlet 'St. Winifride and Her Well' quotes the monk historian Giraldus Cambrensis who tells that bands of armed young men under a leader roamed the countryside in what we might now call war training. They formed a militia to defend the people from danger and aggression. As such they enjoyed the hospitality of any household they visited. This should not be confused with the forced and fearful hospitality exacted by armed bandits or soldiers. The hospitality was freely and joyfully given not only in thanks for their dangerous work but as part of the Christian duty to offer a welcome to the neighbour, the traveller, or the needy, which was foundational to the Welsh society of the time. Caradog's abuse of that hospitality is rightly called by T. Charles Edwards 'an abomination'. But the evil doesn't end there. Winifride had already received her parents' permission to

become a nun. She defended that calling in the only way open to her: she sought the sanctuary of the nearby church, yet Caradog denied her even this. Caradog violated the sacred laws of hospitality, defied Winifride's status as one called to live a life devoted to God and set aside the sanctity of the protection offered by a church. His punishment was suitably biblical! Winifride lived for fifteen more years and did, in the end, become a nun at Gwytherin where she died and where her remains rested until 1138 when they were removed to the great abbey at Shrewsbury.

The shrine, to those who believe, is a memorial to a great miracle. But it is today, and always was, a shrine to the proper expression of Christian faith: duty joyfully performed, faithfulness to vocation and, finally, justice under God. It eloquently tells the ancient message that from faith springs healing. And St. Winifride's Well, although a place of prayer and petition, has always been a place of healing both of the body and the soul. Today, in more sceptical times, pilgrims still come to the one shrine in England or Wales with an unbroken tradition of pilgrimage stretching from its beginning to the present. As always pilgrims bring all manner of things to be healed, not least, perhaps, doubt and uncertainty. Times change and the surroundings to the spring have changed but the desire to pray and be healed remains, and so the pilgrimage goes on.

Dinas Basing (Basingwerk)

The ruins of Dinas Basing (Basingwerk Abbey) now lie within the Heritage site at Maes-glas (Greenfield) just coastward of St. Winifride's Well. This monastic foundation was one of many established in Britain by Norman barons from the mother abbey of Savigny in Normandy. All these foundations came under Cistercian rule, a strict Benedictine order, in 1147. Basingwerk existed in a territory violently disputed and

Basingwerk Abbey

it sought protection and patronage as much from Wales as from England and was generously endowed by both kingdoms. Prince Dafydd ap Llywelyn granted the abbey the shrine of St. Winifride in 1240 and it retained possession of the well until the dissolution of the abbey by Henry VIII.

19

Dyserth

Dyserth is a quiet village just off the A5151 situated two and a half miles east of Rhuddlan. It is the site of a waterfall about forty feet in height. The stream which feeds the falls rises at Ffynnon Asaph (St. Asaph's Well), in the nearby parish of Cwm. There is a small entrance charge to visit the falls and the picnic site beside the stream as it leaves the falls' pool. There is a steep pathway from the foot of the falls to a viewing point for the energetic and sure footed. The stream runs through the village between the road and the ancient parish church and churchyard. The roads from Dyserth on towards Llanelwy (St. Asaph) are narrow but quite driveable through pleasant countryside.

Llanelwy (St. Asaph)

Llanelwy (St. Asaph) is a small, quiet town between two lovely rivers, the Clwyd and the Elwy, the latter giving the town its Welsh name, Llanelwy. But St. Asaph was not always so quiet. Nearby, the great medieval fortresses of Rhuddlan and Dinbych (Denbigh) are a reminder that much of the medieval traffic in this area was the traffic of war. The cathedral suffered at the hands of both the Welsh and the English and was restored by both. The bishops of that time were often hard pressed in the wise or honest choice of where to place their loyalties. The direct route to Llanelwy (St. Asaph) is along the A55. A more interesting route is along the A5151 and through Rhuddlan where the ancient fortress broods above the Clwyd. Happily the castle is now a place for visitors, not a key player in the life and death struggle for conquest or freedom. The cathedral was a foundation of faith and a

centre of learning, its twofold message peace and understanding. Yet religion in these isles has had less peace and understanding than its founders might have wished. Today, however, tolerance and mutual understanding have to a large degree returned and near to Llanelwy (St. Asaph) is the modern Jesuit foundation of St. Beuno's. Persecution, though not forgotten, is remembered differently and reconciliation is possible. The ancient parish church of Tremeirchion, once itself a place of pilgrimage, is close to St. Beuno's and may have been visited by the priest-poet Gerard Manley Hopkins who lived at St. Beuno's for a time and wrote

> 'Away in the loveable west
> On a pastoral forehead of Wales,
> I was under a roof here, I was at rest.'

It may be hard for the modern mind to imagine that great modern city of Glasgow as a quiet, remote monastic settlement. But so it once was. It was known as Carthures, yet even then it must have had its share of strife. For it was from Carthures that the story tells of Kentigern, bishop of the Strathclyde Britons, coming to Wales driven from his diocese by persecution. Having already visited Carlisle he chose the banks of the river Elwy to settle in exile. Kentigern eventually returned to Carthures and was succeeded by Asa or Asaph who became bishop-abbot of the cathedral-monastery which Kentigern left behind him. So little is really known about the founding of the cathedral or about Asaph, the saint whose name it bears, that we cannot be sure whether Kentigern actually founded the monastery or became abbot of an existing foundation with Asaph succeeding him. Although little is

known of Asaph his name features in several local places, Llanasa, Pantasa, Ffynnon Asaph, indicating his local significance.

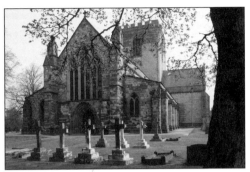

St. Asaph Cathedral

We can be sure, however, that the site around the present cathedral has been a centre of Christian faith since the 6th century. Although Christianity flowered in and spread from the Celtic lands the Celtic Christians of Ireland, Scotland and Wales were cut off from Rome and the Christian world by the pagan barbarian tribes who had swept across Europe and conquered as far west as England. The Celtic people held fast to the faith they had received, spread it and defended it. Llanelwy (St.Asaph) became a 'mother church', one responsible for founding other churches sharing the faith, spreading it and sustaining it. It would have been regarded as holy not only for what it was, a cathedral, monastery and place of learning, but for the tradition of faith and worship it had helped to create. As England became Christian again its holiness would have been recognised and it would have become a natural place for pilgrims to visit either on their way from Treffynnon (Holywell) to Ynys Enlli (Bardsey) or going north from Tyddewi (St. David's) to Treffynnon (Holywell) via the abbey of Ystrad-fflur (Strata Florida).

Today, Llanelwy (St. Asaph) stands for what it has always stood for,

faithfulness to the Christian tradition. That faithfulness has never brought simple answers or easy comfort. Unlike St. Winifride's Well there are no special curative properties here for healing the ills of the body. But there is comfort and support to be found, illustrated not least by the copy of the Bible, displayed in the cathedral, which brought scripture to the Welsh in their own language. Founded out of exile, grown in isolation, matured during bloody war, surviving times of separation and division, the cathedral continues as a place of faith. It tells anyone who will listen of the importance of the message of Christianity especially in the face of foolishness, failure and pride. It speaks of forgiveness after strife and violence. It speaks of the quiet healing that grows out of faith and trust in the final wisdom and mercy of God. The smallness of St. Asaph – it is the smallest of the medieval Cathedrals in England and Wales – is in contrast with the magnificence of its great Gothic cousins of England and northern France. In this small Welsh cathedral God has been glorified by quiet perseverance in the face of difficulty, doubt and fear. Each age expresses its faith in different ways and changes, to some, may seem to change the faith itself. But, just as St. Asaph was once a small wooden structure and grew into the present monument of stone designed and built by many different hands, the desire to keep and pass on the faith, brought by Kentigern and carried on by St. Asaph, makes it still a place of pilgrimage for those who seek to do the same.

Llanelwy (St. Asaph) to Bangor

St. Trillo's Chapel

The chapel of St. Trillo is situated at Llandrillo-yn-Rhos Point just beyond the resort of Bae Colwyn (Colwyn Bay). The fast road is the A55 and the quieter route the old Roman road, the B5381. Whichever route you take join the Marine Drive or Promenade along the sea front at Bae Colwyn (Colwyn Bay) and drive round to Llandrillo-yn-Rhos. This quiet, residential suburb with its neat bungalows separated from the sea wall by Marine Drive, seems an unlikely setting for an ancient chapel. But if you stop at St. Trillo's Drive you will see a low wall on the seaward side of the road. Below that wall, down on the sea front, is the tiny, ancient chapel of St. Trillo. That this chapel should have been preserved, and well preserved, during the development that now surrounds it speaks volumes about the Welsh way of doing things. We know nothing about St. Trillo or the spring that was once inside the chapel. It is said that the monks of the Cistercian Abbey at Conwy prayed here for good catches in the fish weir that used to exist nearby. Today services are still held in the summer months and a sign invites any pilgrim who has found the little chapel to stop awhile and pray.

St. Tudno's Church

Continuing along Marine Drive you will soon reach Llandudno, named for St. Tudno. Like so many early saints little is known of Tudno other than legend but his name lives on, slightly changed, in the place that took his name. Through Llandudno keep close to the sea

on your right until you come to the foot of Penygogarth (Great Orme). Here a toll road takes you round the bottom of Penygogarth (Great Orme). The views you will get make the toll worth while. Not far round the road there is a clearly marked left turn and a steep winding road which eventually leads to the summit. St. Tudno's Church can't be missed standing on the right of the road opposite a bus stop where there is space to park for a while. The church itself and churchyard differ very little from many other small, low, rectangular churches. It is not impressive outside or in. It is, however, a quiet contrast to the busy pleasure resort which Llandudno became in Victorian times and remains today. It sits, quietly, looking out to sea, a peaceful place of prayer in a busy world.

Bangor

The A55 is really the only road to Bangor from Llandudno. One way of getting on to it is to go towards Conwy castle and cross the estuary by the bridge. Choose this way if you want to visit the castle. Another way is to drive straight down to the A55 and cross under the estuary by going through the tunnel. The road hugs the coast because of the mountains and passes through two more tunnels. Near Bangor the A55 meets the A5. You leave here and follow the A5122 into the town. Bangor cannot be described as a resort but it has long been a centre for visitors because of its favoured position between Ynys Môn (Anglesey) and the mountains just inland. Bangor became a University town in the late 1800s and today has over 4000 students resident in term time. Although one of Wales' most ancient settlements Bangor is a modern

city. It has none of the quiet or calm of many of the other holy sites. It is active with all the varied business of modern city life and any pilgrims must squeeze between the bustle and the noise to find an echo of its holy past. And perhaps the obvious place to be quiet, pray and feel some fellowship with those pilgrims of earlier times who came to or passed through Bangor is the cathedral. Because Bangor is so busy, parking may be a problem but the cathedral is quite well signposted in the middle of the city and there are two nearby car parks, a Pay and Display and the cathedral car park, a multi-storey. In fact, you will not be very different from the early pilgrims; they too, had to fit in with whatever they found going on around them wherever they stopped. A pilgrimage is a journey, and both the outside and inside journeys will have their own difficulties; if they did not it probably wouldn't be a pilgrimage.

Bangor Cathedral may be the oldest cathedral in continuous use in Britain. It certainly is an ancient foundation. Like Llanelwy (St. Asaph), its history has been anything but peaceful and calm. Bangor Cathedral's early history is a monument to determination in the face of violence and misfortune. Like many religious sites in Wales, Bangor Cathedral began life as the simple dwelling of a holy man, a monk, in this case Deiniol. He built his cell and wattle enclosure here in about 525. Whether there was already some sort of settlement or whether one grew up around Deiniol, the place must have thrived because about 546 Deiniol was given spiritual oversight of Gwynedd by Prince Maelgwn with whom Deiniol was educated. Whether it was friendship or holiness that made Maelgwn choose Deiniol is not known but Deiniol's spiritual position was confirmed by Dyfrig who consecrated

Bangor Cathedral

Deiniol as bishop and in so doing elevated his church to cathedral
status which it has enjoyed uninterruptedly ever since. St. Dyfrig was a
very important figure in the development of monastic life in Wales
founding many religious houses here and across the border in England.
Like many of the early Saints he passed his last days on Ynys Enlli
(Bardsey) and died there. Bangor is unusual in that it is not named for
its patron St. Deiniol. The word Bangor, not especially common but
occurring elsewhere in Wales, refers to the binding used in making
wattle and St. Deiniol would have built the fence of his enclosure with
wattle.

It is strange how Bangor not only survived but thrived. The
original cathedral, which would have been built of wood, burned down
in 634. In 1073 it was destroyed by the Vikings. In 1210 King John
burnt it down. The central tower burnt down in 1309 and in 1402 the

whole place was badly damaged during the rebellion of Owain Glyndŵr! Although these disasters covered a period of 800 years they serve to illustrate the determination of those living in Bangor to go on celebrating the faith in this particular place. Since 1480 the history of the cathedral has been somewhat happier and is one of renovation, restoration and development. Music has always played an important part in the celebration of the Christian faith and Bangor's tradition of music is ancient and special. Bangor's first organ was installed sometime in the 14th century and was mentioned in a poem by Dafydd ap Gwilym around 1360. One of the cathedral's great treasures is a book of music, the Bangor Pontifical. This manuscript was written for Bishop Anian in the early years of the 14th century and contains words and music of services conducted only by a bishop. After considerable wanderings it now rests in the library of University College, Bangor.

Today, the cathedral still resounds with holy music when services are sung by men, boys and full choirs. The pilgrims would have prayed both when they visited the cathedral and when walking on their journey, but it is also probable that they would have sung as well. Perhaps, alongside the folksongs, they sang the well known sacred music of the time. Bangor Cathedral is a place to be reminded of the importance of music in the life of faith and remember the old saying that 'to sing is to pray twice', in words and music. Bangor Cathedral stands as a monument to continuous worship in one place. It presents a view of the practice of faith which is quite different from that of pilgrimage but, perhaps, more familiar to the modern mind. But each expression of faith complements the other and both give glory to God.

Bangor to Clynnog Fawr

Caernarfon

The pilgrims who had begun their pilgrimage to Ynys Enlli (Bardsey) by visiting Treffynnon (Holywell) and Llanelwy (St. Asaph) would have left Bangor and probably headed for Caernarfon where they might well have joined up with other pilgrims who had come north from Tyddewi (St. David's) and Ystrad-fflur (Strata Florida). The mighty fortress of Caernarfon would have offered shelter, hospitality and, if necessary, protection before the pilgrims set out along the coast. Below the castle there is now a car park on what was the slate quay. From here it is possible to walk across the Aber Bridge on to the seaside road. This seaside road can also be reached by car. Leave Caernarfon on the Porthmadog road and turn right at the first traffic island where Llanfaglan and Saron are signposted. Turn immediately right following the sign for the golf course. This narrow road will bring you down to the Aber Bridge and the seaside road. It is impossible to say where the pilgrim route from Caernarfon would have actually been but the coast is a good guess, since it is flat, easy walking. Today, as there must have been then, there are the sounds of the wind, water and sea birds. It is a wonderful place to stop, rest or reflect. About a mile down the road, in an enclosure in a field, is a small church.

St. Baglan's Church

Llanfaglan Church

The little church and the nearby village take their names from St.
Baglan although, today, we know nothing of the saint other than his
name. The pilgrims' progress would probably have been very slow and
the distances covered in a day quite unlike those which walkers would
expect to cover these days. There would be the sick, the old, the infirm,
as well as the fit and able bodied. The pilgrims would have needed
shelter and hospitality on their journey down the Llŷn peninsula and
they would have found it not at monastic foundations but at the
churches they passed on their journey. The churches became known as
the 'Pilgrim Churches'. St. Baglan's church could have been a stopping
place but, although an ancient foundation, it is not recorded as a
Pilgrim Church. It is, however, fairly typical in size, style and location
of many of the churches of the peninsula. Quite how such places could
offer hospitality to parties of pilgrims may seem a puzzle today, but

provide hospitality they certainly did. If you have walked to the church return to Caernarfon and head out on the A487, the Pwllheli road. If you have driven to the church then drive on to the village of Saron and then join the A487. The lanes are narrow but quite passable.

Clynnog Fawr

The route from Clynnog Fawr to Aberdaron is about twenty miles. There are nine churches on the route identified as 'Pilgrim Churches'. It is rather sad that several of the churches, still active as parish churches, may be found locked outside service times and are not always available to the visitor. There is still plenty of hospitality on the route at inns and hotels but times have changed and not all churches can keep their doors freely open for prayer, reflection and rest. It is a reminder, if one is needed, that progress involves losses as well as gains and not all changes are for the better. You leave Caernarfon on the A487 and then take the A499 signposted for Pwllheli and soon head out into the beautiful landscape of the Llŷn Peninsula. It is a good, fairly straight road and you will often be in sight of the sea. Indeed, the sea is never far away wherever you are on this peninsula. Between Caernarfon and Clynnog Fawr none of the original Pilgrim Churches remain although the impressive Victorian church at Llandwrog, which has replaced the old Pilgrim Church, is well worth a visit. You drive straight down to the small, quiet village of Clynnog Fawr where the church and hotel face each other across the main road. At Clynnog Fawr things begin to change and it is possible to get more of a feeling for the remoteness of the pilgrimage route. Places become smaller, the

The great church at Clynnog Fawr

land emptier of the things that are so much a part of busy, modern life. The skyline of hills and sea cannot be very different today although the details in the landscape would be much changed for an ancient pilgrim. It is still quiet and unhurried, the pace can slacken and the mind turn to more timeless things – our place in this landscape, our aims in life – the thoughts of pilgrimage.

Treffynnon (Holywell), tells the story of how Beuno restored Winifride to life. There are other marvellous stories about this great saint, equally miraculous. It has been said by writers that the earliest chroniclers were not keen to relate the well known but ordinary work of saints but rather fed the popular demand for the marvellous. Then as now, people wanted heroes. However, as J. H. Pollen said, writing in 1894, 'nowadays marvels have become difficulties'. Beuno's miracles may be a matter of personal belief but no-one should doubt that he

was both real and great. As the stones of gothic cathedrals speak for their builders so Beuno's legacy speaks for him. He was Welsh and probably educated at the great monastery of Bangor. He may have established two monasteries on Anglesey before returning to Caernarfon. A story told about him is that he was given a grant of land by a chieftain in order to build a monastery. However, he was approached by a woman with a young child who claimed that the piece of land was the child's birthright and not the chieftain's to give. Beuno refused the land and left the court. A young prince, impressed with Beuno's action, followed him and gave him land elsewhere to build his monastery, the place was Clynnog Fawr. Whatever the truth of the story, Beuno's travels in his work are fully attested to by the many places, churches, wells, fields and other sites which bear his name.

A monastery was established at Clynnog Fawr and it continued to be a holy place inextricably linked with the name of Beuno. The

The main altar, Clynnog Fawr

practices which grew up around the church may be difficult for the modern, rational, secular mind to understand or accept. Local animals born with a distinctive mark were said to carry 'Beuno's mark' and belong to the church. They were given to the church and redeemed by a payment, or they were sold by the church to provide revenue. It may not be wholly rational but

St. Beuno's Well

it worked well enough and was still a practice into the 18th century. The great church at Clynnog Fawr is a monument to its history as a monastic centre, a local church and a place of pilgrimage. The present main building is attached to an older chapel known as St. Beuno's Chapel which is believed to house the last resting place of the saint. Nothing remains of any building of the earliest period although there are reports that a dig discovered evidence of a small rectangular stone building which could have been a 7th century basilica.

What does remain is Beuno's Well. This is not of any miraculous origin, it is a local spring which lies two hundred yards on the left of the road out of Clynnog Fawr and is set just back from the road. It is in a square, stone structure with an iron gate. Why so many early saints were associated with wells is easily explained. Any settlement, even of a single monk, needed fresh water. The water could be used for baptisms, which it undoubtedly was. Beuno's spring still rises and runs down and under the road into the field opposite. Everything else may have changed but the spring itself is the same spring the pilgrims would have visited when leaving Clynnog Fawr and heading off, once more, on the road to Ynys Enlli (Bardsey). They kept their faith in the style of their times, we must keep ours in our own style. St. Beuno, that great traveller, would surely have been pleased that the church he founded is still a place of prayer and hospitality to the traveller, whether pilgrim or visitor or both.

The Pilgrim Churches between Clynnog Fawr and Aberdaron

Llanaelhaearn

The first of the 'Pilgrim Churches' after Clynnog Fawr is at Llanaelhaearn, a village named for one of Beuno's followers who, continuing the work of his master, was probably responsible for the original foundation. The church is still a parish church today and the

The Pilgrim Church at Llanaelhaearn

village lies just after the junction of the main Pwllheli road and the B4417. Take the right turn at the junction and the church is down a left turn on entering the village. There is a small amount of parking by the main gate. The church makes an impressive picture as you walk between the trees that line the path to it. Little is known about Aelhaearn other than he was one of three holy brothers and was a follower of Beuno. According to legend he was torn apart by wild animals and restored to life by Beuno. Lacking a piece of his brow

36

Beuno finished his work with a piece of iron, hence the name, ael-haearn (iron brow). Today it is only a short easy drive to reach Llanaelhaearn from Caernarfon; in pilgrim times it was a long, hard journey.

Perhaps it is a good place to reflect on myths ancient and modern. The ancient myths give us the man of the 'iron brow' restored to life by a great saint. What are today's myths? That getting there quicker is better? That having more makes us happier? Time will tell, but though the future may one day laugh at what we now see as certainty let us hope they will never doubt our commitment to passing on truth, justice and hope.

Pistyll

This wonderful little church is along a right turn just before you reach Nefyn. The turn is unmarked but lies just beyond a lay-by which is on the right of the road. There is also a good lay-by on the left of the main

road but not far down towards the church is a National Trust car park. The church lies just a short walk further on and sits beside a ravine with a stream running through it and has beautiful views out over the sea. This is a typical little medieval-style building similar to what you will have seen before and will see again. Here, as

Pistyll Church

37

elsewhere, there must have been other associated buildings to provide food and rest for the weary pilgrims. The inside of the church is well cared for with a carved baptismal font and a neat little altar. Over the altar there is an inscription – 'Clodforwch yr arclwydd canys da yw' which means – Praise the Lord for He is good. There is even still a place for pilgrim offerings!

This little church is a very good place to reflect on the things we have but do not own. The quiet, the sound of the stream, the view of the sky, bright blue or dull grey, the hills and the trees are all there for you to enjoy. You have your pleasure in them yet you do not own them, they do not belong to you to give or deny to others. The pilgrims praised God as they walked through this landscape. The words over the altar repeat that praise and so can you, enjoying what is freely given to all who visit this little church.

Nefyn

The 'Pilgrim Church' at Nefyn might strike you as either sad or merely a sign of progress. It is no longer a church and hasn't been for some time. The present parish church lies elsewhere in the village, a more modern building able to accommodate a much larger congregation, and the little towered 'Pilgrim Church' sits quietly among the back streets to the left of the main road. On top of the tower there is a ship. The redundant church was converted to a maritime museum which is open in the holiday season. But how long the old church will serve its present function is anybody's guess and what its future would be then is anything but clear.

The old church at Nefyn

There are many ways to reflect on this state of affairs – all things change, purposes change, uses change, a building has meaning and purpose only so long as it stands. So many links with the past get lost; one writer has vividly described this process of change as ' the solvent power that a civilisation exercises on its distant past'. Something will happen to the church at Nefyn. Perhaps it will disappear like the ones between Caernarfon and Clynnog Fawr. Perhaps it will be found a new use and a new life. Only time will tell.

Edern

Edern is a modestly sized village and, as you enter it, you cross a bridge. The first turn on the left takes you along a narrow lane and on the left, behind a farm on the edge of the village, is the church. Next to it, echoing its style, is a private house that once was the local school. The church is a pleasant building dedicated to St. Edern and the village may once have been called Llanedern. Edern the man is substantially

St. Edern's Church

lost to us today. In folklore he was not only a saint but a member of the court of King Arthur whose legend is particularly strong in this area. He is also mentioned no less than three times in the Mabinogion, the surviving collection of ancient myths and tales told originally by story tellers and bards. The church stands surrounded by its churchyard and may give a feeling of being somewhat remote from the life of the village although this might be quite a false impression. Although still a church in use it is no longer a parish church and is served from Nefyn. This is another church in transition. No longer a worship centre in its own right but perhaps more a worship outpost. This may be due to lack of worshippers or lack of ministers but it is not an uncommon feature across the whole of Britain and beyond.

It is, perhaps, a place to reflect on the need to be able to evaluate what we receive as tradition, to know what is myth or legend and what is truth. It is also a place to accept that such discernment is not always easy, especially in times of great change. The pilgrims who called here

40

had a certainty about where they were going and why. Today, many lack that certainty and, even when the immediate journey seems clear, the ultimate destination, where it is and what it will look like, may remain unknown.

Tudweiliog

This village, whose name means 'land of Tudwal', is again of a modest size and the church, dedicated to St. Cwyfan, is the parish church. It stands just off the main road down a left turn opposite the store and post office. There is no easy parking near to the church which stands on a piece of high ground above the road. We know that St. Cwyfan was the patron of three churches: Tudweiliog, one in Anglesey and one in Dinbych (Denbigh). St. Cwyfan was a saint of the 5th century who is credited with the church's foundation. Other than founding this church, why Cwyfan became a saint is not recorded, but we do know something of his ancestry.

St. Cwyfan's Church

He was son of Brwynu Hen and a descendant of Caradog Freichfras. Of all that might have been recorded about this important man his family line alone survives.

Our knowledge of history so often depends on what people of the

past felt important enough to record in some way, in words or monuments. If very little of our times were to survive, what essential thing would we want the distant future to know of us? Long ago they felt the future would surely want to know Cwyfan's lineage. The pilgrim views the future with uncertainty, but it is an uncertainty tempered by hope. No-one can truly know what the future holds, but if one travels in faith one can hope that the uncertainties of life, one day, will be resolved.

Penllech

Now the already quiet landscape is becoming even more empty of people and places. The small, remote, almost forgotten church of Penllech is down a right turn, badly signposted, just after a sharp S-bend about half way between Tudweiliog and Llangwnnadl.

Box pews, pulpit and altar at Penllech

This narrow back lane down to the church doesn't really go anywhere except to another small road which runs parallel to the main road but nearer the sea. As you go down the lane it bends sharply right at a farmyard and a track goes off to the left. About fifty yards down this track is the small church. There is a notice on the door saying that the keys are kept at the farm but the church may well be open. The interior of this church might be something of a surprise: it comes, almost complete, out of another age. At the back, around the carved baptismal font, are benches set against the wall. In front of these are pews with candle-holders on them. Then, nearer the front, are box pews with doorways. The biggest box pew stands opposite the candle-lit, canopied pulpit. A covered altar and a more modern lectern indicate that the church is still in use but the whitewashed, plain interior speaks of a style of worship which is quite remote from much modern liturgy. The wall seating would have been for the poorest worshippers, the benches for the better off and the box pews for those of some local importance. This is all so different from either its pilgrim past or its modern neighbours.

This quiet little church is a place to think, pray and perhaps wonder at how much has changed and then changed again. And to accept that much of what seems so permanent today will, in its turn, change and even disappear.

Llangwnnadl

It is difficult to imagine a church more different from the little church at Penllech than this one at Llangwnnadl. Where Penllech seems to have no settlement, other than the farm around it, Llangwnnadl seems to have two. The first is the village itself on the main road, the other is

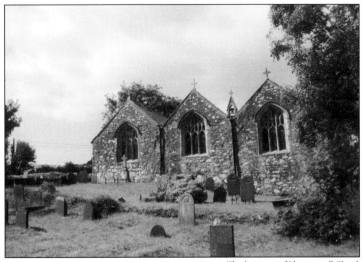

The three naves of Llangwnnadl Church

Pen-y-graig. The fact is that the village must have moved, that is, if the church was ever in the heart of the settlement. It now lies on a little road for which you take a right turn in the modern village. There is a sign on a bus stop for Llangwnnadl and Porth Colmon. This lane leads to Pen-y-graig and the church is half way between the two in the middle of nowhere. It is situated in a beautiful spot and the grounds run down to a tree-lined stream. It is a lovely building, well cared for and much of it is really quite modern. The church at Llangwnnadl was

'restored' in Victorian times. That means it was made to look as people then thought it should look. Whilst this may upset those who think that ancient things ought to be left alone, it may please others who like buildings to be adapted to new ways to show they are alive. Like almost all the 'Pilgrim Churches', it doesn't look as if it could ever have offered hospitality on any scale but, today, it still looks cherished and used. Like Edern, it is no longer a parish church but an outpost of worship and the interior shows that its style of worship is elaborate Catholic rather than plain Protestant.

Perhaps this is a place to reflect on the value of difference, of how different views on the same subject should provide mutual help and support rather than argument and conflict. Perhaps this is a place to feel that, whatever the style of worship, if the essential purpose is the same all can participate in delivering the same enduring message.

Aberdaron to Ynys Enlli (Bardsey)

Aberdaron

Aberdaron is almost at the tip of the Llŷn Peninsula. It is reached by travelling along the B4413 after having left the B4417. It is well signposted and if you pass through Rhoshirwaun and still miss it the only place you can finish up in is the sea! Aberdaron has always been remote but today remoteness is not always a protection from bustle and Aberdaron is busy during the summer months; indeed, in fine weather it can be very crowded. If you begin your visit by looking around the village go first to the church. It is a fine double-naved building and is dedicated to St. Hywyn. He may have been a follower of

St. Hywyn's Church, Aberdaron

the founder of the original monastery on Ynys Enlli (Bardsey) and founded this church, so near to Ynys Enlli (Bardsey), which is dedicated to him. Hywyn is styled 'saint' and, indeed, has his day in the Roman Calendar on January 6th. But Hywyn, like many 'saints' of the 5th to 7th centuries, was known as saint even whilst he lived. In the days of the old Celtic tradition the appellation 'saint' was given to

Y Gegin Fawr, the Big Kitchen

someone who belonged to a monastic tradition and could minister to the spiritual needs of the people. This accounts, in part, for the very great number of 'saints' that are recorded and remembered even though they were not all formally canonised by Rome. Another place to look out for in the village is 'Y Gegin Fawr', the big kitchen. It is believed that this building, although very much changed, is substantially the same building which provided food to the pilgrims. There must have been many a 'Cegin Fawr' alongside the other 'Pilgrim Churches' providing the same service, but only in Aberdaron does one remain so well preserved. Aberdaron is very special as a 'Pilgrim Church' for here the pilgrimage, almost ended, became most dangerous.

Ynys Enlli (Bardsey) cannot be seen from Aberdaron, nor from Porth Meudwy, the nearby embarkation point for the Pilgrims. Today it is possible to get wonderful views of Ynys Enlli (Bardsey) by driving

to the top of Mynydd Mawr, the great hill that overlooks the sound that separates Ynys Enlli (Bardsey) from the mainland. To reach Mynydd Mawr leave Aberdaron along the road over the little bridge signposted for Uwchmynydd. It is a narrow, winding road but quite passable. The road up Mynydd Mawr is a single track road with passing places and takes you up to the top where there is an old coastguard look-out, now an information centre which is occasionally manned. From here there are spectacular views in all directions but especially out to Ynys Enlli (Bardsey). On your way down you will get lovely views in the direction of Aberdaron and the field patterns are a delight.

Aberdaron, a holiday place for many, can also be a place to think of more serious things. Here the pilgrims finally arrived after a journey that may have been long, hard and tiring. There may have been difficulties and problems but there was not usually any great danger. Here things were different. The journey across the sound to Ynys Enlli (Bardsey) was very dangerous, the sea treacherous and the weather uncertain. To finish the pilgrimage meant making the final commitment, placing oneself in God's hands and accepting what might come. Aberdaron is, perhaps, a place to think about final things, about where one is ultimately aiming to go, about what one will venture for faith, about trust and about what trust may demand. Deep thoughts, yes, but pilgrim thoughts. Thoughts for Aberdaron beach before one moves on to Porth Meudwy, the final stage, the point of embarkation for Ynys Enlli (Bardsey).

Porth Meudwy

The tiny cove of Porth Meudwy, which means 'hermit's cove', may have a certain charm on a calm, sunny, summer day when the sea is gentle and everything seems peaceful. It might seem, on such a day, just the place to begin an enjoyable, short sea trip round the headland and enjoy the view of Mynydd Mawr and the surrounding coastline from the vantage point of a boat. Even a trip out to Ynys Enlli

Embarkation beach, Porth Meudwy

(Bardsey) might seem an attractive proposition. It is quite a different place on a wet and windy day when the sea is running and the foam breaks across the surrounding rocks. The pilgrims would have come to Porth Meudwy on foot from Aberdaron. They would have walked along the beach and then climbed the cliffs and followed a small

footpath along the cliff tops. You can still follow this route today but you must negotiate two very small rivers, streams really, which run into the sea here, across the beach. They can be crossed easily but, to avoid wet feet, you need to have good footwear or be very nimble. The steps up to the clifftop path are steep and irregular and harder to come down on the return than to climb up on the outward journey. The cliff path is safe but muddy when wet and not very even. Today Porth Meudwy serves the local lobster fishermen and their boats and equipment stand by the rocks. There is a vehicle track which leads down to the cove from the road to Uwchmynydd which is signposted. This is the best way to reach the cove for those who cannot manage the strenuous clifftop walk but it is still a longish walk and quite hard work coming back up from the cove. There is a National Trust car park at the beginning of the track.

Once in the cove one can reflect that, no matter how much we plan and prepare, there comes a time to act, to translate faith into action. For the ancient pilgrims it was committing themselves to the uncertain sea crossing. Today, as it has always been, faith is not only about reflection but also about action. It is about living as well as thinking, about choosing a way of living that is a sign of belief to others. Any life which is truly a witness of faith to others will have been the life of a pilgrim.

Ynys Enlli, (Bardsey)

Ynys Enlli (Bardsey) is a small, bleak, fairly inhospitable island, not very easy to reach or leave. But it is also a holy island. If Ynys Enlli (Bardsey) had good soil, attractive beaches, a sunny climate and good communications with the mainland, its value and attraction would be clear to the modern mind. But it has little land suitable for cultivation and Swnt Enlli (Bardsey Sound) is a most treacherous stretch of water, dangerous enough today in bad weather and lethal in the days of oars or sail. Yet Ynys Enlli (Bardsey) was inhabited so long ago that no-one can say for certain when the first settlement was. It does seem, however, that Ynys Enlli (Bardsey) has always been a holy place, visited for prayer and lived on by those who dedicated their lives to God. Today, the Llŷn Peninsula may seem remote enough to provide all the quiet anyone might want. But it would have been quite different in the

Ynys Enlli (Bardsey) from Mynydd Mawr

51

5th to 7th centuries. The peninsula would have had many settlements and several religious foundations. Aberdaron and Clynnog Fawr were both significant centres and Mother Churches. Ynys Enlli (Bardsey) may have been a place of seasonal retreat for the early monks, its remoteness and difficulty of access may have been part of its attraction. Getting on to Ynys Enlli (Bardsey), living there for any length of time and getting back again safely must have required a high level of faith.

Whatever the very early history of Ynys Enlli (Bardsey), it became a place of great holiness where many holy men, saints, died or chose to be buried. The legend of St. Lleuddad, an Abbot of Ynys Enlli (Bardsey), states that he prayed that no-one buried on the small island should ever go to hell. And Giraldus Cambrensis, the medieval monk-historian, says that no-one was ever ill on the island and all who lived there did so until great old age. Little wonder, then, that the people of the Middle Ages, for whom death, heaven, hell and purgatory were very real indeed, flocked to Ynys Enlli (Bardsey). At one time the little island ranked in importance with the great shrine of Santiago de Compostella. It was possible by visiting Ynys Enlli (Bardsey) not only to gain remission of sin and its attendant punishments for oneself but for family and friends. It was not uncommon in those times to help pay a pilgrim's costs in return for the pilgrim's intercession at the shrine visited.

But times changed and the world moved on. The old order of intercession and indulgences passed, monastic houses were dismantled and Ynys Enlli (Bardsey) sank back into a remote quietness. It was inhabited and farmed but that simple life eventually ceased around 1970 as the new essentials of modern life became increasingly

impossible to provide on the little island. In 1979 Ymddiriedolaeth Ynys Enlli (the Bardsey Island Trust) was set up to maintain the history and character of the island and develop the study of birds, marine life and natural history. Then its old purpose was slowly rediscovered. Alongside the Nature Warden and the bird watchers the pilgrims returned. They still come to Aberdaron and they still embark at Porth Meudwy. They make retreats of prayer and reflection and the small island chapel has a new life. Ynys Enlli's (Bardsey's) oldest purpose has returned and it is again a place to retreat from the world for a time. It is not a place to be permanently apart but somewhere to seek renewal in order to return to daily life better able to live in faith. Ynys Enlli (Bardsey) is still not nearly as busy or as well known as Santiago de Compostella but it continues its long history as a holy place, a place of twenty thousand saints, a place of pilgrimage.

FROM LLANDDEWI NANT HODNI (LLANTHONY) TO TYDDEWI (ST.DAVID'S)

Llanddewi Nant Hodni (Llanthony) to Llandaf

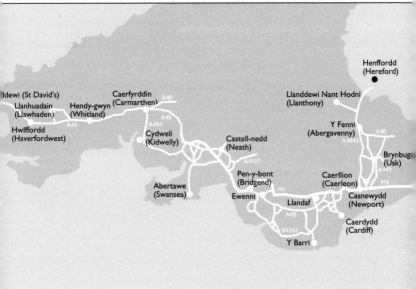

The turn to Llanddewi Nant Hodni (Llanthony) Priory is well marked
on the A465 which runs from Hereford to Y Fenni (Abergavenny).
After leaving the A465 you turn down the lane adjacent to the Skirrid
Inn, said to be the oldest inn in Wales, and follow the clear signs out of

the village. The six miles to the priory ruins run along the lovely Honddu Valley in the Black Mountains. At Llanddewi Nant Hodni (Llanthony) there is free parking and public toilets adjacent to the Priory ruins. After your visit you return by the same route to the A465 and Y Fenni (Abergavenny) is about five miles further on heading south. In Y Fenni (Abergavenny) there are all the facilities a visitor may need including car parking and good tourist information where you can obtain a free and very clear town map. From Y Fenni (Abergavenny) to Brynbuga (Usk) there is a choice of routes. The faster but longer route is along the A40 then the A449, both dual carriageways; the quieter B4598 is the more picturesque. To follow the quiet route leave Y Fenni (Abergavenny) heading south and take the turning for Brynbuga (Usk) signposted at a big junction just after you have left the town. The main A40 can also be taken from this junction. Having taken the road signed for Brynbuga (Usk) take a right turn just after crossing over the A40 and the road runs through charming country and eventually runs alongside the river Wysg (Usk) into the town. There is free parking and toilets situated behind the High Street and the Priory Church is nearby. Brynbuga (Usk) to Caerllion (Caerleon) can again be by the fast A449 or by a quieter back road. To go the quiet way turn left just over the bridge as you leave Brynbuga (Usk). This road takes you through Llanbadog Fawr and Llangybi, both with interesting churches. On entering Caerllion (Caerleon) follow the signposts to the Roman Remains. These are situated in an older and more attractive part of the town and there is a small free car park.

From Caerllion (Caerleon) the best route to Caerdydd (Cardiff)

and Llandaf is the M4 although getting onto it may be considered by many as something of an adventure! Leave the M4 at junction 32 and, at the traffic lights at the end of the slip road, take the A470 signed for Caerdydd (Cardiff). After two miles you arrive at a big junction controlled by traffic lights. You will bear right around the back of the Cross Inn and then leave the A470 to the left and go under the flyover taking the A48 signed for Aberafan (Port Talbot). Strangely, the cathedral is not signposted until you are almost in Llandaf village itself. Not very far along the A48 you will cross a river and shortly after that a sign will show you that to turn right at the traffic lights you must fork left before turning right. The cathedral is now signposted. Once across the traffic lights you take the first right turn. There is a free car park on the right by the Memorial Hall which is very near the cathedral and a few places for street parking adjacent to the cathedral itself.

Llanddewi Nant Hodni (Llanthony)

The key to the importance of Llanddewi Nant Hodni (Llanthony) is in its name but it needs a little bit of explaining. It is nothing to do with St. Anthony. It is an abbreviation – Llanddewi Nant Hodni – The church of St. David on the River Hodni or Honddu. Where better to begin a journey which will end at the city and cathedral of St. David than at one of the places

The ruins of Llanddewi Nant Hodni (Llanthony)

where this great saint once had a cell and established the holy place named for him? Travelling up the Honddu Valley among the Brecon Beacons one is able to appreciate not only the great beauty of the surrounding countryside but also its remoteness. Llanddewi Nant Hodni (Llanthony) Priory, unlike other early monastic foundations, was never likely to become a centre of population. After leaving the Skirrid Inn in Llanfihangel you travel a quiet road, pass the lonely Queen's Head Inn and finally arrive at Llanddewi Nant Hodni (Llanthony) itself. This is a countryside of hills and valleys, sheep and fields, woods and streams and, today, walkers. It is easy to imagine it remote, wild and empty as it used to be.

The priory grew out of a hermitage. William de Lacy, a Norman nobleman, stumbled on the place and found there a derelict little chapel dedicated to St. David, its founder. He repaired the chapel and chose to live in it as a hermit putting his life of privilege and power behind him. Its holy origins, its remoteness and its natural beauty made it a perfect place to retreat to in order to pray and reflect on the glory of God. In 1103 he was sought out by a priest, Ernisius, who was chaplain to Queen Maud. Ernisius decided to join William and they were the first two of what became a small community. The Augustinian Canons of Llanddewi Nant Hodni (Llanthony), as the community became, suffered more than most monastic foundations on the Marches from the troubles of the times. But they also had their times of glory. It was in those times of plenty and temporary peace that the great building, now in ruins, was created. A fine and fitting monument to the glory of God. Yet its size and beauty did not save it. Like many others it passed into secular hands at the Dissolution. But

the little church survived not only as a building but as a place of worship. Where the great priory fell, was forsaken and finally became a hotel, the little church continued. In some ways this is all very fitting. The priory would have been a place of hospitality in these remote parts and given shelter and refreshment to pilgrims and travellers alike. As a hotel, much frequented by walkers, it continues the happy tradition of hospitality and refreshment.

Continuity and tradition can be honoured in unusual ways and the ruins and the little church are a wonderful place to reflect on the proper balance between giving glory and practising humility. The priory buildings were meant to give glory to God by their majesty. That majesty passed, but the glory of God remains all around in the natural beauty of the place and the ruins have now become part of that landscape. The little church remains as a reminder that, however wonderful our expression of praise might be, it is often in the ordinary, commonplace things of life that faith may best be preserved.

Y Fenni (Abergavenny)

Y Fenni (Abergavenny) is a bustling town situated on the confluence of the Gafenni with the Wysg (Usk). It was the site of the Roman fort of Gobanium and there were several sites of Celtic monasticism nearby: Llangatwg (Llangattock), Llangatwg Dyffryn Wysg (Llangattock nigh Usk) and Cleidda (Clytha). The priory, established in Y Fenni (Abergavenny) in 1087, was a Benedictine outpost of the Abbey of St. Vincent at Le Mans in Normandy. The Normans believed in the power of God and the power of the sword and whilst they founded and

rebuilt many centres of religion they also built great fortresses. Y Fenni (Abergavenny) had both priory and castle. The Priory Church, St. Mary's, still functions today, a very beautiful building with a fine collection of monuments. The oldest monument in the church is that of a lady, Eva de Braose, who died in 1265. She was a kinswoman of William de Braose who, it is said, invited the most powerful local chieftains to a Christmas feast in 1177 at Y Fenni (Abergavenny) castle and promptly slaughtered them. This was an act of revenge for the killing of his close kinsman, Henry of Hereford. The result was that the castle was assaulted, taken and burnt with great slaughter by the friends of the slain chieftains.

William and many of the chieftains involved in this tale may well have worshipped in the priory. These were times that could produce beauty and holiness, horror and barbarity all alongside one another. The people who lived in those times could raise up great houses of faith and great fortresses of conquest and destruction. They could be saints and sinners, warriors and pilgrims. They could fight each other to the death and still hope to share heaven. We may think ours to be a more sophisticated and enlightened world but if many of the old superstitions are gone the older tensions between right and wrong surely remain as powerful as they ever were. Y Fenni (Abergavenny), today, welcomes all its many visitors, tourists or pilgrims. Hospitality remains and Y Fenni (Abergavenny) quietly gets on with its daily business. The monks of the priory and the warriors of the castle are both gone, little of their glory or power remains.

The Priory Church was substantially restored in Victorian times and among its treasures is the 'Jesse carving'. This shows a recumbent

Jesse as the root of the 'tree' which gives the lineage of Jesus. It is said to be the finest piece of medieval wood-carving in the world. Standing by this wonderful and ancient piece of religious art it is interesting to wonder why it has survived when so much else was lost. Why do some things survive and others not and what leads to survival? Great fortresses fall and decay, power shifts, violence fades and wealth disperses. Faith survives, hospitality continues, people carry on. Here, one might reflect on the words of Kierkegaard, 'Life must be lived forwards, but can only be understood backwards'. Standing in St. Mary's, so beautiful, so cared-for, with so much beauty from the past well preserved, perhaps one is helped to 'understand backwards'.

Brynbuga (Usk)

If you have taken the B4598 from Y Fenni (Abergavenny) to Brynbuga (Usk) you will approach this pretty little town alongside the wooded banks of the river. St. Mary's Priory church stands quietly behind the main street in Church Street. This fine old building stands near the few remains of the ancient priory, once an imposing foundation. Unfortunately you may find the church locked, like so many these days, but near the main door beside the path is what appears to be a new flat tombstone. It is, in fact, a memorial to a Jesuit priest, David Lewis, who was born in Y Fenni (Abergavenny) in 1616 and who was executed in Brynbuga (Usk) in 1679. It is hard to imagine a quiet, picturesque little place like Brynbuga (Usk), popular with tourists and fishing enthusiasts, as a place of religious divisions so deep and violent that execution was considered necessary for the 'crime' of actively

pursuing one form of Christianity rather than another.

Regrettably, faith and violence have not always been strangers, and the town may be a place where one might reflect on the strength that faith can give and the proper uses of that strength. Many of the pilgrims who passed through Brynbuga (Usk) and sought the peace and hospitality of the priory would have been familiar with the violence of their times and may have been unsurprised had they known of the violence which followed in later centuries. The small monument in St. Mary's Priory churchyard speaks of another kind of strength, the strength needed for reconciliation, the strength needed to pursue peace and justice, the strength to give and seek forgiveness. This strength, to address differences and divisions, is needed by everyone at some time on their journey through life.

Caerllion (Caerleon)

In Roman Britain Caerllion (Caerleon) was a very important place. It was the home of the Second Augustan Legion. From Caerllion (Caerleon) Romano-British settlements of retired soldiers would probably have been established along the river up to Brynbuga (Usk). Apart from being an important fort and centre Caerllion (Caerleon) was probably also a centre of early Christianity. It is recorded that in the Christian persecutions of 249-51 and 257-59 two Christians were executed for their faith, Julius and Aaron. There is no reason to suppose that the Christian faith, soon the faith of the Roman Empire under the Emperor Constantine after his victory at the Milvian Bridge in 312 AD, did not survive in some degree in the Roman settlements

which continued after the legions were withdrawn. But Roman Christianity never moved out of the settlements of south-east Wales. It was the Celtic missionaries of the 5th to the 7th centuries who made Wales a Christian country and Caerllion (Caerleon) may have been the site of a Celtic foundation. It certainly became the site of a monastic establishment when the Normans brought the Cistercians to England and Wales.

Today Caerllion (Caerleon), a suburb of the Borough of Casnewydd-ar-Wysg (Newport), is best known for its Roman remains, not any Celtic or Norman heritage. But the pilgrim can see it is a place where Christianity came in three different ways, Roman, Celtic and Norman. It is a place to remember that the faith we have today is a gift from the past, given by many hands in many ways but a gift which is to be passed on. The faith which the pilgrim carries is not a private possession, it is part of a living tradition, not to own but merely to carry for a time and then to be passed on.

Roman remains, Caerllion (Caerleon)

63

Llandaf

Caerdydd (Cardiff) is an international city, a capital city, an important business and commercial centre. It is also an ancient city dating back to at least Roman times. So why is there no ancient Diocese of Caerdydd (Cardiff)? The reason lies in the way Celtic Christianity came to Wales. The early Celtic missionaries were monks who came from monastic foundations and, as monks, did not normally come to busy settlements to evangelise but rather set up a remote cell and collected people around them. Sometimes these cells became the centre of settlements. Teilo, friend of David and pupil of Dyfrig, those great missionaries, left his name in various settlements. His most enduring monument, however, does not today bear his name. He established a monastic foundation on the banks of the river Taf which was eventually to become the cathedral. For many years it was thought that Llandaf was originally known as Llandeilo Fawr, but it now seems unlikely that Teilo was ever abbot of the monastery or that the settlement ever bore his name. The history of the cathedral that St. Teilo founded is one of struggle for survival. The settlement never grew in importance in the way Bangor did although the Normans honoured the site in the 12th century by raising up a great stone Cathedral, and its history is one of decline, recovery and repair.

In 1815 Llandaf was described as 'a miserable village of mean cottages'. Hardly the setting for a great Cathedral! However, Caerdydd (Cardiff) grew in size and importance and eventually Llandaf was swallowed up. The Cathedral's fortunes revived considerably as Caerdydd (Cardiff) grew and the building, like so many others, was substantially 'restored' in Victorian times. The last violent disruption

of cathedral life came when Caerdydd (Cardiff) was bombed in 1941 and the Cathedral sustained considerable damage. Today the Cathedral, repaired and restored, is beautiful inside and out and has a more comfortable existence after a difficult and varied past. Just how different that situation today is from what has gone before can be illustrated by the tale of

Llandaf Cathedral

Llandaf's connection with the Norman baron, Maurice de Londres. Maurice now lies, under his monument, at the Priory Church of Ewenni. He it was who, among other gifts, gave the Priory at Ewenni to the great abbey at Gloucester. A holy and generous man? Perhaps not, for it is recorded that no less a person than Pope Honorius II, in 1128, condemned Maurice for 'robbing and defrauding the Church at Llandaf and for plundering and killing the itinerant merchants at Llandaf'! Llandaf has clearly not always been the oasis of peace and worship it is today. The Normans, those great warrior builders, were people of prayer as well as war, as at home in the church as they were in the castle. It is interesting to note, then, that the old tradition of

prayer and sword is alive in modern day Llandaf. It is the house of prayer for the Welch Regiment whose regimental chapel is in the cathedral. Where Norman warriors gathered to worship, today's warriors gather still.

Nowadays, we may often feel remote from the past which has formed our times, moved by the beauty of its building and its art but somehow separate from its meaning. We may feel that old problems and difficulties were not only different but simpler. We may feel that those who have gone before could not even begin to comprehend the difficulties we face today. But the truth is, probably, quite the reverse. True, not many of us may have pillaged the church and the merchant, brought the wrath of Rome on our heads or tried to buy our way to eternal happiness by lavish gifts. But our sins, whatever they may be, are still the old sins of pride, greed and selfishness. Llandaf has seen its fair share of human folly, violence and greed since Celtic times but it remains a place of prayer and worship for the warrior, the visitor, the sinner and the pilgrim.

Llandaf to Tyddewi (St.David's)

Ewenni

The medieval pilgrims would probably have walked the flat coastal route from Caerdydd (Cardiff) and it is certainly the route with the better views today although the M4 is available for anybody in a hurry. To take the slower but more attractive route leave Caerdydd (Cardiff) on the A48 and head coastwards by following the signs to Y Barri (Barry) and Caerdydd (Cardiff) Airport. On the outskirts of Y Barri (Barry) head off towards Caerdydd (Cardiff) Airport and then follow the signs to Llanilltud Fawr (Llantwit Major) along the B4265. Llanilltud Fawr (Llantwit Major) was once a great centre of worship and learning named after Illtud. It is now a quiet place by-passed by the main road. Slightly off the route but still on the way to Ewenni is the little seaside resort of Aberogwr (Ogmore by Sea). If you visit Aberogwr (Ogmore) the road to Ewenni will take you alongside the river through attractive countryside and past the ruins of Aberogwr (Ogmore) castle; it is well worth the slight diversion. The village of Ewenni lies just south of Pen-y-bont ar Ogwr (Bridgend) and the ruins are signposted at the Pen-y-bont ar Ogwr (Bridgend) side of the village. You will travel about half a mile along a narrow lane before arriving at the ruins where there is free parking by the side of the road for a few cars.

The Norman Priory at Ewenni was built on the old Roman route from Caerllion (Caerleon) to Caerfyrddin (Carmarthen) which would have continued as the main highway for travellers, including the pilgrims going to Tyddewi (St. David's). The foundation date is

Interior at Ewenni

uncertain, but it was given by the de Londres family to the great abbey of Gloucester in 1141. Ewenni was built in troubled times and was designed as much as a fortress as a house of worship. The ruins today serve an even greater variety of purposes, containing a functioning church, a farm and a very substantial country house as well as being an attraction for visitors. The place is an amazing mixture of the ancient and the ugly, the romantic and the modern, the beautiful and the ordinary. Turner, painting his way through South Wales in the 1790s, painted the ruins at Ewenni and their attraction remains today. One interesting feature of these ruins which might exercise the visitor's mind is to be found across the churchyard and under the old arch which stands against the church wall. There are the foundations of

what must have been a rectangular room. In the wall is a small recess which would have been a piscina, a place for a priest to wash the vessels used when saying Mass. This means Mass was said in this small room. But there is also a small window cut diagonally into the main church wall, a 'squint'. Squints were used to allow someone outside the church to look inside and see the main altar, to see Mass. Why have a 'squint' in a room itself equipped for saying Mass?

Some things about Ewenni are quite clear today, others seem a mystery. The site may be thought of as a place where history has been written over many, many times. In some parts the writing is clear, in others difficult to read and in others quite unreadable. Any pilgrimage will be the same: there will be times of certainty, times of doubt and, perhaps, times of mystery, fear or despair. Ewenni has changed many times and will, no doubt, change again. The pilgrim accepts the changes life brings, holding ever to the same purpose through every different way.

Margam

Leaving Ewenni you head for Pen-y-bont ar Ogwr (Bridgend) and rejoin the A48 heading for Aberafan (Port Talbot). Margam is an ancient and holy site. It is the site of one of the Celtic Mother Churches of Wales and the site of one of the many Norman Cistercian abbeys. The great abbey of Clairvaux was given all the land between the rivers Afan and Cynffig (Kenfig) in 1147 by the mighty Earl of Gloucester to found a daughter house. The result was Margam Abbey.

There will be few, if any, sharper contrasts between past and

present on the pilgrim route from Llanddewi Nant Hodni (Llanthony) to Tyddewi (St. David's) than Margam. To reach the abbey remains today you look out for signs taking you to Margam Country Park near Aberafan (Port Talbot). To visit the abbey you can pay your entrance fee and go into the Park which surrounds

West front of Margam church

Margam 'castle', not a great Norman fortress but a large elaborate Victorian country house. The abbey ruins stand in the grounds beside the 18th century Orangery, built to house a collection of exotic citrus fruits and now used for functions and weddings. If you do not want to visit the park then go on past the gates and turn right just before the motorway junction. A lane will take you to the abbey, now a parish church. The West front will greet you looking, perhaps, more Italian than Norman English, but very impressive. You can actually get into the park through the church but you must still buy a ticket! Where once the monks sang the praises of God, families now come to enjoy

themselves and the ruins are just one part of a day out. But entertainment was never alien to the pilgrim. Chaucer shows pilgrims entertaining themselves and, even if the stories seem inappropriate for people on a holy journey, the tradition of relaxation on a journey is as ancient as travelling itself.

The tradition of relaxation and prayer is still observed here by the park and the parish church and these offer somewhere to think about where God and faith fit into our lives today. Have we, perhaps, lost the old pilgrims' view of God as a very real part of everyday life? Margam Abbey is a vivid reminder of how easy it is to put God and the practice of faith in a separate place from all the other activities of life as if it were a place to be visited if time and circumstances allow. The pursuit of happiness, to the medieval pilgrim, meant the pursuit of heaven and Margam is a very appropriate place to ask where real happiness should be looked for and might be found. Perhaps even to ask if God and faith are ever really a central part of that pursuit in a world so very full of other important and enjoyable things to do.

Nedd (Neath)

Travel on from Margam to Castell-nedd (Neath) on the M4 as far as junction 43 where you leave the motorway and turn right to join the A465. The sign as you enter the slip road will be for Neath Abbey Industrial Estate. Just after you have joined the A465 you turn into the small Neath Abbey Industrial Estate. Drive through the factories and turn right at the T-junction. The abbey ruins lie not far away at the end of this road. There is a small amount of car parking opposite the

Neath Abbey and the Tenant canal

abbey gates and a grassed area with picnic tables. At the little house by the gate you can buy postcards and guide books.

The Abbey began life, like Dinas Basing (Basingwerk) at Treffynnon (Holywell), as an outpost of the mother house of Savigny in Northern France. Savigny was a popular mother house with the Norman barons but the foundations it established all came under the Cistercian monastic rule in 1147. The importance and wealth of Nedd (Neath) Abbey grew as Norman influence in this area was consolidated and it flourished on grants given by powerful patrons. Richard de Granville, constable of the mighty Earl of Gloucester, endowed Nedd (Neath) with 8000 acres of 'waste' land between the rivers Nedd (Neath) and Tawe. Indeed, the rise and subsequent decline of

industrialisation in this area has returned many parts of this land today to the level of 'waste' and there are many places of industrial dereliction nearby. To the visitor the quiet, dignified, majestic remains might seem quite out of place in such a harsh, urban setting. They might resent the railway embankment, the industrial estate, the housing and the busy dual carriageway which jostle the site. Only the quiet disused Tenant canal, with its picturesque little stone bridge, seems to have any sense of what is fitting for a neighbour of these ruins. And such an attitude is understandable; the Cistercians valued peace, seclusion and remoteness. They were great agriculturists.

Nedd (Neath) Abbey today is in quite a different setting from its original surroundings. Yet these remains survive more intact than many in remote locations. Perhaps part of the answer lies in the industrialisation which swallowed the abbey. The abbey was bought, at the Dissolution, by a Tudor magnate and turned into a great house. When this house fell, like the abbey before it, it might all have passed away but a new use was found for the buildings. In 1731 copper smelting was carried out and, later, furnaces were installed. The site of monks' prayer and Tudor gaiety became the humble hostel of industrial workers. Industry, in its turn, moved on and left a ruin and, eventually, Nedd (Neath) Abbey became a 'Welsh Historic Monument'. Nedd (Neath) Abbey has seen money bring great beauty and awful ugliness to this place and is a reminder that wealth is as transient as life itself. To be a pilgrim is to be open to life and understand that change may often be painful if it is to be finally rewarding.

Abertawe (Swansea)

You can travel to Abertawe (Swansea) by returning to the M4 and joining at junction 42. This way will take you to the village of Llangyfelach just off the M4 at junction 46. Here is a church dedicated to St.David and Cyfelach, once a Celtic mother church. The church is interesting today for its tower which has somehow become detached from the main building! Another route into Abertawe (Swansea) is along the A483 which will bring you into the city much nearer its centre. Abertawe (Swansea) is a big, busy city, as different as one can get from the peace and quiet of monastic life and the gentle pilgrim pace. Time and history have, in waves, been kind and cruel to Abertawe (Swansea). Around Castle Square evidence of the city's

changing fortunes abounds. The rather sad remains of the once great Norman castle are rather isolated and ignored. They are surrounded by a variety of buildings, modern glass towers, big shops and the old, shabby buildings of Wind Street which, suffering frequent changes of use, may soon

The castle wall, Swansea

disappear. The elaborate facades of many of these old buildings are a reminder of a wealth that has long since passed away.

But if some things decline and disappear other things can reappear. Near the castle is the parish church of St. Mary's; destroyed in an air raid in 1941 and then re-built, it looks as if it has been there, undisturbed, for as long as the fancy facades of once affluent Wind Street. Also nearby is something that had to wait much longer to reappear, the Benedictine Priory of St. David's. Medieval monastic life came to a sudden and violent end at the Dissolution of the monasteries and there followed a period of religious violence. Today tolerance and, perhaps, a degree of secular apathy mean that a returned Benedictine presence is taken for granted. This new St. David's was built as a local church in 1847 and the Benedictines came quietly in 1873 when it was raised to a 'missionary priory'. The present buildings are a far cry indeed from the magnificence and remoteness that you have seen on your journey. They sit between a massive multi-storey car park and a modern shopping centre.

St. Mary's church and St. David's Priory have lost the city centre housing they once served but both quietly continue to serve God by serving people. They, like the pilgrim, are content to live in the times in which they find themselves. To be a pilgrim is to travel in the present not in any glorious past or golden future. If Abertawe (Swansea) has a lesson for the pilgrim of today it is, perhaps, that what is real and enduring and worth preserving lives in the hearts and the minds of people and that stone and concrete can only ever be a transient reflection of those values and beliefs.

Cydweli (Kidwelly)

To reach Cydweli (Kidwelly) from Abertawe (Swansea) it is necessary to head out through the coastal but industrialised landscape between Abertawe (Swansea) and Llanelli. Once past Llanelli the countryside becomes more gentle. The A484 by-passes Cydweli (Kidwelly) and you leave the main road at a traffic island and follow the local road into the town. The priory church of St. Mary's stands on the right of the main street opposite the White Lion and there is street parking adjacent to the church.

Cydweli's (Kidwelly's) origins may go back to the 6th century but it is noted, today, for its well preserved Norman castle which sits on a

Cydweli (Kidwelly) Castle

hill in what was once known as the 'old town'. The priory church is a lovely building inside and out with many interesting features. On entering you may feel a sense of unusual space. This is because the nave is exceptionally wide and is enhanced by a marvellously low, wide chancel arch. The church was linked to the Benedictine Priory which was established in Cydweli (Kidwelly) in 1130, a small outpost of Sherbourne Abbey. Its main purpose was probably to serve the castle but it would also have served the local population and pilgrims. When the priory was suppressed the church was allowed to continue as the parish church. Whether money changed hands for this transition is not recorded but it is likely that some cost fell on the local people. The church needed the local people's money again in 1884 when the spire fell (for the third time!) after being struck by lightning. This spurred a much needed restoration and it was all paid for by local donations. Today, well looked after, the church, surrounded by its grounds, looks across the river and roofs at the castle on the hill. It is reassuring to think that whilst the church has been maintained to continue its original function the mighty fortress is only maintained as a tourist attraction, its original purpose redundant if not forgotten.

But St. Mary's is a reminder to the pilgrim that just as 'faith seeks understanding', religion needs money. Pilgrims were always happy to pay their way. They well knew that the churches and monasteries where they received hospitality needed to be maintained. Pilgrims were often a vital source of monastic income in medieval times. Faith may be a free gift from God but the pilgrim must accept that wordly things such as buildings, even holy buildings, need paying for. Perhaps Cydweli (Kidwelly) is a place to reflect on the best use of money –

Cydweli (Kidwelly) Church

fortresses, when absolutely necessary, churches, certainly. But as well as buildings there must also be faith, love and justice. For without these, even a beautiful church like St. Mary's could soon be as empty of its original meaning as the mighty tourist attraction on the nearby hill.

Caerfyrddin (Carmarthen)

From Cydweli (Kidwelly) to Caerfyrddin (Carmarthen) you take the A484 for about nine miles. But before going into Caerfyrddin (Carmarthen) itself you might like to visit the old palace of the bishops of Tyddewi (St. David's) along the A40 at Abergwili. It may come as a surprise that, still so far from Tyddewi (St. David's) Cathedral, you might be able to visit the Bishop's Palace. But St. David, one way and another, is never far away and not always just where you would expect him. The old palace was turned into a museum in 1975 but it started life in the 13th century as a college of priests. The present buildings became the Bishop's Palace in 1542.

The museum's pamphlet, 'A Short History of the Building', has Bishop William Barlow as responsible for the move and the pamphlet shows him to be a shadowy figure, whose name is even uncertain. If the description is correct it is a reminder that power, even religious power, is often sought by those not best fit to exercise it. He is charged with removing the lead from the palace roof at Tyddewi (St. David's) to make it impossible to continue using the building, as part of his unsuccessful plot to move the whole Cathedral to Caerfyrddin (Carmarthen). Another, kinder, story is that the Bishop needed the lead because his six daughters all married poor clergymen and it was the only way of providing dowries! Barlow's successor was Robert Ferrar who suffered martyrdom at the hands of Queen Mary's agents, one of the many victims of religious power in the wrong hands. The palace has had an eventful life – decaying, restored, burned down and filled with war evacuees. It ceased to be the Bishop's Palace in 1974 when the Bishop moved to a modern house and office. The museum,

The Old Bishop's Palace, Abergwili

however, is of interest to the pilgrim because when building work and excavation unearthed remains of the two religious houses of Caerfyrddin (Carmarthen), this is where they were kept, together with some remains of Whitland Abbey. When the supermarket, Tesco, was built on the site of the friary they sent what they found to the museum and then decorated the walls of the store's café with monastic scenes. Parts of Caerfyrddin (Carmarthen) castle remain but nothing of the monastic houses.

For the pilgrim Caerfyrddin (Carmarthen) might be a good place to reflect on where pilgrimage should take you. Many tourists today by-pass Caerfyrddin (Carmarthen) as they hurry on into Penfro (Pembroke). But if people ignore what is around them and hold it of little value it may be forgotten and disappear. But the pilgrim is not a tourist. However little remains, there is always something for the pilgrim. Memories enshrined in names like Priory Street, Friars Park, Old Priory Row and even the décor in a supermarket café can speak of a past which continues to live in a present faith. The buildings are gone but the faith remains and so the pilgrimage continues.

Hendy-gwyn (Whitland) and Llanhuadain (Llawhaden)

The A40 from Carmarthen is a good road if rather busy at holiday times. At the traffic island by Hendy-gwyn (Whitland) turn right along the road signed for Llanboidy and turn immediately left. After half a mile down this country road you come to the abbey remains in a field on your left. There is very little left to see and what there is stands in a small walled field opposite a large Victorian house which has taken the name 'Whitland Abbey'. This valley is just the sort of quiet spot so often chosen for a foundation: good land, a stream and far from anywhere. It is a place to picnic or walk or reflect or just enjoy the quietness. The greatness and the beauty of the abbey are no more now than a small pile of worked stone, all that remains of a house established directly from Clairvaux and responsible, in its turn, for establishing Ystrad-fflur (Strata Florida). Only nature sings God's praises now where once the monks sang their divine office.

When you have returned to the A40 head on towards Hwlffordd (Haverfordwest) and take the right turning at the sign for Llanhuadain (Llawhaden) Castle. After a mile turn right signed for the church. Two miles down this winding lane takes you below the great fortress and into the valley of the Eastern Cleddau river. At the bridge leave the road and drive, under the cliffs, to the church car park. There may be more beautifully situated churches than this but St. Aidan's would surely satisfy the most demanding. The church, grounds, cliffs and river make it a special place. Here, pilgrims had the shelter and protection of both castle and church as they headed into the west and Tyddewi (St. David's). The Church is dedicated to St. Aidan who studied with St. David and went to become first bishop of Ferns in

Wexford. In later life he returned to be with St. David. What would they have made of this place today? Each age has its own priorities and problems. For Aidan and David it was establishing Christianity, to the Normans it was the safety of the body and the salvation of the soul. Today it is fishing! On the gatepost the signs say 'Private Fishing' and 'No

St. Aidan's Church

fishing on Sundays'. Apparently the modern sportsman has not always been sensitive to the holy nature of this place and, in 1998, severe restrictions were imposed by the vicar.

What would those who built the fortress-like church tower or those who built the mighty castle think of today's unusual concerns with fishing? Yet life is like that. David taught his followers to be faithful in the little things of life. He knew that very few are called to build great castles or fine churches; most will lead modest lives. Aidan and David both knew that most people's route to paradise lay on an ordinary road, though no easier for that, and that heaven would be reached through the many little things that go to make up a lifetime, even perhaps, by not fishing on Sundays.

Hwlffordd (Haverfordwest)

When you have made your way back to the A40 it is seven miles to Hwlffordd (Haverfordwest). This is a working town with little to detain the dedicated tourists who rush west towards the beaches and cliff walks of the Penfro (Pembroke) coast. There are ruins here, the Norman castle and the priory. The castle is in the town and the priory sits beside the river. The priory was a foundation of Augustinian Canons, as was Llanddewi Nant Hodni (Llanthony), now so far away in the east. How different today these two sets of ruins. Llanddewi Nant Hodni (Llanthony) remote, beautiful and still a place of hospitality and worship and Hwlffordd (Haverfordwest), hidden on the river bank, surrounded by buildings and by-pass roads and, though not at all remote, just as difficult to get to as Llanddewi Nant Hodni (Llanthony). You enter the town on the Arberth (Narberth) Road and take the signs for Town Centre until you get into the one-way system when you turn left into Quay street which becomes Union Hill.

Hwlffordd (Haverfordwest) Priory

83

Opposite some steps, which lead up to a tree-lined footpath, is the entrance to the priory. The priory remains have been recently excavated and restored and, although open to the public, there is only very limited on-street parking by the site or nearby. Visitors might find they have to find parking as close as possible and walk to the site.

Camros (Camrose)

To reach Camros (Camrose) leave Hwlffordd (Haverfordwest) as if you were going to use the A487 Tyddewi (St. David's) road, but at the traffic island where the A487 leaves the town take the B4330 signed for Croesgoch. This country road will take you along the valley of the Western Cleddau river. You will cross the little river three times as it winds along through the pleasant countryside before you see a left turning signed for Camros (Camrose). There is very little to the village of Camros (Camrose), a Baptist Chapel as you enter, the ancient parish Church and the houses. There is a small amount of parking in the village by the telephone and the church is down the lane beyond the telephone box.

Not many churches are dedicated to St. Ismael and they are all in this area of Wales. This is not the Biblical Ishmael but a son of Budic who was a member of the royal family in what is now Brittany. Budic came to Wales but was summoned back to become king in Armorica. Ismael and his two brothers went with their father but eventually returned to Wales and studied with St. David and St. Dyfrig. Ismael was eventually consecrated Bishop by St. Teilo and placed in charge of the Church in Menevia.

St. Ismael's church, apart from its tower, is like so many others across Wales. Yet it is good to pause here because this is the last known place where pilgrims would have rested before Tyddewi (St. David's) itself. Here the pilgrim may reflect on all the unknown or unsung people who carried the faith from David, Dyfrig, Teilo and others on to our present day. Here the great faith tradition, founded in Celtic times, is preserved without splendour or display. Camros (Camrose) is as much part of that tradition as is Tyddewi (St. David's) even if few, today, are aware of its existence. St. David's, rightly, has its place of eminence, but to reach Tyddewi (St. David's) as a pilgrim would have been impossible without all the places such as Camros (Camrose) which lined the route giving rest and refreshment. To go to Tyddewi (St. David's) today, without a thought to places like Camros (Camrose), would be to miss the point completely and be a tourist rather than a pilgrim.

Tyddewi (St. David's)

Rejoin the A487 by way of any of the country roads from Camros (Camrose) and begin the final part of your journey into the western corner of Wales. The landscape takes on that special beauty which attracts so many people to Penfro (Pembroke). This is a country of coastal walks and it may well be that the pilgrims of medieval times completed the final part of their pilgrimage along the strands and coastal paths which are such an attraction today. The pilgrims' progress on foot, often with the sick and elderly, would have been painfully slow by modern standards and many of the places where they would

Tyddewi (St. David's) Cathedral

have stopped and rested are not remembered or recorded and cannot be identified today. But as they approached Tyddewi (St. David's) they would have taken rest and refreshment where they could and you might like to do the same.

If so, a perfect spot is Solfach (Solva), just beside the main road. Today it still offers hospitality in the form of quayside parking, public toilets and a local inn. There is no pilgrimage connection at Solfach (Solva) but it is well worth a visit just to sample the beauty of this coastline before going on into Tyddewi (St. David's). It is a good place to reflect and refresh yourself before journey's end. The journey from the little chapel and the ancient ruins at Llanddewi Nant Hodni (Llanthony), in the Black Mountains, to Tyddewi (St. David's) has

been long and varied and now the destination is very close. You are in the country St. David would have walked, known, loved, left and returned to. There is no need for hurry, it has all been here for a very long time. It has received so many pilgrims in the past and will receive many more in the future. A short pause for reflection and preparation is extremely appropriate and Solfach (Solva) is a lovely place to make that pause.

So much has been written about Tyddewi (St. David's) that it is hard to add anything. But one thing might be remembered: the place was originally chosen because it was so remote. St. David sought to draw followers to him. He wanted a lonely place in order to be apart from the world and therefore closer to God. But why this particular place in those far-off days? The story says he was born here and his mother was Saint Non. Her holy well and the remains of her chapel are only about one mile away towards the coast. Today, St. David's tradition is carried on here by a retreat centre. And there is a small, pretty chapel which looks ancient but was founded only in 1934.

The great buildings of Tyddewi (St. David's), as elsewhere, are more a monument to Norman piety and force than the strong Celtic faith that preceded them and so often outlasted them. To look for David in the monuments and their grandeur may be to lose him, to feel him recede. The pilgrim today might look for St. David, as the pilgrims did of old, in the signs and symbols around them in Tyddewi (St. David's) as it is now. One way to do this is to go to the little city's centre and stand on the steps of the 14th century cross looking out towards the coast. You will look out over the War Memorial Garden with its flag-pole and see the lower town together with the Tabernacle

Chapel dedicated to Non

Presbyterian Church and the top of the cathedral tower. Beyond is the open coastal country. Tyddewi (St. David's) is a very small city, and would even be small as a town, but like many other Welsh settlements of all sizes it has a variety of places of religious worship. But never very far away is the beautiful countryside, a reminder, if one is needed, that man's search for God takes place in God's world and is as much reflected in how man treats that world as the churches and chapels and other buildings that are thrust upon it.

If you leave the cross and go down to the cathedral you will arrive at a great fortress-like gate house. This is a reminder that although faith finds expression in religion, religion can give rise to power, power to greed and greed to violence. We may build to the glory of God in churches and chapels but we often build to other less laudable glories as the route to Tyddewi (St. David's) has shown. For almost every place of prayer and worship you have passed there was almost always a fortress. Today's all too human ambitions may not find expression in castles but they do, regrettably, find expression.

Looking down on the cathedral and its surroundings the pilgrim may ask, "Why has the cathedral lasted and the palace fallen?" "Why do so many have to suffer that so few may prosper?" The tourist doesn't ask or cares little for the answer. The pilgrim needs to ask and try to understand. For everyone, pilgrim and tourist alike, there are guides, pamphlets, books and souvenirs to provide information about Tyddewi (St. David's). But where in all of this is David himself and any answers he might have given? Where is the monk and the teacher who set out on foot to bring a message to all the world he could reach? Where is the faith he brought and passed on so well to others? It is still in Tyddewi (St. David's), very much in Tyddewi (St. David's). But if you have not been to Camros (Camrose) and Hendy-gwyn (Whitland), to Abertawe (Swansea), Nedd (Neath), Llandaf and Llanddewi Nant Hodni (Llanthony) and all the other places, it remains invisible, unknowable.

Those who rush to Tyddewi (St. David's) from wherever see just another place. The pilgrim arrives carrying all the heavy baggage collected on a longer and slower journey. The pilgrim brings the

questions, doubts, and uncertainties which, together with joy and hope, are the inevitable companions of faith. Tyddewi (St. David's) is a place to lay them all down for a brief time and feel the many years of faith that have gone before in this place. To stand silently somewhere for a while, where David might have stood, and be in God's presence and reflect. To ask for the strength to change enough to pick up all that awkward baggage of faith and, with all the hopes, joys and fears of a simple pilgrim, to travel on.

FROM TYDDEWI (ST. DAVID'S) TO YNYS ENLLI (BARDSEY)

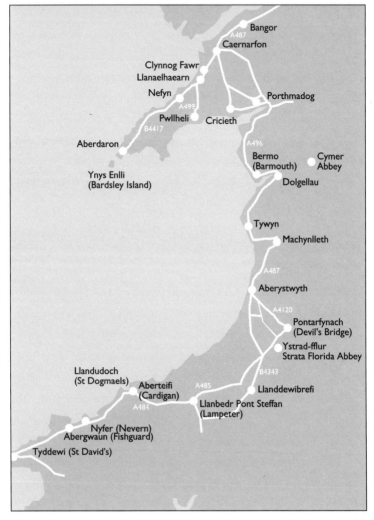

The route from Tyddewi (St. David's) to Ynys Enlli (Bardsey) runs up the western side of the country, often along the coast, to the Llŷn Peninsula. The route begins on the A487 through Abergwaun (Fishguard) and goes on to Aberteifi (Cardigan). From there you follow the A484 and then the A475 to Llanbedr Pont Steffan (Lampeter). After Llanbedr Pont Steffan (Lampeter) you follow the B4343 which stays close to the river until you reach Llanddewibrefi. From Llanddewibrefi you continue on the B4343 through Tregaron and on to Pontrhydfendigaid where a right turn leads to Ystrad-fflur (Strata Florida). Rejoining the B4343 you continue to Pontarfynach (Devil's Bridge) where you turn left and travel alongside the Vale of Rheidol on the A4120 until you reach Aberystwyth. Llanbadarn Fawr is a small village on the eastern side of Aberystwyth. After Llanbadarn Fawr you take the A44 for a short while and turn onto the A4159 which then joins the A487 and travel on to Machynlleth. After Machynlleth you cross the Dyfi river, turn left and follow the A493 through Aberdyfi to Tywyn. You continue on the A493 and, near Dolgellau, briefly join the A470 to visit Cymer Abbey. From Cymer you head out to the coast on the A496 and Llanfair is just off the main road about one mile short of Harlech. Heading north you join the A487 which runs into Porthmadog. Here you enter the Llŷn Peninsula. The suggested route is to follow the A487 and cross over to the north coast and the A499 by the country road from Penygroes. The A499 runs down to Clynnog Fawr and from there you follow the route through the Pilgrim Churches to Aberdaron described in pages 36-45.

What are we to make of those ancient pilgrims who, having made their slow, hard journey to Tyddewi (St. David's) then set out for far

distant Ynys Enlli (Bardsey)? Were they very holy or very mad? By what passes for wisdom today, probably both! It is almost impossible for the mind of one age to understand the mind of any other age. Scholars may learn to feel some real companionship with a distant time but, for the ordinary people of today, the ordinary people of the medieval age can sometimes seem almost as alien in their practices and beliefs as if they had come from another planet let alone another time. For the medieval Christian, heaven, purgatory and hell were as real as life itself. Life after death was much more important than life before death and the agency which governed these divine mysteries was the Church. The medieval Church was not like any Church we know today; it was more powerful than kings and its authority, running as it did beyond the grave, greater than any government.

The Church could and did allocate punishments for sin in this life and the next. It could also remit those punishments. Two pilgrimages to Tyddewi (St. David's) and Ynys Enlli (Bardsey), as already mentioned, equalled one to Rome, ranking them in importance alongside Santiago de Compostella, the resting place of St. James the Apostle. But few, if any, popular writers explain exactly what this meant. What did people actually get? It probably had a lot to do with indulgences. Indulgences were granted by the Church for holy actions such as pilgrimage. Sin, it was taught, attracted punishments in this life as well as the next. Disaster or misfortune could be punishments for sinful living. The worst punishment of all was, of course, eternal damnation. Indulgences could ward off the consequences of sin so both the living and the dead stood in need of indulgences. The holier the place the more powerful the indulgence. First the Holy Land,

second Rome and then places like Santiago de Compostella, Tyddewi (St. David's) and Ynys Enlli (Bardsey). At these places it was believed possible to protect yourself and win the souls of others from purgatory and hell after death. No wonder people flocked to such places. Very much the same was true of relics. Imagine the divine favours that a small piece of the true cross could confer on even the worst sinner.

The Reformation swept it all away, not only the superstition surrounding indulgences and relics but the great monastic houses which sustained the pilgrims. The whole business of pilgrimage came to an abrupt halt. Tyddewi (St. David's) and Ynys Enlli (Bardsey) ceased to be places of importance and sank into obscurity. But although much had become distorted and superstitious there was, at the centre of pilgrimage, faith, and that remained. Slowly this ancient expression of faith began to return.

If you make the long journey, today, from Tyddewi (St. David's) to Ynys Enlli (Bardsey) and pass through the remote remains of Ystrad-fflur (Strata Florida) Abbey you will almost certainly carry your own burden of today's superstitions even if you do not recognise them as such. But you will see the Glory of God in some wonderful country. You will pass through places where God has been praised and faith preserved for over a thousand years. You will be a strange person indeed if the journey does not change you. When you finally stand on the tip of the Llŷn Peninsula and look out to almost forgotten Ynys Enlli (Bardsey) take time to look at yourself as well as the island. And if, in travelling, you have changed it will be because you are indeed a pilgrim.

Nyfer (Nevern)

You leave Tyddewi (St. David's) by the A487 and head for Abergwaun (Fishguard) where the Irish ferry is a reminder that in this part of Wales you are nearer Ireland than England. Following the A487 you pass through the little resort of Trefdraeth (Newport) and a little further on take the left turn signed for Nyfer (Nevern). The road descends into the valley and, after passing an inn, you cross over the river into the village where the church is straight ahead. There is a small amount of parking by the church gates alongside the old mounting block. The river Nyfer (Nevern) runs into the sea at Trefdraeth (Newport) and today there is a designated footpath joining the village and the estuary. It may well follow a similar route to that taken by ancient pilgrims.

Nyfer (Nevern) church has an excellent guide book which takes the visitor around all there is to see in this lovely and interesting church, and there is indeed much to see. Nearby there is what may be a Pilgrims' Cross carved in the rock and there are some ancient bi-lingual

St. Brynach's Church, Nyfer (Nevern)

95

The Celtic Cross, Nyfer (Nevern)

stones which bear inscriptions in Ogham and Latin. Ogham was an ancient writing system used to write Old Irish. The fact that these inscriptions were also in Latin not only provided a clue to their age but helped scholars unlock the Ogham script. The church also boasts one of the most perfect Celtic crosses in Wales, the Great Cross. All of this is of interest to any visitor. Add the old mounting block, the yew alley, the perpendicular architecture of the church with its Norman tower, the beautiful setting, and you have a place of delight. Everyone can come and enjoy what Professor Sir John Rhŷs called 'a remarkable group of antiquities in such a small place'. But the pilgrim may well ask, what has all of this to do with David or with the message he brought? The church is dedicated to St. Brynach. Like many other Celtic saints little is really known about him and what is known somewhat doubtful. Some say he was the St. Brannock who founded a monastery in Devon. The church guide gives him a very varied character – friend of David, Irish by birth, married to a chieftain's daughter, founder of churches and a hermit!

All that can be said for certain is that, whoever founded this church, it has acquired a considerable overlay of people and things. The pilgrim may reflect that personal faith often suffers the same way. The faith is there, somewhere, tucked away but perhaps hidden by so many other things that seem more immediately interesting, important and attractive. These things may not of themselves be wrong or bad, but if they distort or impair faith they can lead down quite a different road from that which faith would lead. So enjoy Nyfer (Nevern), it is beautiful, but see here, among the 'antiquities', the faith that has endured since the days of St. Brynach and St. David.

Llandudoch (St. Dogmaels)

From Nyfer (Nevern) you can continue on the country road, the B4582, until it rejoins the A487 or go back to the main road. At the outskirts of Aberteifi (Cardigan) you will come to a traffic island where Llandudoch (St. Dogmaels) is signposted. The abbey ruins are in what is now really a suburb of Aberteifi (Cardigan) even though it is across the estuary of the river Teifi. As you enter the suburb you will see a sign directing you left to the ruins. Drive round the ruins and, opposite a duck pond, there is car parking by the entrance. What is left of the abbey now shares a site with a church of comparatively recent construction but built to the traditional design. A wall separates the old and the new but a gateway allows you to pass from one to the other.

St. Dogmael was a Welsh monk of the 5th or 6th century who may have belonged to the family of the great chieftain Cunedda. The ruins, however, date from a much later period, established in the wake of the Norman invaders, and the monks who lived here would have been

Ruins of Llandudoch Abbey (St. Dogmaels)

Benedictines. Dogmael, like David and the Celtic monks, followed no founder's rule when they lived in community. The monasticism they followed was very ancient and independent and quite remote from the great monastic orders which had found favour in Rome. The Church which they created in Britain was Celtic and owed little, if anything, to the styles of Rome and when Pope Gregory the Great sent the Benedictine St. Augustine to convert the pagan Saxons of southern England there was already an established and vigorous local Church throughout the north and west of these islands. Regrettably the two traditions found it difficult to co-exist and, whilst they could agree about the beliefs of their faith, they seemed able to agree about little else. They argued about worship, allegiances and even the date for Easter. At the Synod of Whitby in 664 the primacy of the Roman tradition was established and, with the coming of the Normans, monastic life in Wales became what it was elsewhere in Europe and the monasteries were organised by the rules such as those laid down by St. Benedict or the more severe code of the Cistercians.

All of this may seem remote and irrelevant among the quiet remains of Llandudoch (St. Dogmaels) but as Cardinal John Henry Newman said, 'to live is to change'. What Dogmael and David laboured so hard to establish subsequent generations changed to suit their own changed times. Here the pilgrim can reflect on what is needed today to keep faith alive and moving on. The Celtic Church needed courage and sacrifice, the medieval Church needed rules and obedience. What, today, needs to be built-up or pulled down, kept or thrown out? How must our understanding and expression of faith change, not only to survive but to move on into future generations?

Maenordeifi Old Church

Maenordeifi

When leaving Llandudoch (St. Dogmaels) return to the traffic island and take the A478 signed for Dinbych-y-pysgod (Tenby). When you come to the village of Pen-y-bryn there is a left turning signed for Cilgerran. After you pass through the village of Cilgerran, where the remains of the mighty fortress stand high above the Teifi, there is a left turn signed for Llechryd. You will eventually come to a T-junction. Turn left and drive down to the river. On the right just before the bridge is a lane with a sign directing you to a church which is about a mile and a half down the lane. There is parking for one car by the entrance to the church.

Quite why this church survived when so many others like it have disappeared is something of a mystery. As a parish church it was replaced late in the 19th century, perhaps because the site has always been subject to flooding. There is even a coracle at the back of the church as a reminder of this eventuality! The modern, urban eye may

not be able to see what population the church ever served and certainly wonder at what population it might serve today. Maenordeifi is a glorious muddle of a church, its fabric and design are 13th century and the furnishings of the nave 18th century. These box pews, each specially built for the well-off families who would use them, are a wonderful insight into a bygone practice of faith. Especially interesting are those at the front which are furnished with their own fireplaces! Outside there are some splendid Georgian monuments incongruously grafted onto the ancient fabric. And the church has had three different dedications. Originally dedicated to St. Llawddog, son of the Prince of Usk, it was rededicated by the Normans to St. Lawrence and then rededicated in the 12th century to St. David. This insignificant little valley church could well have been host to pilgrims as they made their way along the Teifi valley and it would have been at such little churches as Maenordeifi that they would have sought hospitality. Here, what was on offer would have been quite different from the great monastic foundations. Here, they would have shared whatever the local people had, however little that might be.

At Maenordeifi the pilgrim may reflect on the nature of sharing. It is comparatively easy for someone who has a great deal to give to those in need. To give when there is very little to give from is, perhaps, a truer sign of love. It is in places like this little church that the pilgrim can reflect that, no matter how well off one may be, one always needs others. To be a pilgrim one must learn to be open to receive what even the humblest has to offer. Anyone who feels they have nothing to learn, no need of others, cannot change and anyone who cannot change cannot be a pilgrim no matter how far they travel.

Llanbedr Pont Steffan (Lampeter)

When you leave the little church of Maenordeifi and reach the bridge cross over the river and turn right along the A484 heading for Llanbedr Pont Steffan (Lampeter). It is quite a long run but the road is good and the scenery pleasant. The name Llanbedr Pont Steffan means The church of Peter by the Bridge of Stephen. The bridge referred to was said to have been constructed by order of King Stephen and the parish church is still dedicated to St. Peter. You will see the parish church soon after you enter the town. It stands above the road on the left and is part of an interesting little group of places of worship. At the roadside opposite the church is the Welsh Presbyterian Chapel of Shiloh. On the hill beside the Victorian parish church is a small white church, the Roman Catholic church of Mount Carmel. How is it, one may ask, that a faith can survive and even thrive and yet be so fragmented? What would the medieval pilgrims have made of this little group had it been there as they slogged up the Teifi valley? The idea that the Church could be divided up into sections would surely have been almost unthinkable to them. No trace remains today of the religious foundation which would have been here in those times to offer the pilgrims hospitality. The gothic-style church of St. Peter's only dates from 1870 although the original foundation is much older. But Llanbedr Pont Steffan (Lampeter) is not without religious connections. The university, which is all most people think of if they think of Llanbedr Pont Steffan (Lampeter) at all, was founded in 1822 as a college to provide education for men training for ordination in the Church of England and now offers over fifty undergraduate courses in Religious Studies or Theology.

St. Peter's Parish Church, Llanbedr Pont Steffan (Lampeter)

103

Llanbedr Pont Steffan (Lampeter) cannot offer monastic ruins or medieval churches to aid reflection. It has really very little to offer the tourist. It is a good place for the pilgrim to take a break and some refreshment. The three places of worship, passed as you enter the town, may offer some food for thought. Are they a symbol of how religion can divide as well as unite? A reminder that there is always a need for diversity in any human endeavour? Or a sign of the eventual triumph of tolerance? Llanbedr Pont Steffan (Lampeter) has no special answers; it just sits quietly beside the Teifi, part of the route to Ystrad-fflur (Strata Florida) and, eventually, Ynys Enlli (Bardsey). A place where the pilgrim may pause, rest and then pass on.

Llanddewibrefi

You carry on through Llanbedr Pont Steffan (Lampeter) and, just after you have crossed the river, you turn left on the B4343 which heads off beside the river to Tregaron. You have been following the Teifi ever since Llandudoch (St. Dogmaels), where it enters the sea, but this country road sticks much closer to the river and is very picturesque. It passes through comfortable farm land and there is a feeling of affluence as one passes through the neat, prosperous villages and by the substantial houses. This was once dangerous country where the Christian message was brought only at great risk and many nameless missionaries must have died at their task where others, like David, succeeded and lived. The road eventually runs into Llanddewibrefi and, when you get to a junction at the centre of the village, the parish church is just opposite to the right. You can park by the church gates

and there is also a free car park with a very tight entrance signed just along the road. The church is a massive and beautiful building with a great central tower and stands on a hill which is now the churchyard. The church looks out on one side over the village roofs but round the back the hill falls sharply away down to the river that runs below.

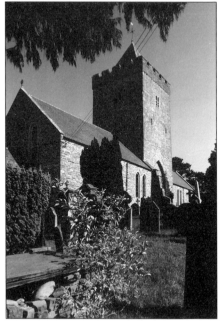

Llandewibrefi Parish Church

Llanddewibrefi is quite a big village but it is hard to imagine it as a place of importance and, today, it would not make any such claim. But to the pilgrim it has considerable significance. It was in Llanddewibrefi that St. David is thought to have conducted his most famous mission. Not surprisingly a miraculous story arose round this great event. It is said that as David spoke the very ground he stood on grew up under his feet and formed a hill so that the great crowd that had assembled could see as well as hear him. This story makes a lovely connection with the situation of the church. David is said to have revisited Llanddewibrefi and spoken to the assembled Welsh Church after a pestilence had swept the land and caused confusion and terror.

What David founded has survived and thrived. Llanddewibrefi has, besides its great church, several chapels. All of these places of worship are a reminder that, although faith is held individually, it finds proper expression communally. David's teachings about Christianity would certainly have stressed that faith must have practical outcomes, that faith must reach out to others. The Christian life was and is one of community, the monastic community for some, but the ordinary community of daily life for most. If you stand under the great church tower and look out across the river below it may be as well to remember that pilgrimage is an interlude, not a permanent state. The pilgrim travels to change but seeks that change in order to return better able to live in and serve whatever community was left in order to undertake the pilgrimage.

Ystrad-fflur (Strata Florida)

Leave Llanddewibrefi along the B4343 heading for Tregaron, a local centre and quite attractive in a quiet sort of way. Continuing along the B4343 you still run alongside the river on your left but the countryside becomes very different. The land on the left hand side of the road is wetland and was described in the Ward Lock Red Guide of 1965 as 'probably unique in England and Wales' where 'trenches from which the peat has been cut and piles of turves drying in the wind and sun are to be seen'. It was countryside which seemed more Irish than Welsh and today is of interest primarily as a wild life sanctuary. Such a bog would have been a dangerous place and pilgrims would probably have avoided it and headed for higher ground on their way to Ystrad-fflur

(Strata Florida). Beyond the wetland you come to the village of Pontrhydfendigaid. Look out for a right turn just past the the war memorial where a sign directs you to the abbey. This lane, lined by small trees, passes through marshy land with the little river never far away until you arrive at the abbey ruins about a mile and a half away.

The west doorway of Ystrad-fflur (Strata Florida)

There is parking and toilets opposite the abbey entrance and a telephone box at the church gate. The abbey shop is by the entrance and beside the abbey ruins, separated by a high wall, is a small church with considerable grounds which spread round behind the ruins.

This once great abbey was a Cistercian foundation, established in 1164, a daughter house of Hendy-gwyn (Whitland) which in its turn was founded directly from Clairvaux. Clairvaux is intimately associated with St. Bernard who was abbot there and one of the greatest saints of the period. The Cistercians were an offshoot of the Benedictines and their name derived from the monastery of Citeaux or Cistercium south of Dijon. Their beginning was anything but promising under their founder Robert and his successor at Citeaux, Alberic, who, in adapting the rule of St. Benedict, made it so severe that many felt the order would never survive. Bernard joined the order at a low ebb in its fortunes in 1112 when there were very few foundations but by the time of his death in 1153 there were three hundred and forty Cistercian abbeys and soon after 1200 there were well over one thousand spread across Western Europe. Such was the influence and importance of St. Bernard that it was said of him that 'he carried the twelfth century on his shoulders'.

The Cistercians, with their strict mode of life, sought remoteness for their foundations and Ystrad-fflur (Strata Florida) is a good example of the situations they chose. Ystrad-fflur (Strata Florida) means 'Valley of Flowers' and it is a beautiful, if wild and remote, place. It may not be immediately apparent how an abbey could not only survive here but become rich. That it was a rich abbey is well illustrated by the great west doorway which still greets visitors after

they pass through the entrance. The monks of this abbey were great sheep farmers and there were many lay brothers to tend the flocks that grazed the high pastures belonging to the abbey here and elsewhere. But if agriculture provided the income it was prayer, praise and worship that were at the centre of the life of the abbey. If you could float above the ruins you would see that, on going through the great west door, you would once have entered a mighty cruciform church. Here the monks sang the daily office and heard Mass. The remains of the three chapels of the south transept are roofed over to protect the ancient tiles which still cover the floors of these chapels. Ystrad-fflur (Strata Florida) was not a Celtic foundation yet in difficult times it allied itself firmly to the Welsh cause rather than the English and it is said that many Welsh princes found their last resting place here. One famous Welshman who may be buried here was Dafydd ap Gwilym, the greatest medieval Welsh poet, whose approach to religion is illustrated in the following lines (trans. Sir Idris Bell):

'Never was Sunday that passed by

But at Llanbadarn* church was I.

To some fair maid turning my face

And the nape of my neck to God's good grace.'

Something of a counterpoint to what some may think of as the excessive piety of the period!

Today Ystrad-fflur (Strata Florida) is still remote and the country round about is still beautiful. There is a local 7-11 mile round walk passing the Teifi Pools mapped out near the entrance for those who want to explore. But it is a walk for serious, well-equipped walkers, not a stroll for the casual visitor. At Ystrad-fflur (Strata Florida) the pilgrim

*Llanbadarn Church is the next step on the journey.

may stand and enjoy the glory of God's creation and man's work among that creation and feel fortunate to stand in such a place. Here the pilgrim may remember the strict rules which once governed life in this place and reflect on the rules which govern lives today. Life needs rules, but rules are meant to serve life not the other way round. If we look at the rules we value we may ask, do they really help us to go where we ultimately wish to go? And if they do not, what then?

Llanbadarn

When you return to Pontrhydfendigaid from Ystrad-fflur (Strata Florida) you will have a choice of routes to Llanbadarn. The pilgrims may have gone to follow the river Ystwyth or headed for the Rheidol Valley. You have the same choice. The B4340 is a left turn just after the village and winds over the hills and gives you a choice of routes along the Ystwyth valley into Aberystwyth. To go via the Vale of Rheidol continue on along the B4343 to Pontarfynach (Devil's Bridge) known for its waterfall and the Vale of Rheidol steam railway. At Pontarfynach (Devil's Bridge) you turn left along the A4120. This road gives you marvellous views as it runs high above the valley. Eventually the road descends into the outskirts of Aberystwyth where you turn right and follow the signs for Llanbadarn. The church stands above the road on the left and there is parking just before you reach it. There is also parking beyond the church in the main street.

Llanbadarn is now firmly part of Aberystwyth although near the outskirts. Yet once it was more the other way round. Llanbadarn was a great and important centre and it was not until the 18th century that

the people of the town felt they needed their own church. As the importance and population of Aberystwyth grew and more parishes were founded, Llanbadarn declined. Just how important Llanbadarn was can be judged by the size and magnificence of its church. Yet even this great church is a mere shadow of what Llanbadarn once was. The church is named for St.

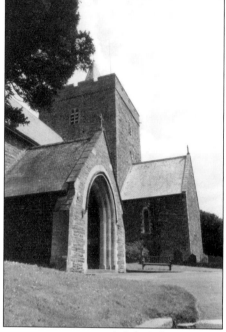

St. Padarn's Church, Llanbadarn

Padarn. Tradition has him as a missionary who came with his monks from Brittany to convert the Welsh but, as with so many of the saints, this is uncertain. He was one of the great missionaries and the monastery that he founded at Llanbadarn became a centre of monasticism and learning. In its great days the library at Llanbadarn was greater than those at either York or Canterbury. The flowering of scholarship and art that took place here in the 11th century is illustrated by the facsimile of a page from the beautiful Rhygyfarch's Psalter (1079) which hangs opposite the door of the church.

The church is wonderfully well kept today, and has made considerable efforts so that what the past has left can be made available to the present. Llanbadarn is a wonderful place to reflect on the importance of giving way and handing on, of allowing new people to find new ways, of valuing the past but being open to the future. Everyone must eventually move on and if one can leave a strong legacy of faith for a new generation to build on, that is as great a personal monument as the wonderful church at Llanbadarn.

Tywyn

Leave Llanbadarn by turning right at the end of the main street and turning left when you reach the main road. You will leave Aberystwyth by the A44. Not far along this road you turn left on to the A4159 and pass through Capel Dewi. Soon after, you join the A487. The pilgrims chose to walk the flat coastland and crossed the Dyfi estuary by boat. There is a coast road, the B4572, but there is no ferry and to cross the river you must go through Machynlleth. Driving straight through Machynlleth you cross the river and turn immediately left after the bridge heading for Aberdyfi. It is a lovely drive down the estuary and Aberdyfi is a charming little resort. After Aberdyfi the road runs on along the flat coastland beside the railway and you soon reach Tywyn. In the Baedeker of 1968 Towyn, the English spelling, is described as 'a popular seaside resort'.

Like many seaside resorts it has seen better days. The church lies on the main street just before the Corbett Arms. It is a reminder that this little town has a history and importance that go well beyond seaside

Norman nave and Victorian tower, Tywyn

holidays. The church is dedicated to St. Cadfan, another Breton monk who came to Christianise the Welsh. He established a monastery at Tywyn and he is associated with no less a place than Ynys Enlli (Bardsey). In Norman times the Augustinian Canons came to Tywyn and established a priory where the old Celtic monastery had been. The church is a reminder of these Norman times. Although an architectural jumble of a church the nave is almost pure Norman. As for the rest, the medieval tower fell down in 1692 and the nave was shortened to build a new tower in 1715. There is a large stone which stands opposite the main door which adds the 8th century to the jumble just for good measure! The Victorians decided to build a central tower and almost all the church beyond the nave is their work. St. Cadfan's has a long history but it is certainly not a museum, it is a working parish church.

If St. Cadfan's church has a varied history then St. Cadfan's Well can match it. Many saints had holy wells and Cadfan was no exception. Pilgrims visited the well for the cures it was said to offer. But times changed and holy wells fell into disuse or disappeared. The well became a spa when that fashion prevailed and when it passed the spa, with the well, became a stable. Horses gave way to cars and the stable became a garage. Today the site is a private house on the right at the end of a lane between the chapel and the National Westminster Bank, quite near the church. Perhaps the pilgrim here might reflect that faith needs to grow and growth involves change. Habit and routine may be helpful in living faith but they are never, themselves, faith.

Llangelynnin

From Tywyn you continue on the A493 which runs inland before turning back out to the coast. You will travel between the flat coastal land on your left and the mountains around Cader Idris on your right, a wonderful journey. When the road reaches the coast you are rewarded with some marvellous coastal views. Soon after reaching the coast you will come to the village of Llangelynnin but before you do watch out for a sign on your left directing you down to an ancient church. Opposite the sign there is a rough lay-by. Do not try to drive down to the church: it is a short, steep and narrow lane and there is no parking. Park in the lay-by and walk down the lane where you will find a little ancient church hanging, it seems, just above the sea.

The history of the church claims that it is on the site of a pathway that existed hereabouts as early as about 700 BC so one might reasonably assume that this church was on the coastal path the pilgrims would probably have used. The church is dedicated to St. Celynnin

Llangelynnin Old Church

115

about whom very little is known and nothing for certain, not unusual with the Celtic saints. He was probably an early missionary and may, like many others, be buried on Ynys Enlli (Bardsey). As you would expect, this little church does not reflect frequent use but neither does it have an air of abandonment. It was unused for a long time but was re-opened in 1917. It is interesting in so many ways. The wall enclosure around the churchyard is an excellent example of what 'llan' meant, a holy enclosure, not just a church. Parts of this building are very old indeed. Most Celtic churches were of wood and were replaced by stone structures but here the situation was unusual: wood was scarce and stone plentiful so parts of this building are very early, from the 8th or 9th centuries. The little guide to the church is wonderfully informative and even notes the miraculous water stoop in the wall of the porch which re-filled itself when empty. Sadly it also gives the explanation of this 'miracle'. The wonder ceased when the drainage behind the porch wall was improved! Inside the church is a horse bier which was still carrying coffins here up to the end of the 19th century.

Of course such a little church, so difficult to get to, could not serve a modern community and if you drive on to the modern village of Llangelynnin, on the right just as you enter the village is the new church that replaced the old. It is built in the same style and is quite pretty. It has a long way to go to have the same history of faith as the old church by the sea but one day it may get there. The pilgrim may, in the old church or the new, reflect on what one must keep, leave, change, re-visit or replace in one's own life so that faith may grow and develop.

Cymer

The pilgrims would probably have continued along the coast and crossed the Mawddach estuary by boat. The modern traveller must go inland and cross the river near Dolgellau although there is a toll bridge at Penmaen-pŵl (Penmaenpool) which offers a short cut and where the George III inn has lovely views over tidal reaches of the river. Not

Cymer Abbey

taking this short cut allows you to visit the remains of Cymer Abbey tucked away alongside the river Mawddach near the village of Llanelltud. Continue on along the A493 and when you come to the junction with the main A470 turn left. The abbey ruins are signed,

almost straight away, to the right. The ruins sit in a delightful spot and are surrounded by dwellings and farm buildings some of which were actually part of the abbey.

It may be hard, today, for the visitor to look at ancient ruins and make any sort of sense of how the original buildings were arranged. It is, however, a bit easier at Cymer than at some other places because it was quite small compared to many of its sister foundations. Cymer was Cistercian but came comparatively late, in the 13th century. The location is typical, 'far from the concourse of men'. The walls that remain standing are those of the church and the ground slopes down to the low remains of the cloister and the little culverted stream which runs so clear and pretty, especially in wet weather, but at one time it was the drain that led from the latrines! Cymer seems never to have been great in size or wealth. The times in which it was founded were troubled and wars complicated the financial problems the monks never seemed able to shake off. Cymer shows that life could be very difficult for the medieval monks and not all abbeys became wealthy and comfortable. Time, that unpredictable agent, leaves us with a lovely ruin at humble Cymer whereas at mighty Hendy-gwyn (Whitland) almost nothing remains. It is not easy to tell from the ruins that this was a poor relation but that is because what wealth can so easily apply, circumstances can so very quickly strip away.

Cymer Abbey is a gentle, beautiful, even romantic spot. It calls out to be walked in on sunny afternoons, to be painted or photographed. It seems totally at peace and harmony with its lovely surroundings. Perhaps the ruins may teach the pilgrim something about happiness. The pursuit of happiness is a lifelong endeavour because moments of

happiness do not last. The search for happiness may be more rewarded if you know what you are really looking for. Rather than striving to surround oneself with the comforts and security that money can provide, happiness may be more a matter of finding harmony with one's situation, however difficult that may be.

Llanfair

When you leave Cymer Abbey and rejoin the A470 you turn right and then left and head along the beautiful Mawddach estuary towards Abermo (Barmouth). This is marvellous countryside and it is easy to see why it has attracted so many visitors over the years. Going on through the resort of Abermo (Barmouth) you drive along the A496 towards Harlech. You will now be running alongside Parc Cenedlaethol Eryri (the Snowdonia National Park) with Yr Wyddfa (Snowdon) itself in the distance and across the sea to the left if the weather is clear you will get views of the Llŷn Peninsula and even, perhaps, Ynys Enlli (Bardsey), your final destination. Llanfair is a small village and is signed just off the main road about one mile from Harlech. Next to the church gate just on the right as you enter the village is a telephone box and car parking for one or two cars. You enter the churchyard through a lychgate and the church awaits you at the end of a yew-lined path. The church is so like many others with its little bell above the main door and simple design. It stands within its 'llan', surrounded by the graves of those that have lived, worshipped and died here. Llanfair is by-passed today. It may have been on the pilgrim route once as they slowly moved on to nearby Harlech Castle

Llanfair Parish Church

and the shelter and protection of the great fortress, but it is not on the route to anywhere today. Visitors still hurry on to visit the great castle but few, if any, stop at the little church.

But something here may be of interest to the pilgrim – the graveyard. The graves inside the old wall filled the space allotted to the church and a new piece of land behind the church has been brought into use for burials. Why is it so important to so many people to lie in holy ground? It surely must say something about belief in what lies beyond the grave. The pilgrim may reflect here on that final act common to every life, death. Is it something pushed away from thought, something too difficult to face? If pilgrimage is about anything it is about travelling and arriving. Every pilgrimage must end, even the pilgrimage of life. Wandering is not pilgrimage, pilgrims have a clear destination. Faith is not vague hopes, it also must have a clear destination. At Llanfair it is possible to look across the sea to your

destination, the Llŷn Peninsula and Ynys Enlli (Bardsey). In this little, rather lonely churchyard, you might reflect on that other destination which lies at the end of every life and ask, is it an ending or a new beginning?

The Llŷn Peninsula and Ynys Enlli (Bardsey)

Return to the main road and continue towards Harlech. At Harlech you can follow the main road onwards or turn right into the little town and visit the castle. True, the castle is not a holy place, but it would have had its priests or monks to serve those who lived there and the pilgrims may well have sought its hospitality on their long journey. If you go through Harlech you can drive on along the wooded B4573 until you come down to the low coastal ground and join the main road. Quite soon you see a toll road signed on the left. Here, the road joins the railway and they cross the estuary together. You run up into

Ynys Enlli (Bardsey)

121

the village of Penrhyndeudraeth where you join the main A487 for the drive into Porthmadog. Before Porthmadog you will pass signs on your left for that modern oddity, Portmeirion. It is interesting to contrast all that you have seen of the Celtic, Norman and medieval building with the fantasy of Portmeirion. If anything remains of it in five hundred years what will it say to the people of that time about those who built it, lived in it and visited it?

At Porthmadog you have a choice. The final route down to Ynys Enlli (Bardsey) is from Clynnog Fawr, the final resting place of that great saint Beuno. This route is described on pages 15-53 in the section on Treffynnon (Holywell) to Ynys Enlli (Bardsey). To get to Clynnog Fawr you will need to cross the Llŷn Peninsula. The simple way is to drive up the A487 towards Caernarfon and turn left in the village of Pen-y-groes and follow the country roads until you come to the A499. Then turn left and run down to Clynnog Fawr. If you feel adventurous you can try to go via St. Cybi's Well, one of the many holy wells that used to abound; this one, unusually, is still in a good state of preservation. It is clearly marked on many maps but is reached through the country roads and you will need time, confidence and a good map to visit it on your way to Clynnog Fawr.

The pilgrims must have felt an enormous sense of elation as their destination grew closer and journey's end was almost in sight. Whatever route you take to Ynys Enlli (Bardsey) enjoy it; the Llŷn Peninsula is a truly wonderful part of Wales. Go to Ynys Enlli (Bardsey) with a sense of joy and achievement. You may not feel it yet but you have changed, you have been on pilgrimage.

Also published by Y Lolfa

Eight day-tours to sites "evocative of the national spirit of the
Welsh people" in the congenial company of Professor Ralph Maud.

0 86243 335 5
£8.95

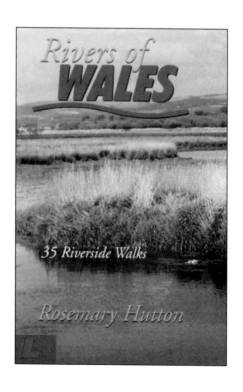

Rivers of **WALES**

35 Riverside Walks

Rosemary Hutton

A voyage of discovery, with Rosemary Hutton, along six of Wales'
most important rivers; with detailed maps and pictures.

0 86243 373 8
£6.95

The Welsh
One Hundred

DAFYDD ANDREWS

Walks to the 100 highest
peaks in Wales

A unique pocked guide, by Dafydd Andrews,
to the hundred highest peaks in Wales.

0 86243 497 1
£5.95